"Jeff was an inspiration to so many individuals within the Boston Bruins organization who met him during his battle with cancer and eventually got involved in the Pan-Mass Challenge. This book allows those who weren't fortunate enough to meet Jeff to understand what a courageous young man he was."

~ Bob Sweeney, Executive Director, Boston Bruins Foundation
Boston Bruins Alumni

"The publication of this important and unique book touches my heart and brings tears to my eyes. The Sandwich Writers' Group offered suggestions and support, but all of the emotional experiences, hard work, and determination were Susan's. Our members simply encouraged a passionate writer's fascinating and worthy project."

~ Ann Shea, Teacher and Member of the Sandwich Writers' Group

"I never knew Jeff, but he came alive for me in "Twelfth Knight." This book is a tribute to a mother's strength and determination to remember her son, and all the people who helped him during his battle—family, friends, doctors, and many others. I visit the Sandwich Boardwalk occasionally and sit on Jeff's memorial bench."

~ Elaine Tammi, Co-Author,
"Scallops: A New England Coastal Cookbook"
Retired Teacher and Member of the Sandwich Writers' Group

"Experience through the eyes of a loving mother the life of a courageous young man who touched so many lives; those of family, friends and a community. Watching a shy young boy become the 'Brave Knight' during his battle is something that will be in my heart forever."

~ Captain John Lessard, American Airlines Pilot

Twelfth Knight

Twelfth Knight

A Mother's Story

Dear Jim —
Thank You for Your continued
Support — Remember #12
All the best,
Susan

Susan Hayes

ISBN: 1511540389
ISBN 13: 9781511540384
Library of Congress Control Number: 2015911491
CreateSpace Independent Publishing Platform
North Charleston, South Carolina

I dedicate this book to my sons and in loving memory of Jeff

Jason, John Jr. and Jeff

Special thanks to

Jeff's many Friends, Coaches and Educators
Our Family and the Sandwich Community
Sandwich Writers' Group
Terry & Judie O'Reilly
Kerry Collins, Director of Community Relations, Boston Bruins
Bob Sweeney, Executive Director of the Boston Bruins Foundation

Nestor Family	Lessard Family	Bridges Family
Tomasini Family	Helms Family	Fair Family
Rubino Family	Cloherty Family	Sullivan Family
Berry Family	O'Connor Family	O'Brien Family
Meuse Family	Robertson Family	Kolb Family

Baseball & Hockey Families
John Hickey, Manager, Gallo Ice Arena
Samuel C. Blackman, MD, PhD | Senior Medical Director
Katherine Baugh and all the Medical Personnel who cared for Jeff
Father Harrison & Father Rodney
Cindy Sullivan, Copy Consultant
Michael Hanlon, Graphic Design
Steve Heaslip, Photographer, Cape Cod Times
Tom Davis, Photographer, Studio280
Ellen Harasimowicz, Photographer
KerriKares, Inc.
Sandwich Enterprise
Cape Cod Times

Nothing is so strong as gentleness, nothing so gentle as real strength

~ Saint Francis de Sales

Table of Contents

OUTSIDE THE LINES WITH
Ted Vrontas

The Friday column of the Sandwich Enterprise sports section, "Outside the Lines," contains conversations with Sandwich High School seniors. Dan Crowley, the columnist, asks, "Who has been your inspiration?" Ted Vrontas replies, "Essentially our entire varsity team, having all sustained injuries this season; they're a tough group of guys, with determination that I admire. My good friend Jeff Hayes, who is currently battling cancer, has been an inspiration to me as well. He's the toughest kid I know, and whenever I'm in the middle of a race, and I feel like giving up, I think about Jeff, and what he's been through, and realize that the pain I'm experiencing is only a fraction of what he's had to endure. Jeff has been the inspiration for some of my fastest times, and many of my most significant victories."

Courtesy of the Sandwich *Enterprise*

C H A P T E R   1

Facebook

I<small>T WAS</small> F<small>RIDAY</small>, January 12, 2007. My beloved son Jeff, age eighteen, had died in the hospital the previous night from cancer. Now we were home. My husband, John was upstairs, and my eldest son, John Jr., was in his bedroom—the one he and Jeff once shared. Jason, my youngest, was sitting in front of our computer in the living room. Our home was quiet with an emptiness that tore at our hearts. I lay on our couch in the den, staring sightlessly at the television screen.

"Mom, it's all over Facebook!" Jason exclaimed, breaking my trance.

"What is?" I asked.

"About Jeff."

"What are they saying?"

"Come here and look!"

I pulled Jeff's blanket off me and got up from the couch and walked into the other room. Jason got up, and I sat down in front of the computer and began to read each message. There were hundreds of messages.

Brittany Whynot (Fountain Hills Junior–Senior High School) wrote:

> *Jeff, you are a true knight. I never got the chance to know you better, but I could never forget watching you and my brother play hockey when you guys were little. You will be in mine and Justin's hearts. We will miss you. Rest In Peace #12.*

Craig Perschini (Saint Joseph, Maine) wrote:

Jeff, there's so much I could say, I don't even know where to begin. It's been a while since we talked but that doesn't mean there wasn't one day you weren't in my prayers. I still remember the first day we met at hockey practice and we ended up being partners. I watched that video the other night of us and the rest of the guys at Hooter's that one time after a game; brought back some funny memories. Jeff you have touched so many lives and inspired every single one of us. I miss you so much man. God bless you Jeff and I know you will be watching over us.

Kim Norton wrote:

We may have lost a fighter, but we gained a hero. Rest in peace Jeff, you are an inspiration to everyone. We miss you bud.

Andrea Gualtieri wrote:

I hear angels have a sweet slap shot. Love and miss you Jeff.

I knew that Jeff's best friends, Brian Tomasini, Matt Melia, Zach Columbo, Will Buckley, Connor Green, and Brendan Kelleher had been called into the main office yesterday morning at Sandwich High School to learn the news from the principal, Mrs. Booras. Then the hockey team had been called down, also to be told, before the announcement was made over the school PA. Father Rodney, our pastor, was called to the high school to provide consolation. Jeff's closest friends, John Lessard and Mike Bridges, had stayed home, knowing their best friend had died; they had been at the hospital.

I looked up from our computer and called out to my husband. "Oh my God, John, you've got to read these messages from the kids."

He bent over the screen and began to read the messages on Facebook.

Doug Parisi wrote:

I love you Jeff and I'll never forget you.

John began to read, standing over my shoulder, and said, "Oh, look, Johnny Muse wrote something."

Jeff, you'll always be the defenseman I'd want out on the ice in front of me. I know you'll be at every college game of mine just like you told me you would so many times before. I'll still get you tickets for every game just like I said I would too. Jeff, you're my inspiration and I'll never forget you. I love you so much and miss you already. Watch over us and keep us safe…

"They loved him, John," I said. We read more, wiping away tears, amazed to learn of the sorrow felt outside our home, in our community, at the high school, from colleges, and friends from afar.

Anna Susko (University of Massachusetts Dartmouth) wrote:

For to His angels, he's given a command to guard you in all of their ways. RIP Jeff, Forever and Always our inspiration.

Brendan Diamond (Cape Cod, Massachusetts) wrote:

Love you man now go play.

"You want to sit down, honey?" I asked.

"They're too hard to read. I'll look again later," he replied and left the room.

I wanted to read more. Deep in my own sorrow, I hadn't realized how deeply so many others felt and how much they too were hurting. I didn't know a lot of the kids who posted the messages.

Megan Welch (University of Massachusetts Dartmouth) wrote:

> *I will always remember his smile, the intense moments of his last time on the ice, the joy radiating from him as he won prom king, and the talks we had in the nurse's office while I was on duty and he was relaxing. You're a great kid Jeff and we miss you so much.*

I sat quietly, thinking about Jeff. I looked at the next message and began to read it, stopping after the first few lines.

"John, you need to read this one," I cried out.

Colin Keohane wrote:

> *It's never fair when the best of us are taken away from us, especially not prematurely. It's never fair when a family loses a son, a brother, and a loved one. It's never fair when a school loses a star hockey player, a good student, a fine young man. It's never fair when someone loses a friend, not someone that's always been there. But it happens. There are those of us who hate it. I hate it too. Jeff Hayes was a person beyond comprehension. I've known him since Kindergarten, and many other people have also. No one can deny his outstanding courage, undying kindness, and perseverance that even the strongest have to admire. His life is not a typical one. He was always excelling. He was always popular and athletic. He had his life ahead of him. He had everything, and we loved him for it. We all loved him, with all our hearts. To first hear of his battle with cancer shocked us all; it made us all doubt a lot. For me to hear of the cancer spreading to his spine was the worst news I had ever heard in my life. I've always been a skeptic when it comes to God, and a lot of people in this situation lose faith in God. For me, Jeff's strength renewed my faith. Jeff wasn't expected to live to Christmas. I prayed to a God I hardly believed in, begging for a miracle, begging that the kid I've known*

4

all my life to at least hold on to see the New Year. God answered me, and gave me an extra eleven days. He gave all of us eleven days. But Jeff's strength, while unbelievable, can't break God's will, and so he took Jeff from us, for what reason I cannot say. But he left us more than just mourning. We are left with the legacy of a kid beyond belief. No one who knew or knew of Jeff, will ever be able to forget his endurance and stamina, his uncompromising optimism in the face of death, and his smile. That smile will last with everyone until they, too, pass away. We can't look upon this event with too much sadness. By all means, we will mourn the loss of a beloved friend, family member, and teammate. We will also honor the memory of him. We will admire him. We all realize the truth that God only takes the best of us away, and Jeff was better than any of us. His smile broke cancer. He nearly beat it, with a smile and a good outlook on life. Let us never forget him. We can only imagine how hard it is for me, for his best friend, John Lessard, for his teammates, for everyone who knew him. We can only imagine how much his brothers Jason and John, and his parents are suffering. But we can offer our support. We can support one another and realize that we are a community. And so I pray for Jeff, his family, and everyone who knew him. We love you Jeff Hayes, #12. We'll never forget you.

There was a break on the Facebook page, and then he continued to write:

At eighteen years old, Jeff had the kind of raw courage that some of us may never find in a lifetime. Jeff has taught us that we are not only individuals, but that we are all part of a greater family. And yesterday morning when many of us learned that a member of our family was taken from us, our hearts sincerely broke. They are still breaking. Even those not personally close with him knew Jeff's story, his courage, and his fight. This is enough to be inspired by him.

Looking around the auditorium there were tears, words of condolence, and loving embraces. For many of us, this is not our first confrontation with death, and the passing or our beloved friend and classmate holds the mirror up to each of us differently. Our personal pain is reflected in each of our eyes; losing a parent, a brother, a friend; we are crying not only for Jeff but for everyone we love who has been lost. There is so much pain and darkness in this world, and this will surely test the courage of all of us who were left behind.

In a world of uncertainty where nothing is guaranteed and tomorrow is never a promise, we have to learn to hold on to each other. We have to hold on to the moments we have together, hold on to the laughter, hold on to the memories, and remember them all not with bitterness or regret, but with love. Always with love. Because we owe it to Jeff and we owe it to each other. Some things are beyond all our control, but our actions and our words in the face of this tragedy will define our character and we must honor our hero. We can honor him every day by the way we treat each other and by the way we live; with dignity, grace, compassion and courage. If we can do this, then Jeff will never truly leave. His inspiration will outlive us all. God bless you Jeff. I am certain that you and your family will be in our prayers always.

I stood up and walked away. I lay down on the couch, covering myself with Jeff's blanket, wrapping it tightly around me. The house was quiet. After the two years we had spent fighting the disease and trying to find a cure, everything had suddenly stopped. All was silent. It was hard to let go. He was gone. It didn't make sense. I took comfort from what Hannah, Jeff's nurse at the Jimmy Fund told me the last day of his life. We were standing outside his hospital room. I said to her, "I don't understand, Hannah; I just don't know why."

"Susan," she replied with a tear in her eye, "he must be needed some-where else."

Last summer during the Pan-Mass Challenge, a Massachusetts statewide bike ride that raises funds for cancer research, the Boston Bruins riding team stopped at the end of our street. Jeff was their Pedal Partner. The Bruins PMC team met with Jeff, our family, and our friends and neighbors. During their brief stop, reporters from NECN, (New England Cable News) and NESN, (New England Sports Network) conducted interviews, took pictures, and shot videos. Later that morning, back inside, after all the excitement, I sat across from Jeff and said, "I'm going to write a book! It's been so amazing these last two years, and now the Boston Bruins are riding in your honor." Jeff looked healthy, sitting across from me. We thought he was in remission. He looked up at me from his recliner and said, "Who would want to read about me?"

John and I finished our meeting to discuss the memorial arrangements at our church, Corpus Christi Parish. At the end of the meeting, John stepped away, and I was alone with Father Rodney. He asked, "How are you doing, Susan?"

"I'm worried. I don't know if Jeff's all right."

"Talk to him," he replied.

"What do I say?"

"Ask him if he's okay," he answered.

"Okay, I will."

It seemed odd and something I wouldn't have imagined myself doing—looking for the hope of a message, a sign from Jeff. On the last day of his life, I'd asked him to let me know that he was okay. Now when I spoke to him, he didn't reply.

Where is he now? I wondered. Is he frightened? Is he alone? Is he lost? It was hard not knowing. I found moments over the first several months to ask. Maybe he was close in spirit; maybe he could hear me.

"Jeff, I want you to know that I'm going to tell our story. It's probably good I can't hear you, but I'd give anything to know what you think. It'd be great to hear your voice again."

CHAPTER 2

❧

Christmas Eve December 2004

"IS IT SNOWING?" I asked.

I was standing in front of the kitchen sink, washing a pan I'd used to boil turkey giblets. My husband came into the house through the side door. He was carrying some shopping bags.

"Smells good in here," he said, picking up one of the chocolate chip cookies I'd just taken out of the oven. "No, it's not snowing, sorry."

He was returning from his usual last-minute Christmas Eve shopping.

"How'd you make out?" I asked.

"All right," he said and left the kitchen carrying the bags. I heard his footsteps going upstairs. "Where's the wrapping paper?" he called down.

"Under the bed," I replied.

"Don't come up!"

"Oh, don't worry; I won't." I heard the bedroom door shut.

My Christmas CD was playing "Silent Night." I stood still. It felt holy. I looked into our living room at the soft lighting and the angel I'd placed on the top of the tree. Earlier, I'd lit candles and dimmed the lights; the Christmas tree had an almost perfect shape this year. The gifts were placed neatly underneath. I smiled with a tear in my eye. "Silent Night" does it to me every time.

Time for another batch of cookies, I thought.

As I placed dollops of cookie batter evenly on the baking sheet, I remembered Christmases past when my boys were young and how tired I would be lying in bed late Christmas Eve. I'd fade into deep sleep only to have my rest interrupted by "Mom! Mom!" I'd open my eyes and turn on my side, facing the edge of the bed to see three small, round faces staring into mine.

"Mom, its Christmas! Come on, get up!"

I remembered being a child and feeling the magical excitement and anticipation of Christmas morning, hoping quietly for the one gift I'd dreamed of for so long. Now as a Mother, I hoped that my sons' hearts were filled with this same anticipation and utter joy Christmas morning.

My husband, John, and our three sons, John Jr., Jeff, and Jason—are the center of my universe. John Jr. graduated from high school last spring and was now working. Jeff was a sophomore in high school, and Jason was in eighth grade.

For the past ten years, John Jr. thrilled us with his lightning speed and skill on the ice. He was fast, a playmaker, and exciting to watch. Jeff became a great defenseman. John a forward, Jeff a defenseman; it made perfect sense. Growing up, the two played hockey all day in our basement on their rollerblades. I saw them only when they needed food and something to drink. They were serious about their game, and they were good. They played on several select teams in the Metro Boston Hockey League. We traveled during the week and on weekends to practices, games, and tournaments. Jason never wanted to play hockey, but he followed his brothers' games, watching intently from the stands. He tracked their plays and goals scored.

Hockey and sports were a big part of my childhood. During the winter, my nine siblings and I spent many winter days outdoors. We all skated. I watched my brothers play hockey. My father, an athlete and a hockey player, would flood the lot next to our house to make ice. He would place bright lights on the outside of our house so we could skate at night. We wore flannel pajamas under our leggings to keep us warm.

Here I am now, standing in the kitchen, wearing an apron and baking cookies. Jason is down the street at a neighbor's house, and John Jr. isn't home yet. The past several weeks had been filled with the demands of a full-time job, shopping, wrapping, parties, Jeff's hockey games and his high school Christmas tournament.

Jeff was still at hockey practice. His teammates who drove would bring him home. He had made varsity as a freshman last year, and he played the most minutes per game of all players on his team, excluding the goalie. The number twelve he wore was the number his brother John Jr. had worn. I asked Jeff why he chose his brother's number, happy that he had, and Jeff replied, "I didn't want anyone who couldn't skate to wear John's number."

I purchased his varsity jacket as a surprise for him after he'd asked a few times. I left it for him when he arrived home after practice. The number twelve is on one white leather sleeve of the jacket, and a large Blue Knight riding a horse is beautifully embroidered on the back.

Jeff with close friend John Lessard

Jeff was proud of John Jr. They were different hockey players. Both handled the puck with skill. John Jr. had great speed and was a goal scorer. Jeff also had great hockey sense but was more defensive, protective of the goal. He could also skate well. They were always fun to watch. With John Jr. out of high school and working, it was Jeff's time to shine.

Lately, however, Jeff had been struggling, puzzling his coach and teammates.

For the last couple of weeks, he had been experiencing pain in his thigh. We had treated his thigh with ice, thinking he had a strained muscle. The pain never ceased, and some days I could tell it was really hurting, but he endured it, thinking it would go away. Last summer, when he played All-Star baseball, he complained of back pain. We took him to a doctor, who found nothing to treat, but we worried nonetheless. Jeff was never one to complain. If he said something was bothering him, it was something to be concerned about.

I heard a car pull into the driveway. It was Jeff's friends dropping him off. A minute later, he came in the house and joined me in the kitchen.

"Hi, Jeff. How was practice?"

He looked at me as I stood next to him and said, "Mom, I think I have a tumor in my leg."

Tumor, I thought, it can't be. I wouldn't let that word or the meaning of the word enter any realm of possibility. It could not be the reason he'd been struggling with pain. The word scared me, and I dismissed it as not possible.

I looked back at him and said, "Jeff, I don't think so, but it's Christmas Eve, and tomorrow's Christmas Day. We'll go see a doctor the day after Christmas to check it out, okay?"

"Okay," he replied and walked away to shower. The oven's buzzer went off. I turned quickly, picked up the hand towel, opened the oven door, and pulled the baking sheet out of the oven. "Oh shit!" My finger touched the hot baking sheet, and I dropped it on top of the stove, slamming the oven door shut. Oh God, I thought, I'm pretty sure you can't swear on Christmas Eve; that can't be good! I turned the cold water on and let it run over my fingertip. Tumor? I tried to get that thought, that word, out of my head. Parents don't think of cancer, or imagine cancer growing in their child. It just doesn't happen to your son. How do we know it won't?

When my kids tell me something is hurting them, I react. I ask questions, I observe, I take them to their pediatrician, and I care for them. I'm thinking bumps and bruises and infections and viruses. I'm not thinking cancer.

What if it was?

I thought about Jeff's courage and the relief he must have felt letting those thoughts out. It was unusual for him to tell me he was hurting in any way; he'd take care of it himself if he thought it was a hockey injury. He just doesn't complain. He's very quiet. How long had he kept this fear bottled up inside him? He was giving up on the hope that his excruciating pain would go away on its own. He'd had enough, I thought. Why did he think it was a tumor? I wondered.

When the cold water had numbed my finger, I shut off the faucet, finished plating my cookies, and cleaned the kitchen.

John Jr. and Jason returned home, and when everyone was asleep, I uncovered the unwrapped gifts I had hidden in our walk-in closet and placed them around the Christmas tree. I heard John snoring from the den.

"Go to bed," I whispered to him; not wanting to wake my sons.

I stuffed the stockings and went to bed. I lay there staring up at the ceiling in the dark. The worry that I'd forgotten someone or didn't do something kept me awake. I thought about Jeff and was frightened, but tiredness overcame me, and I fell asleep.

Christmas day started early. We opened presents, ate breakfast, and went to church. I went through the day trying to convince myself that Jeff didn't have a tumor; it had to be something else.

Family arrived, more presents were opened, and then we sat down for dinner. I could see Jeff struggling with the pain. He was distant and more quiet than usual. Later, when company was gone and our house became quiet again, I looked over at him as he sat on the couch in our living room. He was massaging his thigh, his face stressed.

"Are you okay, Jeff?" I asked.

"Yes, but it's still bothering me."

"Would you like some Tylenol, honey?"

"Yeah."

The day after Christmas, John took Jeff to the urgent care center.

The doctor on duty diagnosed the pain as quadriceps myalgia/myositis, a strained muscle.

No x-ray was taken, and the treatment had no effect on Jeff's condition.

On New Year's Eve, Jeff played in a holiday tournament. I thought it was his best game of the season. I watched from the stands and chatted with the other hockey families. I told them that Jeff had said his leg had been hurting, and he thought he may have a tumor in his thigh. Yet this night, he certainly didn't seem to be hurting. He skated as well as he ever had, cleared the puck effectively, and made quick, accurate passes to his teammates.

"Can you imagine? A tumor?" I asked Doreen Lessard, a longtime hockey friend.

"The way he's playing, it can't possibly be a tumor."

After the game, the Blue Knight's coach, Derackk Curtis, presented Jeff with the "Coaches Tie," an award he gave after each game to the player who played at his best. Jeff would have to wear the tie to the next game. After receiving the award, Jeff turned to his coach and said, "I can't play anymore. I can't even walk."

C H A P T E R 3

Jeff's Birth 1988

THE SKY WAS bright blue on the morning of September 22, 1988. I felt a chill as I opened our front door and looked out at the sea of leaves that had fallen in our front yard; they were still brightly colored, not yet turned brown and brittle. Two towering maples stood at the edge of our lawn near the street. Their long branches reached out over the front and side yards. I felt an uncontrollable urge to rake. I was nine months pregnant. My feet were slightly swollen, my stomach enormous, and the butt I'd never had stuck out noticeably. My biological, hormonal, mother-to-be urge to nest told me to get busy and tackle this outdoor chore. Inside, the nursery was already organized, and my house was as clean as it had ever been. It felt good to be home; I was on maternity leave from my job at Hewlett Packard.

Being home now gave me precious time to spend with my three-year-old son, John Jr. I explained to him again and again that my weight gain meant that his new brother or sister would be coming soon.

John Jr. and I were very close. My affection and love for him came naturally. He was loving and kind, and we had fun together. When I was a child, my parents were busy raising ten children and working long hours. I didn't receive a lot of attention from them. Not that they didn't love us. That wasn't the case. They were from a generation that didn't show affection.

After lunch, I stepped out into our front yard. With the rake in my hands, my arms reaching out beyond my protruding stomach and my feet planted in one spot, I moved my arms back and forth to rake the leaves into a neat pile. I became a pregnant machine out there, raking one section at a time and stopping only for a drink of water.

Hours later, exhausted, I was pleased to see how neat the yard looked. I knew that all the leaves I'd raked would probably blow back into the yard, and I knew that even more leaves would be falling from the trees, but right here and right now, I'd accomplished my task. I headed into our house. John was just returning home from work. He was a supervisor at Poland Spring, a bottled-water company. We ate the dinner that my mother-in-law, Thelma had prepared. She was staying with us to watch John Jr. in case I went into labor.

My doctor had made it very clear when he said not to do any large chores as I approached my due date. "It'll make you tired," he warned. "And if you go into labor, well then, you'll be tired." I'm not a good listener, apparently—stubborn actually. I was pissed at myself. I was tired.

That night in bed, a long and unexpected contraction grabbed hold of me. "Oooh!" Now I remember. Three years from the birth of my first son, and oh, how familiar! My husband lay beside me, sound asleep.

"John, wake up! I think it's time!"

"What?" he mumbled, half asleep.

"Really! Wake up! I think it's time! John, wake up." I had to shout, "I'm nine months pregnant, remember? No, sorry, nine months and three days. I'm not sure how many hours—could be minutes if you don't hurry!"

He jumped up out of bed and called for Thelma. I smiled; he's not that quick, ever. My face tightened, bracing for another contraction. Oh God, I thought, do I start that ridiculous breathing exercise that's supposed to take me through the pain as if it didn't hurt? John was waking Thelma. Thelma had drilled him on the importance of getting me out of the house immediately; she wasn't going to deliver a baby. Within minutes she had my clothes ready to change into and my suitcase by the front door.

"Come on, let's go, hurry up," Thelma insisted, pushing us out the front door.

Jeffrey Thomas Hayes was born just after midnight, September 23, 1988, at Newton-Wellesley Hospital. He weighed eight pounds, nine ounces and was twenty-one inches long. His birth was completely normal other than my stubbornness to not push in the very last moments. "It hurts too much!" I said to the nurse. She was trying to get me to push. "You're going to do some damage if you don't push now," she said as she walked away, leaving me alone in the room. After hearing her loud but fair warning, I went right to it, and Jeff was born.

When I brought Jeff home, I held him all the time. He was peaceful and content. My mom said, "Susan, you can't hold him all day long!" She'd take Jeff and wrap him tightly in his tiny blanket and place him back in his crib.

Scary movies frightened him, thunder and lightning scared him, and loud fireworks hurt his ears. He slept with a night-light on. As he got older, he kept a flashlight under his covers.

Jeff had thick blond hair and big brown eyes. He was quiet, yet he had a kind and pleasing smile that replaced his words not spoken. He was fair-minded, often wise, always sensible, and sometimes more mature than some of his peers. He was playful and always eager to play sports. His first love was hockey.

CHAPTER 4

Mounting Pain, Nor'easter

A WEEK AFTER NEW YEARS' we brought Jeff to see an orthopedic surgeon. Jeff's pain had persisted since the last hockey game during the Christmas tournament, and there was no improvement. The surgeon sent Jeff for an MRI. The technician completed the scans, gave me the originals, and told me to bring Jeff home and wait for the doctor's phone call. When I got home, I looked at the scans of Jeff's thigh. I didn't know how to read or interpret what I saw, but I did see a huge mass encompassing his thigh from his knee up to his groin. I felt a rush of anxiety throughout my body.

"Oh my God, is this a tumor? Could it be this big?"

I sat down at our kitchen table, dazed, the scan on the table and still in my grasp as I stared sightlessly at the kitchen wall.

The phone rang, startling me.

"This is the doctor's office. Is this Mrs. Hayes?" a woman asked.

"Yes," I replied.

"Can you and Jeff come in this afternoon at four thirty?"

"Yes, we can. What did the doctor see on the scan?" I asked.

"He will discuss that with you when you arrive," she replied.

As we entered the waiting room, I could feel the uneasiness of the nurse as she led us into one of the examining rooms. It was just the three of us, Jeff, my husband, and me. Two doctors entered the room, and I became completely still. They put the MRI film up onto the screen, and there it was, a huge white mass. "It's a type of bone cancer, possibly osteosarcoma," The doctor said in a soft voice.

We sat there in shock. I instantly removed my mind from processing what cancer meant. I was outside my body looking on, feeling like a fourth person, feeling invisible. It was the only way I could remain strong in front of Jeff. Slowly I returned to the reality of my son's illness, sitting there quietly and motionless beside Jeff.

John began to question the doctor as if his diagnosis was all wrong. This just couldn't be.

The doctor told us that we needed to get to Boston right away—Boston, where all the renowned hospitals are. He told us about an orthopedic oncologist at the Brigham and Women's Hospital whom he knew quite well. He would make an appointment with him for Jeff on Monday. An oncologist! I couldn't believe I was hearing that word.

Jeff's pain level had increased over the past few days, so the doctor prescribed a narcotic painkiller for him.

We knew we were in for a long weekend. Saturday and Sunday's weather forecast called for a severe nor'easter with near gale-force winds, heavy snowfall, and white-out blizzard conditions. With cancer in our home and threatening our son's life, we were in our own storm of emotions, fearful of the unknown and wondering in which direction that wind would blow us and where we would land in its aftermath.

After we left the orthopedic surgeon's office, we filled Jeff's prescription and headed to a local restaurant to get Jeff something to eat. I left the table after we ordered and went to the corner of the restaurant to use an old phone booth to call my Dad and tell him the news. We had lost my Mom a year before to pancreatic cancer, our first touch with cancer in our large and extended family. "You've got to be kidding," Dad said. He offered encouragement and hope. I asked him to call my brothers and sisters to let them know the news wasn't good. I returned to our table. No one ate much dinner.

We got home moments before John Jr. was arriving home from work. I stood in the living room and approached him when he walked through the door.

"What did they say?" he asked.

I walked toward him. We stood looking at each other. "Jeff has cancer."

"No, he doesn't have that!" he cried.

"They found a tumor in his thigh; it's pretty large. We're going up to Boston on Monday to find out what type of cancer it is." John turned away from me and ran up the stairs to his bedroom, shouting, "No, Mom, he doesn't have cancer!"

Tears filled my eyes and I suddenly felt exhausted.

That night, I slept in the bed next to Jeff, in case he needed me.

I woke Friday morning, checked on Jeff and his comfort level, and then got myself into the shower. I stood there under the water going over all that had happened the day before and the weeks preceding this diagnosis, when suddenly I began to cry, thinking no one could hear me. Tears flowed from me as I tried to control my thoughts. I couldn't believe this was happening to Jeff. How did it happen? What caused it? He was so excited about playing high school sports, going to school, and preparing for college. He's only a sophomore! Then it became clear. He will survive this! I will not let anything happen to my son!

I felt energized and thought of my words directed at cancer as if it were a physical being, an enemy against mankind: how dare you enter my house, touch my family, find your way to my son! You'll have to fight hard against us; we won't give up! We'll beat you! "Yikes!" I yelled. The water temperature had gone from hot to freezing instantly. I heard a bang on the bathroom door.

"Are you okay in there?" John shouted.

"Yes, but there's no hot water!"

I turned the water off and stepped out of the shower. I dried off with a clear head from the jolt of freezing cold water and a will to sacrifice everything I had to save Jeff's life. I dressed to begin the first full day of knowing that Jeff had bone cancer.

Jeff's pain intensified Saturday. It was obvious he would need more medicine, and we'd need to get it soon because of the approaching storm. I phoned the doctor's office and got the answering service. I explained to the operator that my son had just seen the doctor this past Thursday and was in great pain and needed more medicine. She said we could not get any more narcotic medication because according to her schedule, Jeff had not had surgery within the last four days, nor would she give us the name of the doctor who was on call. I told her that Jeff had been diagnosed with cancer on Thursday by the ortho-pedic surgeon and that he was in excruciating pain, but she wouldn't relent. With the storm approaching, I tried again and again, and after several phone calls to the same doctor's office and the same operator, we still could not convince her of the severity of our situation and the need to talk to the doctor on call.

We decided to phone the emergency room at the Cape Cod Hospital in Hyannis. The nurse there immediately told me the name of the doctor on call and said that he just happened to be in the emergency room. The doctor said we could come to the hospital and he would write us a prescription. Heavy snow had started to fall, but John bundled up and drove to the hospital to get the prescription. He left the hospital without filling it there, thinking he could fill it at our local CVS Pharmacy where our medical insurance information would be on file.

While John was driving back from the hospital, the governor of Massachusetts declared a state of emergency due of the impending nor'easter, thus closing all stores and pharmacies. John got to our local CVS only to find it closed. That meant we only had three narcotic pain pills to carry Jeff through until Monday morning. The Tylenol and other low-level pain relievers we had in the house no longer helped. The pain had intensified so much that it became obvious to us that Jeff would need crutches. Luckily, the captain of the Sandwich varsity hockey team had been on crutches the previous year, lived nearby, and brought his over.

The snow was falling so fast that John Jr. and his friends, Johnny and Brian couldn't keep up with it. The wind was howling, and the blowing snow made it difficult for them to see. We heard on television that the winds were gusting up to eighty-four miles an hour, hurricane force, and there were twenty-seven-foot seas. The snowstorm was the worst to hit New England since the blizzard of 1978.

Jeff made it through Saturday night okay, but on Sunday, his pain intensified as I tried to make the pain medication last.

"Mom!" Jeff called out.

I ran up the stairs to his bedroom.

"What, honey?" As I sat down on the edge of his bed, I mistakenly rubbed against his thigh.

"Ouch, Mom! Watch out, jeez!"

"Oh, I'm so sorry, Jeff."

"When can I take another pain pill?"

"I can cut one in half, but I don't know if that will mess up the strength of the drug."

"What do you mean?'

"I think that some pain medication is time released, but I'm not sure whether this one is. Do you want me to try cutting this one in half? We only have one left."

"Yes, then I can take the other half later."

"Okay. Should we try some heat on your leg?"

"Yeah, okay. What's it look like outside?"

"The snow is coming down pretty hard, and John, Johnny and Brian are shoveling and snowboarding. There's at least a foot of snow already, and you can't see; it's a whiteout, a blizzard, honey. But don't worry, they'll plow, and we'll be able to get to Boston Monday morning, first thing. We're usually lucky; our street never loses power. So let's hope we don't this time."

Jeff sat up in his bed, remaining calm but tense with the pulsating pain emanating from his thigh. All day, I was constantly up and down the stairs to his bedroom answering his call for help. I don't recall being tired; I just wanted the day to pass so that we could drive up to Boston. All through Sunday night, I could hear the wind gusting, and I imagined the snow drifts becoming larger, covering over the paths previously cleared. A gust of wind hit against the house and scared me; I hoped we wouldn't lose power. The wind didn't stop, and throughout the night I spoke softly to Jeff, wondering how bad his pain was and wishing the hours would pass quickly for him. My husband, sons, and friends continued shoveling and plowing throughout the night to enable us to make our Monday morning ride. I had packed our suitcases, not knowing how long we'd be in Boston. I counted down each hour and told Jeff to hang in there...just four more hours... just three more hours... just two... just one...

CHAPTER 5

❧

Boston, Dr. Ready, X-Rays
January 2005

IT WAS STILL dark at five in the morning when we got dressed. We slowly made our way down the stairs, Jeff on crutches. We put on our winter coats and hats. We had to exit the house through the back slider because the five-foot drifts blocked the side and front doors. Outside, I looked around and thought we might be in Vermont. Our house is surrounded by trees on a two-acre lot with conservation land behind us. As we stepped outside, it was picturesque but eerie. Nothing was plowed. A blanket of snow covered everything as far as I could see. The sun was beginning to rise. There was a feeling of uneasiness on this quiet and still after-the-storm morning.

We waded through the deep snow and looked around to see tree branches touching the ground. The bitter cold air numbed our bodies.

My husband and John Jr. walked at Jeff's side and guided him slowly and cautiously down the driveway. When they reached our Explorer, John Jr. took Jeff's crutches and helped him into the front seat, saying, "Good luck, kid; I'll see you soon." They looked at each other, too proud to say more. With the car packed and ready to go, I jumped into the back seat. As we looked down our unplowed road, my husband pressed on the gas pedal, and we drove slowly through the deep snow. At the end of our street, a five-foot wall of plowed snow blocked us from the main road. My husband floored the gas pedal and we blasted through the wall, and headed off the Cape. It was like making a getaway. We were on the run, anxious and full of fear, but the waiting was over. All the roads that had been closed due to the state of emergency, including the Sagamore Bridge over the Cape Cod Canal, were now reopened. Clear of traffic on this early Monday morning, we practically flew up to Boston. I could see Jeff sitting quietly in the front seat, fighting off the pain without a complaint.

We were surprised to find the city up and running. My husband dropped Jeff and me off at the front entrance to Brigham and Women's Hospital. I found a wheelchair for Jeff and pushed him into the huge, busy lobby. Jeff barely held on, the pain horrible, but he never cried out, and he remained composed as I completed the insurance intake process in a large, open area whose high ceiling reminded me of Grand Central Station. We were then directed around the corner to the office of Dr. Ready, the orthopedic oncologist to whom our orthopedic surgeon had referred us. We sat in his waiting room for over an hour until we were escorted into a small examining room. We waited again. Jeff sat quietly. He looked pale and tired. I thought perhaps Dr. Ready had made time for us and scheduled Jeff because of his condition, fitting us in when his schedule might have been full.

Dr. Ready entered the room and introduced himself. He turned on the desktop computer and showed us the tumor. We looked at Jeff's tumor on the lower part of his thigh just above his knee. Dr. Ready described in medical terms the location of the tumor and said it was a "better spot" for it. He then walked over to Jeff, who was lying on the examining table. While he examined Jeff's thigh, he began to talk hockey with Jeff. Somehow he knew Jeff played. This seemed to put Jeff at ease. Dr. Ready was Canadian and played "the game."

"So you're a hockey player?" he asked Jeff.

"Yes, but lately I've been having trouble playing with the pain in my leg."

"Well, we're going to admit you so that you can be treated for the pain. We will also biopsy the tumor to find out what kind of cancer it is."

As Dr. Ready walked toward the door, he proudly proclaimed to Jeff, "I'm a Toronto Maple Leafs fan."

Jeff sat up on the examining table. "Bruins fan!" he replied. Dr. Ready smiled and left the room.

I felt relieved that Jeff had been seen by Dr. Ready, in Boston and within a city block comprised of the most renowned hospitals; I knew Jeff would be given the best possible medical care. Oh, thank God we're here, I thought.

We left the examining room and headed to the reception desk in the waiting room.

"We're waiting to hear from the floor to admit Jeff," the receptionist told us. Dr. Ready had given orders to have Jeff admitted for relief of the pain he'd been fighting for several days. We didn't wait long. I found myself thinking that perhaps Jeff had received preferential treatment and attention because his tumor may be in the later stages of cancer.

Once admitted, Jeff was put on a morphine drip. I watched him sitting up in the hospital bed, he looked frightened. He followed all the directions the nurses and doctors gave him. I was relieved that the immediate pain was under control. At least he could rest and sleep.

There was little time to waste. As soon as Jeff's pain was under control, the tests began. As we made our way to radiology that evening, it seemed surreal. I pushed Jeff in his wheelchair through the enormous hospital lobby to the elevators. Neither of us spoke. I kept assuring myself there was a treatment here that would destroy the disease and cure my son. I thought about trying to keep his life as normal as possible during his treatment and recovery. I believed that all Jeff had to do was start the treatment. The treatment would reduce the tumor and kill all the cancerous cells. That was our mission. I didn't think about why or how it happened. I did believe, at some point, I would want that understanding, and would do everything within my power to prevent it from happening to another child or teenager. A tall order, I thought, which didn't scare me; right now was terrifying.

I wheeled Jeff into the radiology reception area. Our x-ray technician immediately escorted us into the x-ray room. Jeff was tired and fearful. He said that the tumor felt like he was carrying a football lodged in his leg. The technician had Jeff strip down to his boxers. It was very painful for Jeff to hold his leg in any position for very long. For a chest x-ray, she had Jeff step out of his wheelchair and lie down on the cold, rectangular metal table. She motioned to me and said, "Mom, can you get behind the glass partition and wait there?"

She continued to position Jeff and then ran over to where I was standing to take the picture.

It didn't work. She tried again. It still didn't work.

Jeff lay there shivering on the cold metal table.

Clearly, she was having problems with the x-ray machine. I wish she knew what we'd been through to get to this point—all that Jeff had endured. If she knew, perhaps she'd understand how difficult and how uncomfortable it was for Jeff. I didn't think to explain. I just watched with empathy for my son and thought, I hope she can get the pictures she needs as quickly as possible.

After several minutes contemplating what she would do next, the technician decided to have Jeff stand up straight in front of another x-ray machine. Standing was painful for him, but he held steady and used all his strength to follow her directions.

"We're done," she said. We headed back up to Jeff's hospital room.

CHAPTER 6

Mite Hockey

I

T WAS AUTUMN and Jeff was five. My sister Kathy was watching Jeff for the weekend while my husband and I attended a wedding. Jeff had a new pair of rollerblades, and he'd brought them with him. On Sunday morning when I returned to pick up Jeff, Kathy insisted that I come with her to a nearby vacant parking lot to watch just how well Jeff could rollerblade. We parked, and Jeff got into his rollerblades. Suddenly, off he went. He was fast, and he moved with perfect, confident strides. He went the entire length of the lot, back and forth, smiling the whole way.

"Look at him go!"

I suppose I wasn't totally surprised. Jeff had been watching John Jr. skate and play hockey for years.

After that, I enrolled him in skating lessons.

Hockey just came naturally to Jeff, so we enrolled him in Mites hockey. Mites is entry-level organized hockey. It's for kids ages seven and under. Within Mites, there are three levels, A, B, and C. In Mites, it's assumed the youngsters know how to skate. The object of Mites-level hockey is to teach individual skill development and not team skills. In Mites, kids will learn how to improve their skating, handle and control pucks, pass, and shoot on net.

Jeff in Mites Uniform

At Mites age, it's hard to determine what position the skaters will play until they've played several games and practiced many times. Jeff was a natural defenseman. My husband disagreed with the coaches and thought Jeff played well as a forward. However, during practice and games, Jeff protected the goalie and the net.

Hockey season is long, from November to March. Mites practiced once during the week and played a game on Saturday or Sunday. The kids improved over the year. When Jeff and his friends weren't on the ice, they were outside playing street hockey.

Judie Duane, a friend of mine and the wife of Kurt Duane, one of the Mites' coaches, approached me after a practice while we waited for our kids to come out of their locker rooms.

"Susan, you must be very proud of Jeff?"

"Yes, I am." I wondered why she'd asked.

"My son told me that during tryouts the other night, when the kids had to get in position for a face-off in their own end, Jeff told my son where to stand and what to do when the puck was dropped." I hadn't seen Jeff coaching her son and began to imagine him showing her son Jimmy where to stand outside the circle, how to hold his stick and telling him to be prepared for a pass. Jeff was one of those kids, unassuming and honest. Judie's son and Jeff were trying out for the same position. It never occurred to Jeff, I thought, that helping Jimmy could hinder his chances of making the team; he just knew that it might help Jimmy's chances.

"He's good kid," Judie said as her son came out of the locker room.

CHAPTER 7

Back from X-rays, First Nights in Hospital

WHEN WE RETURNED from radiology to Jeff's hospital bed, we were glad the day had ended. I tried to stay positive. Jeff was strong and had all the fight in him to battle this disease. He was otherwise very healthy, and because of his conditioning in sports, he had greater endurance.

I helped Jeff into the bed, making him as comfortable as possible. I decided to sleep on a plastic-covered bench built into the wall by the window of Jeff's hospital room. I covered it with sheets and a blanket from the linen room next door. As I tried to make myself comfortable on this cramped sleeping space, my mind searched for some peace and the thought of beating this disease. I fell asleep watching Jeff.

The next day, our first full day in the hospital, Jeff was scheduled for a biopsy. My sister-in-law Patty, who was either by my side or on the phone with me daily, had taken the bus to South Station and a cab to the hospital. She and I accompanied Jeff as he was taken to the operating room. The doctors there explained the procedure. Once Jeff was prepped and taken in, Patty and I waited, thinking that within a reasonable time we would know the type of cancer and the treatment. Jeff returned soon after the procedure. I could hear relief in his voice and see it in his face. He began to talk openly and freely unlike before the procedure. He was so glad to be out of recovery.

"Are we going back to the room?" he asked.

"Yes, honey; we're all done here."

"Good," he replied.

Day three at the Brigham and Women's Hospital, we met Dr. Albritton. She was studying Jeff's case and trying to determine whether the cancer had spread. I saw her several times during the week that followed as she worked to diagnose the exact type of cancer Jeff had. This diagnosis would then determine the most effective chemotherapy treatment.

My husband searched the Internet for information on both types of cancer. We wanted to know which cancer Jeff had the best chance of surviving. We prayed for good news.

During one of her brief appearances, Dr. Albritton said, "Susan, it may seem like things are moving slowly, but behind the scenes, we are moving very fast." I appreciated that news but often wondered why everything required such a long wait. What was going on during the long hours of the day when we didn't see her? We just wanted the treatment to start. Waiting was so exhausting.

One day Dr. Albritton brought me into a small family room down the hall from Jeff's room, and we sat down face-to-face. She told me she was not yet ready to make a final diagnosis, but she wanted to prepare me for when she was ready. She began to tell me about percentages and survival rates, but I stopped her and said, "Percentages don't mean a thing to me." I felt that it didn't matter how many survived or didn't survive; Jeff was not going to be the latter. He was going to survive. I was certain of that. He was going home at the end of his treatment to return to the normal life he once knew. She smiled as the words came out of my mouth.

Dr. Albritton spoke of the possibility of amputating Jeff's leg. I felt overwhelmed by fear, petrified of what else she might say. Oh God, I prayed, please keep Jeff safe. Amputation was too awful a thought to bear. I began to drift away. The sound of Dr. Albritton's voice faded. I could feel the cushioned seat beneath me, but I couldn't hear her voice or any peripheral noise. All I could see was the shape of her mouth and the expressions on her face.

Moments passed. Her voice echoed in my inner ear, and I could hear her again. When she was done speaking to me, she headed back to the lab for more analysis. I watched as she left the room and thought, this cannot be life threatening. I left the family room to go see my Jeff. I sat with him all day, waiting on him and supplying him with whatever he needed.

During this ten-day stay at the Brigham and Women's Hospital, while we waited for Dr. Albritton's diagnosis, our hometown came together to support us and to let us know that we were not alone. Jeff's friends and their parents, his coaches and his teachers, our friends and family showed us how coming together as one could make a world of difference to a teenager diagnosed with cancer. They provided Jeff and our family with everything we would need to battle this disease: a laptop for Jeff, gift certificates, Sunday dinners, and more. Jeff was loved not only by his peers and teammates but also by an entire community of family and friends, even those who didn't know him well or even at all. Jeff and his cancer were the talk of the town. Everyone wanted to help us.

Dr. Albritton's next visit put us on edge again. After studying Jeff's biopsy and viewing the x-rays of Jeff's lungs, she said she still did not know what type of cancer Jeff had or whether the cancer had spread. As she came out of Jeff's room and we walked toward each other in the hallway, she began to say something to me, when a rush of anxiety made me lose my equilibrium. I felt out of balance and dizzy, but I came out of this vertigo and regained my composure without losing a stride. Smiling, I looked at her and said, "Gee, I thought the floor just went out from under me!" She smiled back at me in surprise that I had responded that way. I don't know why she smiled; I just remember she did. I didn't hear or remember what she said to me.

She wanted to speak with Jeff alone, so I sat in the family room again and waited as she went in to see him. I thought this conversation was regarding the sperm bank; it had been suggested that a sample should be stored before the chemotherapy began.

After his conversation with Dr. Albritton, Jeff was very upset, and when I walked into his hospital room, I found him in tears. I asked him if he was all right. He wouldn't look at me. He just asked me to leave. I don't know what she had said to him. This upset me, and I became angry with her. I realized shortly thereafter that she was only doing her job by being honest with him about his condition.

I soon learned that the doctors and nurses who care for cancer patients could not offer what they're not certain of. They had seen children battle cancer for years and survive or not survive. The doctors and staff were always impassive about the results of treatment; if positive results were seen, they gave measurable facts, like, "The tumor has shrunk by twenty-five percent." But they would never say, "Your son is cured." They didn't know. They never gave false hope. They were honest and were taught to keep their emotions hidden even when the treatment was effectively shrinking tumors and killing cancerous cells. In Jeff's case, he had a rare bone cancer where they had little or no clinical data as a resource to actually know the difference between stopping the cancer and just slowing it down. I wondered why there was little known of this rare disease. If it's rare, is it more difficult to find the cause, rather than a cancer that affects more people?

One morning during this time of uncertainty, as Jeff was staring out the window from his hospital bed, his pain under control, and as my husband and I were still waiting for some news, a visitor arrived. We looked toward the door to see Jeff's hockey coach, Derackk Curtis, walk into the room. He was a wonderful and uplifting sight. I gave him a hug. Jeff immediately said, "Hi, Coach!" with a big smile on his face, his first smile in a long time. Coach Derackk was the new Sandwich High School varsity coach, the one Jeff had voted in and had played for until he could play no more. Coach Derackk came from Canada and had run a hockey school and training camp called Puck Masters. Derackk was a great coach, but more importantly he was a wise, kind, and spiritual man.

Jeff and Coach Derackk discussed the coming weekend's hockey game between rivals Sandwich High School and neighboring Bourne. It was called the Canal Cup because Gallo Ice Arena, which was hosting the game, was built on the banks of the Cape Cod Canal. The Canal Cup is a one-game annual tradition that has been played the first weekend of February every year for the past twenty-four years.

Coach Derackk asked Jeff for his advice on this big game, the first Canal Cup for the new coach. Jeff had played in the Canal Cup in middle school and as a varsity player just last year. He had watched his brother John Jr. play for four years as a varsity player. It was hard for Jeff not to play in this game. Jeff turned to him and said, "Just win, Coach."

My husband and I left the room so that Jeff and his coach could have some private time together. Later, I read in Derackk's essay about Jeff that they spoke about the likelihood of chemotherapy and radiation, additional testing, and the possible surgeries that Jeff might be subjected to. Here in the hospital, as far from the rink as you could get, Derackk was teaching Jeff, coaching him and preparing him for what was to come. Outside Jeff's room, Derackk told me that he felt that he was given this coaching position for a reason; that he was brought here to help Jeff through this battle. Derackk had been Jeff's very first visitor and would become one of his most important visitors.

Dr. Albritton became the bearer of bad news. Every time she appeared, we froze in fear. Was it osteosarcoma or Ewing's sarcoma? It weighed heavily on our minds. Which cancer was worse? Had it spread? What was the prognosis?

I found Dr. Albritton and Dr. Ready, the orthopedic oncologist Jeff had seen his first day at Brigham and Women's, standing outside Jeff's room. It was late in the day. My husband and I and Jackie and Michael, our close friends, were in the small family room where we'd been waiting most of the day, waiting to hear if the cancer had spread. Dr. Ready had just left surgery and was wearing scrubs and a Bruins surgical cap. John and I left the family room and approached them.

"The cancer has spread," Dr. Ready began. "We have seen three tiny specks of tumor in Jeff's lungs."

Dr. Albritton said, "These tiny specks might not be life threatening because different parts of the population have these dust particles in their lungs due to where they lived and the environment they lived in. However, we think that the three very small pin-sized spots are tumors."

"Can we treat the lungs?" I asked.

"Yes, we can," Dr. Albritton replied, "but I still don't know what type of cancer Jeff has, and I will continue studying his tissue until I am certain."

Stillness surrounded us. I can't recall what more we discussed and how the conversation ended. I remember returning to the arms of our friends waiting for us in the family room. They comforted us as we stood together, stunned.

"He's going to be okay," Jackie said as I rested my head on her shoulder.

Jackie and Michael left shortly afterward, and John and I returned to Jeff's room.

"Hi, Jeff," I said as we entered.

He was watching the sports channel. It had become dark outside. It seemed more lonely being in the hospital at night.

"Are you hungry, honey? We can go out and get you something to eat."

"Are there any Wendy's nearby?"

"I don't think so," his dad replied. "How about a pizza?"

"Sure."

John left for the pizza, and I sat with Jeff. I didn't speak of the tumors in his lungs.

CHAPTER 8

⁂

K–8 Grade School

ON SATURDAY MORNINGS in the fall, the soccer fields behind the Henry T. Wing Elementary School were packed with young players and their families. John Jr. had long legs and a thin body and could run up and down the field with ease.

In 1991, John and I had coached John Jr.'s team. We taught the kids the basics: where to stand on the field and when to run and kick the ball. That was really all I knew about soccer. When John wasn't there to coach, the kids would all surround the ball and kick it into each other. I'd find myself running up and down the field with the kids, yelling, "Spread out, spread out!"

It was the only exercise I got all week that made my heart race and my face red.

"Mom, you can't run on the field," John Jr. said after the game.

"I know, I'm sorry, but they can't all surround the ball and then kick it into each other. They've got to play their positions and pass the ball."

After one of our games, John Jr. ran off into the sea of colored shirts.

Just then a mother approached me. She was smiling and had also been abandoned by her son.

"Are you Mrs. Hayes?" she asked.

I froze, thinking, oh God, what did John Jr. do? I didn't know why she was asking who I was. I looked back at her and said, "I think that's Mrs. Hayes over there by the playground, near the trees." I pointed to the other side of the field. She looked across the field, and I smiled, thinking, what am I, nuts? I said, "No, I'm sorry, I'm Mrs. Hayes."

"Oh, hi. I'm Mrs. Smith," and she kind of half smiled. "My son, Bryson, loves your son and wanted me to ask you whether he could come over to our house and play?"

I smiled back at her. "Oh, yes, of course." If she'd approached my husband, he would have had a long talk with her and learned everything about her son, their family, and where they lived. He was much more social than I, and he dug deep for any connection he might have with them.

"I'm sure he'd love to play with your son. He's gone off to watch a game still going on. We can ask him," I said, looking back at her and hoping this first impression meant nothing.

Following in his brother's footsteps, Jeff also played soccer. He was good. His face turned purple while he ran up and down the field. He was strong with a powerful kick on the ball.

CHAPTER 9

Diagnosis and Treatment Plan, February 2005

M Y SISTER JANET had reserved a room for John and me for several nights at the Holiday Inn on Beacon Street in Brookline. It was about a mile and a half from Brigham and Women's Hospital, Children's Hospital, and the Jimmy Fund Clinic. Looking out our window at the hotel, we could see Fenway Park and the famous CITGO sign in Kenmore Square. After several days and nights sleeping on the plastic bed in Jeff's room, a real bed was a welcome treat. I showered and slept for a short while, but felt uncomfortable leaving Jeff alone in that hospital bed. In the weeks and months to come, the Holiday Inn became our place to go for a brief reprieve from the onslaught of bad news, tests, doctors, nurses, and the frightening unknown.

On Thursday, February 3, 2005, at eight o'clock in the morning as I walked from my hotel room to the elevator, my cell phone rang. It was Dr. Albritton. She began to speak about the kind of cancer Jeff had. She still sounded unsure, so I asked her straight out, "Is it Ewing's?" John and I had researched the possibilities of osteosarcoma and Ewing's sarcoma and thought Ewing's sarcoma would be the lesser of two evils. Dr. Albritton paused and said, "Yes, I believe it to be Ewing's." I felt relieved for some crazy reason. It's the better cancer, I thought.

Dr. Albritton proceeded to tell me that she was traveling out of town the next day and that I would be meeting with a new doctor, Dr. Holcomb Grier from Children's Hospital and the Jimmy Fund Clinic. I thanked Dr. Albritton for her help and for the long hours she had spent working to determine the type of cancer Jeff had. I would not see or hear from her again. We had counted on Dr. Albritton during those long hours and days waiting for news, good or bad, and had looked to her for answers, for comfort, and for hope. I would sit in my chair next to Jeff as he lay in his hospital bed and look up as she walked into the room, happy to see her and fearful at the same time of what she might tell us. When she wasn't with us, we knew she was there for us, working long hours. Now she was gone. Her job was done, and with her gone, I felt alone and frightened.

With the diagnostic phase now behind us, Jeff was discharged from the hospital. The next day we would visit the Jimmy Fund Clinic. Jeff's pain was under control, so we decided to stay around Boston with our friends Jackie and Michael. It was a welcome break from waking every morning to nurses, doctors, the hospital, cancer, and the upcoming treatment. At our friends' house, we could have peace and normalcy, even if for a short time.

Those who live in New England know about the Jimmy Fund. They have listened to telethons soliciting support for the Jimmy Fund. They know the relationship between the Boston Red Sox, Ted Williams and the Jimmy Fund, and they know why we support this foundation, this cause, and the kids afflicted with cancer. If you've been to Fenway Park, you've seen the picture on the Green Monster of the little boy on the Jimmy Fund sign. You're a part of this cause consciously or unconsciously because if you're a Red Sox fan, you're connected to the Jimmy Fund. If you live outside New England and are a Red Sox fan, then you too are a part of helping children with cancer. It's universal; everyone wants to help.

The Jimmy Fund Clinic is one of the world's leading pediatric centers for cancer research and treatment. It was founded in the 1940s by Dr. Sidney Farber, who used drug therapy to achieve the first-ever remission of childhood acute lymphoblastic leukemia. The clinic now treats every type of childhood cancer.

I used to think that the Jimmy Fund Clinic (JFC) must be a disease-stricken place with little hope for children with cancer. My ignorance changed the instant I walked through the clinic's doors. The JFC had state-of-the-art technology; it was clean and bright, well-staffed, and offered the best standard in health care for infants, children, and teenagers with cancer. Nothing compares to the devastation felt with the diagnosis of cancer in your child, but at the JFC, you'll be down on your knees, grateful there is such a place.

We arrived at the JFC on Friday morning to meet with an intake nurse. She explained to us that Jeff would have a surgical procedure to install a port-a-cath (or port) into his chest. The port was about the circumference of a quarter and about one-eighth of an inch thick. A catheter running from the port would be inserted into a main artery of his heart. The port would be a fast way to deliver therapy into Jeff's bloodstream, and it would be an alternative to putting a needle into a vein each time he needed to receive a chemo treatment or to give a blood sample. The port enabled Jeff to withstand weekly access to his blood and it avoided the possibility of his veins collapsing during treatment or transfusions.

Once the intake nurse finished with us, she brought us to a waiting area where we would meet Dr. Holcomb Grier. This was a small corner room of the JFC where two small couches faced glass windows revealing a third-floor view of the surrounding hospital buildings. We wheeled Jeff into the room, and John, John Jr., Jason, and I sat on the two couches. Dr. Grier entered, introduced himself, and pulled up a chair next to Jeff. He began the meeting by asking Jeff when he had first sensed the tumor in his leg. Sitting in his wheelchair and wearing his varsity high school jacket, Jeff told Dr. Grier how his thigh had become sore and how the pain kept getting worse and worse to the point where it was unbearable.

As I listened to Jeff, I had to wonder what might have happened if he had complained sooner about the pain in his thigh. But that wouldn't have been Jeff. Jeff never complained about anything. He had accepted the pain until it had become too much to bear. It was uncharacteristic of him to bring attention to himself in any way. I understood how he would keep his pain private and not tell us. I couldn't be angry with him for that. I couldn't ask myself, "What if he'd told us sooner?"

As Jeff told Dr. Grier about himself and what had unfolded during the last several weeks, I was proud of him. I listened to him speak politely, explaining how he felt in short sentences and phrases. He was a shy teenager, sixteen years old. I was overwhelmed, but he was very calm as he spoke in front of all of us.

Dr. Grier told us that the cause of Ewing's sarcoma was not from anything Jeff ate, anything he did, anything that I ate when I was pregnant, or anything I did. He said to Jeff, quite frankly, "It was just bad luck." Jeff's cancer was housed in his thigh, in the mother ship, as Dr. Ready had referred to it. The cancer had spread to his lungs. It was quite serious, and the prognosis was not good.

Dr. Grier began to describe the two different types of treatment.

One course of treatment, still in a trial stage, would require Jeff to spend the next nine months isolated in a hospital room with constant and high doses of chemotherapy. This treatment would compromise his immune system and make him susceptible to life-threatening infections; therefore, Jeff would not be able to leave the hospital the entire time and would be allowed only family for visitors. His surroundings would be sterile, and we would need to adhere to strict, limited exposure to Jeff.

The more commonly used treatment, Dr. Grier explained, was fourteen cycles of five different drugs delivered over the course of twelve months. Jeff would receive one cycle of treatment every three weeks.

Dr. Grier recommended the trial treatment. Later I thought it might have been because of the stage of Jeff's cancer. He did not say it would give Jeff a better chance than the standard and more commonly used treatment. We looked at each other, processing Dr. Grier's words when John Jr. emphatically said, "No, that's not an option!" He shook his head in earnest. I silently agreed with him and was proud that he spoke up and felt the need to protect his younger brother. I also thought it was an unimaginable sacrifice for a sixteen year old to be isolated for so many months without his friends, sports, and school. We chose the standard treatment.

Dr. Grier explained the battery of tests Jeff would undergo before treatment could begin. He would have these tests at Children's Hospital and Brigham and Women's Hospital, just across the street from the JFC. These tests would measure how well Jeff's body was performing now and would also serve as a baseline to determine how the chemotherapy was impairing him. Many of the tests would be repeated over the course of treatment to see how well he was holding up.

Jeff would have an audiogram hearing test prior to his treatment as chemotherapy drugs can affect hearing.

He would have a bone scan to see whether the cancer had spread to any other bones.

He would have two tests to assess his kidney function. A creatinine clearance test would measure how well his kidneys were working before treatment; creatinine is a protein, and the level of creatinine in the blood can be measured to monitor kidney function. A GFR kidney filtration test would be done before and after some of his treatments. Before each GFR test, a special dye would be injected intravenously. Then, at certain intervals after the injection, a blood sample would be taken to measure how much of the dye was still in the blood; this would measure how well Jeff's kidneys were working by measuring how quickly they had removed the dye from his blood.

Jeff would also have an electrocardiogram (EKG) to record his heart's rhythm and electrical activity to show whether his heart was able to function normally throughout his treatment. Pulmonary function tests would show how well his lungs were working during his treatment.

The most important test in determining the severity of the cancer and whether it was spreading was the bone marrow test. Marrow is the tissue in the center of the bones that produces white blood cells, red blood cells, and platelets. During the test, a sample of marrow is taken from the hipbone and examined for abnormalities. This is the test whose results would be the most devastating should they prove to be positive. If this test showed that the cancer had entered the bone marrow, Jeff's chances for surviving this disease would be terribly compromised.

I understood the reason and the importance of all these tests, but I was scared, impatient and anxious. I'm the type of person who jumps in the pool without knowing how deep it is. I just wanted to start the treatment right away so we could get through it and get my son back to his normal life again.

It was Friday, however, and the tests and treatment would not start until the following week. "Let's get out of here," I said. I felt somewhat relieved that we knew the type of cancer Jeff had and that we had a treatment plan, but other than that, I would have no idea what was in store for us. This was so upsetting and so frightening. We just wanted to go home.

CHAPTER 10

In Net

J EFF AND JOHN Jr.'s youth hockey, Metro Boston hockey, and high school hockey took up all our time with travel, practice, and tournaments. Their schedules often sent John and me in different directions. After one of Jeff's games, I stood outside the locker room waiting for Jeff to change out of his uniform. My nose felt cold; I imagined it turning red against my white face. From where I stood, I could see the ice surface and the goalie's net. It looked bigger from ice level and more intimidating. I imagined John Jr. and Jeff speeding down the ice and around the net. I had an urge to skate.

I quickly glanced up at the clock on the wall behind the goal, wondering why it was taking Jeff so long.

Robin Bevilacqua approached me. "Do you know what your son did?" Thoughts of the soccer field with John Jr. resurfaced. I knew Robin, so I couldn't pretend I was someone else.

"Hi, Robin. No, I'm sorry I don't. What did he do?" I asked. How did I miss what I missed? I wondered.

"During last week's game, the goalie was called for a penalty," Robin said. In hockey, when the goalie is penalized, he or she stays in the game, but someone from the team has to go sit in the penalty box. "The coach asked my son, Josh, to take the team penalty."

"Yes, I remember." I replied.

Most coaches will pick the player with the least amount of ice time so that the stronger players don't lose a shift with their line.

"My son was upset and crying while he sat in the penalty box," she continued. "Jeff was the only kid on the team who skated over to Josh.

45

Jeff stopped in front of the penalty box. He leaned over the boards and said, 'It's not your fault.' Jeff's a good kid," she said.

Jeff now played Mite A level. His coach was Jack Lessard, a pilot with American Airlines. The team was called the Canal Cobras.

We were at the Hobomock Ice Skating Rink and Pilgrim Skating Club in Pembroke to play a team from South Boston. The rink was old, dark, and cold. It looked like the first rink built on the South Shore. I wondered whether the first settlers skated here. I sat in the metal bleachers with a small group of parents, shivering as I sipped on a cup of hot chocolate.

"John, where are all the kids?" I asked my husband.

"Most of them are sick and didn't come," he said as he walked up the bleachers toward us. I thought about a game we'd played a few weeks ago on Martha's Vineyard when Jeff became sick with an upset stomach. They needed him to play and gave him saltine crackers and sips of water between shifts. After the game, on the ferryboat to Falmouth and still sick, Jeff threw up, but we won the game.

"Where's Jack?" I asked. "Are they going to play?"

"Yes, they'll play. Jack's flying today, but the assistant coach is here. Problem is we don't have a goalie."

"No goalie!"

"I think Jeff's gonna play goalie."

"Jeff!"

"Relax, he's played goalie in our basement with John Jr. for years. He'll be fine."

"What's he going to wear? We don't have goalie equipment."

"Someone on the team has some old goalie pads he can wear."

The game started with Jeff in net for the Canal Cobras versus South Boston. He looked so tiny in front of the big net. The game was played on a full sheet of ice, but all the action was on our end against Jeff. It got to the point in the second and into the third period that the South Boston parents began to cheer for Jeff when he stopped a shot. He was amazing during this shooting gallery. Every time he stopped the puck, shot after shot, the crowd roared. It was so exciting to watch. When the game ended, his teammates circled him.

"Nice game, Jeff!" I heard Jeff's teammates say, one after another.

"You made a hundred saves," another player said when he hit Jeff's goalie pads with his stick.

The referee approached Jeff in short, slow strides and softly stopped with his sharp blades against the ice surface, looking down at Jeff. "Good game," he said and handed Jeff the game puck, patting him on the shoulder. Jeff cupped the puck in his glove and looked up, smiling back at the referee; I could see his big grin through the goalie mask.

"Thanks," Jeff replied.

Officially, Jeff made fifty-two saves and let only six shots in net. The final score was South Boston 6, Canal 0.

"I wish Jack was here to see this." John looked at me, standing against the boards watching.

"Yeah, he would have loved it, being a goalie himself," I replied.

CHAPTER 11

Hockey Lace Bracelets

JEFF WAS CONFINED to a wheelchair and crutches when we returned home. This was his first time home since that horrible Sunday night, the night of the nor'easter. Nothing had changed except that the pain was now controlled by morphine, making him more comfortable and able to speak to his friends, eat, and feel a little at ease. Coach Curtis visited Jeff to tell him that he'd been selected by the coaches from the Atlantic Coast League to be the honorary captain of the all-star team. He wouldn't be skating, but there would be a special tribute to him before the game.

The next day, the whole family drove to Gallo Ice Arena. During the tribute on the ice and as the large crowd of spectators cheered, the teams lined up on the blue lines facing each other. Jeff, dressed in his varsity jacket, was announced and pushed onto the ice in his wheelchair by the Sandwich High captain, Matt Doyle. Matt had given up his role as captain for Jeff. We watched from the stands as the crowd cheered. The players hit their sticks against the ice as the Plymouth South coach presented Jeff with a T-shirt signed by the Wolverines, a semi-professional hockey team from Hartford. He also presented Jeff  with a navy-blue nylon warm-up suit their team wore. In the stands, spectators could buy hockey laces cut into short pieces to make a bracelet with the initials *SHS* and Jeff's number, twelve, printed in the blue of the Sandwich Blue Knights. The Plymouth coach bought bracelets for each member of his team.

The bracelets were designed and manufactured by the Lessard and Iadonisi families in their basements and were being sold in all three of Sandwich's kindergarten-to-grade-eight schools, at the high school, at hockey games, and throughout the town. They sold for five dollars each. Everywhere where we went, we saw Jeff's hockey-lace bracelets. Everyone had to have one. I was overwhelmed by the support.

CHAPTER 12

Pretreatment Tests and Treatment Protocol

"J EFF, WHAT'S THE weather for tomorrow?" I stood in the doorway of his bedroom. He was lying on his back, his head propped up with pillows and his legs stretched out straight. He was on his cell phone. I asked knowing he was on the phone but wondering what weather we might encounter heading up to Boston in the morning. I was in and out of his room cleaning and packing, just hanging close.

"Mom, who do I look like: Barry Burbank?" he asked with a big grin on his face. I smiled and thought, must be his girlfriend on the other end.

"No, honey, more like Bruce Schwoegler," I replied. He was smiling, but not from anything I said. I left his room.

It was Super Bowl Sunday, and the New England Patriots were in the Super Bowl, playing against the Philadelphia Eagles. Patriot's balloons hung from his bedpost. Jeff and his friends ate nachos and salsa, chicken wings, and pizza and cheered on the Patriots. We left them alone, keenly aware that none of them really knew the severity of Jeff's disease. The Patriots won the game, beating the Eagles 24–21.

Monday morning we headed up to Boston to Children's Hospital. Traffic was terrible—two and a half hours of stop and go; a normal, traffic-free ride took one hour. Two days of testing were ahead of us. If the test results showed that Jeff's major organs were strong enough to withstand the treatment, Jeff would receive his first round of chemotherapy on Thursday.

During the GFR test at Children's Hospital, Jeff lay in a small room on a bed as the nurse drew blood and injected dye into his system. His leg was still swollen and painful, even with pain medication, which made him tired and glassy-eyed. I sat in the waiting room with Jason.

"Jason, I'm going to the lobby for a chocolate chip cookie. Want one?"

"Yeah, sure."

"You okay here? I'll be right back."

"I'm okay."

"If they're looking for me, tell them I just stepped out for a minute and will be right back, okay?"

"Okay, but hurry."

I bought a cookie that Jason and I shared. I'd just taken my last bite when, through the window of the waiting room, I saw Doreen and Jack Lessard walking by with their son Garrett. Their eldest son, John, was Jeff's best friend. Steve was their third son. Jeff had spent a lot of time at their home.

The boys played sports together. Jack painted a replica of the Boston Bruins ice surface in the basement of their colonial-style home, and the boys played hockey for hours at a time.

Doreen and Jack had brought Garrett to Children's Hospital that day for a follow-up exam for an injury Garrett had sustained during one of his hockey games. He was a tough hockey player and played on select hockey teams like his brother John and our Jeff.

"Would you like to see Jeff?" I asked.

"Sure! How's he doing?" Jack asked. I explained to them the tests that were scheduled for Jeff over the next few days and the kidney test he was undergoing that day.

We walked into the small examining room. Jeff looked surprised as they walked to his bedside.

"Hey, Jeff," Jack said, standing at the end of his bed. "How are you, buddy?"

"Hi, Mr. Lessard. I'm doing okay, thanks." Jeff's voice was soft, and he spoke slowly. I thought about the time when Jeff was a Mite and Jack backed into our driveway to pick up Jeff for a game off Cape. Jeff picked up his hockey bag and looked up at Jack and said, "Can I bring my homework, Mr. Lessard?" Jeff pushed his huge hockey bag—it was bigger than him—into the back of the truck along with his hockey stick. Jack looked at me and then back at Jeff. "Oh, yeah, sure, Jeff." Jack looked at me, surprised. I shrugged my shoulders and whispered, "His words, not mine."

Jeff looked up at Garrett from the small examining table where he lay.

"Hey, Garrett, are you keeping those water bottles filled?" Jeff asked in his upperclassman voice. Garrett was in eighth grade and was the water boy for the high school varsity team, Jeff's team.

"Yeah," Garrett smiled.

"How's the team?" Jeff asked.

"We're doing fine. We miss you on defense."

Their visit was shortened when the nurse returned to draw more blood.

"Well, we'll see you soon, Jeff," Doreen said. I walked into the hallway with them and watched as they left. They disappeared down the hall and I stared aimlessly, wishing Jeff was here for a follow-up visit for a strained muscle.

We had little free time that day. The doctors had scheduled all tests to be done in a few days so that treatment could begin as soon as possible. Once the nurse completed the first stage of the GFR test, Jeff got back into his wheelchair, and we headed to cardiology for a cardiogram and EKG. When that was done, we left cardiology and returned to test the level of dye in Jeff's system, and when that was done, we hit the road for home.

The next day, my sister-in-law Patty, Jeff, Jason and I drove up from the Cape again, this time to the otolaryngology department at Children's Hospital for Jeff's hearing tests. Patty and Jason stayed in the waiting room as I pushed Jeff in his wheelchair into what looked like the inside of a B-52 bomber from World War II. I had once stood inside the cockpit of a B-52 at the Otis Air Force Base in Bourne during an air show. It was very small.

I hoped the hearing test would be quick and not stressful for Jeff. I pushed his wheelchair into the small room. The walls were quilted with a soundproof blanket. The controls and gauges were old, something out of the 1940s, I thought.

I stood quietly behind Jeff after maneuvering his wheelchair in front of the small window. We could see the technician through the small glass opening. While Jeff raised his hand to the sounds transmitted into his headphones, I remembered hearing tests from my own childhood, when I had sat across from a woman with a big machine on the table in front of me. I put a large earphone up to my ear, listened to a high-pitched tone, and raised my hand. My face remained stoic as I changed the earphone to my other ear. I kept raising my hand and looking for the woman to smile, but she never did.

Jeff's test ended.

"How are you feeling, honey?"

"I'm okay, tired I guess. Are we done?"

"Just one more, the bone marrow test. Then we can go home."

The results of the auditory, kidney, and cardiology tests proved that Jeff's body, his organs, could withstand the high doses of chemotherapy that would be prescribed to beat this cancer.

On Wednesday night, February 9, 2005, we were at home when the phone rang. It was Christie, who was Jeff's Doctoral Fellow at the time, calling to tell us that the bone marrow test results were negative—the cancer had not spread to his bone marrow. Jeff could start chemotherapy.

The next day, Jeff and I met with Dr. Holcomb Grier and Christie at the JFC. They recommended that Jeff receive chemotherapy and surgery (Protocol 01-208). We went over the treatment description and consent form together. Christie read through each page with us.

> The goal of the proposed treatment was to cure Jeffrey of his cancer if possible (CH# 4014097 DFCI #323607 Individualized Treatment Consent for Jeffrey Hayes). Jeff will receive the anti-cancer drugs vincristine, doxorubicin, cyclophosphamide, ifosfamide and etoposide. He will be given the drug Mesna after each treatment to protect his bladder. Because chemotherapy drugs in most cases kill both the tumor and many of the normal blood cells, Jeff will start taking a new drug just recently approved by the FDA called Neulasta which will enable the white blood cells to recover more quickly after chemotherapy. This drug was in the very first stage of usage.
>
> The first cycle will consist of vincristine, doxorubicin and cyclophosphamide. All three drugs will be given over the first two days of treatment. Following this treatment there is a recovery period that will continue for three weeks from the first day of Jeff's treatment. Jeff will stay over one night and on the second day he will be discharged from Children's Hospital to return home where Mrs. Hayes will monitor any side effects or fevers.

Vincristine, doxorubicin, cyclophosphamide, ifosfamide, and etoposide. They sounded like insecticides. They sounded powerful. Vincristine is the female "bad," I thought. The name sounded feminine but evil.

After three weeks of recovery from the first cycle, the second cycle would consist of ifosfamide and etoposide. He would be given these two chemotherapy drugs over the course of five days; the first day would be at the JFC, and the remaining four days would be at Children's Hospital. Jeff would then come home for a three-week recovery period.

The oncologist told us that they alternated the drugs given to Jeff because the cancer cells are so smart; that was the word he used. The cancer cells remember or recognize the last drugs used, and the drugs become less effective. So they hit the cancerous cells when they are "down" with a new and different, effective drug combination.

I found this amazing, and it brought the disease to life for me. Cancer is alive; it's a living creature and able to destroy healthy blood cells and kill an otherwise healthy person. The cancer can differentiate between different drugs and defend itself against them. I realized how frightening this disease was.

The treatment program would have fourteen cycles, alternating between the two sets of drugs with periods of recovery in between. After the first four cycles, we would discuss the options of surgery, radiation, or leg amputation. I didn't think or speak about the leg amputation. We had four cycles ahead of us.

I began to learn the new language of hematology and pharmaceuticals. I began to learn how to administer the drugs. I studied their effects. I became focused. I kept records and learned what I needed to know and blocked out everything else.

At home, KerryKares, Inc. of Sandwich, a nonprofit organization supporting families in Sandwich who are battling cancer, brought us gift cards and food. I never knew this organization existed, and I was grateful for its help. People from KerryKares appeared throughout Jeff's treatment. Their random acts of kindness were heartwarming and uplifting.

One day after I'd returned from the hospital with Jeff, I found a gift that KerryKares had dropped off at our house. It was a large, pewter hanging piece for the front door. The back lay flat against the door, and the front had a pocket that I filled with colorful flowers. I smiled, standing on our front lawn admiring it. I felt normal.

CHAPTER 13

JEFF WAS IN first grade when he started CCD, Confraternity of Christian Doctrine—a religious program provided to children of the Catholic church. One Sunday morning, it was time to leave for church, but Jeff was nowhere in sight.

"Where's Jeff?"

"Still in bed," John replied.

"Still in bed! We've got to go soon."

I ran up the stairs and opened his door.

He was lying on his side facing me as I kneeled down next to him.

"What's the matter, honey? It's time to get ready for CCD class."

"I don't want to go."

"What do you mean you don't want to go?"

His eyes started to water, and I asked again, "Why don't you want to go?"

He shrugged. "I don't know."

"Do you feel okay?" I felt his forehead. He didn't answer, staring back at me.

I stood up. "Come on, get dressed. I'm going with you. Here are your clothes; let's go."

When we arrived at Corpus Christi Parish, Jeff and I entered the rectory and walked toward the classrooms. First graders found their seats, and Jeff sat down at a table alongside the windows. I approached the teacher.

"Hi. I'm Mrs. Hayes," I said, looking at the teacher and wondering what Jeff feared about her class. "I will be sitting in class today, if that's okay with you."

"Hi, Mrs. Hayes. Of course that's fine; please have a seat."

"Good morning, class!" she shouted, and I jumped in my seat at the tone of her voice. She was over six feet tall and thin with short and wavy gray hair. Her flowered blouse was buttoned up tightly around her neck, and she wore dress slacks with cuffs and flat shoes on her feet. With her arms crossed, she started calling out questions and then pointing to students for answers. I began to feel very uncomfortable and a bit nervous. I don't know the answer, I thought. My twelve years of CCD, and I'm drawing a blank.

She called on Jeff.

"God," he replied.

"That's right. Very good, young man," she replied. I tried to match his correct answer to the question she posed. I certainly wouldn't question the answer, God. I lived my life believing in Him.

I smiled in momentary relief as she called on another first grader.

She kept up the relentless questioning, firing out at one student after another without taking a breath. I could feel my face turning red and my blood pressure rising.

"This is worse than getting pucks shot at you, Jeff," I whispered to him, feeling like I might get thrown out of class if I got caught.

"You should have worn your hockey helmet and pads!" I whispered again. He smiled, not looking back at me but concentrating on what the teacher was saying.

Sister Slap Shot, I thought, not wanting to disrupt Jeff's concentration.

I hadn't noticed the clouds approaching until the sun's brightness hid behind the darkened sky and the classroom became more luminous. I glanced out the window, looking up through the glass. I had only turned my head for a moment when the shadow had passed through the room; the clouds had moved silently across the sky.

When the class ended, I approached the teacher.

"My son—and I, for that matter—are very uncomfortable in your class. He was upset this morning and didn't want to come to your class. I don't want my son to be afraid to attend Sunday school. He should feel a sense of well-being and peacefulness as he learns about God, not fear."

"I'll talk to him, Mrs. Hayes; I want him to be comfortable in class," she replied.

"Great, then he'll see you next week."

Jeff and I left the classroom. The room emptied, and the other kids met up with a parent in the hallway. At the end of the corridor and through the door window I could see the rain. When we reached the door, and others ahead of us had exited the rectory, I looked down at Jeff standing beside me.

"We need to make a run for it. You game?"

He smiled back at me. "Yup."

I took his hand, and we made a dash for the car.

The following Sunday I dropped Jeff off at his class. From that Sunday on I never had difficulty getting him to go. I never sat in his class again. On the last day of CCD, I entered the classroom, and his teacher approached me.

"Hi, Mrs. Hayes. Do you have a moment? She motioned for me to come and stand next to her in front of the blackboard, and then she said, "Your son is one of the nicest boys I've ever had in any of my classes."

She was sincere, and I felt she must have made an effort to get to know him. It was satisfying to me knowing she'd discovered his kind soul and genuine heart.

CHAPTER 14

Jeff, Jason, Breast Cancer Scare

J ASON NEVER WANTED to play hockey. He watched his brothers intently from the stands, keeping stats, remembering plays in detail, remembering their goals. He had other interests, and with all the time we'd spent at hockey games and during practice, I had missed recognizing his talents.

"Mom, I have a solo in the school concert," he shouted as he ran up the stairs coming in from first grade one day. "What?" I asked as I walked to the bottom of the stairs. "You have a solo? Wow, that's great! What's the song?" I asked. I thought it would be a popular school song, maybe one I'd sung in elementary school. I assumed he would sing along with a recording.

"You don't know it, Mom," he replied from the top of the stairs.

"I don't! I thought I knew all children's songs."

"Not this one."

"Do you know the words, honey?"

"I study them at night, Mom. Are you coming to the concert?"

"Of course! When is it?"

"Next week!"

The night of the concert, I sat between my mother-in-law, Thelma, and my sister-in-law, Patty. I grew nervous waiting for Jason to sing. He was so shy and quiet.

There were two solos that night. Jason and his classmate were called to sing their solos side by side at the front of the stage. When the first student finished his song, Jason immediately pulled the microphone from his classmate's hands and began to sing. He sang beautifully and sounded like a choirboy. I'd never heard him sing before. I looked at Thelma and then Patty. Both had tears in their eyes. The auditorium was silent. Jason didn't miss a note. I looked around the room at the audience and then back at him. I was amazed and so proud. After that night he never sang publically again. I don't know why; I wish he had. He was really good.

Jason loved sports too and played Little League baseball. He was very bright and very quiet. On the day of his third-grade teacher conference, I walked into his classroom and sat down on the tiny chair at the small, circular table across from his teacher. The classroom was empty. The walls were covered with students' drawings and mathematical equations. Halfway into the conversation, she seemed to become irritated. She said, "Jason never raises his hand in class, so the other day, I called on him. I asked him for the answer to my question. He was sitting with the class on the floor when I called on him, and he looked back at me and said, 'I don't know the answer. When I know the answer, I'll raise my hand.'"

I held back my smile, trying not to burst into laughter. Are you kidding me? I thought. I said the words again in my head: when I know the answer, I'll raise my hand. Jason wasn't a rude child, nor difficult. He was quiet.

"He needs to contribute more to the group," she continued. "He's a very good student, but I'd like to hear more from him."

I was proud of Jason as I walked away from his teacher, my back to her, smiling. What a difference a gene makes.

I worked from March to October in the years 1990 to 2001 at New Seabury, an oceanside resort. During the summer and up until October, my neighbor, Carol Boley, took care of my boys. She had four kids, three about the same age as mine. Our summers were busy with baseball, the beach, and friends visiting and staying for the weekend. It was hard for

John and me—we had to work and host! My time to be with family was during the winter months when the resort closed and the Cape was quiet.

During the winter I'd schedule annual physicals for myself and my sons. At age forty, I scheduled my annual mammogram. I thought nothing of it, as I'd always been healthy. I left the boys at home and traveled to Hyannis for my morning appointment.

The procedure went fine. Back in the waiting room, I was asked to stay and wait for the doctor to speak with me. I began to fear the worst.

"Susan," I heard a technician call my name.

"Yes?" I replied.

"The doctor will see you now. Please come this way."

I followed her into the doctor's office and sat in front of his desk. Is this a movie? I thought. Or am I about to hear the worst?

"Hi, Mrs. Hayes," the doctor said as I sat.

"Hi."

"I examined your mammogram and noticed some cysts on one breast." He paused only a moment. "I don't think it's anything, but I'd like to be sure and have you come back for an ultrasound."

"Okay," I replied.

"You can wait until next week or come back this afternoon for the ultrasound," he said.

"I'll be back this afternoon," I said immediately.

"Good. Please see the receptionist for the time. I'll see you this afternoon."

I drove home trying to process the possibility of cancer. Jeff and Jason met me at the door. Usually all three of my sons would run out to my car to greet me. John Jr. must have been eating or watching television.

I entered the kitchen and told Jeff and Jason that I wanted to be alone.

"What's the matter, Mom?" Jeff asked. He was seven years old, and Jason was four.

"Nothing, honey; I just need some time alone in my room, okay?"

"Okay."

I went upstairs and called Mom. She and I talked at least once a week. We talked until I heard a knock on my bedroom door.

"Mom, it's me and Jason. Can we come in?"

"I'll have to call you back, Mom." I hung up the phone.

"Sure, come on in."

I was sitting on the love seat next to the phone when they entered my bedroom. I looked up and saw Jeff holding a plate with a tuna fish sandwich and potato chips; Jason was holding a glass of chocolate milk.

"Here, Mom," Jeff said.

"Oh wow, you guys, thanks! It's my favorite lunch."

Jeff shrugged his shoulders and smiled. Jason mimicked his brother.

"You're welcome. Come on Jay, let's go," Jeff said, and they left, closing the door behind them.

I looked at the tuna fish sandwich on white bread and took a bite. There were big chunks of white tuna with mayonnaise and lettuce. I smiled while eating the whole thing.

"I saw small cysts. It's nothing but fatty tissue," the doctor said after my ultrasound.

CHAPTER 15

First Treatment

On Thursday morning, February 10, 2005, I drove Jeff to Boston and parked in the parking garage at the Dana-Farber Cancer Institute. The JFC was on the third floor.

We came to a waiting room filled with infants in strollers, toddlers, and teenagers waiting quietly for their names to be called by one of the nurses. There were young girls and boys who were partially bald. There was a little girl with blotches of long, thin strands of light-brown hair that hadn't fallen out yet. I imagined she'd chosen not to shave her head. I smiled at her; she wore a pretty dress with matching shoes. Some kids sat quietly, while others rode around in small land rovers or played or sat cuddled in their mothers' laps. Preteen and teenage girls well into their treatment wore colorful bandanas to cover their baldness. They were all waiting, I imagined, to begin another round of chemotherapy that might make them very sick and take them away from their normal life.

We checked in at the reception desk and received a beeper that would alert us when it was Jeff's turn.

Across from the reception desk was a giant fish tank with colorful fish. Beyond the fish tank was another section for younger children and toddlers. Beyond that, were two doors that led to the other side; the side of treatment and chemotherapy—the clinging-to-life side. The buzzer lit up, startling me. "We're up, Jeff." I said.

I pushed Jeff in his wheelchair into a small examining room to have his vital signs, height, and weight measured. Tracking this information would alert the nurses and oncologist to any changes in the progression of the cancer. Good blood counts and weight stability or weight gain

64

could be a good indication that Jeff was withstanding the treatment and battling the disease with positive results.

Jeff was taken to another examining room so that Hannah, the nurse who would be assigned to Jeff for the course of his treatments, could access his port. I sat across from Jeff. As Hannah placed a needle in Jeff's port, I looked out the door and saw a little girl crying. She was about three years old. She was running in and out of the other examining room, screaming, "I don't want the blue tube; I want the pink one."

I thought, does she know that the blue tube will make her sick? The blue tube must carry the chemotherapy drugs and make her sick. I didn't know. I was guessing. Or is it just that she likes the color pink? She's so young; how could she know? It was our first day. It was all new to us. Her red face, her tears, and her anger saddened me. I wanted to pick her up and take her away from this place. We looked at each other, Jeff and I. We didn't know what to expect or how he would react to his own treatment. We said nothing. The little girl's nurse scooped her up and took her down the corridor. We never saw her again.

Once Hannah finished with Jeff, we returned to the waiting room. It wasn't long before another nurse came and signaled for us to follow her. I pushed Jeff in his wheelchair through the two large doors, down a hallway, and past rooms with beds where I saw younger patients, and then to the back of the clinic. We came to the last room, a large one with two beds on one side of the room and two reclining chairs on the other.

"I'll take the window bed, Mom," Jeff said.

"Honey, why don't you take your shoes off?"

He pushed down on the heel of his shoe with his other foot. He got out of the wheelchair and sat on the bed. I helped him lift his legs onto the bed, and he pulled himself up and rested his head on the pillow.

"Mom, how can I put up the head of the bed?" He studied the hospital bed and the room.

"Push the buttons on the side of the bed. Here's the remote for the television."

"Hey, Jeff!" Hannah walked into the room and came to Jeff's bed with an IV bag.

"Hi," Jeff replied.

"We are going to give you some fluids so that you're completely hydrated before we start the treatment."

"Okay."

"I hear you're a hockey player?"

"Yeah."

"I'm a basketball player," she replied. "So I'm afraid I don't know much about hockey, Jeff."

He smiled. "That's okay; I'm not much of a basketball player."

Hannah smiled. "Once you're hydrated, I will give you some antinausea drugs so you won't feel sick later. We will give you Zophran, Ativan, Marinol, and a patch behind your ear. Next time you come for treatment, you might want to start the hydration on your ride up from the Cape by drinking Gatorade or water. If you're hydrated when you arrive, we can start your treatment right after you get here."

"That sounds like a good idea, Jeff," I looked over at him lying in the bed wearing his white Fighting Irish cap.

"Okay." He watched Hannah while she connected his IV fluid. "We'll do that next time so we can start early and be done early," Jeff replied.

"Yeah, getting done early sounds great. Can he eat anything before his treatment?" I asked.

"Yes, he can, but you might want to have something light."

"Jeff, are you hungry?" I asked, knowing it would be better not to eat, but I didn't know what else to say. Asking questions was a good way to start up a conversation between Jeff and Hannah, I thought. Jeff might have the same questions but be afraid to ask. Then again, he might be pissed that I'm asking too many questions. Just be quiet, I told myself.

"No, I don't want anything right now, Mom."

Hannah began the hydration, and Jeff and I watched the television above his bed for the next hour. We looked away from the television as Hannah approached again.

"Jeff, can you pee in the urinal for me so that I can see if you're hydrated enough to start the chemotherapy?"

I helped him move his legs off the bed and closed the curtain behind me.

It took about two hours for him to become hydrated, and then he was given the Zophran, Ativan, and Marinol orally, and a patch was placed behind his ear. He was also given a strong antibiotic called Bactrim to prevent infection in his lungs. It was a long, white, horse pill.

Hannah then administered the vincristine, doxorubicin, and cyclophosphamide through his port. I watched as the first drug dripped down the line from the bag hanging on his IV pole and into his port. Jeff laid his head on his pillow and closed his eyes as if he could feel the powerful drugs. He slept most of the afternoon.

It was late in the afternoon when Jeff finished this first round of chemotherapy.

"Susan, there is a room ready for Jeff on Six West back at Children's Hospital. We will get Jeff ready to move in a few minutes. Hey, Jeff, how are you doing?" Hannah asked.

He was groggy. He opened his eyes and looked at Hannah and said, "Okay."

We got him up and into the wheelchair to make our way to Six West for the night. Hannah disconnected the IV from the small tube coming out of Jeff's port. The small tube was plugged so that his port was still accessible for his treatment at Children's. We piled my suitcase, Jeff's backpack with his laptop, and Jeff's medical binder onto his lap. Hannah instructed us to take the elevator down to the main lobby and then cross the street to Children's. A catwalk connected the two buildings, but it was a roundabout way; crossing the street would be much faster.

"Are you okay, Jeff?" I asked.

"Yes."

"You did great, Jeff." Hannah said as I pushed him out into the hallway.

"I'll see you in a few weeks. Bye now."

"Thanks, Hannah," I replied for Jeff.

The antinausea medication had made him very drowsy, but he sat upright in the wheelchair for the trip next door.

We entered Children's and headed to Six West, the stem cell transplant floor. Jeff and I entered Children's as though we were invisible. People were coming and going; cars were pulling in and out while valet attendants directed the flow of traffic. The lobby was busy, and an aroma from Au Bon Pain filled the air. I thought there should be a private elevator for patients undergoing chemotherapy, so as not to expose them to germs that could compromise their health, but I didn't see one, so we took the public elevators and went up to the sixth floor. We came to a set of big doors. A sign instructed us to push the large, square button on the wall to open the doors. The doors opened slowly, and as I pushed Jeff in his wheelchair two steps forward toward a second set of doors, the first set closed behind us. We had to wait for the first set of doors to close before entering through the second set. I pushed another square button to open the second set of doors. I didn't entirely realize what the stem cell transplant floor would be like until I entered the first set of doors and waited in silence, frozen in time. Then I pressed the second large, square button to enter a quiet, sterile floor; there wasn't a soul in sight. I would have never imaged life would meet us here, I thought. At this moment I realized, as much as I tried to evade the truth of this disease and its treatment, we were now about to enter the stem cell transplant floor. The moment passed quickly as I armored myself with that invisible shield of mine that kept me focused on what to do next.

We entered Six West. A row of identical high counters ran down the length of a long, curving hallway. Each counter was a small nursing station in front of a glass window that looked into each patient's room.

I pushed on until we met a nurse who showed us to Jeff's room. It was the furthest one down the Six West corridor.

"Jeff will be here," the nurse said, opening a door into a small room; an observation room, I thought. We passed through another door into a small hospital room with a single bed, a computer desk, a television, a couch/bed under the window, and a small bathroom. The nurse explained this was a newly renovated floor for cancer patients needing bone marrow transplants. When I think back, they probably gave us this room so as not to shock us by putting us on Seven West on our very first night. This was a private, quiet floor.

Once Jeff was comfortable and his nurse finished taking his history, I decided to meet up with my husband and sister-in-law Patty for dinner. I told Jeff that I would be back in an hour. He was resting comfortably, so I left for a local Italian restaurant on Beacon Street in Brookline, not far from Coolidge Corner. I thought about my life, years ago, riding the trolley down Beacon Street to an internship as a medical assistant.

"How did it go today?" They asked as I sipped on my apple martini. They had suggested I have a drink to unwind before dinner. It eased the tension and stress I carried. With two sips, I began to relax, waiting for my veal and pasta. "Okay, I guess," I replied. "How's it supposed to go? He's receiving very strong drugs that would make him feel very sick if it weren't for the antinausea meds he takes. He's on Six West. It's the stem cell transplant floor." We ate our meals with little conversation.

After dinner, Patty and John went to the Holiday Inn, and I returned to Six West. Outside Jeff's room I saw a man I thought to be in his thirties. He was short, slim and wore round, black-framed glasses that closely encircled his eyes. He had very short, light-brown hair and was dressed nicely in a suit jacket, not a doctor's white coat. He approached me and said, "Hi, I'm Dr. Samuel Blackman. Are you Mrs. Hayes?"

"Yes." I shook his hand. "Nice to meet you, Dr. Blackman."

"I'm Jeff's oncologist. I have just spoken with him. I'm a Doctoral Fellow at the Dana-Farber Jimmy Fund Clinic." I placed my elbow on the high counter top at the nurse's station feeling the effects of my martini as Dr. Blackman stood across from me. I was tired from everything we'd been through up to this point but wanted to be alert and understand what this new doctor had to say. Our conversation was short, and he assured me I'd see him again in the morning.

"Good night, Dr. Blackman. Nice to meet you."

"Good night, Mrs. Hayes."

Later, I would realize how little this first impression meant to him or to me. We would go through so much together.

I entered Jeff's room to find him angry with me. "Where have you been? You said you were only going to be gone for one hour." I looked at him, knowing how frightened he was, and I sat down next to him on his bed. I lifted my hands, touching each side of his face and kissed his cheek and said, "I will not let anything happen to you."

How sobering that moment was for me. I sat up straight on his bed next to him, and he seemed to relax.

"Can I get you anything, honey?"

"Can you hand me my laptop?"

I passed him his new laptop, a gift he'd received the week before from the Sandwich Little League and Babe Ruth coaches. They had all chipped in to buy the laptop, and they had come over to our house to give it to him. That day, Jeff sat on our living room couch and opened the gift. "We thought you might need a laptop when you're in the hospital and want to e-mail your friends or do some homework," Coach Jim Melia said, smiling as he stood across from Jeff.

"Thank you, Mr. Melia!" Jeff looked away from his new laptop and back at Coach Melia. Jim walked out of our living room and into our kitchen, returning with a wooden bat made professionally by a local company in Barnstable. He handed Jeff the bat. A smile crossed both their faces as Jeff examined the bat as if he were standing on deck and batting next.

Amanda Condon and her mother, Jenni, were also at our house. Amanda was eleven and had just finished her treatment for Ewing's sarcoma, the same cancer Jeff had. She lived within miles of us in Sandwich.

Amanda stood behind Jeff, watching. Jenni gave Jeff a backpack for his laptop that was filled with macaroni and cheese and other things Amanda had found helpful during treatment. Amanda's hair was just growing back, and she was quiet meeting Jeff.

"He's going to be all right," Jenni assured me. We both knew that her daughter and my son were not the only kids in Sandwich with this rare bone cancer. Another young girl who lived close by had also been treated for Ewing's. Jeff was the oldest of the three. It seemed odd and frightening that in one small town on Cape Cod there would be three cases of Ewing's within miles of each other. This question became more concerning. Why have three cases of this rare cancer occurred so close in proximity?

"Is there anything we can watch on television together?" I asked Jeff, sitting next to his bed in the quiet and sterile room on Six West.

"I don't know; there aren't many stations," Jeff replied, not looking up from his laptop. I picked up the remote and slowly changed the channels. He closed his laptop, laid his head down on the pillow, and fell asleep. I covered the window bench with sheets and a blanket and dressed for bed. He'd receive his next dosage of chemotherapy the following morning, and then we'd be able to go home. I fell asleep—so ended the first day of his first set of chemotherapy drugs.

Jeff still felt sick the next day and was unsure of what he might face going home. He asked whether we could stay an extra night, so we did.

That evening, John and I met with Stacy, a social services representative for Dana-Farber. We met in the family room on Six West while Jeff remained in his isolated hospital room. We discussed our insurance coverage and possible assistance from the National Cancer Society. Stacy gave us gift certificates from the food court at Children's and from local restaurants, a gas card, a phone card, and a grocery card, and she told us about hotel rooms available to us for four nights per year at the Holiday Inn. We were allotted these stays at a discounted rate of twenty-five dollars per night.

It was a great relief for us, knowing assistance was available. Everything had happened so fast: the mounting pain, the snowstorm, the diagnosis, and then having to leave home and stay at the hospital for ten days. These gifts were unexpected and helped ease the financial burden that was quickly mounting. Jeff and his treatment were all I thought about, never anticipating the enormous cost.

It was a better-than-expected night, knowing the medical staff were keeping Jeff comfortable and monitoring him. I slept well on that plastic green bench embedded in the wall of Jeff's room, knowing that we were receiving help from the Dana-Farber Cancer Institute and the National Cancer Society. On Saturday, February 12, 2005, we were ready to head home. Before Jeff was discharged, we received instructions for administering anti-emetics, pain medications, and PCP prophylaxis—more precisely, Bactrim, the long, white capsule-shaped pill, a preventative medication for pneumonia. Jeff was given an injection of Neulasta. I read the instructions with the discharge nurse. While I had a good understanding of what to do, I also knew that anything could happen once we left Children's. The discharge plan read as follows:

Admission Date: 2/10/2005
Discharge Date: 2/ /2005 (this was left blank)
Discharge Diagnosis: Metastatic Ewing's Sarcoma
Discharge to home: Yes
Diet: As tolerated
Activity Level: 50% wt. Bear on Right Leg
Return to School on: Will discuss with school and Dr. Blackman
Medications:
Name of Drug—Dose Time—Special Instructions
Bactrim, 160 mg 8am/8pm M–W–F only
Zofran, 8 mg Every 8 hrs. as needed for nausea (start tomorrow)
Ativan, 1 mg Every 6 hrs. as needed for nausea
EMLA Cream Apply 1–2 hours before accessing port
MS Contin 30 mg = 2 tablets 8am/8pm, every day 2x/day for pain
MS IR10–20 mg = 1 or 2 tablets every 4 hrs. as needed for break thru pain
Follow Up Medical/Clinical Appointments: Jimmy Fund Clinic

Date: 2/21/2005
Contact Person: Dr. Samuel Blackman
Additional Discharge Instructions:
Call for: Fever • 100.4 2x in one day or 101.3 1x in one day or shaking or chills
Potential Infection: redness, swelling, drainage of any sore area or wound, including PAC site
Signs of Bleeding: Increased bruising or petechiae, visible blood in urine or stool, a cut that doesn't stop bleeding after 10 minutes or nosebleed that doesn't stop in 15 minutes.
Signs of Anemia: Extreme tiredness, pale skin or short of breath
Signs of Dehydration: Decreased urination or no urine for 6–8 hours, nothing to eat or drink for more than 8 hours while awake; or vomiting.
Problems with constipation or diarrhea
Life Threatening Emergencies, call 911
Medical Issues:
M–F 9:00 a.m.–5 p.m.: Call Jimmy Fund Clinic
Other times: Call Dana-Farber Page Operator and page Pediatric Oncology Fellow on call.

"Okay, aren't you coming home with us?" I asked the discharge nurse. It wasn't as if Jeff had just broken a leg and they were sending him home in a cast. Oh God, I thought. Okay, I can do this. I didn't think about what might happen. When we got home I stayed focused on his medications and stayed with him in case he needed or asked for anything. It helped knowing I was just a phone call away from the on-call oncologist at the JFC in Boston.

The side effects of the first treatment were immediate. The potent chemotherapy drugs were attacking and damaging his cancer cells and his healthy cells. Jeff's immune system was working overtime.

Over the first four to five days, as his body's defenses worked to recover from the toxic drugs, I gave Jeff his morphine and nausea medications as instructed, along with the stimulants for bowel movements and the Bactrim and Ativan. We checked for high temperatures. He had none. Mouth sores were a common side effect with this combination of drugs. Jeff's mouth sores were painful and made it difficult for him to eat. He was pale, tired, and quiet.

During this first week at home, Jason's middle-school nurse called to tell us that a student at the school had contracted chicken pox. Jason would have to stay home from school and quarantine himself from Jeff. The nurse told us that the girl who had the chicken pox had never received her immunizations because her parents didn't believe in them. A nurse from the JFC said it would greatly compromise Jeff's survival if he came down with the chicken pox.

Jeff also could not be exposed to any viruses or influenza. Weeks later, when the Sandwich hockey team came down with whooping cough, the players couldn't visit Jeff. The nurses at the middle school and high school kept us informed throughout the school year of any illness or virus that afflicted the students.

While Jeff recovered from the side effects of his first round of chemotherapy drugs, we could see the swelling in his leg decrease. It wasn't a dramatic change, but it was noticeable. He remained on crutches to get around, but remarkably the pain also lessened. This gave us great hope.

One morning, as I handed Jeff a bowl of cereal, he held the spoon in his hand and looked back at me and said, "Mom, I'm having bad dreams."

"You are? Of what, honey?" I asked. He shrugged his shoulders in reply.

"Umm, try this. If you wake up during the bad dream, put the television on and watch sports or a movie; that might help you forget. It's probably the chemo drugs, honey. Let me know if they continue, and we'll tell Dr. Blackman, okay?"

"Okay," he replied.

CHAPTER 16

Cross-Checking

WHEN JEFF WAS in eighth grade, he was playing his fourth year with the Bridgewater Bandits, a team in the Metro Boston Hockey League. Each player was the best at his position. Jeff was a defenseman. The Bandits' practice was always intense. They skated hard, practiced drills and stopped only at the sound of the coach's whistle. They all looked the same in their black practice jerseys. Many of the players hoped to be recruited by a private school where they could play at the highest level. At the end of one of Jeff's practices, Jason and I were standing in the rink's lobby waiting for Jeff. Johnny Muse, the Bandits' goalie, came out of the locker room. "Hi, Mrs. Hayes."

Jeff holding Bandits' Trophy

"Hi. How was practice?" I asked.

"Good."

"Stop a lot of shots tonight?"

He grinned and replied, "Every practice I choose one guy on the team I won't let score; tonight it was Jeff."

"Really. Did he score on you?"

"Just once, upper left side. The puck hit the top of my glove and went in. He's got a bullet of a shot."

Johnny left, and Jeff appeared. We left the Bridgewater arena and headed to Gallo Ice Arena in Bourne. There were several times, especially when John Jr. and Jeff both played, when we'd leave a hockey event at one rink and drive to another rink for the next practice or game.

One midwinter evening, after Jeff's Bandits' practice in Bridgewater, Jeff, Jason, and I arrived in Bourne for hometown hockey. Hometown hockey was much less structured, and the players were at different skill levels. I pulled up in front of Gallo Ice Arena, and Jeff got out, opened the back of the Explorer, pulled out his hockey bag and stick, and headed to practice. I didn't know where his energy came from, leaving one practice to head to the next.

I parked the car, and Jason and I entered the arena.

"Are you hungry, Jason?" I asked. We hadn't eaten.

"Yes."

"Want some pizza at the snack bar?" I asked.

"Sure." Jason and I ordered our food and then sat down in front of the window looking out onto the ice behind the goaltender. The players began to scrimmage. They wore different-colored practice shirts. There were a couple of girls on the team. I hadn't been to one of these hometown practices yet this year. One kid clearly stuck out and was skating fast and passing the puck. He was a forward.

"Jason, who's that in the black jersey?" I asked. "He's really good." I watched as he passed the puck to one of the girls in front of the net, and she scored. He was all over the ice.

"Mom," Jason replied. "Are you kidding?"

"No, I'm serious! Who is that? He's very generous with the puck."

"Mom, that's Jeff!"

That same season, the Bridgewater Bandits were scheduled to play in a tournament game against the New Jersey Devils, a team known for their scrappy play; tough and dirty. The Bandits knew that, since they had played the Devils before in New York. Over supper before the game, I said, "Jeff, you can't be nice in front of the net." I was walking back and forth from the oven to the kitchen table, serving dinner.

"You've got to push the player out from in front of the net; take him out of the play." Jeff looked back at me, holding it in.

I made a face and started to say something, only I could hear myself about to sound like my mother, so I bit my tongue.

"When was your last game?" my husband John wanted to know, butting in.

"My last game was when you and I laced up for John Jr.'s father-and-son game, or father-mother-and-son game at Gallo. You skated on your ankles and then stayed in one spot like those tabletop hockey games where the hockey figure stays stationary and spins around and around hoping to hit the flying puck. And me? I fell on my butt when one of John Jr.'s teammates skated toward me with the puck. When I sat down on the team bench, Jack Burns, John's coach, asked me if I needed a pillow."

"Just give the guy in front of the net a shove to take him out of the play," John said to Jeff.

We finished dinner and left for the rink.

As expected, the Devils were hitting our Bandits in the corners and against the boards. Sean, Jeff's friend from Sagamore Beach, was one of the Bandits' best goal scorers, and the Devils were all over him, taking him out of the play. At the other end of the ice, our goalie, Johnny Muse, was shifting from one side of the net to the other, outstretched and blocking shots with his stick and glove. The score was tied.

In the second period, Sean skated into the corner after the puck. From the face-off circle, a New Jersey player skated into Sean, hitting him from behind and smashing him against the boards. Sean went down. He didn't move for several seconds. Everyone in the rink fell silent. The referee skated over to Sean, and he got up from the ice and skated to the bench.

The game continued at a fast pace; Sean sat out for a couple of shifts before returning to the ice late in the period. I watched as the New

Jersey player who had hit Sean earlier now skated to the side of the net and chased the puck into the corner. I watched as Jeff skated straight toward him. The kid was too busy trying to move the puck and didn't see Jeff. Jeff checked him hard against the boards. The kid went down and stayed down. Play stopped, and the rink became silent again. Jeff skated straight to the penalty box without waiting to be called by the referee.

"Get up," I said silently. "Get up; please get up." The trainer left the bench and walked over to the player. There was an eerie silence around the rink as we waited for the player to move. Minutes that felt like eternity passed.

He stood up. Oh, thank God, I thought as I watched him skate to the bench. Everyone clapped.

"You were worried about him taking the man out in front of the net?" John said when the play started again with Jeff in the penalty box.

"I don't have a clue, do I?" I said. "I think Jeff gets this from your side of the family."

"Yeah, it didn't come from yours," he replied. "Jeff's tougher than you think," he added, keeping his eye on the game.

CHAPTER 17

High School Sophomore Year, Canal Cup

WHEN WE RETURNED home from Jeff's first round of treatment, the Sandwich hockey team was gearing up for the big Canal Cup hockey rivalry game against Bourne High School at the Gallo Arena. Jeff would be going to the game as a spectator.

On the night of the game, the line to get into the arena circled around the outside of the rink. We parked near the Zamboni garage and took Jeff's wheelchair out of the back of the Explorer.

My husband pushed Jeff as we made our way down into the rink. We took the elevator up to the manager's office where we planned to watch the game. The arena filled. Posters covered the walls, some with the words "Jeff Hayes, You Amaze" and "Get Well Jeff Hayes" and "We love you Jeff Haaaaayes." The words "Get Well Jeff" had been painted under the ice surface where the skaters entered the rink. Spectators were buying the hockey lace bracelets; behind the Sandwich bench, the team had hung Jeff's number twelve hockey jersey.

Jeff sat in his wheelchair up against the glass window in the manager's office to watch the game; his girlfriend sat by his side. He was on pain medication and spoke only briefly to the people who came to see him and to the press who interviewed him between periods.

Sandwich beat Bourne and held onto the Canal Cup title for another year. John pushed Jeff from the manager's office as we walked back around the rink, away from the crowd and to the garage. Jeff's varsity coach from the previous year, Brian Ferreira, approached Jeff as we helped him into our SUV. As a freshman defenseman, Jeff had played the most minutes for Coach Ferreira.

"Jeff, how are you doing?" Brian asked.

"Hi, Coach. I'm okay I guess."

"I wanted to come by to let you know I'm thinking of you and wish you good luck."

OUTSIDE THE LINES WITH
Matt Sarkissian
Dan Crowley, the columnist, asks, "Who has been your inspiration?"

My dad has been my greatest inspiration. He has always supported me one hundred percent. He was my coach for years in soccer, baseball, and basketball, and he is the one that made me fall in love with sports. He did the same thing for my sister, and she has moved on to play soccer and lacrosse in college. He was always there for us growing up, and I am grateful for that. Also, I would say that my good friend, Jeff Hayes has been an inspiration to me as of late. He was recently diagnosed with cancer, and I admire him for the courage that he has had through this tough time in his life. I would like to thank him for being an inspiration to me and to the Blue Knights Hockey Team this past season.

CHAPTER 18

Second Treatment

WE WOKE EARLY on Monday, March 7, 2005, the first day of Jeff's second cycle of chemotherapy. The ground was still covered with several feet of snow. I was nervous about driving on the expressway on a Monday morning. Also, the Patriot's Super Bowl parade was in Boston, another reason not to drive. John had to work. We sat down and talked about an alternative way to get to the JFC.

"John, you sure you can't just drive us up to Boston and drop us off?" I asked.

"I can't. I've got an early start tomorrow. You could rent a limousine," he replied.

"Limousine, can we afford to do that? How much would it cost?"

"Well, it would only be the ride up to Boston. I'd guess maybe a hundred and fifty dollars." He got up from the sofa and sat down in front of the computer in the next room.

"How about a town car?" I asked walking toward him. "It would be easier for Jeff to get in and out of; a limo is too low to the ground."

"Here, take a look." There were a few limousine companies on the Cape, and we chose the closest one in Hyannis. "Since this will be a five-day treatment, we'll be at Children's until Friday; my car wouldn't be parked in the hospital garage all week," I remarked.

"Then it's a no-brainer; let's schedule a town car." John picked up the phone and made the arrangements.

Jeff and I packed one suitcase. Each morning, before leaving for Boston, I applied an analgesic cream over the keloid scar tissue that had formed around Jeff's port after it was surgically implanted. This scarring is not the norm; it's just how Jeff healed but it was extra protection over his port. I then covered it with a thin, small, square plastic piece with adhesive edges. This helped protect his clothing and numbed the area for access.

"Are you ready, honey?" I asked.

"Yeah, let's go."

I told him that Dad and I had rented a town car to drive us to Boston because I was a little nervous about driving on the expressway. He looked back at me with a blank stare.

"Do you have your laptop? How about a Gatorade for the ride?" I asked.

"Oh, yeah, can you get me one please?" he replied.

The town car arrived at our house at seven o'clock in the morning. Jeff put on his red L.L.Bean jacket and grabbed his crutches. I followed him out the door with the suitcase, his laptop, backpack, and my purse. The driver opened the passenger doors for both Jeff and me. As we made ourselves comfortable in the soft leather seats, I felt relief that the stress of the ride was out of my hands. The driver started the town car and pulled out of our driveway.

We arrived at the JFC around eight fifteen. We entered through the front door of the Dana-Farber Cancer Institute and took the elevator up to the third floor. We checked in and were given a beeper. When Jeff's name was called, he and I followed the nurse from the waiting room into a small examining room to record his weight and vital signs. Then we returned to the waiting room.

We waited until Hannah came out from the back of the clinic and approached us.

"Hey, Jeff, how are you?" she asked.

"Good, thanks."

"Ready?"

"Yup," he replied.

"Okay, let's go."

We followed Hannah through the doors to the back of the clinic.

"How did it go at home after the first treatment?" she asked.

"Okay," he replied. "I was tired at first."

"Well, let's see how we do with this different set of drugs. Did you drink on the way up?"

"Yeah, I had some Gatorade."

Jeff sat down on the bed and removed his sneakers.

"Okay, great. I'm going to start you on some fluids anyway, and maybe we can start the chemo earlier if you're hydrated," she replied.

Jeff adjusted his bed and lay with his head propped up with two pillows. Hannah began an IV of fluids. During the first few hours, Jeff and I watched ESPN and NESN, the national and New England sports news stations, respectively.

"Jeff, do you want something to eat?" I asked. He looked back at me, not knowing if he should risk eating before taking these new drugs.

"I don't know, Mom. Should I?"

"I'm not sure, honey. I don't know how you'll feel after these new chemo drugs."

"I'm not hungry," he said, looking up at the television hanging over the end of his bed.

When he had watched all the sporting news from the day before, he began to watch *The Price Is Right*.

Dr. Sam Blackman entered the room and walked up to the side of Jeff's bed.

"Jeff, how are you feeling?" he asked.

"Good."

My one-word son, I thought.

Dr. Blackman noticed the shrinkage of the swelling on Jeff's thigh and seemed encouraged. Then he walked to the end of Jeff's bed and began to speak to him in a more serious tone.

"Most people," he began, "will go through their entire life without knowing what you know right now." He paused. "And that's that there are no certainties in life. I could walk out this door after seeing you, go down the elevator and out the revolving doors, and cross the street." He walked over to the window and looked out onto the street below. "And I could be hit by a truck, ending my life." He looked back at Jeff. "There are no certainties in life."

Jeff and I stared back at him, our faces stoic. I understood the message, but emotionally the words weren't penetrating the thick layer of protection I'd mentally engineered to protect myself from thinking the worst—my invisible shield. We didn't respond but stared back at him.

We talked some more, and Dr. Blackman gave Jeff his e-mail address and phone number and told him to call or e-mail him if he had any questions.

Hannah entered the room. "Jeff, can you pee for me?" she asked.

Dr. Blackman said good-bye, and Jeff got up slowly from his bed and closed the curtain to fill the plastic urinal.

After confirming that Jeff was hydrated, Hannah said, "Hey, Jeff, let's get this chemo started, honey. Okay?"

He smiled back at her as she removed the empty fluid bag and hung the chemo drug. She gave Jeff the antinausea medications Zophran and Marinol, an antinausea patch for behind his ear, Ativan, and Bactrim. She then started the IV of Ifosfamide and then Etoposide.

I watched as the drugs began to take effect. His color change was immediate. His skin turned a yellowish green. I didn't allow myself to be consumed by the helplessness I felt, and I didn't allow myself to get caught up in how I would change places with him at any moment. I just sat next to his bed, waiting and watching over him. It was hard. He closed his eyes and put his head back on his pillow and lay still, as if he could feel the drugs entering his body.

When it came time for us to move from the JFC to Children's, a wheelchair was brought in. Hannah had assigned Jeff to a bed on Seven West. Slowly and carefully, Jeff sat up in his bed. We helped him put his sneakers on and move from the bed to the wheelchair.

Just like the last time, we piled his laptop in its backpack and the five-inch medical binder onto his lap. I carried our suitcase and my purse and we left the clinic for Children's. His IV would come with him and was attached to his wheelchair. I pushed Jeff through the clinic doors to the elevator. And just like last time, we took the elevator down to the first floor, passed through the lobby, and exited the Dana-Farber Cancer Institute. Crossing the street to Children's was a challenge. The street was on a hill so I had to hold back the wheelchair so I wouldn't lose control or my grip while also holding on to the suitcase. I had a flashing image of Jeff's wheelchair getting away from me, and of me frantically chasing after Jeff as he barreled down Binney Street and out onto Longwood Avenue.

Seven West was nothing like Six West. The floor was overflowing with sick children. There were no private rooms that I could see. Each room had two sick children; the nurses were in and out answering calls for attention and care. Toddlers were riding in wagons and Playskool cars as their parents helped them make sense of the reason they were there. There was a sense of urgency. This was the real thing: children fighting cancer. Seven West was like a battlefield. It was the floor where children with cancer received treatment and care; where the outside world comes in wearing clown suits and bearing gifts; where ice-cream-sundae carts arrive, and food comes in from local restaurants; where athletes and celebrities visit; where children live and die.

Jeff was heavily medicated. I pushed his wheelchair into the last room at the end of the floor. The nurse helped him into his bed; an extension had been added so his feet didn't dangle over the end, and I sat in the convertible green chair. It was night. I watched Jeff as he struggled with the side effects of these new drugs. He insisted on getting out of bed and walking to the bathroom. He was unstable as he walked across the room, pulling his IV pole as he and I entered the bathroom together. He wasn't sure whether to vomit or urinate as he swayed and lost his balance. I knew a possible side effect was the loss of equilibrium with these drugs so I was prepared to catch and support him as he stood to empty his bladder. He regained his balance, while swaying a little, back and forth. I wasn't sure how I'd catch him, but I can support his fall I thought. He was lethargic and held onto his IV pole for stability. The IV pole was on wheels but he kept his balance. He felt sick but would not vomit. He had a strong will and determination not to become sick as the drugs began to destroy all his cells; diseased and healthy.

We walked back to his bed, and he sat on the edge and rested. I plugged the IV machine back into the wall and helped him lie down. He fell in and out of sleep, and upon every waking moment, he would ask for the score of the Bruins game. I had to pay attention, not only for the score but because he would ask, "How did they score, Mom?"

Jeff's roommate was a young Brazilian boy. I thought he might be four years old. He was very ill. Throughout our first night, a group of Doctoral Fellows walked past Jeff's bed to the young boy behind the curtain. I listened to them try to explain to the young boy's mother that her son's condition was critical and life threatening; that he might not make it through the night. His lungs were filled with fluid. They described to her the risks, the treatment, and the medication they had collectively decided and agreed upon to save his life. She didn't speak English and didn't understand their explanation of how sick her son was. "Do you understand what we are saying?" they asked. I thought, why doesn't she have an interpreter?

"Jeff, I don't think we should be listening. It doesn't sound good."

"I don't think we have a choice." He turned his head toward me and away from the television above his bed. He was closer to the bed on the other side of the curtain than I was.

I don't recall sleeping in my converted bed that night. It was noisy trying to convert the chair into a bed and trying to position it to allow enough space for the nurse to have access to Jeff's IV so she could administer his fluids and medication. I fell asleep sitting in the chair. When I woke, I dressed in the floor bathroom. Jeff woke when I returned. Thankfully, the little boy made it through the night.

"How are you feeling?" I asked Jeff. He looked fresh, a little medicated, but his color had returned. "Do you feel like eating anything?"

"Can you get me a plain bagel and some strawberry milk?"

"Sure, honey. I'll go down to the food court."

"Before you go, can you unplug the IV pole? I need to go the bathroom."

"Sure." I leaned behind his bed and unplugged the IV as he got out of bed. He was able to walk better than the previous night, and I stayed by his side until he reached the bathroom. When he returned, I plugged the IV back into the wall and left for the food court. He got back into bed and changed the channel to NESN. We watched TV throughout the day.

It was early evening and we listened to the young Doctoral Fellows on the other side of the curtain talking about the sick little boy. I felt empathy for his mother. The next day, I found a moment when Jeff was resting comfortably, and left the room for the lobby to buy the little boy something to make him feel better.

"Can I help you?" the woman standing alongside the toy cart asked.

"There's a little boy I'd like to buy something for; he's my son's roommate, and he's very sick."

"I have balloons and some toys here." She picked up a small metal airplane.

"Oh, I like the plane. I'll take that, and the dolphin balloon, and the star-shaped balloon too." I returned to our room to present my gifts to the little boy. He was a beautiful boy, dark-skinned with big dark-brown eyes. He already had a couple of balloons hanging from his bedpost. He smiled as I gave him the plane, and his mom tied the balloons with the others. She smiled and thanked me, "Obrigada."

It was really a gift from the people in Sandwich: proceeds from the sale of the hockey laces had provided me with extra cash to buy this little boy something to play with and balloons to hang on his bedpost.

The nurse returned and gave Jeff his second dosage of the two chemo drugs. He slept throughout the entire day. I ordered him a Papa

Gino's pizza for dinner; his favorite. He ate a couple slices and watched some television. I gave the rest of the pizza to our roommate, not knowing if he could eat.

"Muito obrigada," she replied.

The boy's mother and I became friendlier, but we couldn't communicate past the common courtesy, respect and sympathy we felt for each other; our sons were ill and we were in an unfamiliar place. She seemed to watch me as I watched over Jeff, getting him what he needed and helping him walk to the bathroom. The next night she bought Jeff a pizza.

"Muito obrigada," I smiled back at her when she handed me the pizza.

That night, a group of fellows walked into our room. They walked by us in their long white coats, not acknowledging Jeff and me as they passed through. They continuously came and went throughout the night and spoke among themselves in front of the little boy and his family, and us. I grew increasingly uncomfortable. I understood their need to speak openly about the boy's illness but didn't appreciate their lack of respect for us. Jeff was very sick and scared too. We weren't prepared to witness anything that might happen to the little boy.

The next time they walked in, one doctor stopped and acknowledged Jeff and me. He apologized to us and then joined the group standing on the other side of the thin curtain. We could hear everything they said about the little boy's illness. I couldn't understand why there weren't single rooms on this floor for all these children and their parents. I looked at Jeff. He was awake and listening too.

"Mom, they're just doing their job." Jeff turned his head toward me as I stood at the end of his bed trying to protect him from what was being said.

"I know, honey; you're right."

On Seven West, most of the beds were for younger children. The nurses saw that Jeff's legs stuck out past the end of the bed, so each stay, they added an extension to the bed. Teenagers were a bit out of place on this floor; there wasn't a more private floor for adolescents. When Jeff was first diagnosed, we agreed with the doctors that it was best for Jeff to be in pediatrics rather than the Dana-Farber for adult patients.

The nurses were very thoughtful and wonderful. They were bright and tireless. I didn't want Jeff to be neglected, and that was never the case. They cared for many children with different life-threatening diseases. The different protocols and medications kept the nurses moving during their entire shift. It was very noisy. With the door to our room shut, we were isolated from most of the noise and nurses answering calls from other rooms.

CHAPTER 19

Father's House

O N WEDNESDAY NIGHT, John came up from the Cape to visit and sit with Jeff. He was staying with a friend for two nights and would be with us when Jeff was discharged on Friday. On Thursday morning, John and I found time to leave the hospital for breakfast. I asked John if he would take me by the house on Carlton Street in Brookline where my father grew up. It was just down the street from Fenway Park, where my father had worked during the summer as a teenager.

I had never seen Dad's house, only pictures of him and his siblings in the house. In these pictures, they were posed in front of a beautiful fireplace. In the background, I could see stained-glass windows. I had always longed to see the inside of the house.

John drove us to the house. There was still snow on the ground. A fence surrounded this small mansion. The front porch wrapped halfway around the left side of the house and a hanging bench, which I imagined would swing when sat in, was still on this cold winter day. I immediately got out of our car and said, "I'm going to knock on the door to see if anyone is home, and if so, maybe they'll let me in." I left the car and crossed the busy street, walked through the fence gate, and climbed up three steps and onto the porch. My heart began to race with excitement and anticipation. Oh, how I hope someone is home, I thought, and I hope they don't have a pit bull. I knocked on the door, which I thought could very well be the original door from the time my dad lived here. To my great surprise, a woman about the same age as me answered the door.

"Hello, my name is Susan Hayes. My father grew up in this house and I was hoping I might come in for a moment to see the inside."

She seemed pleasantly surprised at my request and welcomed me into her home. Thank goodness, I thought, I don't look threatening. I walked through the front door, excited to be inside. The entranceway was a corridor that led to a foyer, which had a fireplace and opened up into three other beautiful rooms. One of these rooms had french doors and a ceramic-tile fireplace. Another was a small living room with a fireplace. Across from the fireplace in the foyer rose a beautiful, wide, mahogany split-level-landing staircase. It zigzagged up five flights to where a mahogany railing extended across horizontally. Above and behind the railing, in the wall, was a large stained-glass window.

I turned to the woman and asked whether I could call my dad on my cell phone. She was excited at the notion and said, "Yes, of course!"

When he answered the phone, I told him, "Dad, I'm standing in the foyer of the home you grew up in on Carlton Street!" I could feel his smile through the phone and hear the amazement in his voice. He chuckled when I described the foyer and the beautiful staircase.

"Do you see a small door at the bottom of the stairs?" he asked.

"Yes," I said. It was a carved mahogany door that could easily have gone unnoticed, as it looked like part of the stairs.

"Behind that door is where your great grandmother, Sarah St. LeCroix put your Uncle Frank when he was bad. I was put there to keep your uncle company." I thought perhaps that was how children were disciplined by earlier generations. It must have been pretty awful to be locked in a dark closet for who knows how long—probably why Dad never did that to us. I imagine though, that with ten children, he must have at times been tempted to lock us in a closet!

When I told this to the owner of the house, she said, "Why didn't I think of that?" She stored her Christmas decorations there.

Uncle Frank and Dad

92

I walked up the stairway and around the corner to a huge room at the front of the house with a very large Palladian window that looked out onto the front lawn and Carlton Street. On each side of the room were rows of small custom windows that opened from the center. Dad told me that was the room he and my mother lived in after they were married and had my eldest brother, before they moved into their own place.

Still describing the upstairs, Dad told me who had slept in each bedroom. I imagined my great aunts sleeping in their beds, the "aunts" that my mom protected my brother from, the aunts that my sisters and I have become aliases to, each of us using their names: Josephine, May, Charlotte, Loreto, and Angela. I'm Charlotte. She was thin with shiny, wavy, short white hair and three-inch-thick bifocals. She wore long floral dresses and big, black orthopedic shoes with laces.

Dad recalled so many details. He told me that their Christmas tree was placed at the top of the staircase in front of the stained-glass window. As I stood at the bottom of the staircase looking up, listening to Dad on my cell phone, I was taken back in time. The lace, the warmth of the fireplace, thoughts of what went on in the dark mahogany-framed rooms in the 1930s, 1940s, and 1950s: I could feel a spirit in that house as I walked down the halls and passed each bedroom. What was it like back then, I wondered?

Dad would become a father who worked long and hard to provide for his wife and ten children. Standing in the foyer of the house where my father grew up, possibly the very same place he once stood as a teenager, I wondered, pausing for several minutes and thought, how did the past, living in this house, form him into the man he became.

Is it the childhood you live through that strengthens who you are, that instills the values that you hold deep within to be true, knowing compassion, honesty and what is right...and what is so very wrong... to be born with an unselfish, genuine, and kind soul that cannot be changed, even when threatened and tested? You know who you are. Nothing changes or should question your righteousness to be that person. Not a home of wealth or poverty, of leniency or strictness should prohibit or prevent you from following what you believe to be good and true, from living with the values you were born to uphold. You are defined by the life you live; by your kindness, strength and dignity; your inner soul. Cancer can't take that away. You are, you. Cancer doesn't change that.

As I walked down the stairs and reached the foyer again, Dad said to me, "Do you see the room off to the right? There are three steps down that lead to another room." I walked to the doorway and was amazed that he had remembered those three steps. I stepped down the stairs and entered another very large room that was a remodel compared to the rest of the house. It was bright and open with a huge skylight that had a beautifully carved wooden frame. The window gave the room character and a taste of the past. It was the room where Dad and his brother stayed as teenagers but the current owners had turned this room into their kitchen and living room.

When I hung up from Dad, I turned to this kind woman who had without hesitation and with complete trust allowed me into her home. I told her the reason I was here in Brookline and the disease my son was battling. She was considerate of my circumstances and listened with sincerity and compassion. She began to tell me a story about a Brookline High School boy who was battling cancer in his neck. She had read about him and his disease and related it to my son's battle. In the weeks that followed, she and I exchanged e-mails until my life became so consumed with Jeff's illness that I lost contact with her. I will always remember the kindness and indulgence she showed me that day.

Afterward, I wondered if Dad ever hesitated before answering his phone when it rang during those months when I was up in Boston with Jeff, pausing to prepare himself for what he would say to me when I told him about Jeff's condition and treatment. I know with certainty, though, that he never expected I would be calling him from the house he grew up in on Carlton Street.

John and I headed back to Children's Hospital. I feared we had been away too long. Back in the hospital, I forgot everything I had just experienced. I was back in Children's, back on Seven West, a world so separate from the world outside.

Jeff continued his treatment until Friday.

That morning, I woke to see the little Brazilian boy, Jeff's roommate, walking to the bathroom with his mother holding onto his IV pole like Jeff did every day. He was up and about; he had survived the week. I was so relieved. I smiled at him, and he returned my smile, blithe to his brush with death earlier in the week. My heart filled with joy and relief. The fellows, obtrusive as they were, had saved his life.

When Jeff woke, he was ready to go home. As usual, I got him something to eat from the food court. When I returned, he began to eat and then turned to me and said, "Don't ever do that again!"

What did I do? I thought. Was it something I had done for the little boy?

He said, "Don't ever rent a town car or limousine for me again; I'm not a spoiled little kid!"

I pushed Jeff's wheelchair through the revolving hospital door and onto the busy sidewalk in front of Children's Hospital. John had driven the car to the front of the hospital and was directed by the valet attendant to the front curb of Children's. Jeff got out of his wheelchair and took the front passenger seat. I got in the back. We headed home, happy to be outside, happy to hear the traffic, happy to smell the fresh air. Not happy to be sitting in traffic on the expressway.

All was quickly forgotten—the little boy, our roommate who almost died; visiting the home my dad grew up in; the long five days of chemotherapy. I left all that we had experienced at the hospital stored in the depths of some cerebral crevice inside my brain that keeps memories locked and safe, not for recall or afterthought. The horrible realities were just too hard to absorb. I used my energy to be with Jeff and care for him.

We followed the same antinausea protocol as before when needed. Katherine Baugh from the Visiting Nurses Association (VNA) arrived in the week that followed to draw blood, check Jeff's vitals, and monitor the side effects from the chemotherapy. We watched for dizziness and confusion, paleness that might mean low blood counts, weakness, and excessive bleeding. We watched for anything unusual or questionable.

It was important for me to understand what normal counts were so I could watch for specific symptoms. The red, white, and platelet counts are what I concentrated on. The normal range for red blood cells is 4.5–6.2. The normal range for white blood counts is 4,000–10,800. The normal range for platelets is 133,000–333,000. An absolute neutrophil count (ANC) or complete white blood count was monitored closely. An ANC below 2,000 is considered neutropenia, which is an abnormally low number of neutrophils. Neutrophils serve as the primary defense against infections; they destroy bacteria in the blood.

I discussed hematology and Jeff's blood levels with Katherine, Jeff's visiting nurse, as if I'd just left the lab. Two months ago, if I'd been asked what neutrophils were, I wouldn't have had a clue.

Jeff's blood analysis gave more indications than just what I watched for. Hannah and Sam studied the page of blood level results taken each time Jeff's blood was drawn. When we were in the clinic, Hannah gave me the results on a full-page computer printout. The paper was folded in half vertically with the actual readings on one side and the normal, acceptable levels on the other. I lived by his blood levels and kept printouts in my binder at home. Jeff's counts usually recovered during the end of the second week, sometimes into the third week, but always in time to receive the next cycle of chemotherapy drugs.

The reduction of the swelling in Jeff's thigh was more noticeable after the second cycle of chemotherapy. He had gained weight with help from a steroid, Decadron. Aside from the chemotherapy treatment and the recovery of his blood counts, Jeff came home to his friends, coaches, and the people of Sandwich. His friends waited eagerly for his return.

I came to realize how important it was for Jeff to maintain his friendships at home and with those of his hockey family. Despite the seriousness of the disease and the treatment, connecting with friends in person was more important to Jeff. He never spoke of his cancer or the treatment to his friends. They accepted it, admired his courage, showed empathy and their friendship became the normalcy he longed for.

CHAPTER 20

Ottawa and Lake Placid Tournaments

WHEN JOHN JR. was twelve, he played for the Bay State Sharks in the Boston Metro Hockey League. Jack Burns was their coach. He'd chosen to play in a tournament in Ottawa. We traveled in a luxury bus with the kids and stayed in a town outside the city.

A light snow was falling as we arrived at the hotel. We checked into our room, unpacked, and quickly returned to the bus to get to our first game. At the rink, the team pulled the hockey bags and sticks out from the baggage compartment on the outside of the bus. As we entered the rink, the players parted and headed for the locker room.

"Good luck!" I said to John Jr. as he walked away.

"Thanks," I heard him say without turning around.

John, Jeff, and I entered the rink to find seats. It was brightly lit, and banner signs hung from the stands. There was loud music. The words "Zero tolerance" were written on a very large sign that hung high in the rink, in everyone's view. "Zero tolerance of what?" I asked John.

"Oh, that. The officials have zero tolerance with the coaches. There's no yelling at the refs or the players, or you're immediately thrown out of the game!"

"Wow! Jack better be careful."

The game fit its Canadian arena. Our opponents skated fast and played with elite skill. We lost our first game.

We boarded the bus and started back to the hotel, but the bus pulled off the highway sooner than I'd expected. "Why are we getting off?" I asked.

"I think the kids are going to play hockey in someone's backyard."

"Really!"

The bus stopped in a neighborhood. Four-foot high mounds of snow had been pushed to each side of the road making a clear path through the neighborhood to a playground behind a row of houses. Bright lights illuminated a large sheet of ice with a net at each end. The boys got off the bus, pulled out their skates and sticks from the baggage compartment, and walked toward the rink. I watched from inside the warm bus. My window fogged, and I wiped it with the sleeve of my jacket. It was still snowing. Tomorrow we'd skate on a river, now a frozen path to the city of Ottawa. All I could think about was sleep; we'd left the Cape in the early-morning darkness.

The next day, with my skates laced, I stood on the banks of the Rideau River. The scene was like a snow globe I'd had as a little girl. Inside the globe, a young boy on skates circled his mother. The snow fell inside the globe, softly touching the sides of the glass and drifting gently, filling the globe as it was tipped upside down and righted again. Now the scene lay before me as if it had magically come to life. I saw people skating in all directions. Thousands of tiny snowflakes fell across the sky. My tongue caught them one by one, and my eyelashes thickened with the flakes. I could hear blades hitting the ice surface as skaters passed by. I wasn't cold, bundled up and blending in with the Canadian folk. Canucks, I corrected myself, smiling.

I looked down at Jeff skating by. "Come on, Mom," he shouted as he skated away, his smile wide and his cheeks red.

"Okay, Jeff, wait for me!"

I figured I wouldn't see much of John Jr.; he was skating up and down the river with his teammates. Meanwhile, my husband, not much of a skater, walked along the riverbanks beneath Victorian-style mansions.

From where we were, it was a three-mile skate downriver to the heart of Ottawa. People of all ages were out skating. The scene reminded me of when I was a little girl skating on Bullow's Pond in Newton on a cold winter day. John Jr. and Jeff skated to and from Ottawa three times before I reached the city. I stopped for hot chocolate and a beaver tail along the way.

"Beaver tail? What's that?" asked Jeff.

"It's a warm cinnamon-and-sugar dough shaped like a beaver's tail. It's delicious. Do you want one?

"No thanks, Mom. I'm heading back to the city. See you there."

"Be careful, Jeff. I'll see you in a little bit. Look for Dad on the side of the river."

"Okay!" He skated off to join up with John Jr.'s friends and I lost him in the crowd. I made my way to the city. When my husband arrived, we changed into our boots, which he'd carried in a backpack. We then met up with the team at a tavern for lunch. After lunch and a short walk in the city, we put our skates back on and ventured back out of the city, the way we had come, three miles back to the bus.

That night, the team was going back into the city to see the Ottawa Senators game. Jeff was going with Dad and John Jr.'s team. He was so happy to be hanging out with the big kids.

"Jeff, stay close to Dad, okay?"

"I will, Mom."

I stood by the hotel window, watching the three step out and join the others. I closed the drapes. I thought about a nice hot bath. I turned on the hot water to fill the tub, adding just a little cold water, enough not to scald myself, but wanting to keep the bath as hot as possible for as long as possible. It wasn't often that I took time for myself.

John Jr.'s team lost the first two games and was eliminated from the tournament. Matt Green, the team's center on the first line, was chosen best skater in the tournament and received an award.

When he was eight, Jeff also started to play on select teams. He played for the Whalers in 1998. Then, during the 1999/2000 season, he made the South Shore Dynamos select team. The Dynamos entered the CAN/AM Challenge Cup in Lake Placid, New York. John, Jeff, and I went on this trip together. John Jr. had games he couldn't miss, and Jason stayed with my parents.

It was November, and we were excited to be staying in the tiny mountain town of Lake Placid, home of the 1980 Winter Olympics.

It snowed our first night in Lake Placid. I walked down Main Street, imagining the crowded sidewalks in 1980 filled with the greatest athletes from around the world. We visited the rink, the same rink where the US Olympic team beat the Soviets. It was empty. We walked through the stands and sat in a row of empty red seats. I was surprised at how small it was. John got up and walked down to the ice while I sat alone. In the quiet emptiness of the rink, I envisioned the United States playing the Soviet Union, and the exhilaration of that time. In my mind, I was there, watching the game, feeling the excitement, the jubilation of winning! The fans were screaming and waving the American flag. I remembered the words I'd read when Herb Brooks spoke in the locker room to the US hockey team before the Soviet game.

"You were born to be hockey players, every one of ya. And you were meant to be here tonight! This is your time. Their time is done!"

"Susan, come on! Let's go!" I heard John's voice call out to me as I sat alone in the empty arena. I walked down to ice level and met up with him.

"The game was played eight years before Jeff was born, and I can still remember watching the US hockey team beat the Soviets. I think I need therapy," I said to John.

"Yeah, you do. Come on, let's go back to the hotel."

Jeff's team won every game they played and earned the Challenge Cup's gold medal.

On our last night in Lake Placid, I stood at the end of Main Street, away from the stretch of shops and pubs on each side of the street. A mile down the road, beyond our hotel, the bright lights and traffic diminished, and the road curved along the lake and toward the mountains. Jeff was with the team.

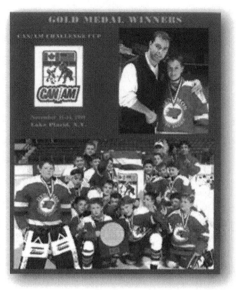

I was waiting for John to join me for dinner at a pub tucked into a small cove on the lake. The sun was setting behind the mountain. Its orange color against the gray sky mirrored through the mist on the lake, and as the sun set, the colors changed and the glass lake turned gray; the bare branches on the trees in front of me turned black in the foreground and against the fresh white snow that had fallen during the day. It was breathtaking and a call to the wild.

During Jeff's sophomore year in high school, while the undiagnosed pain mounted in his thigh, Coach Curtis, the new coach, took the team to the movie theater in Sandwich to watch the newly released, *Miracle on Ice*.

"How was the movie?" I'd asked Jeff.

"They played terrible hockey," he replied.

"What do you mean? They beat the Soviet Union. They were the best in the world."

"Yeah, they did, but hockey was different back then; it's not how we play now."

I didn't ask how they played differently. Mothers don't ask those questions. I'm staying away from that one, I thought.

The next week, John and I took Jason to see the movie. I quietly cheered from the last row at the top of the theater. I spent the last part of the movie on the edge of my seat. I watched the US team take the lead over the Soviets, and I became nervous in the last minutes of the game, hoping the Soviets wouldn't score.

"Mom," Jason whispered. "Relax. They win the game."

CHAPTER 21

First Transfusion, First Buzz, First Time Driving

Two cycles down, and all the new drugs were no longer new. It was March. Dr. Blackman was now Sam to us. He and Hannah continued to alert us to watch for the ensuing side effects of mouth sores, elevated temperature, racing heart, nosebleeds, and infection. The Neulasta shot gave way to new white cell growth, keeping at bay possible infection in the susceptible and vulnerable parts of Jeff's body.

"Jeff, I was thinking," I said, sitting on the edge of his bed in the bedroom that he shared with John Jr. "What if we did over the basement and turned it into your own living room, bathroom, and bedroom?" John and I had been thinking about this for a few days and had talked to my sister, Janet for help with the financing.

Jeff's eyes widened and he smiled. "Yeah, that'd be great!"

"You could have privacy and your own space for your friends to visit. You could fill the room with all your baseball and hockey awards, trophies, plaques, everything. It would be your own place."

"When can you start?" he asked.

"I'll ask Uncle Marty to build it and Freddy O'Connor to do the plumbing," I replied. "I'll get your brother and his friends to start cleaning out the basement so we can start as soon as possible."

As the week progressed, I kept an eye on Jeff. He had stopped using the crutches but walked with a limp. I asked him whether he was feeling any of the side effects that Sam and Hannah had warned us about. "My heart feels the way it does when I am sprinting up and down the ice during hockey practice. It's beating very fast." He had just walked back from the bathroom. I called Sam.

It was Saturday morning and Sam wanted us to drive up to Boston to Children's Hospital for a blood transfusion. With Jeff's heart racing, we could assume his red blood count was low. He asked us to go straight to the emergency room at Children's, not to the clinic, which was closed on the weekend. The emergency room at Children's Hospital would be a long wait, I thought.

"Susan," John said, "Call Sam and ask him if we can take Jeff to Cape Cod Hospital. Tell him it's twenty minutes from our house. See what he says." I picked up my cell phone and pressed speed dial for Sam.

Sam was reluctant. Before Jeff started his treatment, John and I had asked whether Jeff could receive his treatments on the Cape. Sam said the hospitals outside of Boston are considered community hospitals and are not capable of treating Jeff's cancer. "Why would you want to go anywhere else, when the best hospitals are here in Boston?" he'd said. But this time he relented.

"I'll call Cape Cod Hospital," he told me.

His orders were accepted by Cape Cod Hospital, and my husband took Jeff for a blood transfusion.

Jeff and John returned home three hours later. Jeff was considerably better and was noticeably stronger. His heart was no longer racing.

The swelling in Jeff's thigh continued to lessen. His thigh looked almost normal. Sam worried about the strength of his thighbone, but the cancer had not penetrated enough to pose a threat for a break. We put Jeff's crutches and his wheelchair in storage.

It was March, and Jeff was sixteen and a half. He began to study the Massachusetts state driver's manual. John promised Jeff many hours of driving lessons whenever possible. Cancer treatment wasn't going to interrupt his right to drive, and my sister Janet was buying him his first car. Jeff googled different car types and came up with a new favorite car or truck every week.

"Mom, look at this one," he said when he heard me coming up the stairs to his bedroom. I looked at his laptop screen; it showed an enormous, flashy yellow pickup truck that cost $59,000.

"I don't think so, honey."

He kept looking.

I remembered a hot summer day, Jeff's first time behind the wheel. He was four years old. My sister-in-law, Patty and I were making tuna fish sandwiches and packing up the car to head to the beach. I looked around for John Jr. and Jeff while I stood in the kitchen. It was unusually quiet. I walked into the living room and looked out the front window. Our car was no longer parked at the top of the driveway. "Oh shit!" I ran out the side door and saw our car wedged in the brush at the bottom of our driveway. I ran toward it and opened the driver's side door to see Jeff standing behind the steering wheel. "I backed the car up for you, Mom."

Jeff's hair began to fall out at a fast rate after the second treatment. His facial hair, his eyebrows, his eyelashes, and his goatee disappeared.

"Mom, Jeff wants me to give him a buzz," John Jr. said. John Jr. had given many buzz haircuts before and was pretty good at it. I'm sure Jeff knew this, or he would have never asked.

"Wait a minute," I said. Thoughts of him cutting his head and bleeding profusely scared me. I thought neither of them understood the risk, but they did.

"Okay, John, but I'm not watching." I left the room and went as far as I could away from them. "John, please be very careful, you cannot miss and cut him," I called out.

"Don't worry, Mom!"

After the sound of the clipper ended and the buzz was done, I went back in. Jeff looked pretty good, no pools of blood, no need to call Sam.

Winter was turning into spring. Hockey season had ended. When he felt well enough, Jeff went to the high school baseball practices and games. Many of the players were friends he'd played baseball with since he was eight years old. These friends were the same friends that he had spent a week with in Cooperstown, New York.

A year before his diagnosis, during practice, Jeff's Babe Ruth baseball coach, Don Bolton, timed each player as he ran from home plate to first base and then around the bases. The fastest player could replace the one on the bench. No one had a faster time than Jeff, and he sat alone on the bench for the entire drill.

I knew how hard it was for Jeff to have to watch and not play this year, and I was amazed at how he stood quietly and watched his teammates, keeping stats on the game and talking to his friends, never showing the eagerness he must have felt to go out there and play. God, I thought, I hope he'll be back out there again when his treatment is over.

CHAPTER 22

Third Treatment

ON MONDAY, MARCH 28, 2005, we headed up to the JFC for the start of Jeff's third treatment. I drove this time. Not renting a town car—got that message, loud and clear. So the heck with it, I thought; I can overcome my fear of the expressway. Jeff had an incredible memory and sense of direction, so I knew he could get us there.

This would be a short, two-day treatment, so it was easier knowing we would be back home on Tuesday afternoon. Jeff began hydrating on the ride up so that the treatment could start sooner, we could be assigned a bed at Children's sooner, and the whole process could begin sooner. The expressway north to Boston on a Monday morning gave him plenty of time to hydrate.

When we arrived at the Dana-Farber, we parked in a garage adjacent to the building. My car would stay in that same parking spot for two days on the short treatment and five days on the alternating cycle. It was never moved, and sometimes it was the only car in the garage overnight, untouched until I came to retrieve it. I never left the hospital during Jeff's stay. I never had trouble finding my car after a long week; I always remembered where I'd parked. I found that remarkable for me because I had trouble finding my car in the parking lot after shopping for one hour in Stop & Shop.

When we entered the clinic, we followed the usual protocol of checking in at the desk and waiting for Jeff's turn to record his vital signs and weight. There was no need for a beeper this time. Hannah came to greet us shortly after Jeff's vitals were taken, and we walked past the fish tank and through the double doors heading down to the end of the hall, into the infusion room, and to his bed beside the window.

Hannah was perfect for Jeff, smart and energetic. She always put us at ease. The sight of her familiar, friendly face was always reassuring. I felt I could face this treatment with a little more confidence and less fear, especially since we were employing the same drugs as the first treatment and we knew how Jeff would respond.

We were beginning to recognize some of the patients that we had seen before. I wondered what type of cancer they had and how their treatments were going. I wondered if their lives had changed as much as ours had. There was the boy who was younger than Jeff and had leukemia. He played hockey for Medford and wore his team's hockey shirt. There was another boy, a teenager Jeff's age, who had osteosarcoma. His leg had been amputated, and he was undergoing chemotherapy.

Jeff sat up in his usual bed in his stocking feet, wearing his white cap with the Fighting Irish of Notre Dame clover on the front. Hannah accessed Jeff's port, and Sam arrived soon after to examine Jeff before he started the treatment. Sam was animated and funny and made Jeff laugh. Jeff trusted him and listened to him carefully.

Jeff had mouth sores from low blood counts but no other symptoms other than the racing heart he'd experienced two Saturdays before. Once Sam left, Hannah administered the preventative nausea meds and the Bactrim dosage, and then she gave Jeff the three chemotherapy drugs: Vincristine, Doxorubincin, and Cyclophosphamide. I could now easily pronounce these drugs and knew their side effects, but they sounded just as horrible. Jeff rested his head back on his pillow, closed his eyes, and lay still as the drugs entered his system.

With a bed available at Children's, we made our way from the JFC, across the street to Children's, and onto Seven West. As we settled in, we heard our roommate from the other side of the curtain and his parents speaking Chinese. Jeff turned to me and whispered, "Mom, are there any other Americans in this hospital?"

"Yes, honey, this hospital is world renowned, giving care to children from all over the world. It's not unusual for you to have a roommate from a different country."

Jeff wasn't hungry that night, and we watched television. I converted my chair into a bed, gathered my linens and pillow, and made my bed.

At the end of the day, I imagined that people back home were finishing their day of school or work, arriving home to their family, having dinner, talking about their day, doing their homework, watching television, living their normal lives, and continuing their routines. Our days and nights were anything but normal. It was lonely at night and scary facing this disease. I looked out the hospital window to see the streetlights go on. I watched people leaving for home, rushing in the cold to get to their cars. The traffic had diminished. Big stacks of white smoke came from the roofs of the hospital buildings that surrounded Children's Hospital.

Later, as Jeff slept, I lay awake listening to the sound of his IV pump. Our room was dark, lit only by the lights on his pump and the light that shone in from the street below. The nurses came in and out of our room throughout the night to change Jeff's fluids and check his vitals. Every time I nodded off, an IV alarm—Jeff's or his roommates—jerked me awake. It was hard to find rest. I opened my eyes every time the alarm sounded and looked up at the clock, trying to force myself back to sleep. Eventually, I could see the shapes of the buildings outside the hospital window as the sun began to rise and the sky took color. Rest couldn't be measured by the sunrise.

I sat up. It unusual for me to get up early in the morning. At home, I loved lying in bed on a cold winter morning, waiting for the last possible moment until I would have to get up. But in the hospital, I would wake early and immediately look to Jeff to see if he was okay. He always was, even in that bed with IV tubes connected to his port and the top of his bed elevated. I couldn't imagine that was comfortable for him but he never complained, not once.

At seven o'clock the nurses changed shifts. It was a bit livelier as the next nurse arrived to assess Jeff's condition. I dressed, converted my bed back into a chair, and waited for Jeff to wake up. He always wore his glasses during treatment and not his contacts. When he woke, I handed him his glasses, and he instantly turned on NESN and ESPN to get last night's sports news and game scores. He was hungry and asked for cereal for breakfast instead of his usual bagel and strawberry milk. Before leaving to get his cereal, I unplugged his IV pump, and he walked slowly to the bathroom. I waited for him to leave the bathroom and helped him back into bed, plugging his IV pump back into the wall before leaving for the kitchen on the floor. The routines of Seven West became very familiar to me, and I began to move around the floor more freely.

We preferred the two-day treatment, although these three drugs were strong and cousins to poison. Judging from the decreased swelling in his thigh, we felt that the therapy was working, but that was the only measurement of progress we would have until the scans that would be taken after his fourth treatment.

Tuesday morning progressed, and Jeff was given the chemotherapy drugs. We waited for a few hours until the discharge nurse came with our instructions and the okay to leave. He was given the Neulasta shot and his port was de-accessed. He dressed and got ready to leave in his wheelchair.

On our way out, one of the nurses noticed my pocketbook. "Wow, I love your Coach." It was a gift from Nancy Bridges. I'd never owned one and hadn't realized its value until people had started complimenting me on it. "Thanks," I replied. Later the same day, a woman behind the pharmacy counter in CVS at Children's Hospital said the same thing. I smiled and began to admire my bag. Okay, I thought, stay focused and don't forget the medicine.

The week that followed saw Jeff's blood counts drop again. He didn't leave our house and rested in bed. His appetite was good, and he drank Gatorade. We had met with a nutritionist. She wanted Jeff to eat healthy, but her real message was to eat anything, if he felt like eating.

By the end of the second week home, Jeff felt well enough to go to school and to watch his friends play sports. The basement was under construction. Everyone was working after hours to get it done.

During this brief respite, Jeff travelled back to Boston to the TD Bank Garden Arena to receive the Sportsmanship Alliance of Massachusetts award from the Boston Bruins. He had been nominated by Coach Curtis. He would be one of many athletes nominated from boys' and girls' ice hockey leagues across the state; Jeff represented the Atlantic Coast Division. Jeff proudly wore his Sandwich varsity jacket. At the presentation, the league divisions were announced alphabetically, beginning with the Atlantic Coast Division. That brought Jeff onto the ice first, as his proud father pushed him out in a wheelchair.

"It was one of the proudest and saddest moments of my life," John said when he called me from the Garden. I'd stayed home. I thought this would be a good night for Jeff and his dad. I was tired and needed a break.

The next player called onto the ice was from the Bay State Division. This was the same boy that I had learned about from the woman who lived in the home my dad grew up in. He was from Brookline High School and was battling cancer in his neck. He and Jeff were side by side and talked while the other recipients were announced. I'd never told Jeff the story of this boy and his cancer.

Because of the NHL strike, the Bruins didn't play that night. Instead, the Division I and Division II High School Championship games were played. Five of the Duxbury High School players had played on the same Bandits team with Jeff. They heard Jeff was there to receive the award and came to see him after their game. They hadn't seen Jeff since they had heard the news of his cancer diagnosis. For Jeff it was a great surprise to see his old buddies and a great moment out on the ice.

Jeff would proudly display his Bruins Sportsmanship gold medal with all his other awards when his basement renovation was complete.

The next day, Jeff's blood counts were good: red = 3.5; white = 1,400; platelets = 98 (98,000); ANC = 9936. He weighed 153.6 pounds, and his temperature was 97.6 degrees. Tuesday, he ate a meatball sub and roasted chicken and rice for dinner. No meds, just a vitamin. On Wednesday, he had Bactrim and Benadryl and went to Friendly's with his friends. Thursday, a vitamin again, and John Lessard came to visit him at seven o'clock; no blood was drawn. Friday, Saturday, and Easter Sunday he was in good shape but not well enough to participate in our traditional family Easter egg hunt. He sat on the sidelines and watched.

CHAPTER 23

Fourth Treatment

IT WAS THE beginning of April when we returned to Boston to start the fourth cycle. The forecast called for higher temperatures than normal; it was a beautiful spring day. The traffic was at its usual slow pace on Route 3 in Hanover, and the expressway was backed up. It took us two and a half hours to get there, plenty of time for Jeff to drink his Gatorade.

Jason and Patty came with us. They would stay at the Holiday Inn on Beacon Street in Brookline where John and I had stayed in January during Jeff's diagnosis period. Jason and I planned to meet our friends, Jackie and Michael, and see a Red Sox game that night. Fenway Park was within walking distance of the Holiday Inn and the JFC. Patty would watch the game with Jeff from his room at Children's.

We entered the JFC. Jason and Patty were quiet and sat down on the sofa with Jeff as I checked in. Jason and Patty became familiar that day with Jeff's treatment. It was the usual long day for Jeff, hectic and busy.

After receiving his antinausea meds, Jeff was given the two chemo drugs, Ifosfamide and Etoposide. As before, the effect was immediate. He turned green. "Oh God," I thought, "he's so sick."

It was warm in the late afternoon when we crossed the street from the JFC to Children's. "I can't believe you push Jeff and carry all this stuff down this hill to Children's by yourself," Patty said while I held on tight to Jeff's wheelchair to control the speed I was gaining heading downhill. "Can't someone, a volunteer, come with you?" she asked.

"I've never asked. I thought this was what everyone did. I think if the JFC had volunteers, they would have assigned one to us," I replied.

We entered Seven West. It was hot in the doorway of Jeff's room. He sat in his wheelchair. The heat made Jeff feel worse. He liked his hospital room at a cool sixty-five degrees. His bed was short, without an extension, and unmade. The nurses hurried to add an extension and make his bed. When they finished, they helped him out of the wheelchair and into the bed.

Jason and Patty waited in the doorway. I stood alongside Jeff's bed. On the other side of the curtain, a little boy screamed horribly. A large group of family members dressed in long dark robes stood around him. They had placed religious statues in the window. The boy screamed again, louder. This was awful, and Jeff was feeling the worst he'd felt thus far. My thoughts lit up in my mind like fireflies on a hot summer night. Why aren't these kids battling cancer in private rooms protected from the possibility of exposure to germs from their roommates or visiting family and guests? I couldn't understand the medical reasoning for no privacy in a place where children were fighting for their lives. I paused and thought, this is Boston Children's Hospital—they know our needs; maybe it's funding or lack of space. I didn't know.

I looked over at the family of our roommate. The little boy let out another frightening scream and brought me back to real time. I left Jeff's room and walked to the nurse's station.

"Is there another room available for my son?" I asked.

"No, I'm sorry, there aren't any other rooms available," the nurse replied.

When I returned to the room, Ann, a supervisory nurse from the JFC, met me. She had been promoted to assist Dr. Holcomb Grier, the Head of Oncology, Sam's boss. She was standing alongside Jeff as he lay in his bed. When I saw her, I stood on the other side of the bed over Jeff. She began to tell us that we had been selected to be the first patient and parent ever to receive outpatient chemotherapy. Jeff would come to the JFC, receive his treatment, then return home, drive up to the clinic the next morning, receive treatment, and then go home the next night. She told us we were chosen because Jeff was such a good patient and I was able to take care of him so well. She spoke of this as if it represented a new era in treatment. They wanted us to be the first trial. I thought the current treatment was enough to make anyone crazy and overstressed. To take on complete control alone at home was too much for me.

Jeff turned to her, very ill from the strong drugs he had just received. He politely and quietly said, "Can we discuss this when I feel better?" Ann and I looked at each other. I didn't say anything but looked down at Jeff with pride and empathy. Just then, the boy on the other side of the curtain began to scream again. I turned to Ann and mouthed, "Please get us another room." She whispered, "I'll see what I can do."

Patty and Jason stood in the room watching; wondering if this was how it was all the time. I assured them it wasn't, but that didn't assuage their shock. I told them that I would not be comfortable leaving Jeff tonight.

Later on, Jeff asked, "What's the matter with Jason?"

"Jason has never seen you receive your treatment. It's all new to him. He worries. Also, I think he wants me to go to the Red Sox game with him." I paused. "Jeff, I won't leave you in this room alone. Jason and Auntie can go to the game, and I'll stay and watch it with you."

"Mom, go. I'll be okay," he replied.

"That's okay, honey; we will all go to a game together after treatment."

Patty and Jason met Jackie and Michael, our friends who owned season tickets. They left the hospital, checked into the hotel, and went to dinner and the game. After the game they would return to the hotel for the night.

Within an hour Jeff was moved to another room, the same room that we had shared with the Brazilian family at the end of the floor. Once we were settled in, I quietly put our suitcase and Jeff's 2004 Red Sox World Series commemorative hardcover book on a chair by the window. On the other side of the room, I saw a young boy lying in his bed. His dad and his two brothers were sitting in chairs beside him. They were wearing Red Sox shirts and baseball caps and watching the Red Sox game on television.

During the week and from time to time, we'd hear the screaming boy. They didn't put another patient in the room with him.

Ann didn't approach us again to ask about Jeff becoming an outpatient. "They'd miss you too much on Seven West!" Jason said. I smiled back at him, and he continued, "Mom, when the nurses see that Jeff is scheduled for treatment on Seven West, all of them check their schedules to put in for vacation time."

"Very funny," I replied. "I'm not bothersome for the nurses, Jay. I just think we should be afforded privacy. Not just us, but all the families on this floor. Besides, if it was you in that bed, I'd be doing the same thing."

The next day Jeff came down with the hiccups. He hiccupped every four or five seconds. He had nonstop hiccups for three days until his dad arrived on Thursday and called Sam. Every nurse tried to come up with a remedy, but no one could figure out how to stop them. Sam arrived immediately; he was not the doctor on Seven West during any of the time Jeff spent there. "Dad, this is worse than the chemotherapy itself," Jeff said.

It was awful.

Dr. Grier came by and couldn't offer any advice other than the usual stand on your head or drink from a cup upside down or eat a little sugar. Patty continued to give Jeff small packages of sugar. He found no relief, and sleeping and eating were nearly impossible.

Finally, it was discovered that Jeff had reacted to the combination of the drugs he'd been given. Kerry, Jeff's nurse at Children's for most of his visits, came up with the cause. We were grateful. She was extraordinary caring for Jeff. After this cycle, he never had the hiccups again.

Friday we were ready to go home.

CHAPTER 24

———— ✇ ————

Baseball

I T STARTED WITH T-ball—baseball fundamentals and learning to bat and field the ball. "This is relaxing for me, John," I said to my husband as we sat on the grass across from first base. No stress, an introduction to the game of baseball for these little all-stars.

The miniature baseball player swung at the ball sitting on the tee. He hit it past the pitcher's mound and darted toward third base.

The following year, Jeff played little league. John and I watched from the bleachers. Jeff's team was up. A ball was hit to right field. It was a fly ball. The right fielder watched as it came toward him. He sat down, right there in right field. Everyone looked on as the coach walked toward the third base line. "Stand up!" he yelled. The little boy shook his head. "NO!" he shouted back at the coach, still sitting.

The ball bounced behind him. The center fielder ran toward the ball, trying to catch it before it hit the ground again. "Stand up!" The coach shouted again. I looked at John, smiling and thinking this poor little boy doesn't want to play baseball. The coach walked out to right field and talked to the little boy. "That's his son," explained a parent sitting near us. The boy stood up, and the coach walked back across the field to the bench. The second time the ball was hit in the direction of right field, the little boy sat down again. Finally, the coach took him out of the game.

Jeff was up. After the first two pitches, Jeff hit a long fly ball into left field, behind the outfielder. He ran around bases, a home run. When the all-star team was selected, Jeff was chosen.

The first time I realized Jeff had a good throwing arm was outside our church. It was after CCD, on a Thursday afternoon. Jack Lessard and his sons, John and Garrett were with Jeff, Jason, and me out in the parking lot. The boys began throwing rocks toward an open field. Jeff threw a rock that flew...and flew...and flew. I didn't see where it landed. Jack and I just looked at each other. We said nothing. No one said anything. The stone disappeared into the field. We stared as Jeff kept throwing stones that flew out of sight.

Jeff could throw a baseball eighty miles an hour at age twelve. He had a fastball and a natural curveball. His Little League team was filled with talent. The Sandwich Little League all-star team won every tournament on the Cape and in Southeastern Massachusetts and made it to the "Final Four" playoff in Lynn. If they won there, they would have a chance to play in Williamsport, Pennsylvania, for the Little League World Title.

During the playoffs in Lynn, the Sandwich team roomed with the families of Lynn players. Jeff and Brian Bodjack stayed with the same host family, and they invited our families for dinner on Saturday night. When we arrived, Brian's dad asked, "How did you sleep last night?"

"Good, Dad," Brian replied. "But there must be a hospital nearby because there were sirens going off all night."

I smiled. The host family team didn't live near a hospital; our kids are not city folk.

Sandwich lost in the Final Four in Lynn to a team from Pittsfield, Massachusetts. Instead of going to Williamsport, the Sandwich team hit the road to Cooperstown. They finished in sixteenth place out of sixty-five teams from across the continental United States and Hawaii. Jeff hit three home runs, which we were told would remain in the Cooperstown Hall of Fame.

Jeff pitching at Cooperstown Dreams Park

In Babe Ruth, the team traveled around the Cape on the weekends to play in tournaments. Today they were in Rochester to play against Middleborough. Middleborough was always competitive in Little League. They were better at this level.

Jeff was pitching. He was the third-string starter in the bullpen. When he didn't pitch, he played third base or center field.

John and I sat down to watch from the grass along the third base line with other parents.

It was a hot afternoon. Jeff had started and was still pitching as the game went into the top of the seventh with a tied score. As Jeff stood on the mound, Middleborough's best hitter approached the plate. There were runners on first and second with two outs. The count went to 2–0. Jeff wound up and threw his best pitch, a changeup. The batter swung.

"Strike!" the umpire yelled.

My heart was pounding.

Jeff wound up again and threw one outside. The umpire raised his fingers, 3–1. The catcher threw the ball back to Jeff.

I could see Jeff's red face and the sweat that separated pieces of his hair below the rim of his baseball cap. He needed a haircut, I thought.

The batter fouled off the next pitch: 3–2.

I changed my sitting position. I was on my knees as Jeff wound up and threw his fastball. The batter swung and tipped it foul. The first and second base runners walked back to their bases. Jeff wound up again. The base runners took a big lead. Jeff threw another fastball, and the batter swung hard and missed.

"Strike three!" the umpire yelled.

I sat back down and sighed silently. It was worse watching him pitch than watching him play in goal that one time. The team ran off the field while Middleborough grabbed their gloves and hurried back onto the field. The game was still tied.

Sandwich had two men on base when Jeff walked to the plate. After three pitches, the count was two and one. I watched anxiously, hoping for a hit.

"Come on Jeff, you can do it!" His team stood in the dugout and cheered him on.

He swung hard at the next pitch. The ball sailed high over the second baseman and into the gap between center field and right field. The second base runner was rounding third and heading home; trailing him was his teammate. The center fielder chased down the ball, picked it up, and threw it to the cutoff man, who threw toward home. The runner slid under the catcher, his leg stretched out over the plate.

We watched the umpire's arms as he watched the play. Slouched over, he raised his arms, and in one swift move, his arms straightened out.

"Safe!"

The team jumped up from the dugout and raced to the field. Jeff was running around second when the play ended the game. We stood up and cheered. The teams came together at home plate, lined up for the traditional handshake and high fives, and mumbled, "Good game."

After the team dispersed, I walked behind Jeff and his friend, Mike Bridges as they walked toward the snack bar. Jeff was head and shoulders taller than Mike as they carried their bat and baseball bag. Their uniforms were dirty. Jeff's hair and face were wet with sweat.

"You did it all," I heard Mike say to Jeff before they approached the window of the snack bar. They had been best friends since Little League. Jeff didn't reply, and they didn't speak again until they ordered a drink. I imagined a little bit of a smile on Jeff's face that I couldn't see. It was a hot day, and the sun was beginning to dip in the sky, cooling the long day and the end of the game.

It was the first time that his teammates and classmates had seen Jeff since his treatment began. Jarod Larocco, a senior and captain of the hockey and baseball teams, organized a baseball game between the two Sandwich High teams. It was a fundraiser for Jeff, the hockey team against the baseball team. Jarod designed T-shirts, white for the hockey team and navy for the baseball team. Parents and classmates came to watch.

Jeff was bald and without facial hair—no eyelashes or eyebrows. His face was round, and his weight had increased from the steroids. I wondered which shirt Jeff would wear. I don't know how he decided hockey or baseball, but it was a minor decision compared to the ones he'd made in the last two months. He wore the hockey shirt, his true passion.

Parents who knew Jeff wanted to know how he was doing. We talked to our friends we hadn't seen since Jeff had been diagnosed. It was our first public appearance. Jeff couldn't play, but he was up and out of a wheelchair, free to walk around without crutches, and free of pain.

It felt good to be outside watching baseball and watching Jeff with his friends.

At the end of the game he came to me and said, "We're all going to Twin Acres for an ice cream." I smiled. He looked happy and not tired and weak. I handed him the money raised from that night, a couple hundred dollars. "Thanks!" he exclaimed and headed toward the parking lot with his friends.

CHAPTER 25

❦

Amputation, Replacement, or Radiation, April 2005

A FTER THE COMPLETION of the first four cycles of chemo, the doctors wanted to scan Jeff to measure the tumor in his thigh for shrinkage and to see whether the three small tumors in his lungs had been destroyed. A decision would then have to be made, not just by the doctors but by Jeff too, on whether to amputate his leg or to use radiation to kill any cells lurking in the mother ship, the original mass in his thigh.

"We can kill hundreds of thousands of cancerous cells, but it's that one cell that escapes or survives the treatment that we worry about," Sam told us. Sam had also stressed to John and me, privately, that this had to be Jeff's decision, not ours. Both John and I agreed.

We were excited to find out from the scans that the small tumors in Jeff's lungs had disappeared. However, the bone scan of his entire body showed that tiny tumors had traveled to his knee and that other spots of various sizes had moved up his leg to his hipbone and to his growth plate. This was unusual for Ewing's. Usually in Ewing's, the cancer metastasizes from the original tumor and then to the lungs. In Jeff's case, it had spread in the opposite direction from the original mass. We grew silent; processing the news, knowing a difficult decision would need to be made. We were advised to talk as a family and that Dr. Grier would be calling us shortly.

We received a call from Hannah. She had five front row seats to a Red Sox game, which had been donated by one of the club's minority owners. The front row seats were directly in front of the Red Sox on-deck circle. Parking was included. Perhaps this is just what Jeff needs right now, I thought. Hannah left the tickets for us at the front desk of the Dana-Farber.

We got into the car for our ride up to the game. John drove, and Jeff, Jeff's friend Ian, and Jason sat in the back. I sat in the passenger's seat. I knew Dr. Grier would be calling us on my cell. I thought that having this discussion during our ride to Fenway instead of in the confines of a secluded room in the JFC would be less scary. Sometimes difficult medical decisions are better made in lighter, less threatening and nonclinical surroundings.

"I am not getting my leg amputated!" Jeff declared from the backseat. I looked back at Jeff and said, "That's your decision, honey." It was clear he was steadfast in his decision.

When my cell phone rang, everyone became quiet. I looked out at the water of Quincy Bay as I opened my cell phone. It was Dr. Grier.

Dr. Grier told me about the amputation and what it would involve and then discussed radiation. Jeff's leg could be radiated only once. Radiation now could cause other types of cancers later in life. He spoke in detail, and I listened. Without knowing what Jeff's decision was, Dr. Grier continued, stating that at their meeting, he, Sam, and other oncologists and specialists, knowing Jeff and his athleticism, all agreed that Jeff would be miserable with the amputation. He said if it were another teen who wasn't as active in sports as Jeff, amputation might be the right decision. The fact that Jeff's cancer had metastasized to his lungs was another reason not to amputate. If the cancer had not spread to Jeff's lungs and his leg was amputated, there was a 90 percent chance that he would be cured. However, it had spread, and Jeff's chances of survival had dropped to under 30 percent. He was serious and straightforward about how aggressive Ewing's sarcoma was.

That afternoon, at that moment on the expressway, we knew the severity of the decision. My thoughts were to radiate and kill any living cancer cells in his thigh, and since the tumors in his lungs had disappeared, Jeff might then be free of cancer. I thought radiation and the possibility of killing any cancer cells left behind in his thigh outweighed the risk of a secondary cancer showing up later in Jeff's life. That was a risk I could live with at that moment. Let's try to kill the cancer now, and perhaps ten or twenty years from now a cure will be found for any type of cancer that might occur as a result of this radiation. Radiation was a better alternative for Jeff than amputation, which would then mean a total hip and a total knee replacement. It was much more practical than amputation. It was the best decision for Jeff, by Jeff, with all that we knew up to that point.

I told Dr. Grier that we were on our way to the Red Sox game. He said he too was heading to Fenway Park for the game.

"Jeff has decided not to amputate his leg or to have any replacement surgery."

"Is this Jeff's decision?" he asked.

"Absolutely," I replied.

It was a relief ending that phone conversation; a huge relief for Jeff. I said good-bye and "Go Sox."

"I can't believe that he is on his way to the Red Sox game," I said to Jeff.

"Mom, he needs time off too. He's at the hospital all the time," Jeff's voice raised from the back seat.

"I know, you're right, he does."

The Red Sox won with a walk-off home run.

The next day, just to be sure, John phoned Dr. Ready, the orthopedic oncologist surgeon who first saw Jeff the morning after the snowstorm.

"If it was your son, what would you do?" John asked.

"I wouldn't put him through that surgery," Dr. Ready replied.

CHAPTER 26

Baltimore with Jason

"**M**OM."

I jumped up at the sound; I'd fallen asleep on the couch in our living room.

"Jeff? John? Jason?" They sounded alike.

"Mom, it's me, Jason."

"Oh, honey, what is it?" I sat up, still dazed.

"Can you drive me to CVS? I need some index cards."

"Sure, Jay, let's go." I got up, found my keys, and we left the house. Index cards for class—wow, that's a relief. I usually go straight to the pharmacy.

I felt bad I wasn't giving Jason the attention he needed during Jeff's illness. It was April. I thought about the time I'd been to Camden Yards in Baltimore with my two brothers, John and Paul, and Dad. It was the year before Jeff got sick. "Fenway South" they called it. I remembered that at the first game I stood next to my brothers and Dad, watching Pedro and Varitek warming up in the bullpen. When Pedro wound up, he looked back at us and then turned and threw the ball. He did this every time, and I started to feel awkward. We stayed in Baltimore for a couple of games before returning home. A few weeks later, I received a signed picture of Pedro. I'm pretty sure it was Dad, but the three of them never came clean.

I decided this would be a great trip for Jason and me.

We flew into Baltimore and took the train to Camden Yards.

Jason and I checked into a hotel around the corner from Camden Yards. That night, the park was filled. We sat at center field, enjoyed the game, and ate roast beef sandwiches and homemade french fries from the stand behind our section, the same sandwiches I bought for Dad and my brothers.

The next morning, we took a duck boat tour of Baltimore, went to the aquarium, and walked along the harbor before heading back to Camden Yards to purchase two tickets at center field—fifteen dollars each.

After the game that night, we went to the Cheesecake Factory on the harbor. We stood waiting for a table when one emptied in the lounge, and Jason and I sat down.

"Mom, there are some Red Sox players here."

They'd walked past our table, but I didn't see them.

"Who?"

"Papa Jack, Wily Mo Pena, and Willie Harris."

"I'm going to get their autograph," I said.

"Oh no, here we go. Mom, don't. I knew I shouldn't have told you!"

I did. I approached Papa Jack, the batting coach, and Wily Mo Pena and got their autographs on a napkin. Willie Harris stood alone. He was my height and had stolen a base that night. I got his autograph too. When I returned to our table, I called Jeff.

"Jeff, I just got autographs from Papa Jack, Wily Mo Pena, and Willie Harris!"

There was silence, and then Jeff spoke. "Mom, are you done ruining their night?"

"No, not yet, honey."

CHAPTER 27

Road Test and Blood Counts

THE FOLLOWING WEEK Jeff had a small window of time to get his driving learner's permit. John had been taking him driving whenever he could. I took Jeff to the registry for the written test. When Jeff gave the clerk his social security number, she entered it into the system and immediately looked back at Jeff with concern.

"What's the problem?" I asked.

"It looks like Jeff is a victim of identity theft. Someone else is using his number," she explained.

I had Jeff's original social security card and handed it to the clerk. She got up from her chair to look for her supervisor. When she returned, we continued with Jeff's intake. She said he was all set. Jeff was then called to take the computerized test, and he passed.

When Jeff was scheduled for his road test, the state trooper assigned to him was a Sandwich resident. His sons had played hockey with John and Jeff. We knew him from the years of hometown and select hockey. He had just lost his wife to brain cancer. The state trooper turned to Jeff and said, "Today's your lucky day." Jeff took the road test and passed. He was a good driver.

Jeff began radiation treatment. Blue markings were made on his thigh so that the technician could precisely radiate the correct spot. A leg piece was molded to his leg for him to wear during each treatment to protect him.

Radiation also reduces blood counts. Each week, Jeff had his blood drawn by Katherine Baugh, our VNA nurse. She sent Jeff's blood samples to a local lab or to one of the local hospitals if she thought Hannah would need to see them immediately. After several weeks of radiation, Jeff's blood counts remained steady. At first, I was pleased that they remained constant and were not sinking below normal levels or affecting his bone marrow, but then I began to worry.

Why weren't his counts going down? I thought about it every day. Weeks went by without a drop in counts. What if the radiation wasn't working? And then it happened. They plunged! I called Hannah.

"Hannah, Susan Hayes."

"Hi, Susan," she replied.

"Jeff's blood levels finally dropped. Were you worried? I was told that radiation would also lower his red and white blood cell levels and lower his platelets as the chemo drugs did."

"Yes, we were waiting for them to go down," she replied.

"You were?" I questioned.

"Yes."

"Okay, but I don't want to know why." I answered.

"Keep an eye on him," she said. "He needs to be kept away from any potential germs that could compromise his health."

When the radiation finally scored, his marrow was hit hard. But it was a long wait for his bone marrow to react. I thought as Jeff's blood was drawn and the counts were read each time that his immune system was strong and that it was a good sign, but on the other hand, not knowing what it meant when his counts didn't react worried me. How did I know something wasn't right?

As a parent of a child undergoing chemotherapy, you need to ask, "What does this mean?" When alone and faced with the unknown and uncertainty of the effects of the treatment, you need to ask questions. When you're the person in charge, alone at home with your child, remain confident and follow your instincts because you're not an oncologist, and the effects of the treatment are not the same for any one child. React without fear and remain calm. It's your child's life at hand; this holds true for me in the morning, however at night I was less confident and more tired and fearful. My hope comes from knowing that tomorrow morning, when I awake, it can be a better day.

Jeff drove himself from the Cape to Brigham and Women's Hospital for some of his radiation treatments. When he was unable to make the trip because of his chemotherapy cycles, friends and family took him.

Our friend Michael, who lived outside of Boston, took Jeff to one of his treatments. Jeff entered radiology and slid his magnetic card through a small scanner at the reception desk and sat with Michael while waiting to be escorted to the treatment room. The radiation treatment, on a good day, took about fifteen minutes.

Moments after Jeff was called for his radiation, a fire alarm went off, causing immediate panic in the waiting room. This was the nuclear medicine floor, and it was located in the basement. Patients waiting for treatment became frightened. They were unable to use the elevators to get to the street floor. Michael stood up and tried to calm everyone. He was worried about Jeff and couldn't get to him. The alarm kept sounding and causing panic. No one could leave the basement floor. Michael persuaded the patients to return to the waiting room and wait for an announcement. The alarm silenced. Michael left the waiting room and went down the corridor looking for Jeff. When he made it to the nurse's station, Jeff appeared. Michael was relieved that Jeff was safe and sound while on his watch.

Jeff's cousin, Julie, took Jeff to his next radiation treatment. It was a good day. Jeff's wait was short, and he was done in fifteen minutes. Julie wanted to do something more to help, so while they were at Brigham and Women's, she decided to give blood. Jeff waited for her. After donating blood she became weak and ended up needing to stay and rest.

For Jeff's next treatment he stayed with my brother John and his family who lived in Norwood. My other sister-in-law, Patti, took Jeff the next morning for his scheduled treatment. They sat in the same waiting room for the first hour and then were told that the radiation machine was broken and they didn't know how long it would be until it was repaired. Jeff wanted to wait. After three long hours, a technician told them they would have to reschedule.

On days when Jeff and I waited for him to be called for radiation, I would control the television so that he could watch his sports, and when I wasn't there with him, he would control the remote to watch his sports. He learned, watched, and took control as his treatment progressed.

CHAPTER 28

Fifth Treatment, May 2005

AT HOME, THE normal morning routine no longer existed. The words *rise and shine* were hardly spoken. *Rise and shine for chemo* wouldn't inspire anyone. I recalled one of the nurses at Children's Hospital telling us that Jeff's outlook and positive thoughts were effective during his treatment, and that it's important to believe that the chemo is killing the cancer cells.

"Jeff, think of the chemo as little Pac-Men opening their mouths wide and swallowing the bad cells." He had that look: I don't think so, Mom, but okay. "Or," I said, "Think about an army of soldiers invading enemy territory. The enemy is the bad cancer cells, and the chemo is the army taking down the city or the tumor that houses the cancer cells. We can always rebuild the city after we kill the bad cells."

"Okay, Mom, I got it!" he replied, annoyed.

Jeff began his fifth treatment at the JFC, and then we traveled across the street to Children's where we were assigned to a room with a young toddler and his mother. Jeff had the bed next to the door. He turned to me from his bed, his head elevated with a couple of pillows. He had learned precisely how to set the bed in the position he was most comfortable and could watch television from.

"Mom, I'll be okay if you want to spend the night at the Holiday Inn."

I felt good that he wasn't afraid to stay alone anymore. "Okay, Jeff." I was happy to sleep in a real bed. That night, my sister Kathy was coming up to stay with him, and she encouraged me to take the night off. I went to the hotel, checked in, and went to the lounge for dinner and a glass of wine. I spent time calling my friends and family and was grateful for some quiet time to myself.

I got up early the next morning and took a hot, cleansing shower that washed away the hardness of my days and stripped my body of the stress. I stood in the shower, recalling the last months of a changed and unexpected life. I resisted turning the water off, not wanting to leave my safe place; I knew I'd have endless hot water. I wondered what kind of night Jeff had, hoping it was uneventful. I packed up and took the shuttle back to Children's.

I walked into Jeff's room. I was surprised to see him awake this early. "Hi, honey. How are you?"

"Hi," he replied. "It's a good thing you didn't stay last night."

"Why, what happened?" I was standing next to his bed.

"The boy in the other bed threw up all night next to my bed," he replied.

It had been a horrible night. The mother of the little boy came over to me from the other side of the curtain, and I walked to the end of Jeff's bed.

"I feel bad for your son. It was a bad night for my son; he was sick all night," she said.

"Oh, I'm sorry. How is your son doing?" I replied.

"He's sleeping."

"Oh, that's good. Maybe he'll feel better when he wakes."

"I hope so," she replied.

I walked back to Jeff's bedside, feeling guilty I'd left him last night. "I'll be right back, Jeff."

"Where are you going?" he asked.

"I'm going to see if there's another room with an empty bed. I promise I'll be right back."

"Okay."

I walked down the hall looking for another room. I found a couple and went to the nurse's station to ask that Jeff be moved. Without resistance or delay, they moved Jeff to an empty room. He was relieved. He closed his eyes and soon fell asleep. I stood next to him for a long time, not allowing anyone or anything to disturb him as he lay sleeping. The sun was shining in the window, and I sat for hours on the bench in front of the window. He was safe and able to sleep now. That was my job, to keep him safe. I found resolve and a renewed conviction to never leave him for any selfish reason again. I was overwhelmed with contentment and love just watching him sleep in peace. It was so little to ask for so much suffering.

Many young cancer patients were left alone on Seven West. Parents have to work, and siblings need care. I'll never judge a parent who lives this battle with his or her child and cancer; it's incredibly difficult. I'm thankful to my employers, my family, my friends, and my community who enabled me to care for Jeff.

That night at Children's, a fellow assigned to the floor came to examine Jeff.

"Hi, Tom, how are you feeling?" he asked as he walked up to Jeff's bed.

Jeff and I looked at each other, and I stood up next to his bed. I looked at the fellow and said, "His name is Jeff."

"Oh, yes, I'm sorry. Hi, Jeff. I just have some questions, but first let me listen to your heart." He moved closer to Jeff and placed the end of his stethoscope on his chest, listening carefully. Then he stood up straight and asked, "Do you play hockey, Jeff?"

"Yes," Jeff replied.

"I can tell. You have a strong heart." He continued to examine Jeff and asked many questions. Jeff answered what he could, and I listened, filling in some of the answers. That night when the room was dark, lit only by the IV pump, I fell asleep on the plastic-covered bench under the window. The fellow and Jeff's nurse came in and out of the room throughout the night. I thought they were doing the usual vital signs and changing his fluids, so I fell back to sleep.

When morning came, the fellow came into the room again to check on Jeff. He told me that Jeff's blood pressure and heart rate had become dangerously low throughout the night. I sensed his deep concern. I don't know what they did to treat it, but that morning when he awoke, Jeff's blood pressure had increased, and he was out of danger.

Clearly the fellow had been on alert all night and had monitored Jeff's condition. I was grateful.

"Thank you, doctor," I said and smiled, thinking, I don't remember his name either.

The day after we arrived home, Nancy Bridges came by. She visited regularly to help me while Jeff recovered at home. Her son and Jeff were close. When Jeff was first diagnosed, she gave him the silver medal of Saint Peregrine, the saint of cancer victims. He wore it around his neck all the time. Nancy was a nurse at Carney Hospital. Her hours at work in Quincy were erratic, so on her days off, she came by to stay with Jeff. On some occasions she'd bring her husband Mark's meat sauce. It was delicious and my favorite.

It was good to see Nancy. It was a break for me. I always feel more at ease in the company of a nurse or doctor. We had the best of both in Boston and here at home. We were fortunate.

She sat down next to Jeff and asked, "How are you feeling, Jeff?"

"Okay, I guess."

Looking back at him, she suddenly cried out, "Susan, Jeff's eyes are dilated!"

"What! They're dilated?" I knelt down next to Jeff and looked into his eyes.

"Nance, why are they dilated?"

"I don't know. Call Sam now!"

I speed-dialed Sam's number and he answered.

"Sam, Jeff's eyes are dilated."

Sam paused. "It could be the anti-emetic patch." That medication helped to control vomiting. "Did Jeff touch the patch and then scratch his eyes?"

"I don't know." I turned to Jeff and asked him.

"I could have, I guess," Jeff replied. I told Sam.

"That's it!" Sam said. "Ask him not to touch the patch, okay?"

"Got it."

It was several hours before Jeff's pupils were normal again. Nancy stayed seated with him. Instructions were given at the JFC to the nurses to instruct all cancer patients wearing a patch not to touch it.

CHAPTER 29

Sixth Treatment

"Concert Helps Sandwich Teen"—Courtesy of the Sandwich *Enterprise*

"Jammin' for Jeff," a concert featuring four rock bands, a DJ, and pizza, will be held from 7 to 11 PM on Saturday, May 6, 2005 in the Corpus Christi Parish Center at 324 Quaker Meetinghouse Road in East Sandwich. His friend, senior Tom Prendergast, is producing the concert to help raise money for Jeff's family's medical bills, the Jimmy Fund, KerryKares, Inc., and a scholarship fund.

S CHOOL WAS ENDING, and many of Jeff's friends were graduating. It was the end of Jeff's sophomore year. The basement was complete. The ceramic tile in Jeff's bathroom was installed by Brian Boley, whose wife, Carol, had taken care of my sons in daycare while I worked at the New Seabury Resort. All the specs for the doorways and shower were made for wheelchair access. We installed french doors that led out into the backyard. The floor throughout the rest of the basement was set in a checkerboard-patterned tile. We purchased an oak bar with bar stools for the mud room. Jeff's friend, John Lessard, framed the Wolverine-signed T-shirt given at the all-star game, and we hung it in the mud room.

My brother-in-law, Marty, installed shelves that he had custom made for Jeff's trophies, awards, autographed hockey sticks, baseball all-star certificates, the Cooperstown Dreams Park plaque, his Barnstable wooden bat, and his Cooperstown wooden bat. Jeff placed all the trophies

in order by height, spaced equally on the shelf, and hung his signed baseball caps on the horizontal rack where the sticks were hung. The front
of one his baseball caps was covered with baseball pins he'd swapped in
Cooperstown; many of the pins were given to him by his friend, John
Muse of Falmouth, whose team had been in Cooperstown at the same
time. Each pin was placed touching another in a collage on the front of
Jeff's baseball cap from that tournament.

It took us a few weeks to find a big screen television that fit in the
corner of his hall-of-fame living room.

"What do you think we'll have for dinner tonight?" I asked John as I sat
down beside him; he was reading the Sunday *Cape Cod Times*. We never
knew who would be coming by our house on a Sunday afternoon with
a homemade dinner for us until we saw a car drive up our driveway. A
friend or family member would come to the door carrying aluminum
trays of hot food, fresh rolls, salad, a dessert, sometimes a bottle of wine,
and sometimes a bouquet of flowers.

"Lasagna or chicken something," he replied, turning a page of the news-
paper and not looking back at me. Chicken was one of Jeff's favorite dishes.

For me, it was the best day of the week. We were home, and I didn't
have to cook.

Tonight's meal came courtesy of Diane Iadonisi: meatballs with sub
rolls and a salad, another favorite of Jeff's. I called Diane to thank her.
"Do you secretly own your own restaurant?"

She laughed. I remembered her last dish, a chicken casserole with
stuffing and gravy and all the trimmings; it had been delicious.

We headed up to Boston for the two-day treatment. We followed the
same routine. Jeff now looked like the rest of the young patients in the

waiting room at the JFC. We knew the receptionist, the intake nurse, and most of the other oncology nurses. Jeff received the three chemo drugs in his same bed as always, and we left the clinic for the short and always eventful trip to Children's. After the last treatment, when I'd crossed the street pushing Jeff in his wheelchair, I'd hit a pothole. Jeff had put his foot down immediately, stopping himself from pitching forward and falling face first in the street. "Mom, what are you doing?"

"Sorry! I didn't see the hole."

Arriving at Children's, we were surprised and comforted when we were assigned a private room. It was a warm afternoon, and I got Jeff an ice cream from the food court, his favorite hurricane ice cream mixed with Reese's Peanut Butter Cups. He devoured it in minutes. "That was delicious," he said, licking his lips. It was the most I'd ever seen him enjoy any food. I laughed to myself and asked him if he'd like another.

We watched television together that night and felt good in the privacy of our own room, knowing we would be leaving tomorrow. It was a great night, a relief not having to share our chemotherapy treatment with another patient and family. The next day we were discharged after Jeff received the chemo drugs, and we left for home. He knew now how he would feel after these drugs, and he chose not to take some of the antinausea drugs so that when he got home he could drive to his friend's house and play Wiffle ball.

Jeff made a special effort to watch Stevie Lessard play his Little League game. Stevie was Jeff's best friend's youngest brother, and Jeff had spent a great deal of time at the Lessard home playing with Stevie. His mother, Doreen, said, "It was like the president coming to his game!"

Jeff woke one morning and came upstairs and into the kitchen. "I don't feel good," he said. I was getting ready to go to work. I was surprised; he hadn't complained up to this point.

"Lie down on the couch, and I'll check your temperature." Jeff's normal temperature was 97.6 degrees, always. I took his temperature, and he was at 99 degrees. His temperature was elevated for the first time during his treatment. I immediately phoned work to tell them I wouldn't be in. Jeff stayed upstairs and lay on the couch. I stayed with him, and within the hour I took his temperature again. It was now at 100 degrees, and I phoned Sam. Sam said, "If his temperature goes up to 103.1, get in your car and drive to Boston." I changed my clothes and packed a suitcase.

Jeff's temperature continued to rise. Early that afternoon, it reached 102. I paced and cleaned all day, watching Jeff closely and waiting for each hour to pass so that I could take his temperature again. I couldn't wait that long, and after thirty minutes, I'd take it again. I couldn't give him Tylenol or aspirin because it would mask his fever, and we wouldn't know whether an infection was growing. Sam and Hannah worried about an infection in his port. His temperature was still 102.

Jeff didn't eat or drink anything; he lay still and slept on and off all day. I could feel myself becoming anxious. I remained calm and concentrated on taking his temperature at regular intervals and prepared to drive to Boston. Another thirty minutes passed, and I took it again; it was 102.7. I thought if we did have to make the drive, traffic would begin to get worse mid afternoon, and his temperature could rise during that drive while we were caught in traffic. I wasn't sure what to do. Leave now and risk traffic and a high temperature on the expressway, or wait it out at home? I could always go to Cape Cod Hospital, I thought. I waited. I took his temperature every twenty minutes. It reached 102.9.

At three o'clock his temperature dipped slightly, reading 102.1. I questioned the reading and waited a few minutes and took it again, 102.0. In twenty minutes it was at 100. At four o'clock it was at 99 degrees. By five o'clock it was back to 97 degrees, and he said to me, "I'm hungry." I called Hannah at the JFC.

The receptionist paged Hannah.

"Hannah, how are you?" I was thinking that she might be alarmed by me calling her because I seldom call.

"Good," she answered. "How's Jeff?"

I told her about Jeff's day.

She was very calm, and I began to relax hearing her voice.

"What's his temperature now?"

"It's back to normal."

"An infection was starting in Jeff's body due to his low white blood count, but at the same time, because of the Neulasta shot, which speeds up the growth of new white blood cells, well then, these white blood cells fought off the infection." I could hear the relief in her voice.

I replied, "Are you kidding, Hannah? That's what was happening!" I found this remarkable, and I couldn't believe it had just happened to Jeff.

"Yes, Jeff's body was fighting off the infection throughout the day," Hannah confirmed.

There was silence over the phone for a moment, and then Hannah spoke, "Someone up there was watching over him."

"Yes," I replied and thought about my mother.

CHAPTER 30

——— ✲ ———

Mom

Diagnosis

IT WAS ABOUT two years ago, in May 2003, that Mom's health changed. "This is your mother calling," I heard when I turned on the answering machine. I smiled after a long day at work. How could I not recognize her voice? She hadn't been feeling well for several months and had been suffering from rheumatoid arthritis. When she started having other symptoms, I began to worry. The last time we'd been together was when we met for a Mother's Day brunch with my sisters. Mom had given each of us a red rose she had grown in her garden. She could make anything grow. Her impatiens grew so beautifully between the bushes at our home in Newton, and they spread across the beds in our front yard in bright pink and white, filling every open space. I'd tried to reproduce that memory by planting impatiens in the rich soil in my front yard, but the plant flowered only long enough to humor me, as if to say, "Nice try."

"Susan, can you call me when you get a chance?" There was a long pause as she waited for me to pick up. "Okay, thank you. Bye now." I called her right back.

"Hi, Mom," I said when she answered the phone. "How are you feeling?"

"Okay. How are the boys?" She always asked.

"They're fine, Mom. What's up?"

"I called because Dad and I wanted to meet you and Joanne either at your house or at Joanne's. We'd like to talk to you and Joanne first, and then meet everyone else at Kathy's." They had retired in Eastham, a small town thirty-five miles down Cape.

"Okay. Have you talked to Joanne yet?"

"Yes, she said we could meet at her house."

"Okay, when?"

"Tomorrow night if that's okay with you."

"Yes, that's fine. What's the matter?" I asked.

"Oh, we'll talk tomorrow."

"Mom." I paused for second. "Is everything okay?" I asked. It was sudden to call a family meeting, which in itself was unusual. I felt something was seriously wrong.

"I'll see you tomorrow night, okay?"

I left work the next afternoon at five o'clock and drove to Joanne's. When I entered her house, Joanne was in the kitchen preparing small pizza appetizers. She had just placed them on the table when Mom and Dad entered the front door.

"Hi, Susan. Hi, Joanne," Mom said, walking through the living room. Dad nodded. He was a proud man and spoke little; Jeff was a lot like Dad. They sat down at the dining room table.

We passed the small pizza bites, and I sipped from my glass of water, waiting for Mom to speak.

"I have cancer," Mom looked at Joanne and me. I looked back at her and then across at Dad. "It's in my liver. They don't know where it originated from, but they have found it there. They'll need to do more tests." She spoke slowly and carefully as if she had rehearsed this several times before our meeting.

"Oh, God," I thought. In the liver, that's cancer's way of saying we've broken through the battle lines and we're now taking down the fort.

Mom sat at the table teaching us about pride and strength by not showing any emotion. I knew how serious it was, but she was telling us this news as if she had a bad cold.

"Please don't call anyone when we leave; I'd like to tell them myself."

"No, of course not, Mom," Joanne answered.

Joanne's three kids, Jerome, Angela, and Josh, were outside playing soccer.

"How are you feeling?" Joanne asked.

"Oh, not so great."

It became still inside the room where we sat. Time seemed to have stopped. I felt our family strength.

"We're gonna fight it, Mom," I said with certainty. "And beat it!" I added.

"Yes, we are." Dad looked back at me.

"What can we do to help?" Joanne asked.

"Nothing now," Dad replied. "She'll have more tests tomorrow."

They were eager to get on the road, so we left the table, and Mom and Dad walked out the front door toward their car. Joanne and I stood in front of her bay window, staring out at them. I ran out the front door and to their car while Mom opened the passenger door. She turned and looked back at me. We stood feet apart without speaking for several seconds.

"I'll call you tomorrow." I didn't know what else to say.

"Okay." She stepped into the front seat and sat down.

Dad started the car, and they pulled away, heading off Cape to break the news to the rest of my siblings.

After more tests, Mom was diagnosed with pancreatic cancer. It was July and very warm. I sat on the couch in the living room of Mom and Dad's house in Eastham. Mom sat at the kitchen table taking small bites of toast with jelly. She was thin and ill from the strong chemotherapy. It was the first time I'd seen her this sick. She'd always been healthy.

"You don't need to stay," she said from her seat in front of the kitchen sliders. The sun shone in brightly, warming her back. She wore short cotton pajamas with a tiny pink rose pattern.

"I want to, Mom," I replied. "It's so hot; why don't you put an air conditioner in your bedroom?" I asked.

"Oh, no, I don't need one."

"But you'll be much more comfortable." She had moved downstairs from their master bedroom to the first floor bedroom with a half bath.

"I don't like air conditioning."

Dad was the same way. It was a generational thing, I thought. They'd learned to live without many luxuries. We didn't have fans when we were young. I remembered the hot nights when I'd lie on the end of my bed waiting for a hint of a breeze to come through my window. Unable to sleep, I'd look up at the moon. I'd hear the branches swaying slightly, and then I'd feel a cool breeze; ah! However small it was, it felt so good.

"Is there anything I can do for you?" I asked.

"No, I'm okay. You don't need to stay."

She wanted to be alone, and I thought she was sitting up only for my benefit, so I knelt down by her side and said, "Please have Dad call me if you guys need anything. I know you don't feel good, so I'm going to go. I'll see you again soon."

"Bye bye, Susie." Her voice was weak and she spoke as if I were a child.

My sister Kathy insisted that Mom have air conditioning and bought a unit. Dad placed it in the window of her bedroom during the remainder of the hot weather.

Mom had treatments every Friday at noon at the Davenport Mugar Center at the Cape Cod Hospital. I'd sit with her during my lunch hour while Dad left for his lunch. She looked pale and thin. She sat in an oversized green cushioned recliner while the chemotherapy dripped into a vein in her arm. The lunch hour passed quickly for me. The chemotherapy drug was administered for several hours; the nausea last-ed for several days.

Dad returned from lunch, and I said good-bye to Mom and walked with Dad to the exit. I turned to look back at Mom. I could see the sadness on her face as she began to cry. We looked at each other from across the room. I quietly said good-bye as I waved softly to her. I hated to leave, remembering her look as I left the room and walked to the elevator and through the doors.

I couldn't go to visit Mom one Friday morning because I was ex-tremely busy at work.

"Are you coming today?" Mom asked over the phone before she left for the hospital.

"I don't think so," I replied. "I'm too busy today to leave."

"Okay," she replied, and we said good-bye.

At work, I found myself anxiously thinking about Mom. I had to be with her. I left work, stopped for a bouquet of flowers and drove to Cape Cod Hospital.

When I arrived and walked out of the elevator, Mom and Dad were sit-ting in the waiting room with their backs to me. I walked up to them and presented Mom with the flowers and sat down next to her.

"Susan," Mom looked up at me in surprise. "I thought you weren't coming!"

"I lied." I could sense the comfort she felt when I sat down next to her. The comfort I'd felt from her all my life.

It was halfway into September, and I hadn't heard from Dad in a few days until he called me at work. I had gone to lunch and the post office, my daily routine. When I returned, Margo, my assistant, gave me the mes-sage that Dad had just called. I sat down at my desk and returned his call.

"Hi, Dad; it's me."

"Hi. I called to tell you that your mother was just taken to the emergency room at Cape Cod Hospital. I stayed behind to clean up. She'd been throwing up all morning. Can you go to the hospital right away?"

"I'm on my way, Dad."

"I'll be there as soon as I finish cleaning here."

"Okay, I'll see you there." I hung up the phone and told my bosses I was leaving and why. They knew Mom was sick.

I went straight to the emergency room and searched for her until I saw her in one of the cubicles wearing a hospital johnny.

"Hi, Mom."

"Susan?" Her eyes looked up at me.

I walked up to her bed and stood beside her. She had fought hard all summer. Now I could see the fight was gone.

Dad entered the room and stood beside her. I was amazed at his demeanor. He was quiet, worn, and stoic.

"Are you okay?" he asked Mom.

She nodded, and then after a long pause she turned her head slightly to Dad and said, "I'm going fast."

I left the room and walked outside the emergency room entrance and called Joanne. When she answered, I began to cry.

"I'm at Cape Cod Hospital. Mom was taken here by ambulance, and she's not doing well." I then called my sister Kathy and told her.

"It's time to call everyone," I said.

"Do you think I should call Marianne and Tom?" Kathy asked. Marianne lived in Colorado, and Tom was in California.

"Yes, I think you should," I replied.

"I'm coming down right after I call everyone." Kathy lived in Needham.

Mom's oncologist didn't show up until early evening to speak to her. Where had he been? Mom had been in the emergency room since eleven thirty that morning.

"I think the treatment is too much for you now," he began. "We are going to admit you for a couple of days. You've suffered a stroke and have lost strength in your right arm. Fluid has built up outside your lungs. We'll need to drain that first before you're admitted."

He didn't stay long. Kathy and I stayed with Mom while another doctor drained a liter of fluid from a tube inserted in her back. It looked very painful.

Mom was admitted. That night, she fell out of her bed. Kathy stayed with her the next night, and my brothers, Jimmy and Johnny and I took the third night's shift sleeping in Mom's hospital room. The night was long. Jimmy and I switched between one chair and the floor, while Johnny sat in a recliner next to Mom's bed. Mom slept great, but we didn't. We watched her all night.

"How did you sleep, Johnny?" I asked after Mom woke.

"Not so great; I was afraid to move. Every time I did, the chair squeaked. I stayed in one position the entire night watching Mom, afraid I would wake her." I smiled. Johnny always made me laugh.

Marianne flew in from Denver, and Tom arrived from California. Mom and Dad had visited Marianne last year but hadn't seen Tom in years. When Tom arrived at the hospital, he entered her room and leaned over Mom's bed.

"Hi, Mom. It's me, Tom."

"Oh, hi, Tommy." She stared back at him while he talked to her.

That day, on the way to the hospital, I stopped at Procuts. My hair was very long, the way I liked it, but Mom had told me over the past several years that I should wear my hair short; she loved it short. I told the stylist to cut my hair short, above my shoulders. I walked into Mom's hospital room and sat on the edge of her bed. I spoke to her, waiting for her to notice my new short hair; she never did.

We decided it was time to bring Mom home. She would be transported by ambulance. Johnny, Paul, Dad, and I stood outside the emergency room next to the ambulance.

"I'll ride with Mom," I said to Dad.

Mom appeared through the hospital doors and was guided by a nurse and a volunteer pushing her gurney. They placed her in the back of the ambulance, and I pulled myself up inside and sat down next to her. She lay quietly without speaking. I thought maybe she'd been given painkillers and was unaware of where she was.

The ambulance left the hospital parking lot. During the ride, Mom kept her eyes closed and her arms crossed over her stomach; the blanket kept her warm.

In that moment, and for the first time, I remembered an early memory of Mom from when I was very young.

"Susie!" Mom had called my name. "Come sit down on the floor next to me while I lay on the couch. Come here, sit down." She repeated. "I just want to shut my eyes for a couple of minutes." She lay down on the white vinyl couch in our living room, and I sat down on the linoleum floor in front of her. I watched as she closed her eyes and placed her hands across her stomach. She fell asleep. I looked around the room and then back at her. I don't remember how long. I didn't move.

I watched Mom, her eyes still closed as she lay still next to me in the ambulance. I didn't move.

A hospital bed was delivered and set up in the family room. Hospice had been notified by the hospital. My brothers and sisters were there. The house was still and quiet, even though we walked through the rooms and outside onto the deck, filling her home with our presence. Each of us searched for something meaningful to do for Mom, wanting to make this time, however long or short it might be, something extraordinary. Now was the time when we could give back to Mom, speak to her in a private moment, and collectively give her all our love, for as long as she was here.

Thumpertown Beach

Everyone had gone to bed. It was quiet and my turn to sit with Mom while she slept.

My mind began to drift back to the times we'd spent with her at Thumpertown Beach. In the early 1960s, when Mom and Dad rented a cottage there, I was a kid. I remember watching the planes from the North Truro Base fly over us on their way to bomb the target practice barge miles out in Cape Cod Bay. Years later, Dad bought a small parcel of land in Eastham, and he and my two brothers built a Cape-style summer home on Edgewood Drive.

Thumpertown Beach on the bay side of the Cape had calm waters. Low tide there was perfect for John, Jeff, and Jason when they were toddlers wading in the puddles of ocean water. The Atlantic-facing Cape Cod National Seashore had the surf and the excitement. The water there was rough, and many times when I'd gone swimming there as a young girl, I'd been tossed about by the waves and rolled along the sandy floor with my bathing suit falling off, weighed down by the sand. I was completely disoriented, like being tossed around the inside of a washing machine. It was fun until a huge wave washed me ashore, telling me, "Get out while you can." When my sons had outgrown the safe and shallow waters of the bay, we took them to the National Seashore beaches. I remember Dad taking me, John, and Jeff to Coast Guard Beach one cloudy day when the beach was mostly empty; Jay was a toddler and stayed at home with Mom. Not many tourists came to Coast Guard on cloudy days, but we knew that days like this had the best waves.

I stood at the edge of the breaking tide, facing Dad and a lifeguard, my back to the ocean's fury. A storm was brewing, and four- to five-foot waves rolled in, crashing against the shore.

Dad and the lifeguard looked on. One at a time, John and then Jeff jumped into the surf and were washed back to shore by a wave. Standing at the water's edge, I scooped them up quickly and stood them on their feet before the next wave broke and pulled them back into the ocean. I looked up at Dad as if to say, "Well, can you help me?" He just watched. "It's your turn," he said, reading my face and smiling, he knew how scary it was; many years he had watched his own kids swim at this beach.

Jeff giggled and gasped for more while John ran back out to catch the next wave; I watched them closely and caught myself laughing as the waves broke at my feet. I'm not doing this much longer, I thought, knowing how powerful the surf can be. Once you're tired, that's when it's time to come out. "Okay, guys, that's enough; out of the water." Next to me a lost beach toy rolled onto the beach, caught in a wave, it toppled onto the shore, and then was quickly pulled back in by the ocean. The tide was changing.

"Let's go!" I said again. I was tired, but they wanted to stay in. "It's going to start raining soon," I said as I turned toward them with my hands on my hips, dripping from the waist down.

"We're already wet, Mom," John replied.

Jeff dodging waves at Coast Guard Beach

Car Ride to Church

Mom had been prescribed Dilaudid and was sleeping soundly in the hospital bed we'd positioned in the corner of the family room.

My brother Johnny had drilled a hole through the wall behind her bed to feed the long oxygen tube into the garage and then into the tank. He sealed the hole around the tube. It kept the room quiet. My brother Tom had placed an assortment of hearty yellow, orange, and maroon mums out on the deck for Mom to see when she opened her eyes in the early morning hours; she could see them perfectly through the french doors. Their colors were stunning in early autumn. I knew in my heart that she wouldn't be getting up from her bed today or, sadly, ever.

It was night now. Mom was sleeping. She liked sleeping with her feet uncovered and wore socks. I sat in Dad's soft cushioned recliner in the corner of the room. I could see the stars shining through the skylight above the doors. This is too far from Mom, I thought. I pushed the afghan off me and quietly walked to the other side of the room. I slid one of the matching pink cushioned chairs across the hardwood floor and placed it alongside her hospital bed.

I sat down. I didn't want to fall asleep keeping watch my first night with Mom. What if something happened and Dad came walking into the room with me snoring away? I looked around the darkened room lit only by a set of recessed lights high above Mom's bed. It was hard not to think about all she had done for us; watching over her seemed much less in comparison. I stared up at the ceiling but avoided watching the rotation of the fan, afraid it might cast a spell on me as I fought off the blanket of sleepiness that was beginning to fall upon me.

I stayed awake by remembering our Sunday morning ride to church, Dad's station wagon packed tightly with my siblings and me. Dad drove with my oldest sister, Kathy, sitting next to him and Mom with a baby on her lap sitting next to the window. My eldest brother, Bobby, always sat in the seat behind Dad. I thought he was pretending to be the driver with the view from his seat. Janet and I sat sandwiched between Bobby and Jimmy, who sat next to me and the other window. They always got the window seat. Janet and I never fought for it; we knew we'd never win, especially on a Sunday morning going to church. Tommy and Johnny sat in the "way back" with Joanne.

We'd walk in one straight line into church following Dad, who would look for an empty pew. He'd stop in the aisle, and we'd move one by one into the pew. Dad sat on one end and Mom on the other. Half the mass was in Latin, so it didn't mean much to me. After church, Dad drove us to Cumberland Farms to buy the Sunday *Globe*. Next to the convenience store was Patty's Donut Shop, owned by my Aunt Patty and my Uncle David.

"What kind of donut do you want, Kay?" Dad would ask Mom before leaving the car. Kathleen Emma Fay—Kay Fay—my mother's name.

With his hand on the door handle and looking back at mom, he waited for her answer. Would it be jelly or honeydew, I wondered.

"I don't know, Bob, hmm…" She'd hesitate, and the after-church mood would inevitably end with Dad's lost patience. Just say jelly, Mom, I thought.

"Oh, Bob, get me a lemon one," she finally answered. Oh, no, I thought, that'll throw him off, a different kind of donut; oh, boy.

"Lemon! You want a lemon donut, not a jelly?"

"Yes, Bob, lemon," she answered.

Where Do Babies Come From?

Mom moved in her bed, and I looked back at her. My heart raced for a moment as I rose from the chair to stand next to her. She didn't open her eyes and seemed to fall back into a deep sleep. I looked around the darkened room and saw my reflection in the french doors; outside was pitch black, as if there were nothing beyond the doors. I walked into the kitchen to see what time it was. The clock on the stove read two thirty. It was very quiet. Someone was sleeping on the couch in the living room across from the kitchen. Dad was upstairs in their bedroom.

I went back to Mom and sat down. Again, my thoughts drifted back to when I was very young. I was standing next to mom while she stood washing dishes at the kitchen sink. Staring up at her, I tugged on her dress.

"Where do babies come from?" I asked.

She looked down at me, turning off the water. She dried her hands on the dishcloth and knelt down next to me. "From God," she replied.

Oh, I thought as she stood up again. After a moment, I walked back into the other room. I started writing in my spiral binder of paper. I filled the pages with script, and when I was done, I wanted Mom to see my work. She was sitting at the kitchen table. "Mom, look what I did!" I handed her my book with the story I'd written. She took the book from me and opened it. The pages were filled with different shapes of circles that connected across each line and filled several pages.

"Wow, that's very good, Susie," she said, leaning over and smiling back at me.

Blizzard of 1978

I smiled with a tear in my eye as I looked at Mom sleeping soundly. How had she done it? I thought. I have three boys and find little time to try to teach them anything other than what they observe. She'd had ten of us! Most of her time was spent making sure we were clean, clothed, and fed. The values she instilled in us were not always clear when she spoke them. She was busy all the time; I don't know how she got through to us.

I'm now sitting in her home, later in life as a wife and mother, watching over her alone and in the middle of the night, living in the same house again with my parents and all my siblings. It's a great sense of family and incredibly meaningful at a time of deep sadness. I got comfortable again in the pink, soft cushioned chair next to Mom. I covered myself with the afghan. I began to think more about my childhood and growing up in a home with nine brothers and sisters. I was right smack in the middle, number five! I had a taste of the older half and a piece of the younger.

I thought about the blizzard of 1978.

Then, I was the oldest sibling still living at home; it was me, Tom, John, Joanne, Marianne, and Paul. I'd been home for several months after graduating from Lasell College. I worked for a group of oral surgeons.

During the blizzard, my brothers and sisters and I dressed to venture out into the storm. "Be careful and stay together," Mom insisted.

I stepped out the front door and was immediately blown back by a gust of wind and snow. I lifted my scarf over my nose, leaving only my eyes exposed, and followed my brothers down the front walk, which was covered with snow. We walked down the street toward Albemarle playground, where the wind blew more freely and fiercely; it was blinding.

"Look out!" Johnny yelled. "There goes Marianne." She looked like a tumbleweed blowing across the white opening before the protected path of woods that led to the brook. "I got her!" Tom dove toward her. We took small steps through new snow that was above our knees. We moved onward in the black and white, colorless storm. I could see the small bridge over the snow-covered brook that led us to Gath pool, which was now filled with snow. As we made our way over the bridge, we climbed up onto the roof of the building adjacent to the pool and jumped into the deep snow. Boy, we were lucky not to get hurt. It was tiring to push against the high winds, and the cold began to penetrate our winter jackets. As the day started to darken, we fought the elements to make our way back home.

The city was closed for a week. Phone lines were down. Driving was prohibited, and emergency vehicles were the only cars on the roads. We walked to the local grocery store on the corner for food. Everyone had to walk, there was no other way to get around. I smiled, remembering when we jumped off the back porch roof; Mom took pictures with her Polaroid.

I remember bonding with my family then. It was the time in my life when I was ready to leave home but hadn't yet. Boy, I thought, I'll never have the chance again to jump into deep snow from our small porch roof—or any roof, for that matter; it was amazing. I looked up at Mom. She was still sleeping soundly. I pushed myself back in the chair to lay my head on the back of the chair.

I thought about Thanksgiving and the twenty-seven pounds of fresh turkey Mom cooked every year; it was delicious. One year she gave my brother Tom the turkey gravy to carry from the kitchen to the dining room. Wow! Who lives after dropping the turkey gravy on

Thanksgiving Day when everyone is seated with full plates just waiting for the hot gravy?

I thought about the traditions that Mom upheld each holiday. She taught me everything. She cared for all of us, cooked, cleaned, made our Halloween costumes, shopped, and worked—she did it all, and she did it with a song in her heart.

I had to get up out of the chair. I needed to move to stay awake longer. Mom looked comfortable and lay on her back. She had short, dark, wavy hair with gray showing through. Her skin was soft with very few wrinkles for a mother in her early seventies with ten children. She was a very pretty woman. I hoped I had her skin. Of the five daughters, I looked the most like her; we were so much alike that sometimes I'd look twice at myself in the mirror.

I took another walk into the kitchen to check the time. It was three o'clock. My brother was going to relieve me at four o'clock. I can stay awake for one more hour, I thought, and I returned to my seat next to Mom.

I heard my brother John walk into the room. It was four o'clock in the morning.

"How's she doing?" he asked.

"She's been sleeping all night," I replied.

"Okay, I'll take over now."

I walked down to one of the bedrooms at the end of the hall and got into the twin bed.

It was noon when I woke. I could hear people moving around, but their voices were soft and low.

It was Saturday. I looked out the kitchen window at Tom and Paul working in the yard. Tom had picked some of the tomatoes from Mom's garden.

"Want some eggs?" my brother John offered.

"Are you having some?"

"Yes. How about some scrambled with tomato?" he offered.

"Sounds great, thanks." I left the kitchen and walked toward Mom.

"Hi," I said. Kathy, Janet, Joanne, and Marianne were hovering around her bed.

"Hi," Mom replied, turning her head slightly toward me.

Her eyes moved across the room toward the deck. "The mums look so pretty from here. Yes, nice." She paused for several seconds and asked, "Where's your father?"

"He's around somewhere," I answered softly. "He always is. And if not, he's going to the store for something." I turned and looked up as Dad walked into the room. Mom looked at him, and they gazed silently at each other. I felt their deep connection.

"I'm going to the store. Do you need anything, Kay?" he asked quietly. I returned to the kitchen and ate the first bite of the eggs John had cooked. The garden tomato was the sweetest I'd ever tasted.

"Susan?" Kathy softly called my name.

"Yup, I'm coming." I'd just cleaned my dish and was about to get into the shower.

"Come and sit down with me for a minute."

I sat down in the living room beside Kathy on Mom's couch.

"Hospice dropped off a binder for us to read. They have volunteers and nurses who can help us take care of Mom."

"Oh, I don't think we need a stranger to come and take care of Mom," I said.

"Yes, I know, but they're trained to do this kind of thing."

"Mom sacrificed everything for each one of us, all the time. I'd drop everything, paint stars on the walls, color my hair a vibrant pink, and sit up all night with her if that's what she wanted; we all would."

"Of course we would," Kathy replied.

"Being here with Mom and Dad and all of us, well, it's bittersweet. The disease is horrible, pancreatic cancer; who survives that cancer? I can't understand it. She has eleven siblings, and none had the disease.

Why Mom?" I paused and then said, "The other side of it is, all of us have left our families and jobs to be here. That's extraordinary—all of us together for the last time with Mom."

She looked back at me without speaking, making me think more about Hospice while she turned the pages in the binder. I couldn't absorb any of it and just nodded. I was stubborn. I didn't want to look into the future. I lived only in the moment and hoped for as much time as possible, time when we could all be together for as long as Mom was here with us. Kathy always planned ahead for everything.

"Okay," she said. "We'll try to take care of Mom on our own, for now."

I left the room to take a shower. I changed, put on Mom's bathrobe, and put my dirty clothes on top of the washing machine on my way to the bathroom. John was in the kitchen, Marianne was with Mom, Joanne was dusting, Tom and Paul where still outside, and Kathy got up to start the laundry. It was Saturday, cleaning day.

Fayway Park

"You dust Mom and Dad's room; I did it last week," Janet exclaimed. I was eight years old. Janet was two years older than me. I hated dusting their room; it took too long. Mom's bureau had all kinds of stuff on it. Dusting the parlor and living room was quick and easy.

"Janet and Susan, take the wash out of the dryer and fold it," Mom yelled out.

"Susan, you go get it."

"Where are you going?"

"Nowhere. I'll stay here."

I opened the door to the basement. It was cold and dark, and the stairs were old and dirty.

I turned on the light switch at the top of the stairs to light the landing where the stairs turned. I touched the cold cement foundation and walked down the last set of stairs. I could smell the dampness and the dirt. Down here on rainy days, we'd ride our tricycles around the furnace, putting our feet down to steady ourselves around the turns.

I ran to the dryer and pulled out the clothes, putting them into the laundry basket. Oh, good, I thought, it's a dark wash. There were too many clothes, underwear and socks to match in a white wash.

Upstairs, Janet and I folded the clothes and left the clothes that belonged to our siblings on their beds.

"What do you want to do now?" I asked Janet.

She had an idea. "Go downstairs," she instructed me, "and get Bobby's shin pads."

"No, you go downstairs!"

"What if he catches me?" Janet asked.

"You can do it; I went last time."

Janet left our bedroom, and I followed. She paused at the top of the stairs.

"What are you doing?"

"I'm listening; what do you think I'm doing?"

"Just go. I'll get some belts."

"Tommy and Johnny are playing floor hockey in the kitchen in front of the radiator," she whispered.

"So, they won't see you. Go ahead."

Baseballs, gloves, bats, hockey sticks, skates, shoes, tennis balls, and shin pads; everything was downstairs in the hall closet.

Janet returned with the shins pads, and with the belts we tied the shin pads to our backs.

"Is this Dad's belt?" she asked.

"I couldn't find one upstairs, so I got Dad's."

"Do you see any sharks?" I asked. We were on our stomachs on the floor with our tanks on our backs, sliding under our beds playing *"Sea Hunt."*

"No, just little fish, but I'm looking for the treasure."

"What are you two doing up there?" Mom yelled. "Is your room clean?"

"Yup."

I could hear Bobby, Jimmy, Tommy, and Johnny rumbling down the stairs from the third floor.

"Janet and Susan, come on; we're going outside," Bobby said as he passed our room.

"Let's go!" Janet turned to me from under the bed.

We took off our tanks and hid them under the bunk bed and ran downstairs and out the back door. The back steps faced Mr. Ed's backyard. I turned to the left past the heavy steel lid of the in-ground garbage bucket where Dad put the small bags of garbage. A man came every Saturday to empty the bucket. I'd watched him one day and saw little white worms under the lid. I'd stepped on top of the lid many times while running across our backyard, but never again after that day.

I ran in front of the garage and jumped across from one strip of cement to the other. We named the field next to our house Fayway Park because our last name was Fay. In the winter, Dad made a miniature ice rink in the center of the field. In the summer, Fayway Park was our Fenway Park.

We lined up along the edge of the field: Bobby, Jimmy, Janet, me, Tommy, and Johnny.

"Hey look!" Jimmy said, facing us. "It's David Dog Dew and Steven Dirt." They lived down the street, David and Steven McGowan. David was two years older than me, and Stephen just one year.

"You can't say that to them," Janet said. David and Steven walked up to us.

Bobby and Jimmy picked the teams. Janet was always picked last.

"If you hit the house, it's an automatic out," Bobby said, blurting out the rules. "If you hit the glass, it's two outs. If you break a window, then run." We looked at each other.

"Okay."

I looked at the garage and then back at Bobby while he explained the rules. One of the six garage windows was broken at least a couple of times each year. I remember when my younger brother Johnny and I played catch in front of the garage. I threw the ball to him, and it went past him and broke the glass. Dad came running out. "Who broke the window?" he yelled.

"Johnny did!" I looked back at Dad.

"I did not! You threw the ball at the window," Johnny said.

"Ya, but you didn't catch it!" I argued.

"Clean it up now," Dad yelled and mumbled something about going to the store again.

We started to play baseball. I was playing third base when the ball was hit, and my brother Tommy came running fast to the hole on the side of the cement strip of the driveway—third base. He ploughed into me and kept running. I lay on the incline next to third base looking up at the sky. I couldn't breathe. Janet and Jimmy were standing over me.

"She's okay. She just got the wind knocked out of her. Now who's gonna play third?" They looked around the field.

I couldn't speak. I was looking up at the blue sky and thinking, oh no, I'm in trouble if I get hurt. I stood up.

"Okay, let's play," Jimmy said as he walked back on the mound.

Jimmy raised his knee and tucked the ball into his glove and then swung his arm around and threw the ball toward home plate. David swung and missed. "Come on, David, keep your eye on the ball, you can do it," Bobby yelled as he threw the ball back to Jimmy. Jimmy wound up again and threw another pitch. We looked on, waiting for David to swing. His bat hit the ball into the air. Our heads turned, and our eyes widened as the ball headed toward the side of our house and smashed the window. I heard the back door slam as Dad came running out. "Who broke the window?" He yelled.

We ran in different directions. "We can play kick the can after we clean up the glass," Jimmy said, as we ran off the field.

"Let's play steal the flag."

"I wanna play red rover or red light; one, two, three, red light!"

Dad yelled, "That's it; game's over. Now get over here and clean this up now!"

Bobby starting counting to one hundred, and we ran in different directions from the front yard to play kick the can. His foot sat atop an old can that was placed in the middle of the front walk.

"Seventy-two, eighty-one, eighty-five, ninety, one hundred," Bobby yelled.

We scattered and hid. Bobby walked back and forth across the front yard until he spotted someone and then ran to the can to call that person's name.

I ran down the side of our house alongside Mr. Ed's bushes to the end of the walk.

Mr. Ed's house was the last house on the street and next to our house. His beautifully landscaped yard was the same size as our Fayway Park, but our lot was mostly dirt with grass edging. Mr. Ed's yard was bordered by tall hedges that were perfectly manicured in front and alongside the yard that abutted our house. A narrow cement walk ran adjacent to his hedges. I never saw Mr. Ed. We weren't allowed in his yard.

Stooped over, I snuck around the end of Mr. Ed's hedges and hid. My brother Jimmy was in front of me.

"Don't go over to Mr. Ed's garage," he said. We could see the garage directly across from where we were crouched down and hidden. The second floor of the garage had a window that overlooked our house.

"I won't," I whispered.

"Do you see the window up above the garage?"

I nodded. The garage looked like an old barn. I looked up, keeping close to the hedges so not to be seen. Jimmy pointed toward the window.

"There's a mad man who lives up there, so don't go over there."

I looked up at the window. "No there isn't," I said.

"Yes there is!"

"I've never seen him."

"He's there."

I stared up at the window and looked back at my brother. "I don't see anyone."

Jimmy had run alongside the hedges toward our front yard. I followed him.

When he got to the front, Bobby was walking on the other side of the house. Jimmy went through the bottom of the hedges and ran to the front walk to kick the can. Everyone caught ran to hide again.

"You better not be in Mr. Ed's yard," Mom yelled from the window.

I looked at the round hole and the loose dirt at the bottom of the hedges across from our front yard where we crawled through into Mr. Ed's yard. There was silence at the sound of Mom's voice, and everyone stood still for a moment. No one answered.

My brother, Jimmy-
Yvonne's front porch

I turned around and ran back along the hedges in Mr. Ed's yard. When I came to the end, I turned back into our yard. I ran past our back porch and into the yard. David ran in from the other side.

I stopped and said, "Ferme la bouche, ferme la bouche," I started to run again as I repeated it a second time. I ran past the clothesline and the round bush in the corner of the yard. I'd hidden in that bush last year and had sat on a bee's nest. Mom put ice on my bum, and I cried for a long time.

"Do you even know what that means?" David shouted.

"No." I ran toward the back of the garage and disappeared. David's mother had said those words to us when we'd spent an afternoon at their house.

Long boards were placed along the back of the garage, and I ran over them and out the other side. I was standing behind home plate. I saw Tommy standing against the side of the house, peeking around the corner to see where Bobby was. At the end of the field and across the street, Yvonne sat in her rocking chair on her front porch, cranking out two afghans a day while she watched us play. She was a seamstress and Mom often benefited from her advice. I too, visited Yvonne for her expertise when I was working on a project; a garment I was getting ready to sew. I didn't know how lucky I was! She lived across the street from us!

It was an automatic home run when my brothers hit the ball onto her porch. Not so lucky for Yvonne!

"Time for supper!" I heard Mom's bell ring from the back porch. The first ring didn't stop the game; it took several rings after that and a yell from Mom.

I went upstairs to wash my hands and then went to my bedroom. I opened the window that faced Mr. Ed's garage. I knelt down and stared at the window across the green lawn and behind the house. It was newly painted brown like the house. A man's face appeared.

"Oh! I see him," I said softly.

"See who?" Janet asked. I didn't know she was in our room and standing behind me.

"The bad man."

"What bad man?"

"Jimmy said a scary man lives in Mr. Ed's garage."

"There's no one living in his garage."

"Yes there is. I saw him."

"Come on, it's time for supper."

I knelt there until I thought I saw his face appear again, and then ran downstairs to the kitchen.

Every Saturday night we ate hamburgers. Hockey pucks, Jimmy called them. Then one by one, a bath, and Lawrence Welk before bed. Dad would be drinking a beer, and Mom would be in the kitchen singing along with the Lennon Sisters.

It was never a quiet Saturday night when we went to bed. Kathy, Janet, and I slept in the bedroom at the top of the stairs across from Mom and Dad's room. Their room was the only bedroom with a door. Our brothers slept above our room on the third floor.

"I'm not tired, are you?" Janet asked me. Kathy could stay up later than we could.

"No. What do you want to do?"

"Listen."

"What?"

"I thought I heard something."

"What!"

The hall light was off, and our room was dark; moonlight shone in through our window.

"Ahhhh!" we screamed and giggled.

"Who is it?" I said.

"What's that?"

"It's a dirty sock."

"Get out!" Janet yelled softly.

"If I have to come up there," Dad yelled, "you're gonna get the belt!"

We froze for a minute, waiting for Dad to clear the bottom of the stairs and sit back down.

"Go to sleep!" Mom yelled.

I could hear our brothers laughing and running back upstairs.

"Let's sneak upstairs and throw the socks at them," Janet said.

I took the top of the dirt-stained white sock, careful not to touch more than what I could hold with two tiny fingers. The third step squeaked as I stepped up to the first landing.

"Who's that?" Tommy said.

Janet and I threw the socks up the stairs and ran back down.

"Can you do somersaults on the bed?" I asked.

"I can; can you?"

Janet fell off the side of the bed.

"That's it, I'm coming up," Dad yelled.

Janet and I got under our covers and lay silently with our eyes closed when we heard Dad's steps getting closer. He was at the top of the stairs and next to our bedroom doorway.

"Kay, where's my belt?" he shouted to Mom.

My eyes popped wide open.

Treasure Chest

The day had turned into late afternoon, and any chores Dad needed done were complete; the house was clean.

Mom was awake. I brought her a small bowl of Ben and Jerry's sorbet and gave her a very small spoonful.

"Mmm, that's delicious," she said after the first taste. I fed her a couple more tastes.

Mom fell back to sleep.

"Marianne, do you know where the treasure chest is?"

"I don't know, maybe in the hutch," she said quietly.

I opened the doors beneath the hutch next to Mom's bed. Inside I saw the square wooden chest.

"Here it is!" I pulled it out and walked into the living room across from the kitchen and away from Mom to let her sleep in silence. I sat down and opened the chest. Inside were slips of colored paper, each one folded several times. Twenty years earlier, Marianne had sent each one of us sheets of colored paper and asked us to cut the paper into strips and write down some of our childhood memories. The inside cover of the chest read, "Memories are the bonds that tie us together." There were hundreds of folded pieces of paper in the chest. My siblings joined me as I picked out one to read.

"Dad, going to the Boston arena to watch Bobby and Jimmy's high school hockey games. One time we were standing at the glass and they skated up and sprayed us."

I picked out a green folded one.

"Mom and Dad washing little babies in the sink."

Kathy sat down next to me and picked one out of the chest.

"Eleven years old, Little League with the Yankees. Mom trying to show me how to wear a ball cap. It took me a few years to realize she was right. But I will never forget the day she showed me in the front hall."

"That was me." Paul walked into the room and sat down.

"Anyone want a glass of wine?" Tommy asked from the kitchen.

"Yes, I'll have one."

"Red or white?"

"If there's a red open, I'll have that," I replied.

"Anyone else?"

"Yeah, I'll have red too," Marianne replied.

"A beer, thanks," John said.

I picked another.

"Mom, I remember you at the sink around dinnertime, and I came in from the field saying that Bobby had done something wrong, and you said, 'If it's too rough, then don't play.'"

We read one message after another.

"Mom, visiting you at the Cahill House in Cambridge after you had a baby by waving to you up in the window."

We weren't allowed inside and could only wave from the parking lot below.

I took a sip of my wine and picked up a folded pink slip of paper.

"Mom, waiting for you guys to leave so we could play tag with a wet cloth in the house."

We kept reading.

"Dad, do you remember the year you bought three Christmas trees across the street from our church and tied them together to make one beautiful tree?"

"Buying the Admiral color TV at Lechmere after our hockey game at the Boston arena to watch the first televised Bruins game on Channel 38."

"Dad was so nervous. He knew he was in trouble with Mom, but he bought it anyway," Bobby laughed.

"She was pissed," Jimmy recalled.

"Oh yeah, she was gonna kill him."

"I'm sure there were a lot of other things they needed before a new television," Kathy said.

"Yeah, like new clothes," Janet added.

"The first televised Bruins game. Wow, what year was that?"

"In the early sixties, I think. Most people already had a color television."

Joanne stood up and picked out a green slip of paper and read, "Dad, we got the word on Easter Sunday at 1:33 p.m. that you had a new baby girl (Marianne). You asked for a frappe. We had peanut butter and jelly sandwiches for Easter dinner."

"I remember that day," I said. "I visualized Dad standing in the hall on the phone next to Mom's hope chest. Marianne, was number nine. Dad's ulcers were probably flaring up, hence the frappe."

"Well, me next." Marianne pulled out a blue slip.

"Mom, I remember you at my swim meets, especially the regional's— standing outside the fence, waiting for my race. It meant a lot to me to have you there!" I wrote that one.

I picked one. "Getting new shoes and sneakers for school at The Barn Family Shoe Store."

Kathy picked out a folded yellow piece and said, "This was terrible. Mom was so angry."

"Mom, you at eight months pregnant with Joanne, and we're out Christmas shopping at Grover Cronin's in Waltham. You're trying to find the last two blouses to go with the teal corduroy jumpers you have made for Janet, Susan, you, and me. We take a break and wait for Dad to pick us up at Liggett's Drug Store. You take a seat at the counter. The lady next to you makes friendly conversation. Dad picks us up. We get home and find out that the lady shoplifted your bag and took the blouses."

"Wow, I didn't know that. How awful."

"I remember the corduroy jumpsuit," Janet said.

"Figures, Waltham."

We kept reading.

"Black and white frappes at home."

"Vaseline cheeks to survive the New England cold."

"When you go for your morning swim."

"We swam all the time. I thought that's why we never got sick, all that chlorine!" Joanne remarked.

"I remember when everyone got the chicken pox except me. Mom kept checking me. After two weeks passed I broke out on a Sunday, the day before vacation week. I was so mad. Everyone was outside playing, and I had to stay in. Then on Monday morning after vacation, Mom came into my bedroom and said, 'I know you feel better, but you can stay home from school today.'" My eyes watered as I read from the pink strip of paper.

Johnny chose from the treasure box.

"Dad, the day at Seabrook beach when you talked to me while I was on my raft so that I wouldn't disturb the shark that you could see swimming underneath my raft."

"That was in the early days, Kathy." He picked another and then another.

"Hockey at Larz Anderson."

"Dad peeling potatoes before the New York Giants game."

"Christmas morning, meeting at the top of the stairs."

"Remember Christmas morning! Wow, that was awesome. I don't know how Mom and Dad did it."

"At four in the morning I'd knock on Mom and Dad's bedroom door. I think Mom had just gone to bed, and I'd asked if we could go downstairs," Kathy said.

"Then, in the dark, we stampeded down the stairs, stumbling and trying to beat each other to the bottom."

"It was pitch-black as we waited at the bottom of the stairs and in the hallway for Bobby or Jimmy to plug in the tree. When the lights went on, my eyes widened, still filled with sleep as they adjusted to the

Christmas lights. I could the smell the tree. The floor in the parlor and the other room were filled with toys. New skates, a Radio Flyer, a toboggan, baby carriages, dolls, new baseball glove, hockey sticks—so much stuff. Remember our stockings hung along the stairs in the hall?"

"Yes, they were filled with a winter hat, gloves, or socks and underwear."

"They were the old-fashioned, red felt Christmas stockings. Where are they now?"

"Mom still has them with the Christmas stuff above the garage."

"I remember trying to get to sleep Christmas Eve. Kathy told Janet and me that if we got on our knees and put our foreheads on our pillows and rocked back and forth, we'd fall asleep."

"Yes," Janet continued. "We had plastic pink curlers in our hair around the base of our heads. We could never sleep with them digging into our head and neck."

"I don't remember that," Kathy said.

"It's true; you told us we'd fall asleep that way."

"Or lose circulation in our extremities with all the blood rushing to our heads," Janet finished.

"It seemed like each Christmas one person would get more gifts," Johnny said.

"That was you every year, Johnny."

"No, he's right. I remember I got more presents than everyone a couple different years."

"That's because you counted," Johnny said.

We laughed.

I picked another; it was hard to stop.

"When President Kennedy got shot."

The room became quiet.

"I was in kindergarten," I broke the silence. I came home from school, and Mom was crying. So I cried too."

"I was in second grade. We went into the auditorium for an assembly and were told the president had been shot. We said a prayer."

"I remember watching the funeral procession. We sat in the parlor in front of the television for hours."

"I remember Caroline and John John standing in front of Jacqueline Kennedy and John John saluting the casket. I think that's why it affected me so much when John was killed in the plane crash," Janet recalled.

"I remember Dad calling us in from the field. 'You need to see this,' he told us. We came in and sat in front of the television. I, too, remember Caroline and John John standing and watching as children," Bobby said.

"Then Bobby Kennedy was assassinated; it was incredible. Mom and Dad supported the Kennedys. It was very upsetting for them."

"Where is Dad? Paul asked.

"He's in with Mom."

Joanne picked another.

"Dad, it meant so much to me to be at home with you while you were recovering from surgery. You continue to teach me about courage and strength—and more importantly how we all must lean on one another from time to time, and that this is where the strength of our family is."

I remember walking upstairs to the second floor, and as I turned the corner on the last flight of stairs, I looked up and saw Dad straight ahead. The bathroom door was open. He was sitting on the toilet throwing up blood. I ran to him, and he said, "Go call Mom." She was at work.

The room was quiet, and I picked another—a pale-yellow slip of paper.

"Tappen Zee Bridge, Pop Warner football trip in New York. Over the Tappen Zee Bridge four times!"

"Dad would never stop for directions," we agreed.

"Just a couple more, then we'll read more later."

"I'm gonna start dinner," Tom said as he got up and walked into the kitchen.

Joanne read, "Mom, I catch myself saying, 'You're full of old shoes' to the kids in my class. I have to explain what it means the first time, and then they know they have to fess up if they hear it again."

"I wrote that. I was in second grade. My friends didn't know what the heck I was saying," Joanne laughed.

"Full of old shoes. I didn't understand at first. I thought about the bottom of my closet."

She chose another and then another.

"Mom, I remember you throwing a hairbrush at me while I was sitting on a chair in the parlor. That was your best throw."

"Mom, we had the best Sunday dinners. You could smell them from Albemarle."

"Mom, remember playing cards with Grandma Sousa down in Florida? She would always complain about her eyes and how they bothered her and how she could hardly see the cards...Gin!"

"Dad, I remember you driving me to church to confession, and you said, 'You first.'"

"Mom, letting me watch you tease your hair before going out on Saturday nights. I remember just being able to peek over the top of your dresser to see you in the mirror."

"Banging, clanging, and loud noise from the radiators at night—how come always at night?"

"Playing music after Saturday night dinner."

"Mom always said, 'Boots come off in the hall!' Trying to hit the radiator from the other side of the hall."

In the kitchen, Tom was making one of Marianne's recipes from Colorado.

I picked a folded green piece of paper. "Oh, this is a good one!"

"Mom, remember the time Jimmy squirted you with red dye from a squirt gun—all over your Easter dress and right before we left for church. You were ready to kill him. Jim quickly asked you to look at your dress again because the dye had disappeared. Did we ever laugh!"

"The 1975 Red Sox, and being able to stay up late to watch the ballgame sitting on the floor in the living room."

"Wow, I'd just graduated from high school, Paul."

I remember staying up late to watch *The Wizard of Oz*. We'd have our bath and sit in the living room in our pajamas, and Mom from the kitchen would sing "Somewhere Over the Rainbow" along with Dorothy. She'd hum some of the verses until the end, and then she'd sing, "If happy little blue birds fly beyond the rainbow, why, oh why, can't I?"

"I watch it now when it's on, only to hear Judy Garland sing, and then I change the channel."

"You know, if Glinda, the good witch, had just given the wicked witch back the ruby slippers when they were standing in Munchkin Land looking at the fallen house, then we wouldn't have had to go through that yellow brick road trip," Janet said. "No, the slippers ended up on Dorothy's feet, then Glinda leaves, and all hell breaks loose."

"Yeah, but we never would have met the Scarecrow."

"Oh lee oh, lee ooooh. Oh lee oh, lee ooooh," my brothers started to chant.

"I liked the part when they discover the wizard isn't a wizard at all, and he gives each one a gift. He hands the Tin Man an ugly looking plastic heart then says, "A heart isn't judged by how much you love, but how much you're loved by others."

"Who wrote *The Wizard of Oz*?"

"I don't know. Go online and check it out."

Joanne picked another.

"Mom, making cheerleading pompoms out of yarn for our sneakers and sewing the letters onto our sweaters."

Paul walked over to the chest and picked a blue slip.

"Practice slap shots in basement; let Mom pass with the laundry."

He picked another. "Oh, this one I wrote."

"Gath pool, no matter how many people were at the swim meet you could always hear, 'Pull, pull, pull, pull' from Mom—every breath I took."

"Watching the Bruins on Sunday after a huge Sunday dinner."

"Did the Bruins play on Sundays?"

"I don't remember. Ask Dad."

"Janet and I clearing the table after dinner and Dad washing the dishes."

"One more, guys. Dinner is almost ready," Tom said from the kitchen.

Johnny leaned over to reach the chest and chose a slip.

"Mom, quote: 'You boys had better get to bed before your father gets home!' Tom and I would wait until we saw the headlights of Dad's car pull into the driveway then run up to bed before Dad came in the house."

"Boy, did we run up those stairs!"

"Couple more, that's it," Joanne said.

"Saint Bernard's hockey." Paul chose another.

"In the early years of youth hockey when I scored a lot of goals, I'd look up to the left corner of the stands and get the classic salute from Dad."

"Dad, remember me, you, and John Jr. that one summer night swim at Thumpertown Beach—great night!"

"Trophy's last supper." We laughed hysterically.

"Oh my God, remember that day. We could never have a dog. Dad didn't like animals. But for Paul we got one."

"What do you mean for me?"

"Dad would never let us have a dog."

"We had chicks one year, remember? The milk man gave us three chicks, and Mom put them in a big cardboard box."

"I remember Dad was heading out at noontime to pick up Mom at the The Barn Family Shoe Store for lunch. She was going to make him a roast beef sandwich when they got home. Dad left. The leftover roast beef was on the counter, and Trophy jumped up and pulled it off the counter and ate it all! Dad was so pissed. We never saw Trophy again."

"And the chicks turned into chickens, and I never saw them again."

We finished dinner and gathered around Mom's bed. The lights were dim in the family room. We talked softly. Tom began to sing "Amazing Grace," and we joined in.

At the end of the night, I said good night to everyone and went to the twin bedroom. I walked up to my bed and noticed the pile of clothes I had put on top of the washing machine earlier that day were clean and folded neatly on the end of my bed.

"Can you put on *My Prayer*," Mom asked. It was her favorite song by Celine Dion and Andrea Bocelli. We played it for her many times during the day when she was awake. She never got up from the hospital bed.

I sat with Mom and Kathy one afternoon, listening to Celine and talking about our childhood. I was finding it difficult to put together the right words I'd want to say to Mom when I'd have a quiet moment alone with her. I wanted to tell her about some of the dear memories I had of her, and I wanted to thank her for her endless care for all of us. I wanted to tell her how remarkable she was, how great a mother she had been. My words should be comforting to her, not just words that would benefit me. It took me days of watching from a distance, thinking of a way to say good-bye.

Trip to the Beach

It was a beautiful and warm Sunday morning in October 2003. We were taking Mom to Thumpertown Beach to see what she called "my beach" for the last time.

"How are we going to get her out of bed? She has a catheter."

"What if we pick up the mattress and put it in the back of Dad's Sable wagon?"

"I don't know. What about her oxygen tank?"

"We can do it. We'll surround the bed and pick up the mattress and go out through the garage door; it's just around the corner."

And that's exactly what we did. We positioned the mattress so Mom faced out the back of the station wagon. We put the oxygen tank in the car. Dad sat in the driver's seat, and I sat with Mom in the back. I could hear car doors closing from the cars parked in our driveway and on the street. Within moments, a procession of cars escorted Dad down the road to Thumpertown Beach. Dad backed in so that Mom could look out onto the beach. She didn't speak; she stared out at the view.

The tide was out. I left Mom's side to join my brothers and sisters on the beach. Just before the top of the steep staircase down to the beach, I saw a row of sneakers and sandals lined up in the sand. This was the same view and the same spot where I'd stood as a young girl. I left my shoes next to the last pair and walked down the stairs. We played football. It wasn't long before we knew we had to return home. I walked past a family sitting and watching. A man sitting on his towel smiled and asked, "Who are you? The Kennedys?" I smiled back and reached out my hand to him and said, "Hi, I'm Caroline. Nice to meet you."

"Theodore Roosevelt." He shook my hand and smiled. I continued walking toward the stairs, suddenly very sad. I held it back. Mom was dying; it wasn't fun.

I realize now that we didn't take Mom to the beach that day for her sake; she did it for us.

On the morning of Wednesday, October 29, 2003, we lost our beloved mother.

Family Football Game

During Mom's memorial mass, we played "Somewhere Over the Rainbow" and "The Prayer." I looked up at the skylight over the altar during most of the service, stopping the tears from falling as my sister Janet's poem was read, "The Very Heart of Our Family." She was.

A week after Mom passed, I was upstairs in our second-floor bedroom, standing in front of my bureau, brushing my hair and getting ready for work. Something caught my eye, and I turned toward the window. It was a tiny gray bird, maybe a chickadee, I thought. It was hovering outside my window. Can chickadees hover like that? I don't know. I'd never seen a bird do that. Hummingbirds, yes, but they're tiny. I don't know. It's November. Shouldn't they be heading south?

The little gray bird continued flapping its wings so quickly that I could see only their color shifting up and down, like the blades of a fan rotating on high; you know they're there moving, but you can't see them clearly. I stared at it for what seemed like minutes until it flew away. I became still. At this moment and for the first time in my life, I began to believe that there was more beyond this life. This was something that I could have easily missed in my very busy life, but this particular day, I became acutely aware of noticing what was right in front of me.

Jeff's symptoms began a year later.

CHAPTER 31

Seventh Treatment, June 2005

THREE WEEKS HAD passed, and we were on our way back up to Boston for Jeff's seventh treatment. This one would last five days. We were in the middle of the fourteen cycles of treatment.

We entered the JFC, and Jeff's vitals, weight, and height were recorded. Jeff took his bed by the window. Sam arrived to examine Jeff, and then sat down in the chair next to his bed. "You are the only patient I have with very few written notes." He pulled out his pen and began drawing on Jeff's sheets. "There's nothing there, Jeff! Look, zero on the chart." He was confirming that Jeff hadn't suffered any life-threatening side effects, hadn't needed transfusions, and was never in danger from an infection. Up to this point, Jeff had mouth sores and one blood transfusion early on.

We looked up from Jeff's sheet, noticing Jessica Robertson and her mother, Lisa, walking toward us. I stood up from the infusion chair across from Jeff. I had e-mailed Hannah and Sam to ask their permission for Jessica to come visit the JFC on a day that Jeff was to receive his treatment. Sam had checked with Dr. Grier, Head of Oncology.

"Sam," I said, "This is Jessica Robertson, Jeff's friend from Sandwich High, and her mother, Lisa. Jess has been accepted to the nursing program at Simmons College; she wants to be an oncology nurse."

"Hi, nice to meet you," Sam said, as he walked toward them, shaking their hands.

"Hi, Jeff!" Jess walked to his bed. "How are you feeling?"

"Pretty good right now. I haven't started the treatment yet," he replied.

"So, I understand you want to be an oncology nurse." Sam turned to Jess, now standing at the end of Jeff's bed. The room quieted when he began to speak. "There is nothing greater and more satisfying that you will do in your life than caring for these kids. I would do this without pay, although pay is nice. Yes, there are times when I want to jump out the window, but that is outweighed by how I feel most of the time."

Jess smiled. Sam looked at Jeff and back at Jess. "Why a nurse? Why not an oncologist? We need more oncologists!"

Jess shrugged. "I don't know," she replied.

"Well, I've got to be on my way," Sam said. "Jeff, e-mail or call me if you have any questions or want to talk."

Hannah returned and walked up to Jeff's IV pole to check his fluids. She looked down at the end of Jeff's bed and said, "Jeff, who's been drawing pictures on your sheets?" Jeff laughed.

Jeff preferred that his friends visit him at the JFC clinic before the treatment began, when he was feeling his best. He didn't ask them to visit him at Children's. I don't know whether Jeff insisted that his friends not come or whether he didn't want them to make the trip up from the Cape. He kept his treatment private, and when he returned home, he never spoke to his friends about his cancer or his treatment.

Jess and her mom left to tour the clinic before Hannah gave Jeff his pre-chemo drugs and administered his chemo. When it was time and a bed was available, we made our way from the JFC to Children's. We shared a room with a little boy. Patients were always paired with one of the same sex. I made myself comfortable in the chair-bed and tried to remain still; it was difficult for me to stay seated, not having anything to do. I was always running in so many directions. Working, cooking, cleaning, going to games, keeping up the pace, and being on the run all the time; sitting still and having time to think made me restless. This was the time when I would leave Jeff's room to make calls to my family. I called John or he called me daily to see how things were going.

Dinner was brought in from Bertucci's, an Italian restaurant across the street from Children's. I sat with some patients and parents in the activity room for a buffet of pastas, salad, and fresh-baked rolls. I didn't know how to ask, "Why are you here? What kind of cancer does your son or daughter have?" How do you ask, I wondered, how would you ask such a question. I looked around. I saw some parents walking from a room where a child lay in a bed. I saw some parents walking their son around the floor pushing an IV pole. I saw many toddlers riding Playskool cars. I didn't see many other teenagers.

The next morning, I sat in the chair next to Jeff while he searched for NESN. I watched him as he lay in bed. I didn't think about the seriousness of his disease. He's going to beat this, I thought. His immune system is remarkably strong; he seems resilient to the many side effects. He'll be all right. He'll finish the fourteen cycles of treatment in December, and that will end his temporary life spent at Children's. He'll be able to resume a normal life. I focused on his treatment and didn't allow myself to think about anything else.

I decided to take a walk outside to get some fresh air. I left Seven West, walking past each room filled with children lying in their beds sleeping or sitting up watching television. I walked past the nurse's station, out the main doors of Seven West, past the "tubby room," and past the activity room to the service elevators.

I pushed the elevator button and the doors opened. I walked in and the doors closed. As I looked up, "Oh, jeez!" I was startled; standing next to me in the elevator was a short robot, and he was standing in front of the elevator buttons! Oh, God, how do I push the lobby button?

"Lobby, please!" Oh great, I'm talking to a robot, I thought. Yeah, that's me; here I am.

I smiled and thought, no one is going to believe this. The elevator moved downward. I wondered how the robot got there, how he knew what floor he was on, and how did he push the floor buttons?

I called John. "I'm alone in the elevator with Gismo!" I said.

"Gismo?"

"Yes, a robot!"

"Does he speak?" John chuckled over the phone.

"I don't know whether he speaks. I asked him to push the lobby button, but he didn't respond." The elevator stopped and the doors opened. The robot started out of the elevator, then stopped. "I've got to go," I said to John. "I think Gismo is getting off on this floor."

"Okay," he laughed.

"Obstruction, cannot proceed," said Gismo.

"Oh, so you can speak!"

"Obstruction, cannot proceed," he repeated.

"For heaven's sake, you're always whining!" I laughed. "All right, all right, okay," I said. Just outside the elevator I saw the hall was filled with tall metal baby cribs that blocked the robot's path. They looked more like cages than cribs. No one was around; the cribs had just been left there. I became a little anxious as the robot kept repeating those words, "Obstruction, cannot proceed." I quickly pushed the cribs back out of his way, and he immediately went through the open elevator doors and turned down the hall.

"You're welcome!" I called out. "I may not be there next time to help you, Gismo!" I shouted, looking around to see if anyone was near. "R2D2 is better looking and polite," I added, walking back into the elevator smiling—that's me, taking care of everyone else; kids, family, friends, clients…robots! I pushed the letter *L*. The doors closed. Where was I going? The doors opened to the lobby and I walked out into the crowd of parents and children coming and going, seemingly programmed to follow their own path.

During the week, a notice was left in our room for neck massages that would be made available in the teen room. I had never had one before, so I scheduled time in the afternoon. When I got there, the massage therapist had me sit on a chair with my chin resting against a soft padded face cradle open to the floor below. She began to massage my neck and shoulders.

"Boy, you sure have a lot of stress in your neck."

It hadn't occurred to me how much the stress was affecting me physically, too.

"You must feel a lot of stress in some of the patients on this floor," I asked.

"Yes, most."

The massage wasn't long enough, and when she stopped, I wanted more.

Children's Hospital and the Jimmy Fund organized many activities for children with cancer and separate events for parents. We received a notice to sign up for an afternoon ride on the *Spirit of Boston*, a small cruise ship that toured Boston Harbor. It was a lobster buffet tour with live music and entertainment, and it was scheduled for September. I signed John and myself up.

Jeff's treatment continued for the week without any issues.

At home, our close friend, Chuck Nestor, began to organize the First Annual Jeff Hayes Golf Tournament at the town golf course, Sandwich Hollows. Friends from off Cape and friends living in Sandwich formed a committee that met throughout the summer to plan the fundraiser.

Chuck and John attended high school together. Chuck played baseball at Bentley College and followed Jeff's teams from Little League to his freshman year in high school. When Jeff was first diagnosed, Chuck gave him his father's gold cross and chain. Jeff wore it always and only removed it during radiation treatment. The gold cross and Nancy's silver medal were visible around Jeff's neck throughout his entire two years battling the disease.

Chuck's was the hand that held ours. John and Chuck spoke all the time during Jeff's treatment. Chuck and his wife, Kathy, showered Jeff with gifts: a Red Sox windbreaker, a Boston College windbreaker, a subscription to *Fantasy Football*, whatever they thought Jeff would like.

Many people were constant in our lives: Patty, Joanne, Janet, Kathy, Johnny and Patty, Paul, Marianne, Brian and Mike, John, all of Jeff's close friends, Nancy Bridges, Nancy Helms, Angelo and Jane Tomasini, the Lessard family and Tom and Peggy Fair. They played important roles in our lives. They were family, and along with our families, they pulled us through the hard times.

Back in February, during Jeff's first treatment, I met with the social worker at the JFC. She spoke seriously and said, "Do you have family or friends who can help you and your family through this?" I smiled. I was proud to tell her that I had enough family and friends to help support all the kids in the clinic, and I would gladly share that support with all of them. My family was very large, and we had many friends and an entire community backing us. We'd received such an outpouring of help and support already, even before Jeff's treatment started. I don't know how other families with a child battling cancer do it without this kind of love and support, and the genuine desire of so many people to help in any way they can. We were lucky and incredibly fortunate.

CHAPTER 32

Nine West, Eighth Treatment, July 2005

FOR HIS EIGHTH treatment, Jeff followed the same routine at the JFC. We waited for a bed at Children's. We always believed there'd be a bed available, but this day we waited longer than usual. Finally, we were instructed to go to Nine West at Children's.

Children battling cancer were sent to Seven West first, and then to Nine West. We'd never been assigned to this floor. I thought Seven West was frightening, but the nights spent on Nine West were filled with code blue alarms that went off throughout the night, almost every night. A flashing blue ceiling light lit up the hallway with the sound of an alarm. It woke me throughout the night, and I sat up from my reclining chair imagining a child fighting for his or her life. Some nights I'd see nurses and a doctor running down the hall outside our room. When the lights stopped flashing and the sound of the alarm silenced, it became very quiet. I could feel my heart racing as I sat up, covered by my white blanket. I didn't know the patient for whom the alarm sounded, and I never asked our nurse, but I felt frightened at the thought of a child in danger of dying. Our room remained dark; only the lights on the IV pump created shadows around the room. Jeff woke, and we stared silently at each other. Soon he'd fall back asleep, and I'd wait, making sure he had, before allowing my eyes to close.

The next morning, before Jeff's chemotherapy, I went to the food court for his strawberry milk and plain bagel. When I returned, he was watching ESPN. While he ate, I asked, "Jeff, Jess is the only friend who's visited you here. Do you want your friends to visit?"

"Is it okay?" he asked.

"Of course it's okay, honey. Your friends are probably waiting for you to tell them they can visit. They don't know what happens when you come to Boston or anything about how you feel. E-mail them if you want, and tell them they can visit you."

My phone rang. It was in my bag across the room. I scrambled to get to it. I opened the bag and reached in, careful not to squish my two Three Musketeers bars. Finally, I put my hand on my cell phone. "Ah, here it is!"

"Hi!" It was Nancy Helms. "I'm here at Children's with Josh. We're on Ten West," she told me.

"You're here?" I asked, surprised she was in the same hospital.

"Yes. This morning we were driving home from our cottage in New Hampshire. Josh was lying down in the back seat. I pulled over to the side of the road to look at Josh's knee—he had surgery on it a few weeks ago. His knee was all red and swollen and looked infected, so I thought we'd better get to Boston right away. I called the police, and they sent an ambulance to get Josh while we waited on the side of the highway. I drove to Children's while the ambulance took Josh to the emergency room here."

"How is he now?" I asked.

"They've got him on heavy antibiotics. He's in a private room on Ten West, which is a brand new wing. How's Jeff?"

"He's doing well. He's waiting for more chemo this morning. We're here for the week. We're on Nine West. You're right above us, Nance."

"We are? I'd like to come see Jeff; can I come down now?"

"Sure, he's awake. Come on down."

Josh and his older brother, Chris, played hockey with John Jr. on select hockey teams. They both attended Bridgeton Academy. Most of the athletes from Sandwich High hung out at the Helms' house after school and during the weekends.

When Jeff got sick, friends from Sandwich contacted Nancy to help us. She rarely called with questions. She seemed to know what we needed. She always found a way to make things at home easier for us. She was our liaison, the person who stood between us and the community. She organized our Sunday dinners. "People can't do enough for Jeff and your family; it's incredible," she told me.

"Hey, Jeff! How's it going?" Nancy asked when she entered our room. Jeff had the first bed.

"Hi," Jeff replied. "How's Josh?"

"His knee—I must admit it looked very bad. He was screaming from the pain. He has to stay isolated from any germs and can't have many visitors."

"Do you think I could stick my head in his room to say hello?" I asked.

"Yeah, I think so. I'll stay here with Jeff. Go ahead."

"Okay. Jeff, I'll be right back."

"Tell Josh I said hi," Jeff replied.

I took the elevator one floor up and walked out toward Ten West. There was no one around. The nurse's station was empty. The hall was spacious, and I could smell the newness from the recent construction on the floor. Everything was upgraded and clean. I walked by rooms with empty beds. The floor shined, and the rooms looked like hotel rooms. I came to one occupied room; the television was on. I saw Josh lying in bed.

"Hi, Josh! How are you?" I said, as I entered his room. His leg was propped up on pillows.

"Hi, Mrs. Hayes, How's Jeff doing?"

"He's doing well. He's had few side effects so far, so that's been pretty good, but the chemo is strong, and they give him lots of meds to get rid of the nausea. He's right below you on Nine West. Boy, I wish he had a room like yours! This is nice."

"Yeah, it's new, and I don't think there are any other patients on the floor."

I stayed far enough away from Josh so not to spread any germs that could worsen his infection. I'd just come from a floor full of very sick children. I walked around his incredibly large and private room that resembled home. His television was housed in a cabinet that matched the counter, and another cabinet held a refrigerator and microwave. The room was spacious enough for a large number of guests, with a couch, two chairs, and a large private bath.

I said, "You should see the room Jeff's in. It's half the size of this, and it's a semi-private room, and most of the time the other bed is taken. There's lots of commotion on his floor. It's much quieter here."

"How long are you here for?" I asked.

"It all depends on the infection. I have to stay until it gets better."

"Well, I hope that isn't too long."

"How's John Jr. doing?" Josh asked.

"He's working. I don't see him much with all the time I spend here with Jeff."

"When's his last treatment?" Josh asked.

"Well, he has fourteen cycles, and the last one is the first week in December."

"That's a long time."

"Yeah. Jeff's been very patient. He seems to be fighting it well. This is a long week for him; he'll go home on Friday. Well, I'd better get back. Take care, Josh, and we'll see you later."

"Bye, Mrs. Hayes. Thanks for coming by, and say hi to Jeff for me."

On my walk back down to Nine West, I couldn't help but imagine a room or a floor like this for the children on Seven West and Nine West. Life at Children's during chemotherapy treatment would be private and comfortable for the children, teenagers, and parents. It would make an enormous difference on so many levels.

I returned to the hustle and bustle of Nine West, one floor down from privacy and sanity.

The word was out, and that week Jeff's friends came to visit.

CHAPTER 33

Harbor Cruise, August 2005

T HE SUMMER WAS coming to an end, and Jeff wanted to start school in the fall. He and I met with Ellin Booras, the Principal of Sandwich High. We enrolled Jeff in courses that he thought he could handle during treatment. The history teacher, Mr. Linehan, was Jeff's favorite teacher, and his history course slot fit Jeff's schedule. Jeff smiled, not letting on how he would coast through this course with his friend and teacher, Gary Linehan.

The flyer for the first annual Boston Harbor Lobster Luncheon Cruise was posted outside the social director's office at the JFC. The cruise was on a Saturday afternoon in September, open for all parents of a child battling cancer. I had already signed up.

The day before the cruise, on the Friday of Jeff's last five-day treatment, my brother John and my sister-in-law Patti picked Jeff up from Children's Hospital. They were taking Jeff to their home in Norwood to care for him over the weekend. Jeff felt comfortable with them, and he knew what meds to take and when to take them. John and Patti went to Seven West at Children's and were given the discharge instructions. I had told the floor nurse that they would be picking Jeff up on Friday. I had left the day before.

When they arrived at their home in Norwood, Jeff walked slowly down the stairs to the living room in their basement. The room in the basement was small and had a sofa and a flat-screen television where Johnny and Niki, Jeff's cousins hung out.

"Where's Chief?" Jeff asked. Chief was their golden retriever. Jeff was not fond of dogs, just like my dad. He wanted to make sure Chief wouldn't jump up on him while he tried to keep his balance walking down the stairs. He was still heavily medicated and feeling the effects of the chemo.

"Chief's outside," Patti replied. "Don't worry, Jeff."

Jeff made himself comfortable on the sofa and said, "Okay, Chief can come in now."

When Chief came into the room, he went right to Jeff, sniffed him cautiously and lay next to him and the two fell asleep together. It was remarkable how Chief instinctively knew to be gentle with Jeff. After that, each time Chief would go outside and come back in, he'd find Jeff, and put his head down and lay next to him.

"What would you like to drink, Jeff? I've got lots of blue Gatorade; would you like some?" Patti asked.

"I'd like the red Gatorade, please."

"But your Mom said you like the blue Gatorade!"

"That's all they have at the hospital."

"Jeff, would you like a turkey sandwich?" my brother John asked. He had just carved an entire turkey for Jeff.

"No, thank you. I don't like turkey sandwiches."

"What! You don't like turkey sandwiches? You can't be your mother's son…Okay, what would you like?"

"Hot dogs."

"I just carved a whole turkey, and you want hot dogs!" he said smiling.

"Yes, Uncle John. Sorry."

"Hot dogs it is!"

Patti left to go buy red Gatorade and hot dogs.

John and Patti's two teenagers, Johnny and Niki, were close to Jeff. Johnny and John Jr. were the same age and spent their younger years together whenever possible. Niki was Jeff's age. When they were young, Niki and Jeff played together while John Jr. and Johnny fought off bad guys while dressed in their Ninja Turtle shells and masks. When they weren't saving the city from destruction, they played mini hockey.

Johnny sat with Jeff in their basement while Jeff rested.

"Are you afraid of dying?" Johnny asked.

"No," Jeff answered. "I have some good doctors taking care of me." He paused. "No, not really," Jeff said again. "I'm not afraid. I go through each treatment thinking the chemotherapy is going to work. At the end of this year, I'll be done, and I can have my life back. I can play hockey again."

"You bet, kid," Johnny replied.

"Are you okay, Jeff?" Patti asked, as she checked on him again and again over the weekend.

"I'm trying to sleep," he replied.

"Johnny, go down and check on Jeff."

"He wants to be left alone."

"I know, but I need to know he's okay."

Johnny walked down the stairs.

"Jeff, you okay?"

"I'm okay, Johnny."

We met the social director at the dock and walked toward the ramp. We stopped alongside the *Spirit of Boston* cruise ship for a picture and then boarded. We were given two drink tickets and escorted into the dining room. We chose a table by the window with a view of Boston Harbor. I approached the bar.

"What can I get you?" asked the bartender.

"Apple martini," I replied, "and a Michelob Ultra."

It was two o'clock in the afternoon. Our table began to fill with other parents. It was a beautiful, warm September afternoon. John and I went to the buffet in the front of the ship.

I gave John my lobster and feasted on the rest of the buffet. We didn't recognize any of the other parents. We made casual conversation with parents at our table, but none of us really wanted to talk about the personal battles our sons and daughters were facing. Why open that wound, when it was bandaged for the afternoon. This was an afternoon with a purpose; specifically planned to ease the stress of what we were all facing.

The show began after lunch with a master of ceremonies, a DJ, and dancers dressed in satin dresses and high-heeled shoes. Oh, God! He's coming up to me with the microphone to finish the words to the song! Luckily, I was able to finish the verse. John shook his head. "I don't know where that came from!" I said, and then I joined the train dance that went out of the dining room and onto the deck.

After the train dance, John and I walked up to the upper deck to take in the sights of Boston Harbor. We could see Logan Airport, and we watched planes take off and land. We saw Old Ironsides, the shipyard in Charlestown, the Boston skyline, and a group of sailors learning to sail. As they came closer to the ship, one began to sail right toward us, out of control, barely missing our port side. Other parents on the deck began to yell out to the sailor, and somehow, frantically, he managed to avoid striking our port side.

"Wow, do you think he'll pass?" I asked John.

"Pass what, the ship?"

The cruise was ending, and I could see the Seaport Hotel from the harbor as we headed toward the pier. The ship pulled in and we docked. John and I walked off the ramp and down the pier. The pictures that were taken as we boarded were displayed on the side of the pier on a table. I picked up our framed picture, with a photograph of the *Spirit of Boston* on the front cover. I opened it and looked at John and me smiling close together. I could see the stress in our tired eyes. Our smiles wrinkled our faces. I could see the effects of the last several months. I put the picture in my bag. Although I wasn't looking so great, I felt rejuvenated. We said good-bye and thanked the social director. We walked across the street and entered the lounge at the Seaport Hotel. We sat at the bar and ordered another drink. The Boston Red Sox were playing the New York Yankees. We watched most of the game and then left for our room.

Later that evening, we returned to the lounge to meet up with our friends, Jackie and Michael. The lounge began to fill with people from a wedding at the hotel and another large group of guests just getting off the evening cruise on the *Spirit of Boston*. I looked around the large room with couches and tables that were filled with patrons and noticed my Uncle David, Dad's youngest brother, standing in the crowd. I hadn't seen him for several years. I approached him; we were so surprised to see each other. I told him about the day I had visited Carlton Street, and the hidden space under the stairway, and the Christmas tree at the top of the stairs. We laughed. He knew of my son's battle with cancer, and we talked for quite some time until a wave of exhaustion hit me, and I had to say good night. The thought of sleeping in a bed without IV alarms going off and nurses interrupting my sleep was so comforting.

Sunday morning we picked Jeff up in Norwood. He was anxious to go home, back to his friends.

CHAPTER 34

First Annual Jeff Hayes Golf Tournament, September 2005

LOCAL RESTAURANTS, INCLUDING the Dan'l Webster Inn, Marshland, the Dunbar Tea House, the Sandwich House of Pizza, and Anna Belle Bed and Breakfast, as well as several golf courses around the Cape, donated gift certificates as raffle items for the tournament. American Airlines donated a free round-trip ticket to London courtesy of Captain John (Jack) Lessard. Donations and hole sponsorships were received from local businesses, and private contributions came in from on and off the Cape. The social director from the JFC donated an autographed NFL football, and some families in Sandwich donated two framed, autographed pictures of athletes from the Patriots and the Red Sox. Many valuable raffle items filled the front of the banquet room, including a four-wheel ATV displayed at the entrance to the country club.

Two hundred and fifty guests and golfers were in attendance. It was a beautiful sunny autumn day. There wasn't a golf slot available. Golfers who hadn't registered in advance were turned away. Jeff had his own foursome of his closest friends. Each golfer received a gift box with a golf shirt and a cap packaged inside. The navy-blue collared golf shirt had the Jeff Hayes Golf Tournament logo

Uncle Chuck and Jeff

(two hockey sticks crossed with a baseball and the number twelve on each side of the sticks) embroidered onto the front upper left side of the shirt.

John and I stood at the front of the banquet-sized room inside the clubhouse during registration. People approached us with more valuable raffle items to be displayed around the room. Items that weren't expected and listed in our program were brought in before the first tee off. We were amazed at the generosity and outpouring of support. After registration, the golfers gathered outside and filled the rows of golf carts. John and I stood in front of the carts. The manager waved on the first row of carts, and John and I waved to each foursome as they drove out onto the course.

The day was long. I watched foursomes stop on the green outside the clubhouse and waited during the afternoon with my friends for the golfers to finish the eighteen holes and then gather for dinner. John and I had decided we would both say a few words. I was frightened at the thought of speaking in front so many people at a time when I was so vulnerable.

After dinner I stood at the front of the room. I knew I wouldn't make it past "hello" and "thank you for coming," staring out at the people who meant so much to our family and who had come to support Jeff. I can't remember what I said, but I felt I delivered my message of deep gratitude, thanks, and appreciation for everyone who helped make this day so very special for Jeff and for us.

Then John spoke. He was fluid and articulate as he talked about the importance of raising awareness, being supportive, of being thankful and true friendship. He then introduced Jeff's closest friends and asked them to come up to the front of the room. He praised them for the companionship they bestowed upon our son. Jeff's friends stood

Mike Bridges, Jeff, Brian Tomasini, Connor Green

196

at the front of the large banquet room and looked around the room. Each stood still, stoic, nodding their heads when John called out their names: Brian Tomasini, Mike Bridges, John Lessard, Ted Vrontas, Will Buckley, and Connor Green.

John continued speaking; his glasses hung below his eyes and on the end of his nose, and sweat started to drip from his brow as he ended his speech. Jeff's friends returned to their table. It was a long, moving speech.

Angelo Tomasini, Brian's father, then called Jeff up to the front of the room. Jeff was wearing the golf shirt and hat, covering his baldness; he was still sporting a few extra pounds even after Sam had stopped the steroids. Jeff's weight reached 196 pounds. He was tipping the scales and jumping up in pant size.

"Jeff, go for the lettuce when you open the refrigerator door," Sam said.

Jeff's weight slowly began to drop after Sam stopped his steroid dosage, and his appetite diminished. His weight when he started his treatment was 157 pounds.

He looked pale from the chemo. Everyone clapped as Angelo and Chuck presented Jeff with a hockey stick signed by Derek Sanderson, the last stick he used in the NHL. Jack Lessard played a video with pictures of Jeff's youth, pictures of hockey, a baseball video, and family pictures. The silent auction began. Bill O'Brien, one of my bosses, began drawing raffle tickets. He has a great stage presence. He starred along with Rex Trailer in the children's television show *Boomtown*. He was Sergeant Billy. I had been on the show as a young girl. It was a special bond we shared.

Toward the end of the silent auction, Nancy Bridges approached Jeff's table with her son and all of Jeff's friends.

"Hey, Jeff, what a day! How are you feeling?"

"Pretty good, I guess," he replied.

"Look at all these raffle items. So, tell me, which one would you like? I'll get it for you."

"I'd like the Miller Lite neon sign. I can hang it up in my basement," he said, smiling.

"Oh, yeah, your Mom would love that! All right, I'm gonna get that for you," she said, and left to bid on the Miller Lite sign.

There were many items that people purchased and gave to Jeff. Jimmy Fucci, John's friend, had the highest bid for the New England Patriots portable gas grill and gave it to Jeff. Someone else gave him a Heineken golf bag, and he also received Patriots game tickets.

The raffle took many hours, and the tournament ended late in the evening. It was an amazing day. Hannah, Jeff's nurse, had traveled down to Sandwich for the tournament.

When the evening came to an end, I looked for Jeff at the back of the room.

"Jeff," I called to him as I approached his table. "If you're feeling tired, it's okay to leave." He looked up from the table where he was seated with his friends and said, "Mom, I'm not leaving until the last person has gone."

CHAPTER 35

Ninth Treatment, October 2005

THE NEXT TREATMENT was a two-day cycle, and again, Jeff and I made the trip up to Boston.

We shared the treatment room at the JFC with a teenager we'd seen a couple times before. He had osteosarcoma and had his leg amputated. He and his mom always seemed upbeat and appeared to be very close. I was amazed with his good humor while battling his cancer, especially after losing a leg. It was a reminder to us that amputation had once been an option for Jeff.

Today the boy and Jeff received their chemo in beds next to each other, separated by a curtain. When they finished the chemotherapy, we waited for a bed at Children's. The day was coming to an end.

A Jimmy Fund nurse entered our room, and I heard her inform the boy's mother that the hospital was having difficulty getting approval from the family's insurance company for her son to be admitted to Children's. I recall Sam telling me that I must have had good insurance because he never heard a peep from them. I had Blue Cross Blue Shield and a caseworker assigned specifically to Jeff. She had contacted me in the very beginning to introduce herself and to let me know I was to contact her with any questions regarding coverage. Joe Sullivan, my other boss, told me that if we had trouble with our coverage, he would change it.

Our roommates continued to get updates from the nurse regarding approval from their insurance company. Listening to their nurse return with troubling news, I thought that maybe their insurance representative should come sit with them at the JFC to witness firsthand what it's like for a child with cancer to have to wait for treatment and care, or be denied a bed because of a delay by the insurance company. A delay in approving treatment should never be an issue for any child with cancer. It infuriated me that an insurance company could dictate and interfere with this child's undeniable need for treatment. It was more stress in an already overwhelmingly stressful state for a parent.

Jeff's room was ready, and Hannah de-accessed his port and helped me get Jeff in his wheelchair. The mother looked at me as she waited.

"You got a room?" she said.

"Yes, finally," I replied. I was happy to be on our way to Children's but felt sad to leave her behind.

When we got to Children's, we entered a room that was unoccupied; both beds were empty. An aid was still cleaning the room. A nurse I didn't know entered the room after us and told us specifically to take the first bed, not the bed by the window. The bed by the window was the most desirable bed because it would prevent Jeff from being exposed to people walking by us all night. She was very stern, and I was ready to follow her instructions.

When the nurse left the room, the aide turned to me and said, "You take whatever bed you want. The rule is the first one to arrive gets first choice." I don't why this woman told me that, but I was grateful. I phoned my husband to ask him what I should do. I told him what the aide had said, and he immediately said, "Take the bed you want." So I did.

Shortly after, the same woman and her son who were having difficulty with their insurance entered the room. She looked at me and said, "So, you took the bed by the window." Apparently, the nurse had been trying to save the window bed for them. I felt awkward and guilty, so that night I shared my stash of Hershey's kisses with the mother.

The next day, Jeff was given his chemo and the Neulasta shot, and I was given the discharge instructions. We made our way to the parking garage to find our car and go home.

During this two-day treatment, and after Sam had examined Jeff, he and Jeff talked about school.

"Would you like me to come down to your school and talk to your classmates about how you've been skipping class to receive chemotherapy?" Sam asked Jeff.

Jeff smiled, "Sure, that would be great."

The next day I phoned Ellin Booras, Jeff's high school principal and we arranged for Sam to speak in front of the Junior class, during an assembly on October 4, 2005. I didn't know until that day when Sam asked to speak with Jeff's class that he had lectured high school and college students before becoming a doctoral fellow.

Jeff began to complain of a toothache. It was his wisdom teeth. We scheduled an appointment with Dr. Lane, an oral surgeon in Sandwich. Jeff had x-rays taken to see how the four wisdom teeth were growing in. His upper left third molar was slightly horizontal and pushing against his second molar giving him pain. He wasn't taking any pain meds at this point in the treatment, just the antinausea meds and Bactrim. Dr. Lane decided to remove that one upper molar that was causing trouble.

It was a procedure that any other teen could endure, but a teenager undergoing chemotherapy was at a much greater risk. Wisdom teeth can grow horizontally when impacted and could be very difficult to remove. If the tooth split during extraction, it could be difficult to remove the roots left behind. In Jeff's case, the real concern was infection and excessive bleeding from low blood counts. We were hoping that the molar could be extracted in one piece with little bleeding, so the extraction had to be scheduled for a time when Jeff's counts were at their highest.

Sam phoned Dr. Lane to discuss Jeff's case and the extraction procedure. We scheduled the surgery in the surgeon's office in Sandwich. Jeff started taking an antibiotic a few days before the extraction.

I needed to be at work, so Patty took Jeff for the procedure. Jeff was given a Novocain shot. The extraction went well, and the wisdom tooth came out all in one piece. That day when I returned home, I changed his gauze and looked at the socket. His bleeding was somewhat slow, but I still needed to change his gauze throughout the night until the bleeding stopped completely. I kept a close eye on the bleeding and his pain level. He was tough and a great patient. At the time of this extraction, we were relieved it had gone so well, but in the year that followed it became a means for Ewing's to find new life.

The week followed with the usual blood count recovery. Katherine came by on the first Thursday to draw blood. On Sunday, Jane Tomasini made us dinner—baked ham, mashed potatoes, squash, green beans, applesauce, and fresh baked rolls—which we ate on the run. John, John Jr., Jeff, Jason, and Brian were going to the New England Patriots game. The social director from the JFC had called and invited us to watch Tom Brady and the New England Patriots from a luxury box at Gillette Stadium. It was the night of October 16, 2005, just eight months after the incident when Tedy Bruschi, a linebacker, took the field again for the New England Patriots after suffering a stroke.

I filled my plate with Jane's delicious meal, happy to watch the game from home.

Sam's Presentation to Sandwich High School

ON THE MORNING of October 4, 2005, Sam traveled to Sandwich High School to talk about cancer to an assembly of the junior and senior classes. The school nurse introduced him. "It is my great pleasure to present Dr. Samuel Blackman, a Pediatric Oncologist from the Dana-Farber Cancer Institute in Boston. He's here to talk to us about the implications of having a disease such as cancer."

Sam took the stage to a polite applause. "It's very interesting for me to be up here to talk to you about cancer, a word that people are not too keen on saying. It's a word that scares people and has scared people for hundreds of years. It is important to talk about cancer. I don't want you to go home with a big, black cloud over your head, but I want you to be aware that cancer is something that may happen to people around you, may happen to people in your family, and may happen to you, unfortunately, or any of us at some point in the future."

The students listened attentively as Sam talked a little about the science of biology, but it was Jeff they wanted to hear Sam talk about.

"Jeff's been a patient of mine, and it's been an absolute, extreme pleasure getting to know him and his family. I'd like to talk to you a little bit about Jeff, and with his permission, I'm going to share some information about what's been going on with him, so you can understand a little bit more about what he's been going through."

"Jeff came to us after noticing swelling in his leg and some pain and really no other symptoms. So what we found were these small round tumors, and we did some special scans in the laboratory. Based on Jeff's age and the location of the tumor, it looked like it was consistent with the disease, Ewing's sarcoma. Ewing's sarcoma is named after a guy and refers to a family of tumors. I'm aware of a couple of other kids in Sandwich who had Ewing's sarcoma." Sam looked around the room; the students remained quiet and attentive.

"Ewing's happens in about one in one million people, and it's about two percent of all cancers we see. It happens to patients that are between eleven and eighteen years of age. You see it in adolescents, but you don't see it in old people. Most of the patients who have Ewing's sarcoma are under twenty years of age, and it shows up in a variety of different places in the body. More importantly, how do you fix it? Really, this is what it boils down to."

Sam talked about cancer treatment and about the kinds of chemotherapy that Jeff had undergone. He concluded, "Cancer in children and adolescents isn't anybody's fault. It happens. I wish we knew a little more about why. It's really nobody's fault. Cancer is not contagious, but ignorance about it is. You're not going to get it from touching or being around someone who has cancer or from sharing a hamburger with that person. But ignorance about cancer is contagious. Please be informed. Really, the most important thing is that people with cancer are people first. I started out by titling my talk 'My Friend with Cancer,' but that violates what I just told you. So, I think the more appropriate title for my entire talk should be, 'My Friend, Jeff Hayes.' Thank you!"

When the applause settled, Sam fielded questions from the students about Ewing's sarcoma. Many students wanted to know whether there was a causal link between Jeff's cancer and the PAVE PAWS radar installation or the polluted groundwater from nearby Camp Edwards. Sam explained that studies to date had shown no connections.

"Are you able to play athletics?" a student asked.

"Yes, absolutely. Because of receiving chemotherapy for a long time, most of our patients don't have the energy and can't go full tilt, but we certainly encourage them to do as many of the things they're capable of doing as they can. There are things we specifically ask them not to do because the chemotherapy makes their counts go down and makes them a little more susceptible to bleeding—so things like juggling chainsaws, playing with knifes, jumping over sharp rocks, and other things that would increase the risk of bleeding, we ask them not to do, but within the limits of normal human behavior, they can do pretty much whatever they want."

Sam looked over at the principal, Ellin Booras, and said, "I think I've run out of time. Thank you so very much for listening and allowing me to come here to talk." Kathy Grant, the school nurse, approached the podium and took the microphone. "Thank you very much, Dr. Blackman, for coming in and talking on behalf of Jeff's family."

Jeff stayed at school for the day. He had another week before he had to start the next cycle.

CHAPTER 37

Tenth Treatment, October 2005

THE TENTH TREATMENT was a five-day cycle. It was routine for Jeff; he knew what to expect. He got up early and got dressed, and with our suitcase packed, we left the Cape.

I had a large supply of Gatorade for the ride up. My boss's wife and my friend, Cindy Sullivan, phoned me at work asking if we needed anything. I thought she and Joe had done so much for my family up to this point that all I could think of was Gatorade for Jeff. When I left work that night, I walked down the sidewalk to where my car was parked. I slowed down as I approached, looking into the backseat. Several stacked cases of Gatorade filled my backseat. Oh wow, I thought. I smiled, and tears suddenly began to fill my eyes; like so many other times, I tried to hold them back.

I kept a full-time job during Jeff's treatment. Joe Sullivan and Bill O'Brien were partners and owners of the financial planning firm in Sandwich where I'd worked for the past five years after leaving New Seabury. They considered Jeff's battle against cancer a struggle we'd bear together. "We're in this together," they'd say. When I had to leave work at a moment's notice, their response was, "You know how we feel about this. Now go!" They assured me I would always have my job when I returned. I can't imagine any other employer showing the immense compassion and generosity they did.

Jeff drank as much Gatorade as he could during the two-and-a-half-hour drive up to the JFC.

When we arrived at Dana-Farber, we parked in the usual garage above the clinic. While Jeff sat on the couch in the waiting room, I went outside the clinic and down the hall to the ladies' room. On my way back to the waiting room, I saw Dr. Grier at the other end of the hall. I remembered I'd brought copies of the letter that the Sandwich High School Principal, Ellin Borras had written to Sam. I wanted Dr. Grier, Sam's boss, to see the letter and see how much Sam's presentation had left an impression on the students.

"Dr. Grier!" I shouted as I ran toward him; his back was to me. "Dr. Grier!" He turned and looked at me. I slowed and approached him.

"Hi. I'm Mrs. Hayes."

"Jeff's mom, yes. How are you?" he asked.

"I'm well, thanks. I wanted you to see this letter that Jeff's high school principal wrote Sam after his lecture at the school. Sam was amazing that day."

Dr. Grier took the letter and began to read it.

I stood next to him, anxiously waiting as he read the letter. I wanted to see his expression as he read about the student who informed his physics teacher after the assembly that he wanted to become an oncologist, and about the other student who told Mrs. Booras that Sam's presentation was the best assembly she had ever been to. When the principal asked her why, she replied, "Because it gave us hope that we can all make a difference, and it helped to connect us all to Jeff even more than we already were." And there was more, I thought, waiting as he read. There was the teacher who, later that day, commented in front of his peers that Sam's presentation was outstanding and that he was very proud of the students' level of attention.

After Dr. Grier finished reading, he looked up at me and asked, "May I have this copy?"

"Yes, of course," I replied.

"Thank you. I've got to get to a meeting, so I must be on my way." He turned and walked a few steps then stopped, and looking up from the letter again, said, "This is very good."

"Yes," I replied. "Thank you."

I walked back to the JFC and waited with Jeff. It was good to see Hannah greet us when she came through the two large doors from the back of the clinic. She was coming to take care of Jeff. For me, it was a day of respite, where I could sit and observe. There was time before Hannah was going to administer the chemo, so I took the elevator to the street floor for my usual walk to CVS for two large Three Musketeers bars. I left the clinic and took the elevator to the street floor. I walked around the elevators past the stairway that led to the Jimmy Fund Hall of Fame and entered the seating area. I glanced over at the chapel. My pace slowed. I've passed this way before and never stopped. I stood still. People were sitting in cushioned chairs in this open area and I didn't know if they had noticed as I stared at the closed chapel doors. No, I thought. I can't go in there. I walked slowly on. It was unthinkable; that I might lose my son.

I sped up as I approached the corridor. Once in the wide corridor, I stopped to look at the large, bright, and colorful mural of a crowd of people walking through Boston. It was the Boston Marathon Jimmy Fund Walk. I'm going to do that, I thought, admiring the faces in the mural. What a great thing to do. Twenty-six miles—oh yeah, I can do that. I had made it past the chapel and that was difficult.

When I returned from my trip to CVS, I sat in the chair next to Jeff's bed.

"You always get two candy bars, but I never have one," Jeff said, when he looked at the two large Three Musketeer bars inside my bag.

"Do you want one, honey?"

"No thanks, not now."

"I'll save you one."

"No, you won't."

Sam entered the room. "Hey, Jeff. How are you?"

"Pretty good," Jeff replied.

"Any new side effects?"

"Nope."

"That's good," he said and then began checking Jeff's leg. "Okay," he said, I've got a joke for you; want to hear it?" He stood, leaning over the tray next to Jeff's bed.

"Sure," Jeff replied.

"All the organs of the body were having a meeting, trying to decide who was in charge. And the brain said, 'I should be in charge, because I run all the body's systems, so without me nothing would happen.'" Sam stood up straight. "'I should be in charge,' the heart said, 'because I pump the blood and circulate oxygen all over the body, so without me you'd all waste away.'

"'I should be in charge,' said the stomach, 'because I process food and give all of you energy.'

"'I should be in charge,' said the rectum, 'because I'm responsible for waste removal.'" Sam raised his hands and moved them back and forth, imitating each organ. "All the other body parts laughed at the rectum and insulted him, so in a huff, he shut down tight. And within a few days, the brain had a terrible headache, the stomach was bloated, and the blood was toxic. Eventually the other organs gave in. So, they all agreed that the rectum should be the boss. So, Jeff, the moral of the story is, you don't have to be smart or important to be in charge...just an asshole." We laughed.

"What's going on in here?" Hannah said, as she entered the room.

"Nothing, just discussing anatomy with Jeff," Sam replied.

"Oh, anatomy can't be that funny!"

Jeff was smiling back at Sam.

Hannah checked Jeff's fluids.

"Call me or e-mail me, Jeff, for anything," Sam said.

Hannah gave Jeff his antinausea drugs. He was hydrated, and his blood counts were at an acceptable level to start this treatment. She administered the chemo drugs, and later in the day we made our way to Children's.

When we entered the lobby at Children's, the aroma from Au Bon Pain made me nauseous as I pushed Jeff toward the elevator to Seven West. On Seven West, a floor nurse took us to our room. Jeff had the bed next to the door. We settled in. This week, one of the networks was showing a *Rocky* movie marathon. Jeff and I watched the original *Rocky*, and then I converted the big green chair into a bed and covered it with sheets and a blanket. Jeff and I fell asleep.

I woke during the night feeling a warm sensation below my waist. The room was dark, but I had a direct view of the large clock on the wall across from Jeff's bed. The light from outside the window shone on the clock. It was eleven. I looked down at my sheets; they were saturated in blood. Frightened and shocked by the amount of blood, I got up and could feel blood clots expelling. I was hemorrhaging. No way, I thought, this cannot be happening! I immediately got up and pulled off the sheets and the blanket from the makeshift bed and threw them in the dirty linen holder outside our room. The lights on Seven West were turned down low. The floor was quiet. I grabbed a change of pajamas and hurried to the linen supply rack down the hall and got all new sheets, a blanket and a bunch of facecloths. I placed the sheets and blanket on my converted bed and quickly walked down the hall to the bathroom right outside the floor and in the corridor that led to elevators—the tubby room. I changed, cleansed myself, and returned to Jeff's room. I made my bed again. As I lay there, the bleeding intensified. Once again, I had to remove the linen and head back to the tubby room. I sat there for hours passing clots. This had come so suddenly and unexpectedly. I thought to myself, I can handle this; I'll get through this and I'll be okay. When I returned to Jeff's room, I covered the bed again and lay down. Our roommate's nurse entered the room, and I stopped her before she made her way to Jeff's roommate. My chair was next to the door.

"Excuse me," I said quietly, looking up at her in the dark. "I am hemorrhaging badly. It's been going on for several hours."

She looked back at me and said, "You can call your obstetrician, or you can go to the emergency room," and she walked over to her patient on the other side of the curtain. Um, okay, I thought. Those are my options. I understood that I couldn't receive any medical attention from her right then and there, but felt she could have shown a little more empathy. I contemplated going to the emergency room, but I didn't want to leave Jeff for any extended period of time. I thought I was in a good place, though, for what was happening. I can take care of myself. I lay there while Jeff slept, hoping the bleeding would subside.

I didn't follow either of her suggestions. I didn't call my obstetrician or go to the emergency room. I wouldn't leave Jeff. Eventually I fell asleep for the rest of the night. It was four in the morning.

The linen holder outside our room was filled with sheets and blankets saturated with blood. With the nurses changing shifts at seven o'clock, I thought no one would know of the night I had. The soiled linen went unnoticed. Jeff's nurse didn't ask, and I didn't tell her, thinking that our roommate's nurse never mentioned my conversation with her to Jeff's nurse.

When I awoke again, it was nine o'clock, and I looked up at Jeff. He opened his eyes and turned to me and said, "Mom, what was the matter with you last night?"

"Nothing. I'm okay, honey."

He turned his head and fell back to sleep. I got up slowly and showered. The bleeding had stopped as if it had never happened. I hadn't realized Jeff was aware of me getting up several times during the night and leaving him. I felt better that morning so I went to the food court to get him his bagel and strawberry milk. When I returned, I positioned myself in the chair next to Jeff and made myself lie still for the rest of the day. I thought about many things. I had never noticed any symptoms that would have caused me to even consider that I may have been pregnant. I couldn't imagine myself going through a pregnancy at forty seven years old while trying to save the life of my sixteen-year-old son. What thoughts would Jeff have seeing me carry another child into the world while he was fighting for his life? Clearly my body wasn't capable of maintaining a healthy pregnancy and I could accept that. My focus and attention was directed where it needed to be; on Jeff and that's where it would remain.

The rest of the week Jeff continued the treatment. We watched *Rocky* and all the sequels through *Rocky V.* We never saw Sam or Hannah during the week. The floor doctor cared for Jeff. Jeff was assigned the same nurse each time when possible. Her name was Kerry. We saw her when Jeff received his chemotherapy and during the day or evening during her shifts, when his fluids and his other medications were needed. She was the nurse who had cured Jeff's hiccups. She was pregnant. When Jeff was scheduled for his chemotherapy, another nurse administered it. Pregnant nurses didn't administer chemo, and several of the nurses were pregnant. When we left Children's Hospital, Sam and Hannah were Jeff's primary caregivers. We were instructed to call them or the JFC after hours as needed. Jeff's care at Children's ended when we left the hospital, and we didn't have the same relationship with the doctors and nurses at Children's as we did with Sam and Hannah.

When Jeff and I returned home late in the afternoon on Friday, Jeff entered the side door of our house, walked carefully into the kitchen, and then walked slowly down the stairs to his living room. I joined him after I'd unpacked. He sat in his recliner and I on the couch next to him.

"Mom, do you want to watch *Rocky*?" he asked. I looked back at him and smiled. "Yes," I said, knowing he didn't remember we'd watched *Rocky I* through *V* the entire week. It was first time I realized he probably didn't remember much of the time he spent on Seven West.

"Which one is on?"

"The first one," he said, pushing his recliner back and elevating his legs.

"Are you hungry?" I asked.

"What do we have to eat?" he asked. "Do we have strawberry milk and peanut butter crackers?"

"Yup, I'll be right back," I replied. "Don't worry about me missing anything. I'll catch up." I walked up the stairs.

"I can pause it, Mom."

"Okay." Great, I thought. I have a feeling I'll be watching the entire series of five movies again.

I brought down his strawberry milk and peanut butter crackers. After his first sip, he looked at me sitting on his couch and asked, "How come Grandma's strawberry milk tastes different? Can you make it like Grandma did?"

"I don't know, honey; all her stuff tasted better." I thought for a moment. "I can make it like Grandma did. Hold on; I'll be right back." I went back upstairs and added a spoonful of vanilla ice cream, stirring until the strawberry milk was smooth, and brought it back down to him. The secret strawberry milk ingredient: I should have known—Mom loved ice cream. Thanks Mom, I thought.

"Here, honey, try this."

"Thanks." He took a sip. "Yeah, that's good."

It felt good to be home again. I had a lot of help. Our friends, Judie and Jerry Meuse had hired a cleaning service to clean our house. My sister Joanne and Patty were there to help cook and take care of John, John Jr., and Jason. I thought about that long night on Seven West and decided to concentrate on the lives of the sons I had.

CHAPTER 38

Waterville Valley

JEFF, JOHN JR., and Jason left for the Sandwich High School Thanksgiving football game. After the game, we ate our Thanksgiving dinner then packed our Explorer. We were going for a long weekend to Waterville Valley, located in the heart of the White Mountains of New Hampshire. Lisa Raposa, whose son had played hockey for Falmouth and knew of Jeff's battle, had offered her condo to us, and we had rented another unit for Jeff, John Jr., and their closest friends. My sister-in-law, Patty and her husband, Marty, and Jeff's grandmother, Nana, would be staying with us.

It was dark and snowing when we pulled into the Waterville Valley Condo Association. I phoned the manager from my cell, and when he arrived, he gave us the key and directions to the condo.

It was a three-bedroom unit with an open living room and kitchen with a cathedral ceiling and a fireplace. The deck off the back looked out onto a small yard, and beyond that was a steep drop down to the road below. It was night, so I could only imagine the view of snow-topped mountains we'd see the next morning. Marty placed wood in the fireplace and started a fire.

John Jr., Jeff and Mike Bridges arrived the next day. Their condo was two doors down from us. John Jr. and Mike snowboarded most of the day while Jeff watched from the lodge. Friday night, Patty and I checked on the boys. We knocked on the door. No answer. We waited and knocked again. The door opened and a girl holding a mascara applicator stood inside the doorway.

"The maids are here!" she shouted, turning her head away from us.

I looked at Patty and smiled, "Did you bring the vacuum?"

"No, and I don't have my broom either," she replied, laughing. "I didn't know girls were coming too."

"Neither did I," I replied.

The girl turned around toward us, still standing in the doorway.

"I'm sorry," I said, "but I'm Mrs. Hayes. Are Jeff and John Jr. here?"

"Oh, hi, Mrs. Hayes! I'm so sorry; come in."

The next day, Jason and I went swimming at the athletic club. It was nice to spend time with Jason. Later, we all went to Waterville's small village to shop while we waited for the lighting of the Christmas tree. We met up with Jeff and Mike, who had just come from the ice skating rink. Jeff didn't skate, with his low counts and fatigue, he couldn't do anything strenuous. After the lighting of the Christmas tree, we all gathered together in our condo for a wonderful pasta dinner. It was so nice to have everyone together in this winter wonderland.

CHAPTER 39

They Play for Coach Curtis and Jeff

THE SANDWICH HIGH School Blue Knights hockey team opened the 2006/07 hockey season against neighboring Barnstable, a Division I team. The Blue Knights hung Jeff's number twelve jersey behind the bench and laced up their skates with their teammate Jeff on their minds; his designated seat in the locker room remained empty. Senior and close friend, John Lessard and his brother Garrett, Casey Helms, Craig and his brother, Connor LaRocco, and Bryan Bolton, along with the all the Blue Knights varsity team, played with heart and motivation, not just for Jeff but with a new inspiration: their Coach Derackk Curtis had been diagnosed with a brain tumor.

John Lessard scored midway through the first period with a blast assisted by Craig LaRocco. The Barnstable Red Raiders came back to tie the game, but John's younger brother, Garrett put Sandwich back on top, assisted by Connor LaRocco. With less than two minutes left in the second period, John picked up his second goal of the game with assists from Ryan Williamson and Garrett. Craig teamed up with Bryan Bolton to score just seventeen seconds later. It was now 4–1. Adding to the game's emotional load for Sandwich's Assistant Coach, Jordan Mohre, was the fact that he was facing his old high school coach, Scott Nickerson.

Andrew George made it 6–1 on an assist from John Lessard. Barnstable slipped their second goal past Sandwich's goalie, Kevin Desmarais, ending the second period. Casey Helms, who was named one of the team captains prior to the game, then "put on a show," according to *Cape Cod Times* columnist Dan Crowley, beating Barnstable twice in the third period to collect a hat trick. Coach Mohre was quoted in the article, "Casey created both of those goals on his own. Casey stuck with the puck and wasn't going to settle for anything except seeing that puck in the net. Casey leads by example."

The victory was special for the Blue Knights, the article read. With thoughts of Jeff Hayes and Coach Curtis on their minds all night, being able to open the season in this way meant a great deal to the team. "This was just a special game," Mohre said. "This was for Derackk and Jeff. We found out about Derackk the Thursday before the game. We took it pretty hard, but we have a lot to play for. Jeff is still battling. The kids draw a lot from Jeff's strength. We'd love to have them both here."

Jeff sat at home, and when I told him the news about Coach Curtis, he picked his cell phone and dialed his coach's number.

Coach Curtis had surgery the following Monday. His tumor was benign.

CHAPTER 40

The Christmas Season, Eleventh Treatment, November 2005

JEFF AND I headed up to Boston, still anticipating that a cure was within reach, hoping there were no more tumors. Jeff still presented no severe side effects and looked and felt the same after this two-day treatment.

When we returned home, he chose not to take all the antinausea meds and drove to see his friends. Hockey and the chance to play again was all Jeff thought about.

During the second week of the cycle, we received an invitation for a weekend retreat for Jeff and me at a resort hotel on the Cape for kids battling cancer. Jeff wanted to be with his friends, so Jason accompanied me. Friday night on our way to the resort, we stopped at the Christmas Tree Shop in Yarmouth and bought a large red basket and enough Christmas ornaments to fill it. In our hotel room, we wrapped all the ornaments and placed them in the basket to bring with Jeff and me when we returned to the JFC. My husband joined us on Saturday morning, and we met other parents and kids battling cancer and received a gift from the sponsors of the retreat. We swam in the indoor pool during the day, and then Jason left with John; I stayed. John dropped Jason at his friend Casey Rutherford's house at the end of our street and then returned alone to the retreat.

"What are you watching?" John lay beside me. I was under the covers, propped up on the bed with all the pillows, staring at the television but not watching.

"Give me one of those pillows, will you!" he pulled one out from under my head.

"Where's Jeff? Is he okay?" I asked.

"He's staying at the Tomasinis' house. Angelo said he could wear a pair of his pajamas."

I laughed, thinking of Angelo and Jeff wearing his pajamas. "Are they okay watching him? That's a lot to ask of them, don't you think?"

"Jeff said he was feeling fine. I thought it would be good for him to get out of the house."

"Well, he's past the low counts; I guess it's okay. I don't know. I kind of feel a little irresponsible leaving them to watch him. They might be uncomfortable and worry that something may happen." I began to feel guilty.

"Angelo will call us if Jeff feels sick," John replied. "Jeff needs to be with his friends. Don't worry."

"I know, but I'll wonder whether he's okay, and I'll think about it all night."

"Want a glass of wine?" he offered.

"Sure. I got some Michelob Ultra Lights, too," I said.

The colder temperatures had forced us to forget the warmth of summer and the beauty of autumn. On the Cape, the trees were bare and the sky gray. It didn't feel like Christmas. The television ads gave me advance notice of how many shopping days left till Christmas. John Jr. and Jason were spending Christmas with my family in Colorado and staying at my sister's house in Denver.

Jeff and I drove to Boston for the next treatment—two more to go, but this was the last of the five-day treatments. We entered the JFC. I carried the large red basket filled with small wrapped ornaments. Jeff and I said hello to all the nurses, and after Jeff was weighed in and his vitals were taken, he and I made our way to his bed by the window. I placed the basket on the long, horizontal, adjustable table above Jeff's bed. I was happy to give each nurse a gift. They seemed excited. Everyone should feel appreciated and receive a gift at Christmas. Each wrapped ornament was different. Hannah asked if she could have another for her daughter, while Sam, who was Jewish, declined his. Jeff gave Hannah a Cape Cod hooded sweatshirt for Christmas and Sam a Sandwich High navy-blue hooded hockey sweatshirt.

Jeff felt relieved. His body was a bit worn from the chemo but his spirits were good. The three tiny pin-sized spots in his lungs had disappeared, and by now the radiation treatment and chemo should have killed any cancer cells that remained. The end of treatment was within reach, and he had made it through this year without most of the side effects the doctors had warned us about. He complained of nothing and tolerated mouth sores and fatigue. He had missed some of the school year, times with his friends, and his greatest love, hockey.

When Jeff was hydrated, the antinausea drugs were administered, followed by the chemo drugs. Even after of all these cycles, the sickness never became less; the drugs were still strong as they entered into Jeff's system once again. His skin color immediately changed to a sickly greenish yellow, and he closed his eyes and rested his head back on his pillow. Even with the knowledge that this was his last five-day treatment and the last time he'd take these drugs, he still had to endure it.

Jeff's treatment had started late, and it was dark outside when we got him into his wheelchair and headed for Children's, the basket of wrapped ornaments, along with everything else, in his lap.

At Seven West, we waited in the hallway for a bed until we were told that Jeff's room was at the end of the hall, the last room, a room we had never seen before. I was pleasantly surprised to see that it looked like a hotel room. Jeff's bed was a double bed on the far side of the room, near the window. His television was encased in a wooden cabinet, not above his bed. There was a couch, an end table, and a coffee table in the room. Across from the coffee table was another large wooden cabinet that encased another television, a refrigerator, and a microwave. I helped Jeff into his bed and gave him the remote, and then I walked out of the room. From the hall, I called Hannah. I wanted to thank her for this different and wonderful private room. When she answered, I thanked her for the room, she responded, "It's the end-of-life room."

I was stunned. "Oh," I said and quickly ended the call.

Thoughts that I never let enter my mind now consumed me. I was terrified when I walked back into the room. Then I rationalized, thinking this must be the only room available.

Jeff lay in the double bed. I saw the relief and excitement in him with the privacy we were afforded in this room, for whatever reason. Suddenly, I realized why the bed was a double. I sat down on the couch, unable to move. It became late. My cell phone rang, and I pushed Ignore.

Jeff's nurses changed throughout the week, and we gave them each a wrapped ornament from the red basket.

Watching a Bruins game, Jeff would ask, "What's the score?" but then fall back asleep.

Each morning when the chemo was administered, Jeff would sleep most of the day. At night family would visit. I would go for walks during the week. The lobby was filled with homemade Christmas crafts and jewelry for sale. An enormous, beautifully decorated Rockefeller Center–style Christmas tree stood in the center of the lobby. People came and went all day long. It seemed like the beginning of a movie. I watched and wondered what their stories were. Why were they here? Let me tell you my story, I thought. There is good news of children overcoming disease, repairing broken bones, or going home with the hope of a cure for whatever may have afflicted them. At night, the flood of patients, family, doctors, and nurses lessened. Security guards manned the desk and sectioned off the lobby, stopping anyone entering, giving each visitor a name tag, and checking the computer for the name of the patient being visited.

One night, too restless to sleep, I left Seven West and walked to the lobby. I looked up as I sat alone. I could not see the guard station or the closed gates of Au Bon Pain. I felt like I was sitting on center stage. The theater was quiet. There were no voices. The room was dark, with one dim light shining on me. I had no fear. There were no sounds or voices or disease to scare me. Time had stopped. It was dreamlike. Then the revolving doors to the lobby opened, and a cool breeze fell upon me and brought me back to the reality of Jeff's disease.

I got up and walked toward the elevator and wondered whether Gismo would be there when the elevator doors opened. Maybe I could talk him into having a drink with me at the Longwood Grille.

CHAPTER 41

The Last Cycles, Results, Lung Surgery, December 2005

A FTER JEFF RECOVERED from the second week of this last five-day cycle, he started to travel with the hockey team and keep the stats on the game. He would occupy his seat in the locker room before a home game. No one else was allowed to sit in his designated spot when he wasn't there; the players wouldn't allow it.

Jeff had gone through the treatment amazingly well. We wouldn't know until the scans were done after this last treatment whether the chemo had destroyed all the cancer, every last cell. There were no signs, and no tests had been done since after the fourth treatment in April to prove otherwise. Jeff and I were anxious for this last treatment to end.

We entered the JFC for the last time; nothing was different, and Jeff followed the normal routine. He was weighted in and his vitals were taken. His blood counts were high enough to receive the treatment. He walked through the double doors, entered his room, and walked over to his bed by the window. Sam came in to examine Jeff and wish him a Merry Christmas. "Jeff, I was jogging down Longwood Avenue the other day, and every time I passed someone on the sidewalk, they backed off when they read the front of my sweatshirt, *SANDWICH HOCKEY*."

Jeff laughed.

"I had to fight off my wife for the sweatshirt, too; she wanted to wear it."

After hydration, the premeds were administered, and then the IV with the three chemo drugs was pushed into Jeff's port. When it was time to go to Children's, Hannah stopped me and asked, "What are your plans for Christmas?" I told her that my other two sons were going to Colorado for Christmas. They were flying out on Christmas Day. She placed her hand on my arm. "Don't have too much family together with you over the holidays, as the news of Jeff's scans may not be good."

I looked back at her, startled again. I didn't know what to say. I was worrying now more than I had in the first eleven months with the recent not-so-subtle hints from Hannah. It was getting harder to shield myself from the fear of losing my son, but I knew I had to. I loved him too much to allow myself to think of anything but him beating the disease.

Jeff was out in the waiting room and was not able to hear Hannah. I said good-bye and walked away from her, pushing open the door to the waiting room. Jeff sat in his wheelchair parked next to the reception counter.

The anticipation of the results became much more frightening. If they came back without any signs of more tumors, then Jeff would be tested every six months, then every year until year five. Even after this year with clear scans, he would face periodic tests and fear the results each time. That would be his life, the fear of relapse or a secondary cancer from his radiation. It would be our fear for the rest of his life. I was beginning to think that hope was futile with a cancer this relentless, no, stop, I thought again, I'm keeping hope in my back pocket.

Early Christmas morning we opened our gifts. Jeff stayed at home while John and I drove John Jr. and Jason to Logan Airport for their trip to Colorado. John Jr. was a very talented snowboarder and was looking forward to snowboarding in the high mountains. I spoke with him later that day. My brothers and sisters and nieces and nephews had played football in the open field behind my sister Marianne's house. It was seventy-four degrees on Christmas Day; the snow-topped mountains were hundreds of miles away.

John, Jeff, and I had Christmas dinner with John's family. That night, Jeff and I watched a movie together on the couch in our living room. It was quiet and peaceful. He was tired and content to be in the comfort of his home without a room filled with relatives.

The scans were scheduled during the week between Christmas and New Year's. Jeff's lungs were x-rayed, and a bone scan was done. After New Year's Day, Sam called and asked us to come up to Children's for the results. Jeff and I drove up to Boston to meet with Sam. He asked us to meet him upstairs behind the lobby at Children's Hospital in the small auditorium designed for young children. We sat in child-sized chairs at the back of the large and spacious children's auditorium above the tall tree still decorated for the holidays. I wasn't sure why we met there. People walked by us, and some stopped to sit in the large theater-style room. Sam sat down with Jeff and me.

"We saw a small tumor in the x-ray we took of your lungs," he said. "After fourteen cycles of the most powerful drugs we could give Jeff for his size and weight, to see a small tumor at this time is not good. It had managed to evade treatment." He continued, "There is nothing else we can do for you."

Frozen with the fear of losing Jeff, I stared back at him. This couldn't be the end. Jeff had done so well the entire year. What had happened? The lungs were clear in April.

"Can we do a lung transplant?" I asked. "Can we enter into a clinical trial? We must keep trying!"

Sam thought quietly for a moment. Then he said, "Let me see if I can find a surgeon right away to remove the tumor, and then we'll try to get Jeff into a clinical trial." I began to thaw, sitting in the child's chair. We needed to try everything to save his life, I thought, and we need to start now.

"I'll see what we can do," Sam said. "I'll call you later." He stood up and walked toward the elevator.

Jeff was quiet. I could only imagine the fear he felt. Why did Sam think that we'd give up that easily, that we wouldn't search for more treatment? I was certain we'd find a trial that Jeff would respond to. We had to.

I called Hannah. She said, "Sam came to see me this morning. He told me he'd seen a small tumor in Jeff's lung, and we just stood there in the hall, staring at each other, not saying a word for a very long time."

On Thursday of that week, Sam called me. Excitedly he said, "I have a surgeon, one of the best from Children's Hospital, to remove Jeff's tumor on Monday, January 11th."

The news spread fast. Soon everyone knew that a tumor had withstood the yearlong treatment and that Jeff would have surgery within a week to remove it. If he was frightened of the surgery, he didn't let on. He was accustomed to hospital surroundings and had been in surgery before when his port was inserted into his chest. He didn't speak about the relapse.

John, Jeff, and I drove up to Boston Monday morning for the surgery. After preop, we hugged Jeff and wished him luck. He was then wheeled into the operating room. John and I sat in the waiting room. A woman in a closed-door glass cubicle took phone calls from nurses reporting on surgeries that were being performed throughout the morning. We watched as she passed along news to families that were waiting. Our wait was long. We were told before surgery that what they thought was a tumor might turn out to be scar tissue. It wasn't likely, but we hoped for that news. After several hours, a nurse told us the surgery had gone well and that the surgeon would be up shortly to see us. When Jeff's surgeon arrived in his scrubs, we went into a small room down the hall to discuss what he had discovered.

It was a tumor.

Jeff recovered from surgery on Seven West for the rest of the week. He had a tube in his lungs for drainage. It protruded out through his chest.

Later in the week, another surgeon came to remove the tube. She explained the procedure to Jeff and me as she, two nurses, and another doctor stood beside his bed. As they prepped Jeff for the procedure, she warned Jeff that the removal would be uncomfortable, if not painful.

When she pulled the tube out, Jeff had no reaction, as if he didn't feel a thing. They watched in amazement, waiting for Jeff to react. They praised him for his bravery and began to bandage the small opening. They quickly cleaned up, and when they were done, they swiftly left the room, on their way, it seemed, to perform another procedure. I followed the doctor to the nurse's station. I looked into her eyes as we stood facing each other. She said, "What we just did to your son is a very painful procedure, and he remained stoic throughout the entire process when we would have expected him to cry out. He is truly remarkable."

"Do most patients react from the pain?" I asked.

"All patients do," she answered.

"Oh," I said, looking at her but thinking about Jeff. "Okay, thank you very much. I'm going back to his room. Thanks." I left the nurse's station, and she left the floor. We never saw her again. I went back to be with Jeff. He was watching television. I sat down next to his bed in awe of his strength, courage and resiliency.

The tumor was removed successfully, and Jeff was recovering well. His hair was slowly growing back, and Sam was working on getting Jeff into a new clinical trial with different drugs. After a week at Children's, we returned home. Jeff spent time with the hockey team, going to games and hoping that he might get back onto the ice to play. He continued to take Bactrim to protect him from pneumonia. Time was critical. We didn't know whether Ewing's would show up again in Jeff's lungs, so he needed to start combating his disease again and as soon as possible. Jeff was not on chemotherapy, so he wasn't experiencing sickness and low blood counts. He felt stronger and started to look normal. His facial hair grew back.

Jeff and I went back to the JFC to meet with Sam and another doctor who specialized in chemotherapy drugs, Susie Sherman. She was an expert on the use of different chemotherapy drug combinations. She and Sam discussed drug combinations that might be effective against Ewing's. Jeff would receive the treatment at the clinic but follow the regimen dictated in the clinical trial. The treatment in this clinical trial required us to follow the protocol and report Jeff's progress as a participant. Jeff would follow this trial for several weeks before scans would be taken to measure his progress.

At home, our friends, our family, and Jeff's friends watched and waited for word of his progress and what would happen next. The chemotherapy drugs in this clinical trial were not as strong as the previous drugs, and the protocol wasn't as rigid, so Jeff wouldn't be bedridden. He would still experience the nausea and low blood counts, but the side effects would not be as severe.

Sam gave Jeff permission to skate during practice. He wanted Jeff to get out there and do what he loved. Jeff was going to skate in the upcoming Canal Cup.

OUTSIDE THE LINES WITH
Connor Green
Dan Crowley, the columnist, asks, "Who has been your inspiration?"

My inspiration has been and will always will be my dear friend Jeff Hayes. The way he carried himself on and off the ice, in and out of therapy, has inspired me to perform at my fullest and give it my all, every single time. Jeff is a hero in my heart, who I often look to for guidance and help. Just picturing his smile and laughter at his most difficult times of pain has highly influenced me to perform my best but never forget to smile. He has taught me a significant lesson that no matter what you do, give it one hundred percent, never lose focus and keep a positive attitude. I love you Jeff.

CHAPTER 42

Twenty-Seven Seconds, February 2006

I
T'S TRADITION. THE high school hockey team meets at the Sandwich British Beer Company restaurant for a steak dinner the night before the Canal Cup. Coach Derackk had recovered from his surgery and was back coaching the team.

Jeff sat at a table with his teammates in a private room in a corner of the restaurant.

"Jeff!" Coach Derackk shouted from his table after they'd eaten and while the players chattered among themselves, excited about the next day's big game. "Do you have a few words for the team?"

His teammates cheered, "Jeff Hayes! Jeff Hayes! Jeff Hayes!" egging him on to speak. Jeff's face turned from a pale, pasty look to an embarrassed red. Hesitantly, he stood up, looked around the room, trying to find the right words, and said, "Just win, boys."

Coach Derackk asked for more, pushing the envelope and hoping to get Jeff to speak. "What do you predict for the final score?" he asked.

Still standing, Jeff replied, "Seven to one." The team let out a romping cheer.

Jeff smiled and sat down. His teammates sitting at his table patted him on the back, knocking him slightly over his half-eaten dinner.

On Saturday morning, the day of the Canal Cup, Jeff returned from a team breakfast.

"How are you feeling, honey?" I asked.

"I'm okay," he said.

"Ready for the interview?"

"I'm ready, Mom."

Tracy Jan from the *Boston Globe* had driven down from Boston that morning to meet Jeff at home before the game. Jeff's friends were at our house, sitting with Jeff, also there to answer her questions. Tracy sat next to Jeff. He looked pretty tired.

"So, how many guys are on the ice at the same time?" she asked.

"Five." He then quickly followed up with, "Five, plus the goalie for each team." I thought, maybe I should give him some pain meds just for the interview.

Tracy asked Jeff about the big game tonight and about his battle with cancer. All she had to do was look around the room to see the story of Jeff's life, including his achievements and championships: trophies, plaques, and awards filled his room.

I heard the door from the kitchen to the basement open and foot-steps coming down the stairs. It was Nancy Helms.

"Hi, Jeff," Nancy said. Realizing she had interrupted the interview, she apologized for her intrusion. She was carrying Jeff's shoulder pads and showed me where she had sewn more padding in the front shoulder to protect Jeff's port.

"Wow, Nance, that looks great! Thank you!" I said.

"I can't stay," she said. "I've got a lot to do before the game. I'll see you later."

"Good luck, Jeff!" she said as she headed back up the stairs.

The Boston *Globe* reporter walked around Jeff's small apartment with John and me. She tried to learn as much as she could about Jeff. She stayed for an hour and then drove back up to Boston; she wasn't able to stay for the game.

Jeff left for Gallo Ice Arena to meet up with his teammates. We saw him there before the start of the varsity game. I watched him from the other end of the ice. He stood with his friends, half-dressed from his waist down in the Sandwich High hockey uniform, watching the end of the JV game, his jersey no longer hanging behind the bench.

I thought about the coldness of the rink and wondered whether Jeff would be warm standing at ice level. I worried about the possibility of his loss of coordination, a side effect from the chemotherapy. It had been only three weeks since his lung surgery. It had been over a year since he'd played a game.

I chose to watch the game from inside the manager's office. John stood at ice level, along the boards with our friends.

The rink walls were blanketed with posters for players from both teams. Bourne and Sandwich alternated each year for the home and away benches. Sandwich was the home team this year.

The arena filled with students and spectators. Everyone knew Jeff was returning to the ice, and people came from near and far to see him. The excitement began to escalate as the JV game ended and the Zamboni left the ice.

I watched in anticipation as I had last year when Jeff was pushed out onto the ice in a wheelchair by his teammate and captain, Matt Doyle, during the all-star game. This year was different. Today, Jeff was bald, standing on his skates, and dressed in his team uniform. He was out of the wheelchair and ready to skate and play.

The music stopped, and the announcer welcomed the fans to the twenty-third start of the Canal Cup. The crowd roared as he called the Sandwich High Blue Knights and the Bourne Canalmen onto the ice. When the Sandwich locker room door opened, Jeff and his teammates walked through the blue and white balloons that towered above them and encircled the outside of the door. It was the entrance into the arena. They walked toward the gate and onto the ice.

Jeff was wearing his number twelve jersey with the letter *C* for Captain on the front shoulder. It was as if he'd never missed a stride when he stepped out onto the ice with his team.

The crowded chanted, "Jeff Hayes, Jeff Hayes, Jeff Hayes, you amaze!" as he and the Sandwich Blue Knights and the Bourne Canalmen skated around the rink and began shooting on their goalies.

I watched him skate beautifully around the net and up to the blue line for shooting practice. I couldn't imagine how he found the strength. This was his night!

The teams ended their warm-up and lined up alongside the net as the announcer called the Sandwich senior players to center ice. He then called out Jeff Hayes. With his helmet in one hand and his stick in the other, Jeff skated to center ice to another deafening roar and a standing ovation.

"Jeff, Hayes, Jeff Hayes, Jeff Hayes!"

Players from both teams slammed their sticks on the ice. I imagined a few tears flowed from the packed crowd; I could feel them as I looked out from the manager's office and into the stands. Jeff stood there, smiling but humbled by the cheers from the crowd. The announcer continued, and the crowd settled down to hear Bourne's team announced. Each player skated to center ice. The national anthem was sung.

I learned after the game that the Bourne coach had told his team not to touch Jeff, not to go near him. The teams lined up for the face-off at center ice, and the puck was dropped. The Sandwich center won the face-off and directed the puck to Jeff. As he received the pass, he started to move his feet while handling the puck, but lost his balance and went down on the ice. The crowd fell silent. I thought every mother in the stands must have been reaching for her cell phone to dial 911, except for me. I'd seen him overcome so much during his treatment with amazing resilience, never faltering. I knew he was okay; he was always okay.

Jeff got up so quickly it was as if he hadn't fallen.

Coach Derackk shouted, "Hayes, off the ice! Hayes, off the ice! Jeff Hayes, off the ice!"

Jeff didn't want to leave the ice and resisted, staying in the game, but he couldn't ignore his coach for very long. Finally he skated to the gate and sat on the bench. His coach turned to him and asked, "So how was it?"

"Great, Coach!"

Twenty-seven seconds was all he had that night. He had waited for one long year to get back onto the ice, and he did it without letting on how much physical strength it took to skate and do it in front of thousands of people.

Jeff remained on the bench for the rest of the game, laughing with his teammates and happy to be there.

Sandwich lost the game.

I waited for Jeff outside the locker room while the spectators left the arena.

When he appeared from the locker room, I asked him how he felt.

"I'm hungry and have a headache," was all he said.

What I was thinking and wanted to say to him was that it had only been three weeks since his lung surgery and that he wasn't in condition to play. But I couldn't. He had spent yesterday morning in Boston for a blood transfusion so that he could play in tonight's game. The headache, I thought, was from pushing himself too hard.

At the restaurant, Bob Corradi, the athletic director of Massachusetts Maritime Academy and the coach of the Post 188 baseball team, approached Jeff. He coached a select team of baseball players during the summer months and knew of Jeff's battle. His son was a great athlete and had played hockey and baseball for Sandwich High years ago. His son wore the number twelve.

"I was very proud of you tonight," Coach Corradi said. Jeff stood up and shook his hand. "Thanks, Mr. Corradi," he replied. He wished Jeff good luck with his treatment and talked a bit to those at the table and then left, returning to his table. I knew how Jeff hoped to play baseball for Coach Corradi someday. You had to play hard and be the best at your position to be chosen to play for the Post 188 team.

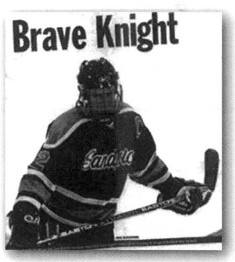

The *Cape Cod Sunday Times* sports page headline read in large letters, "Brave Knight" above a picture of Jeff skating in his Blue Knights uniform. Behind his face guard, you could see his wide smile and his eyes looking out at the crowd. Twenty-seven seconds doesn't sound like much time. But for Jeff it was twenty-seven seconds born from courage, determination, and the desire to reach a goal that had nothing to do with winning or losing a hockey game.

Tracy's article appeared in the Sunday *Boston Globe*.

CHAPTER 43

—— ❦ ——

Kathy Grant, High School Nurse

A T SCHOOL, JEFF spent hours during the day with Kathy Grant and Debbie Lynch, the school nurses. They tried to help him manage the side effects and give him a place to go when he felt weak and tired. When I was at work, away from him, I'd worry.

"Hi, Kathy. This is Mrs. Hayes." I said when connected to the nurse's office. "I'm just worried about Jeff and how he's been feeling at school. I worry about his tiredness and his low blood counts. I worry about him picking up some germ that might make him more sick."

"He comes to see us a lot. We talk about things, not just how he's feeling certain days but about his cancer. I tell him, 'Jeff, we have a lot of hope, because we know that Ewing's is treatable.' I know he thinks about this, so I give him hope. I told him last year, I said, 'It's going to be one bad year, but we're going to get you through this; you're going to be okay. You're going to come out on the other side of this, after a horrific year of chemotherapy, surgery, and radiation, and be okay. You'll have tutors and home schooling to help you with school work.'"

"What did he say?" I asked.

"Well, mostly he smiles, but he also makes it look easier than it is. I think he feels weak a lot of the time. Recently, we talked again after the tumor was seen after Christmas. I told him, 'You know, Jeff, you have this one spot, but the chemo will probably get it, and we'll continue to fight this.'"

"I'm so glad he can come to you and that he feels comfortable talking with you," I replied. "He keeps all this from me. He's quiet and doesn't react while I'm with him, so I don't know how he's feeling or what he's thinking."

"Well," she continued, "there are days when Jeff comes into our office very sick with mouth sores and very weak and fatigued, and we put him at a desk in the back office with all his work. It's private there, and he's away from any germs. I worry about his health and his white blood count. We'd always joke. 'You go sit back there!' When I'd go back there to check on him I'd say, 'Jeff, are you okay?' and he'd smile. That smile, it's a smile that radiates a room. He would grin, ear to ear with his big eyes, and say, 'I'm good, Mrs. Grant.'

'Do you need water?' I'd ask.

'No, I'm fine, Mrs. Grant.' He'd pause and then say, "I'm hot, though. I think I'll take off my hat and show my bald head.'

"The kids have had several hat days for him," Kathy said. "Did you know that? All of the kids wear a hat on Fridays. It's a school rule that hats are not allowed, but Jeff is exempt from that rule, and on Fridays, so are all the students."

"Really! I didn't know that. He never told me."

"Yes, they do. They all wear hats." She paused and there was silence for a moment. "Jeff is the silent rock of the class. He's a strong kid, an athlete, and he has a lot of friends. He's done a lot of things to help the class and reached out a lot. He's a wonderful person."

I listened, trying to imagine him walking through the halls, talking to his friends and shielding them from his pain.

"He has this whole spreading of friends, and when they see what he's been through, and with such dignity and such grace, he gains even more friends. Kids say to me, "Mrs. Grant, I didn't know Jeff Hayes before, but I knew him when he got sick, and I've seen him in class and in the cafeteria, and I just can't believe how well he's done."

"You see, I don't know any of this," I remarked. Then I thought about the students. I had to ask her about Sam. "Did you get any feedback from the students after Dr. Blackman's presentation? What did they say? How did they feel about him?"

"Oh, gosh, Mrs. Hayes. Dr. Blackman spoke to those kids on their level, and he spoke to them as adults. His message was incredible."

We both took a long breath, and there was silence on the line until she spoke again.

"You're probably aware of Jeff's faith in God, but I…" She paused. "I asked him one day, 'Jeff, I noticed the cross you wear around your neck. Do you have faith in God and pray that he is with you?' He looked right at me and said, 'Absolutely, I have great faith in God, and I believe he is with me all the time.'"

"The gold cross and chain were a gift from a friend we refer to as Jeff's Uncle Chuck," I replied. "Chuck isn't related to us. He's a close friend and very close to Jeff. When Jeff was first diagnosed, Chuck gave him the cross; it was his father's. You know, Kathy, Jeff and I never talk about God; I'm glad you did. Sometimes I wonder." I paused. "I pray like the dickens for God's mercy with this disease, but I keep that private and only pray alone. I think it might frighten Jeff, if he saw me praying."

"Yes, yes, I understand," she replied.

The subject changed, and Kathy talked more about Jeff's days at school. I knew so much about what Jeff went through at the JFC and Children's and at home, but so little about his time at school.

"Everybody sees Jeff's smile. He has a presence about him of calmness, of peace, of strength, and of compassion for others. It isn't just about Jeff. He doesn't make it about himself. He's very humble. He really wanted to make it about other people, even when he got to skate on the ice for twenty-seven seconds; it was all about his team. Everything is about other people. It's not a normal way of thinking for teenagers, let alone how society thinks. A teenager's growth and development is narcissistic, so we expect that from a teen, but Jeff isn't like that. He isn't your average teenager saying, 'It's about me.' It's really all about other people with him. It's so rare. I've been working with teens for twelve years, and it's all about them, which is perfectly normal growth and development for teens, but not with Jeff. And kids see that in him. Another student said to me, 'I don't know Jeff, but I know what a hero he is.'

"I always ask him every time I see him, 'How are you today?' And he replies, 'I want to try to get through today.' He is able to always live for today. 'When I get through today, then I'll see about tomorrow.' But he never frets about tomorrow. 'I'm going to try today to be who I am,' he says."

"You know," I replied, "he battles this disease with such maturity that I'm always amazed."

"Yes, Mrs. Hayes, you're right. And he has a really great sense of humor. He has a fun, dry sense of humor, so we joke a lot. I'd say, 'We're going to get through today,' and he'd say, 'Who cares about tomorrow.' And then there's that smile again."

"Last year I remember talking to all the hockey players. It was during the winter when some of them came down with whooping cough. I told them, 'If you don't feel well, don't go to practice, and stay away from Jeff.' The players were wonderful. They backed down, and I remember telling them that this could kill Jeff, and it could. If he got whooping cough, he could die. They looked at me and said, 'We didn't realize that, Mrs. Grant.'"

Her words "could kill him" passed through my veins like ice water.

"Do you know how much he loves you?" she asked me. "He wants to protect you, and he said, 'You don't have to tell her this right now, Mrs. Grant.' He wants to be strong for his mother."

Oh, God, I thought. He doesn't have to be strong for me.

"Well, I'd better get back to things here at school. Don't worry, Mrs. Hayes. If he needs anything, we'll take care of him. I'll call you if I feel something's up."

"Thank you so much, Kathy. You've been so great to Jeff. You talk about the hard stuff with him, things that are too difficult for me, and I thank you."

"Oh, please don't worry, Mrs. Hayes. We love him too."

Cape Cod Times

On Tuesday, February 7, 2006, the front page of the *Cape Cod Times* read, "Cape to Pursue Cape Cancer Study: Unusual Pattern of Childhood Carcinoma Cases Is Found in Southeastern Sandwich." The story by staff writer Robin Lord was as follows:

> SANDWICH—An in-depth study of cancer rates in children on the Upper Cape will be launched in the upcoming weeks after state health officials found elevated rates of the disease in the southeastern section of Sandwich.
>
> "In this particular case, it deserves a follow up," said Suzanne Condon, Assistant Commissioner of the State Department of Public Health. But she stopped short of saying there is a cancer cluster in that area of town. "We choose to take a more cautious approach—what we've elected to call this is an unusual pattern," Condon said.

Concerned Parents

> The study that led to the report released yesterday began in 2004 after concerned parents contacted county and state officials about the unusual number of childhood cases they were seeing in town. Researchers found that from 1995 to 2002, 10 children were diagnosed with five different types of cancer, as opposed to 7.5 children that would be expected based on the state average. According to the town Website, Sandwich has about 22,000 residents.
>
> In its study, the department took a cursory look at data from several areas of environmental concerns in town, including toxic chemicals flowing in the aquifer from the Massachusetts Military Reservation and microwaves emitted by the Air Force's PAVE PAWS radar station in Sagamore.

None of the plumes of toxic chemicals in the groundwater from the military reservation have affected the houses where the children with cancer are living, she said. And the houses are in the Sandwich census tract farthest from the PAVE PAWS facility.

Cape Cod Times

The very next day, February 8, 2006, the *Cape Cod Times* front-page headline read, "Sandwich Cancer Study 'Significant': Expert Says the State Seldom Launches In-Depth Reviews of Childhood Cancers." Again, the story was by staff writer Robin Lord.

SANDWICH—The state health department's decision to take a closer look at childhood cancer rates in Sandwich is "significant" on its own, according to a former state public health researcher. "It's pretty uncommon," said Dr. Richard Clapp, one of the founders of the Massachusetts Cancer Registry and now a professor of environmental health at Boston University School of Public Health. "If I was a parent in Sandwich, I would say, 'We were concerned and now it's clear we had a right to be concerned.'"

State public officials announced Monday they will launch an in-depth study of elevated rates of childhood cancer cases in the southeastern section of Sandwich.

The announcement came about 18 months after the department began a preliminary look at childhood cancer rates in town, which was prompted by concerned parents.

Jenny Condon, whose daughter was diagnosed in 2004 with a rare bone cancer, Ewing's sarcoma, said she is unsure how many answers the department can find by interviewing parents. "I know almost everything there is to know about Ewing's sarcoma and they have no idea what causes it. So, when they say they're going to do follow up work, what good is that going to do? she said.

Clapp, whose research interests include the health effects of dioxin, radiation and environmental exposures to toxic chemicals, disagreed with Condon's pessimism. He said if state researchers are alert to potential risk factors during the interviews, important new information could be found.

"It's like the 'white elephant' in your living room that no one wants to talk about," said a father of two children who lives in Forestdale. "It's the military base and until someone can stand up to the government, the families and kids will continue to pay the price."

The state has not pointed to any particular cause of the elevated cancer rates. In fact, they say none of the homes of the children with cancer are affected by the base pollution and tract 0135 is the farthest from the PAVE PAWs radar station.

Health officials plan to do a follow-up study by interviewing parents of children with cancer. Johnson-Staub, who is President of the Oak Ridge School Parent Teacher Association, a school at the center of the study's area, said like many parents she just wants more information as quickly as possible. "If we knew it was well water, we'd know what we could do," Johnson-Staub said. "We don't have anyone we can be angry at yet."

CHAPTER 44

First Clinical Study and Pan-Mass Challenge, February 2006

CLINICAL STUDY, PROTOCOL Title: Phase II Study of Sequential Gemcitabine Followed by Docetaxel for Recurrent Ewing's Sarcoma, Osteosarcoma or Locally Recurrent Chondrosarcoma (Other Bone Cancers).

Jeff started this clinical trial in February 2006. It would run for four weeks. These drugs weren't nearly as strong as those used in his first course of fourteen treatments. When the trial concluded, a chest x-ray was taken. Jeff, John, and I sat in the JFC waiting room to meet with Sam for the results of the clinical trial. We were quiet, sitting and waiting until one of the nurses asked us to follow her to a small examining room on the other side of the clinic. Sam entered the room and sat down on the round cushioned chair with wheels and slowly rolled himself over to Jeff. He looked up at Jeff and said, "Another small tumor has showed up in your lung." Jeff sat on the examining table, his sneakers untied and dangling above the clinic floor.

"Jeff, we won't be continuing in this trial because you're not responding to these drugs." He paused, looking for a reaction from Jeff, but Jeff just listened. "However, there is another trial. Hopefully, we will see a response from this new trial to reduce the spread of new tumors."

Sam discussed the drug combination and the protocol. He then brought Dr. Susie Sherman into the small examining room with us to give us her opinion on viable drug combinations that would be part of this new clinical trial. The only other obstacle was Blue Cross Blue

Shield. These drugs were $10,000 a dosage. This was the only phone call I had to make to BCBS during Jeff's treatment. Our case manager questioned the drugs, and I referred her to Sam; they were approved immediately after they spoke.

On the first day of treatment with these new drugs, Jeff was given the same antinausea drugs, Zofran, Ativan, Marinol, and the patch for both trials, as they worked well during the first standard fourteen-cycle treatment. He never stopped taking Bactrim. He began the prescribed treatment. My husband was with us this time, and Jeff lay in the bed next to the window at the JFC. The curtain was closed between his bed and the bed next to his. I heard another patient arrive and settle into her bed. Her parents were with her. I recognized the mother's voice.

"Jeff, do you want anything from CVS?" I asked. "Dad, need anything?"

"No, I'm good," John replied. "Are you coming right back?"

"No, I think I'll go the movies while I'm here. There's got to be a theater somewhere in Brookline." I paused. "What do you think? Of course I'll be right back." I knew he was nervous.

"Well, I never know with you," he replied.

"Jeff, anything you need, honey?"

"No thanks."

As I walked away from Jeff's bed, I saw Mr. and Mrs. Young sitting next to their daughter's bed. I'd recognized the voice, but when I saw Mrs. Young, I knew I'd met her before, but where? I stopped and turned back to John and whispered, "John, I think I know the people right next to us. I think they're from the Cape."

"Is it the Young's?" he asked. "They're here with Holly, I imagine."

"Yes, that's who it is! How do you know that?" I asked.

"I'd heard a teenager from Dennis was battling cancer. I think it's Ewing's too."

"Wow, you're kidding."

Dennis is a small town twenty-five miles down Cape from Sandwich. Holly was diagnosed the week after her nineteenth birthday during final exam week amid her first semester at the University of New Hampshire. She had started experiencing pain in her leg six months earlier and had attributed it to running in the sand while training for lifeguard competition. Holly was quite an athlete. She had played volleyball for four years at Dennis-Yarmouth High School and had also played for the Cape Cod Juniors, Pilgrim, and Coastal volleyball clubs. She was named to the Massachusetts Girls Volleyball Coaches Association's First Team and was given the *Boston Globe* and *Boston Herald* All Scholastic Award. She led the Coastal Region team to the gold medal in the Bay State Games and was a redshirt freshman on the UNH volleyball team when diagnosed.

"Hi, I'm Susan Hayes and this is my husband, John," I said. "We're from the Cape."

"Jeff is fighting Ewing's sarcoma," John said.

Bernie seemed surprised. "So is Holly!"

"There have been two other cases in Sandwich within the past couple years too," I explained.

"Really," he replied. "We were introduced to Jordan Leandre and his family early in Holly's treatment because the nurses thought we were both from Dennis. I don't know if you knew that, but Jordan has Ewing's as well."

"Yes, I knew," John replied.

"Knowing how rare Ewing's sarcoma is, I thought it strange that two people living less than two miles apart were being treated for the same disease at the same time, and now Jeff and two other cases in Sandwich." He shook his head and continued. "I'm an educated and experienced research scientist. I'm used to gathering and analyzing data; this is very interesting and alarming."

We agreed. Hannah entered the room, and we excused ourselves and returned to Jeff's bedside. I abandoned my walk to CVS. I couldn't stop thinking about what was causing this rare cancer. Was a cluster forming?

While Jeff was recovering from the new combination of drugs, I received an e-mail from Sam. He told me that the Boston Bruins were looking for a Pedal Partner for the Pan-Mass Challenge. A Pedal Partner is a pediatric oncology cancer patient, usually a young child, whom the nurses and doctors at the JFC try to match with a rider or a team of riders.

Once chosen, the Pedal Partner becomes the PMC team's inspiration. The riders learn about their Pedal Partner's disease and their personal struggles; it gives them motivation and incentive to ride and raise money for the Jimmy Fund. It is the largest athletic fundraiser in the country.

Billy Starr, along with thirty five other riders, started the PMC thirty-six years ago. Billy's mother passed away in 1974 from cancer. Today, there are six thousand riders. The 192-mile bike ride begins in Sturbridge, a town in central Massachusetts, and ends in Provincetown at the tip of Cape Cod. It takes place the first weekend in August. At the end of the first day, the riders pedal into the Massachusetts Maritime Academy campus in Bourne to rest for the night. At four thirty on Sunday morning, they rise for a quick breakfast and start the route from Bourne to Provincetown, weaving their way through the several small towns of Cape Cod.

When Sam received an e-mail from a representative of the Boston Bruins inquiring about a cancer patient, he immediately thought of Jeff.

"This is the first year that the Boston Bruins Foundation will ride in the PMC," Sam wrote in his e-mail.

Sam was a spinning instructor and a mountain biker before his fellowship began. He was aware of the magnitude of the event and the impact this fundraiser had on the Jimmy Fund. He was also riding in the PMC this year.

My mind began to race with thoughts of how pairing Jeff and the Boston Bruins PMC team would be an enormous boost at a time when it appeared he was losing the battle against Ewing's. Sam wrote, "Please don't tell Jeff. I'd like to ask him."

Anyone partial to the game of hockey can say, "Yeah, I like the Bruins; I'm from Boston." Not Jeff. He belongs to a die-hard fan club that watches every game regardless of the Bruins' standings in their league. His love for the team and the game is not influenced by me, nor by his grandfather or his uncles. He was born with that gene, the hockey gene. He was born to play. In his first-grade school picture, he's wearing a Bruins black-and-gold sweatsuit with the Bruins round logo on the right side of the jacket's chest. He is smiling, sitting in the center of the class picture. The Bruins are his team, no doubt, I thought, but he'll be humble and shy when he's asked to be paired with their team. I know him; he doesn't like attention, and he especially doesn't like special treatment.

The following week, Jeff and I sat on the couch at the JFC waiting for Jeff's name to be called. We saw Sam walk out from the back of the clinic. He was excited and couldn't wait to tell Jeff. He approached Jeff and knelt down on one knee in front of him.

"I have been asked by the Boston Bruins for a Pedal Partner for the Pan-Mass Challenge. I told them I knew of a perfect match; I told them of you."

Jeff tried so hard to hold back his smile but couldn't. His face lit up, and then his glorious smile broke through. It made me laugh out loud. Inside, my heart was exploding.

"I know that smile is a Jeff-Hayes-really-excited reaction," Sam said. "Okay, I'll let them know you're the one."

Jeff and I drove up to meet with the Bruins PMC riders at the Prudential Center in Boston in March of 2006. I didn't know how to get there, but Jeff gave me directions. I found his sense of direction remarkable. John had told me that his friends call Jeff when they're lost or need directions. This is a trait he most certainly gets from his father.

"Mom, we just need to go the same way we go to the Jimmy Fund, except we take a right onto Huntington Avenue, and that will take us to the Prudential Center."

"Okay, you can show me the way, honey," I replied.

When we arrived, we parked in the garage below the Prudential and made our way up the elevator and followed the signs to the Pedal Partner Pairing. Jeff was among many children with cancer who were meeting their Pedal Partners for the first time. Jeff was wearing his Bruins jersey. The first Bruins rider was Steve Caldwell. He was a golf pro. When he saw Jeff in his jersey, he approached us, and we spoke until others from the Bruins Foundation arrived.

When they approached, Steve introduced us and said, "I think we have the perfect match."

We met Kerry Collins, the Director of Community Relations; and Kim Jacobs, Charlie Jacobs's wife and the daughter-in-law of Jeremy Jacobs, owner of the Boston Bruins.

Jeff and I stood with Kerry, and I told her that the Bruins had generously given the social director at the JFC ten tickets to a Bruins game last year during Jeff's first year of treatment and that he was lucky enough to go to the game.

"I was the one who gave the tickets to the Jimmy Fund," she said, surprised and smiling. "It's so great to see it turn full circle."

Jeff and I, Kim Jacobs, and Steve Caldwell posed for several pictures. Most of the other Pedal Partners were young cancer patients, running around with their faces painted, hairless, with food in hand from the buffet as they met the PMC team riding on their behalf. Jeff posed for pictures with the other patients, and we ate from the buffet.

Jeff looked strong and healthy when he met the Bruins representatives that day. I wondered whether, in their first year as a PMC team, they might have wanted a younger cancer patient. I know they didn't realize when they met Jeff that day that he was not only a good hockey player and a nice kid but also the closest cancer patient they would find who has been a Boston Bruins fan his entire life.

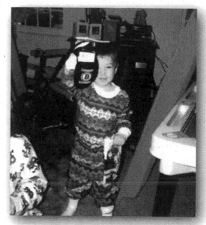

Jeff Christmas Morning

When Jeff and I left the event, he directed me back to the Prudential Center parking garage. I followed his lead to the garage and back to the expressway that led us to Route 3 South. It was a Sunday, with no traffic, so we made it home in an hour. When we walked into the kitchen, I could smell the hot dinner spread out on our kitchen counter. It had been prepared and just dropped off by a family from Sandwich. A bottle of wine and a bouquet of flowers stood next to the containers of food. My eyes watered, and I thought about someone cooking all morning in their kitchen, preparing a meal for us so that we wouldn't have to prepare one ourselves. One year of Sunday dinners, it was truly wonderful. Can this last forever? I thought. I picked up the flowers, placing them near my face to smell their fragrance; I cut them and put them in a vase while Jeff, John, John Jr., and Jason scooped the dinner onto their plates. I opened the wine.

March was chaotic with Jeff's new treatment and meeting the Boston Bruins PMC team. Jeff had now become the subject of a Channel Five "High Five." Each Friday, during the five o'clock and eleven o'clock newscasts, Channel Five produced a five-minute clip of a high school athlete. Jack Lessard had contacted the station's sports department to inform them about Jeff, his battle with cancer, and his career as a high school hockey player. Mike Dowling arrived with a cameraman at the

Dana-Farber Cancer Institute on a day Jeff was receiving chemotherapy. They filmed Jeff walking into the Dana-Farber and interviewed him as he lay in his bed at the JFC. He was also interviewed outside the Gallo Ice Arena in Bourne and in the Sandwich Blue Knights locker room. Film clippings were shown of Jeff's twenty-seven seconds on the ice during the Canal Cup.

It was all a great distraction from unbearable thoughts. In March we also began meeting with a representative from the Make-A-Wish Foundation, Mrs. Hein. Her son, CJ, had played baseball with Jeff. The Winter Olympics had begun, and Jeff questioned whether we could go there. They were held in Italy that year.

"Jeff, you need to choose a place where you can relax and have fun. If you choose the Olympics, you will be moving from place to place to see certain events. You will be in another country without immediate access to Sam if we need him. I think your first choice of Disney World is perfect. It's warm, and it's only a two-and-a-half-hour flight from Boston. You can stay at any Disney resort; you can stay at the most exclusive hotel." I also told him that I would pay for two of his friends to fly down and stay close by so he could hang out with them and really have a great time. He opened his laptop and started searching the Disney website for a listing of their accommodations.

Six days before our Make-A-Wish trip to Disney World, Jeff began to feel very sick and suffered severe headaches that were constant. Dr. Holcomb Grier gathered his staff, including Sam, to discuss how to stop these headaches and give Jeff relief from his pain.

I phoned Sam and asked him to do a brain scan to determine whether the cancer had spread to Jeff's skull. When Jeff and I drove up to Boston for the scan, by chance we met Sam in the elevator. "This is a good idea, as we haven't scanned Jeff's skull," Sam said. He looked rushed and carried a thick patient binder under his arm.

After the scan, we waited at the JFC until late in the afternoon for Sam to return with the results. There were two computers in the JFC waiting room, and Jeff went online to talk to his friends.

When Sam entered the clinic, he approached Jeff and stood next to us while we remained seated.

"The brain scan was clear." We were very tired but thankful not to have to face more bad news. The brain would stay intact or untouched by disease, but the skull is bone and a place for the disease to spread, I thought. I didn't ask.

"Jeff, you have a huge brain!" Jeff smiled back at Sam. Sam's specialty was brain tumors.

Jeff's headaches continued, and our Make-A-Wish trip was put on hold until the day before we were scheduled to go. Dr. Grier, Sam, and the oncology staff prescribed Celebrex to rid Jeff of his headaches. Dr. Grier told me over the phone, "Susan, we worked for long hours on Jeff, for several days; we just couldn't let him miss his trip."

CHAPTER 45

Make-A-Wish Trip

A T SEVEN O'CLOCK on a cold March morning, the sky was gray, and the ground was still covered with snow. We didn't care; there was a limo in our driveway to take us to the airport for our trip to Disney World.

The ride was an hour long to Green Airport in Rhode Island. We were dropped off at the airline terminal, and the driver emptied the trunk and placed our suitcases at the curbside check-in. As our luggage was scanned, mine was tagged for a random security search. I walked through the upright metal detector and was escorted to the back of the security assembly for a more thorough search.

They rummaged through my large shoulder bag and found the ziplock bag filled with Jeff's prescriptions, but they didn't question it. I thought the medicine would be a problem, but the Make-A-Wish badge that I wore explained the medicine cabinet I carried. "Okay," I said, "let's go."

"You're the one who's holding us up, Mom!" Jason said.

I was carrying a bag full of tickets and passes. Just before the trip, Mrs. Hein from the Make-A-Wish Foundation had come to our house with a check for spending money as well as the Make-A-Wish badges, park passes, airline tickets, rental reservations, and instructions for the entire trip. The day before we left we gave Jeff one thousand dollars to spend.

Jeff and I had studied the Beach Club Resort and Yacht Club and had been impressed by the pictures on the website, but we couldn't have imagined the casual beauty of the resort. We could see a large lake and a boardwalk that circled the lake. The ESPN Club, Jellyrolls, small restaurants, and many other attractions were visible from the front of the resort. A ferry went across from our hotel to the other side of the boardwalk. "New England Clambake Every Wednesday Night," was posted outside the front of the restaurant inside the lobby. Our rooms had standard double beds and a balcony. John and I had one room. John Jr., Jeff, and Jason shared the room next door. We changed into our bathing suits and left to check out the three pools. Cold New England seemed so far away. Jeff's friends Brian and Mike would arrive in two days.

Walking to the pools, we saw a large shipwreck that was broken in half, leaving the middle arch of the ship a passage where guests walked under; it was part of the boardwalk. Spiral stairs led to the top of the pirate ship, and a long slide ended at the edge of the pool. My husband started to climb the spiral stairs to the ship's deck and to the top of the slide. He'll never do it, I thought, watching from the other side of the pool. He looked out onto the pool below and sat down. I saw him look for us and then push off the top of the water slide; he was fast and broke the water's surface like a bombshell, showering anyone close by and splashing water over the lounge chairs on the pool deck. Jason and I looked at each other.

"They'll be closing that slide today for repairs!" Jason said.

I laughed and looked over at John Jr. and Jeff, watching them smile in embarrassment, looking back at me. He may have broken the slide, I don't know, but he certainly took away any apprehensiveness we were feeling.

Between the pools was a small beach area and a kiddy pool. I sat on a raft, and my three sons hung onto the edge. As we drifted, Jeff let go; I looked at him, and he stared back at me. We held our gaze; no words were spoken.

"Dude, you need your hat. Where's your hat?" John Jr. said, breaking our stare as he looked out at Jeff while still hanging onto the side of my tube. John Jr. moved the tube closer to Jeff.

"Want me to get your hat?" he asked.

"No, I'll get it after," Jeff replied, and John Jr. and Jason let go of the tube to swim.

I looked back at Jeff as the tube floated away with the current; it was as if I was losing him and he was fading away from me. He was only a few feet away in a moment's time, but it tore at my heart.

My husband walked up to the side of the pool and said, "You must be in your glory, in a pool, surrounded by your sons." I looked away from Jeff and smiled. "Yes, I am."

I'd been in my tube for a while when I heard Jason's voice: "Mom, Jeff rented a Boston Whaler. Come on, let's go; they're waiting for you." John, John Jr., and Jeff were sitting on the boat docked at the pier at the yacht club. Jason and I got on board. John Jr. started the engine. We cruised the open lake and the riverways that gave way to the two majestic hotels, The Dolphin and The Swan. It was still warm, and the cool breeze off the lake was refreshing. Jeff was content and proud to have rented the whaler with his own money and, in his quiet way, to have surprised us.

After getting off the boat, Jason headed for something to eat at the outdoor restaurant. John Jr. and Jeff went back to their room. John and I walked off the pier toward the pools. "How about a piña colada, Mom?" my husband asked.

"Oh, yes. No wait, a margarita, no salt. Thanks!" I replied. "I'll be sitting by the pool."

The next day we were given instructions to register at a place outside Disney World, miles away, called "Give Kids the World." It was a small version of Disney World for young children. We drove up to the security gate and needed approval to enter. As we drove through the gate, we saw a castle and towering prehistoric dinosaurs, kiddy rides, and housing for the families who visited the park. This was our check-in location for our Make-A-Wish trip, and we were greeted by volunteers. Jeff, John Jr., and Jason were given T-shirts with the words *Give Kids the World* written on them. Jeff received small gifts. We were scheduled to come back the next day to the small theater on the grounds for pictures with Mickey and Minnie Mouse; other families would join us.

We headed back to Disney World. The weather was perfect: sunny and in the eighties. We walked over to the small pier of the yacht club where a fleet of small one-man motorboats bobbed. I approached the gentleman running the boat rides and told him we were here on a Make-A-Wish trip. The gentleman called his manager, and we were given the normal thirty-minute ride for free. The lake and riverways went for miles, and we all set out in different directions. The next day, John, Jeff, and I returned to *Give Kids the World* to meet for pictures with Mickey and Minnie. We entered the small theater and sat watching and waiting for Jeff to be called. I looked around at the younger children, wondering about their illnesses. I saw their excitement as they sat restlessly waiting to meet Mickey and Minnie. Jeff was the only teenager. When the volunteer called Jeff's name, we walked to the side of the stage and waited on the stairs. At center stage was a little boy with his parents. He was beautiful, with dark hair and big round eyes. He had an enormous smile as he stood there waiting. I smiled with him from across the stage, hidden within the darkened stairway. I thought he might be five years old. He was small, thin, and fragile. When Mickey and Minnie walked onto the stage, he looked at them, still smiling and laughing as he looked back out into the theater. He stood with Mickey and Minnie as if all of his dreams had come true.

"It's TJ's birthday tomorrow, so today we're going to sing 'Happy Birthday' to him." The Master of Ceremonies, a volunteer, I imagined, looked up at center stage. TJ and his parents were standing with Mickey and Minnie. The volunteer paused and then began to count. "One, two, three, happy birthday to you..." Everyone in the theater began to sing. I could hear Jeff singing loudly to the little boy on stage. I wanted to embrace TJ, pick him up, and give him the world. His smile was enormous, and it exploded into laughter as we sang. When the song ended, we clapped; Jeff clapped hard and loud.

It was as if Jeff wasn't sick at all that week, or he didn't appear to be. He took his medicine and kept up with all he wanted to do. He covered himself with sunscreen and avoided what might make him tired or sick. I never saw him in pain, nor did he complain at any time during the trip. Waking up to the Florida warmth and sun and living at a Disney's resort allowed Jeff to live without restraints, boundless and happy, with his family and friends, away from the JFC and Children's, doctors and nurses. He was out of bed, walking around and driving. You can't possibly know what freedom is until it's no longer yours.

A cancer patient must feel isolated no matter how much they're surrounded by those who love them; they still face the thought of their own mortality. It's a very private and scary place. Disney took all that away.

It was difficult to think about leaving to return to a life we didn't choose, a life thrust upon us without reason, a place no one wants to live. It was sad to see it end, and it was hard to leave.

Brian and Mike left on Friday, the day before we left for our last stop at SeaWorld. They had driven around, played miniature golf, and eaten out. Jeff said it was one of the best times of his life.

We drove back to the airport, and when we landed at Green Airport in Providence, a limousine picked us up and took us home.

CHAPTER 46

Results of Second Clinical Trial, March 2006

THE MONDAY AFTER we returned from Disney World, Jeff continued with the second set of drugs from the second clinical trial. The combination of these drugs had shown positive results with good percentages of survival rates among children with Ewing's. With a rare bone cancer, there weren't many teenagers or young adults to test, and there isn't enough interest, I thought, in testing these drugs when the number of Ewing's cases, in comparison with the number of other childhood cancers, was much lower.

One day, during this clinical trial, CNN aired a story about a young girl in Texas with Ewing's sarcoma. Sanjay Gupta was the commentator. The girl's treatment hadn't been working, and the disease was spreading. In desperation, the family tried a drug manufactured by a pharmaceutical company in Texas; the drug had failed in clinical trials. Miraculously, the girl responded to the drug almost immediately and was cured. I was shocked. I called CNN the next day. Oh my God, how come we don't know about this drug? CNN was very accommodating in helping me find out more about this drug. The drug was called Immither. I was told that the pharmaceutical company no longer manufactured the drug because there wasn't enough need for it. There weren't enough patients stricken with Ewing's to make manufacturing this drug for profit possible. As I probed further, I was told that this drug had to be given at the onset of the disease and that it would not be effective if other chemotherapy drugs had been used beforehand. That wasn't the case in the story of the girl cured by this drug that was aired by CNN. It didn't make any sense.

I asked Sam about Immither, and he had no knowledge of it. Dr. Grier investigated my story and told me it could have been an experimental drug. I let it go because I trusted Dr. Grier and Sam. The first day we'd met Dr. Grier, he had told us that he met each year with scientists and oncologists from around the world to discuss any new breakthroughs in Ewing's and other childhood cancers. If there were something new and that effective, they would know about it. He also said that the protocol for Ewing's hadn't really changed in the last twenty years.

In April, the social director from the JFC contacted Jeff and asked if he would like to go to the Boston Red Sox spring training camp in Fort Myers, Florida. It was the first year that the Jimmy Fund, along with the Boston Red Sox, was sponsoring cancer patients from the JFC to travel to spring training and meet the players. Jeff didn't want to go. I understood that he would rather spend any free time at home and with his friends. As great a trip as that would be, it wasn't what he wanted to do.

I watched the telecast as the kids we'd seen in treatment boarded the bus from outside the JFC. Some were hairless and wearing Red Sox caps and T-shirts. That was our life too. Our life and their lives were a world apart from other kids.

As the Red Sox season began, Jeff's nurse, Hannah, called and said, "I have been selected with other nurses here at the JFC and Children's Hospital to choose a cancer patient to throw out the first pitch at a Red Sox game. I have chosen Jeff's name to be put into a pool with the other patients. Please don't tell Jeff because his name may not be chosen."

I pictured Jeff on the mound at Fenway Park. I imagined his slow wind-up, his leg lifted, his glove placed just above his chest, and then as he brought his arm up and forward with the release of his grip on the ball, he let go. His upper body moved forward in one single motion; his arm followed through swiftly, as one leg was planted in front of him and the other behind him, a foot off the ground, adding speed behind the ball. I pictured Jeff's natural curveball, as I'd seen it many times, spin and curve at eighty-four miles an hour as it moved over home plate and into Jason Varitek's glove.

It turned out that Jordan, the little boy from Cape Cod who was also battling Ewing's sarcoma, was picked to throw out the first pitch. Jeff was glad he hadn't been chosen.

It was time to measure the results of the second trial drugs, and Jeff and I made this trip alone for the x-ray and the results. After the x-ray, Jeff and I waited at the JFC. Jeff looked as he did before the first year of treatment. He was strong, and his weight remained constant throughout these trials. His eyebrows and eyelashes had grown back, as did a trace of his baseball goatee on his chin. I wondered whether this was a bad sign. If his hair was growing back, then his healthy cells were not being destroyed. Did that mean the cancer cells were still spreading?

Jeff and I were escorted into the dreaded small examining room on the dark side of the clinic.

Sam entered the room. He said hello and sat down next to the computer. He looked up at Jeff and said, "There isn't any good way to say this." He paused. "Two more tumors showed up in your lungs, one where we first saw a tumor and a new tumor in your other lung."

Jeff had a stoic look on his face, a mask that hid what he was feeling. He didn't look my way; he stared at Sam, not speaking a word.

How many more trials and drugs were available to stop his cancer? He had gone through so much pain and sickness and had sacrificed so much since his treatment began eighteen months before, and still the cancer had continued to spread. For the first time, the possibility of losing his battle started to sink in. Anger inside, I looked at Sam and said, "What can we do now?"

We were interrupted by a knock on the door, and Dr. Susie Sherman entered the room. The look on her face mirrored Sam's. She said, "We still have some drug combinations we can try, and we will keep trying them." I tried to concentrate as she spoke, thinking maybe we still had a chance. Jeff and I left the examining room with the hope that she and Sam would come up with another treatment plan; one that would work.

Once in the waiting room, I hugged Jeff tightly and said, "We're going to get through this. We're going to try another trial and may be this time it'll work." He sat down on the couch.

"I have to go outside for a minute. Sam will keep trying. I know he will. I'll be right back. I couldn't speak again. I left the clinic and headed for the parking garage to call John.

When I got back to the clinic, I met up with Hannah in the corridor. I felt defeated. I began to cry. Sam approached me as Hannah stood by my side. He hugged me, and I whispered in his ear, "I love him so much."

"I know you do," he replied softly. We stood facing each other, and he said, "I'm going to make some phone calls to hospitals around the country to find out if there are any new clinical trials that are showing a good response to Ewing's."

With tears in my eyes, I said, "Thank you, Sam."

Jeff and I headed home without a new treatment plan. It was Monday. On Wednesday evening we received a call from Sam. He was excited. I could hear it in his voice as he explained that he had phoned a friend and colleague who was in Cincinnati and was leading a clinical trial with a new combination of chemotherapy drugs that was showing a 50 percent response in Ewing's patients. This was the greatest response currently in trial. Sam wanted to try these drugs on Jeff immediately.

The following Monday we arrived at the JFC. Jeff's blood levels, vitals, weight, height, and hydration were checked. One of the chemo drugs needed to be measured and put into separate vials so that I could administer it at home. The other drug was a pill. It was a five-day treatment plan, but it would be six weeks before we could measure the results. That day, Jeff received the first two doses at the JFC. We headed home with hope.

The chemo needed to be stored in the refrigerator. Jeff had his own refrigerator in his basement apartment, and I used his refrigerator for the chemo, Gatorade, water, and juice. I was extremely vigilant keeping the chemo separate from anything I had in the refrigerator so that it wouldn't come in contact with the surface of a bottle or a drink. It was a powerful drug newly prescribed. I heeded their caution, not completely understanding the hazard should a drop of the drug escape our prudence and make skin, mouth or eye contact. We couldn't risk anything happening to disrupt this new treatment.

I followed the instruction I'd received at the clinic to prepare the liquid chemo. I emptied one vial into a plastic cup with one to two ounces of cranberry juice. I could then blend the cranberry juice with apple or grape juice. Jeff and I needed to wear non-latex gloves while handling the drugs, and I needed to wear a mask when preparing and administering the drugs.

It wasn't very complicated, yet it was hope for us. I was somewhat nervous, but didn't worry about doing this alone. I wasn't alone—Jeff was completely aware of what needed to be done. He would question me if he thought the timing of the medicine was wrong, and he helped me remember what to do. His calmness and maturity gave me the confidence I needed.

"Mom, can you get me just one glove?"

"Oh, sorry, yes of course; you only need one."

With gloves on, I prepared a nonsterile working area by covering the bar with paper towels; I thought of it as a clean surface from which to work on. I took one vial out of the refrigerator and transferred the chemo to a cup with two ounces of juice, measured by eye. Then I took one of the chemo pills out of the prescription bottle and walked over to

Jeff. He sat up in his recliner, and I knelt down in front of him with the pill in the center of my gloved palm. Jeff picked it up with his gloved hand and swallowed it with water. Then I gave him the cup of juice with the chemo. When he finished, he pulled the glove off inside out and handed it to me.

I put his used glove on my working surface at the bar and then wrapped everything up in a ball and put it in a plastic bag. I pulled my gloves off inside out and put them in the same plastic bag. That plastic bag I threw in a garbage bag isolated in the basement until the week of treatment ended.

Jeff's bar provided me the perfect setup to facilitate all my needs in administrating his drugs. The bar was in the room directly outside his bedroom. He also needed to take the prechemo, antinausea medicine throughout this treatment. I kept all his medicine on the shelves below the bar along with my binder that organized the daily sheets I kept to record when I had given Jeff any medications. This binder was specifically made for me by Nancy Bridges. She was able to provide me with the medical records forms, and I used them to keep an accurate account of Jeff's treatment. I prefilled the times when I knew Jeff's medications needed to be administered so that I could adhere to the treatment exactly as instructed.

I also recorded his temperature, bowel movements, and general well-being. I noted everything I thought was important as well as what he was able to do physically during the treatment. When I remembered, I made notes of what was going on in his life.

The fluid and the pill tasted so horribly that after taking them the first time Jeff asked, "Next time Mom, can I have some of the mouthwash for the bad taste?"

"Oh, yes, good idea, Jeff."

Jeff had been prescribed an oral analgesic for the pain he started to feel in the upper corner of his mouth where his wisdom tooth had been extracted. He wanted the analgesic to coat his mouth so he couldn't taste these new chemo drugs. He rinsed his mouth out with a small cup of mouthwash and spit in a cup held with his one hand gloved. I held out my hand, and he took the pill then the chemo and juice. By the look on his face, I could see how strong the drugs were when he swallowed them, even with the analgesic.

We told Sam about the mouthwash, and he said, "Wow, what a great idea! I hadn't thought of that."

As Jeff and I became more confident about taking this new drug combination and how he would feel afterward, Jeff's friends started visiting him. It was great to see him with his friends. I went down only to offer food and drinks or to give Jeff his medicine and chemo. If friends were in his room when Jeff needed to take his chemo, he and I went into his bathroom for privacy. His room was filled with five or six girls and boys who visited for many hours. The walls and shelves in his room were still filled with trophies, plaques, a Boston Bruins jersey signed by Patrice Bergeron and Chara as well as signed hockey sticks and baseballs. New gifts arrived almost daily. Throughout the last few months, Jeff had received a football autographed by Dick Vermeil from Paul O'Connell, a wholesaler from work; the book *Fred Cusick: Voice of the Bruins* signed by Fred Cusick from my brother-in-law and Jeff's godfather, Peter Macleod; the book *Searching for Bobby Orr*; a painting done by a teacher at the high school; new baseballs signed by different Red Sox players; and numerous "get well" cards that filled our mailbox daily.

Katherine Baugh, Jeff's VNA nurse, continued to come by to check on Jeff daily and draw blood to check his red, white, and platelet counts. Katherine sat at the bar with her laptop to record Jeff's progress and then report back to Sam.

CHAPTER 47

———— ❈ ————

Prom Night, May 2006

I RAN HALFWAY UP the stairs from Jeff's basement apartment and then stopped. I turned back to look at Jeff sitting in the middle of the couch watching one of his favorite shows. It was a reality show featuring a father and his two sons who assembled custom motorcycles, or choppers. Until I had watched the program with Jeff, I couldn't understand his interest in the show. Motorcycles, I thought, were so out of character for Jeff. But his interest was not so much in motorcycles as it was in the dialog and play between the father and his two sons and the small group of mechanics who creatively and skillfully designed and built unusual and magnificent choppers. During one show that Jeff and I watched on my lunch hour, they custom built a motorcycle and brought it to a benefit to raise money for cancer research. I watched the show several times with Jeff, wondering each time what the end product would look like as custom-built parts were delivered to the set and welded onto the bike during the show.

From the open stairway, I stood and asked Jeff, "Do you want to go to the prom, honey?"

I walked back down the stairs to sit with him.

"No, it's too expensive," he replied, not looking at me but staying focused on the television show.

"I don't care how much it costs. If you want to go, then you should go."

"No, I don't want to go."

The show ended, and I went up the stairs to finish the laundry and start dinner.

It was May. I continued to give Jeff the antinausea medicine and the oral chemotherapy.

I called Sam during the weeks of this treatment and asked, "When can we have an x-ray taken?"

"Susan, we have to let it work; we have to give it some time," he replied.

I was anxious to see whether Jeff was responding. If he wasn't, time would be crucial. We would have to try something else. What I didn't realize was that Sam knew there wasn't much more they could do if this didn't work.

Life seemed closer to normal only because Jeff didn't have to spend any nights at Children's Hospital. We only revisited the JFC when Jeff finished the week of chemotherapy and after the second week of recovery. This was the third combination of chemotherapy drugs after eighteen months of treatment without a break from the toxic drugs. I was thankful when Katherine came frequently to draw Jeff's blood, which was monitored by Hannah at the JFC. Katherine was always close by and gave me the confidence to care for Jeff while he was home.

I continued to work full-time. At noontime, I called Jeff to see if he wanted me to bring him some lunch. He was alone at home. I knew he'd be hungry. "Can you get me a ham and cheese sub from the General Store on 149?"

The General Store in Barnstable had his favorite sub rolls and cold cuts. I left work and brought us both home a sandwich, and we ate our lunch together watching a motorcycle being designed and built from two wheels and a frame.

The next day at noon, I phoned Jeff from work.

"Hi, Mom." His voice was different, and I sensed from his tone that he wasn't lying on the couch in his basement living room.

"Where are you, Jeff?"

"I'm with Greg Iadonisi at a tux shop in Hyannis. Greg bought me a ticket to the prom, and the tux shop donated a tux."

"You are! Wow, that's great, honey!"

The day of the prom Jeff asked me to meet him at Greg's house for pictures. Greg's house was on a hill, and you could see the ocean in the distance. Ten couples posed outside on the Iadonisis' front lawn dressed in their gowns and tuxes. The high school men in black, wearing sunglasses, posed with their arms over each other's shoulders.

Jeff's date was Holli Bridges, Jeff's best friend's sister and a senior. Jeff was a junior. Holli's boyfriend had graduated the year before, and she had asked Jeff if they could go together. She was petite and tanned. She had blue eyes and auburn hair that was perfectly done up and pushed back off her beautiful face. She wore a green satin strapless dress that illuminated her eyes and fell just above her knees. They looked happy together; they were good friends. I walked around the lawn and inside the house taking candid and formal shots while other parents pinned corsages and took pictures.

When it was time to leave, I drove home to pick up my husband and headed downtown to the Grist Mill, a historical town landmark where the kids all gathered with the rest of the class for more formal pictures. It was a beautiful sunny day. Jeff posed with his family, his nana, and more friends.

We walked away, and Jeff and his friends were off to the Junior Prom.

During the night, two of the teachers chaperoning the prom sat alone at a table, distant from the students, tallying the ballots for the couple who would be crowned Prom King and Queen.

"Jeff Hayes," was written on the first ballot as Jan Simpson, Jeff's homeroom teacher, began to tally the votes.

"Jeff Hayes," the other teacher announced after pulling out another ballot. "Jeff Hayes," Jan said, placing another ballot down on the table in front of her. "Jeff Hayes," she announced again. "Jeff Hayes," she said again. Every piece of folder paper they opened for Prom King read, "Jeff Hayes."

"We stared at each other in silence," Jan told me. "Our eyes were filled with emotion as we looked back at the kids eating dinner in their formal wear, smiling, laughing, and enjoying the night they had planned."

Jeff smiled with joy and surprise when the announcement was made and he was called to be crowned. Everyone stood and cheered. He stood up and walked around the tables and up to the stage. He hadn't suspected a thing. They had planned the entire night for him. They bought him a ticket. His tux had been donated. Holli was his date, and they crowned Jeff their Prom King.

I waited up until midnight for him to come home. My husband was sound asleep waiting for me to wake him when Jeff came home.

I heard the car doors shut and I ran to the front door. Jeff limped quickly up the driveway to our front door. Holli was behind him in bare feet, carefully walking over our pebbled driveway; the tiny stones piercing the bottom of her feet as she tried to keep up. Jeff's face was lit up. He was wearing a tall red velvet crown and a sash over his shoulder that read, "Prom King."

"Wow! You're the Prom King!" I held back my tears and asked him and Holli to pose together in our kitchen. I pushed the button down on my camera, but the flash didn't go off. I was standing there in front of them in my pajamas and bathrobe, frustrated, thinking I was ruining the moment. They stood posed for several minutes as I tried again and again to get a shot.

"It's okay, Mrs. Hayes. I've got lots of pictures," Holli said.

They went downstairs, and Jeff changed into his shorts and T-shirt.

"Should I wear the crown to the After-Prom Party?" he asked me.

"Yes, of course you should," I answered.

He put the sash on over his T-shirt and then put the crown back on.

He looked a little tired, I thought, so I said, "You don't have to go to the After-Prom Party if you don't want to."

"No, I do. I want to win the car!"

"Do you want me to drive you and then pick you up later?"

"No, I'll be okay."

They headed back out to the high school; Jeff driving.

I was accustomed to sleeping on the couch. I heard his car drive up at three o'clock in the morning. He went straight downstairs to bed.

On Memorial Day, Jeff and the Prom Queen sat up on the backseat of a white convertible as they drove through the streets of downtown Sandwich in the Memorial Day parade. They threw small pieces of candy out into the crowd. He looked very happy.

In June, we heard from Kerry Collins, Director of Community Relations for the Boston Bruins. The PMC was the first weekend in August. She called me to ask what Jeff's jersey number was. They wanted to make him an official Bruins jersey for the day when Jeff and his friends would skate at the New England Sports Center in Marlboro with former Bruins star, Terry O'Reilly. It was a hot and humid day in Marlboro when we drove up from the Cape to meet with Kerry Collins, Jay Southwood, Steve Caldwell, and Kim Jacobs.

John, Jeff, Jason, Patty, my two sisters, Kathy and Janet, and I entered the Sports Center. This was our first meeting with the Bruins since last March when we'd met at the Prudential Center in Boston.

Kerry handed Jeff the Boston Bruins jersey with his number twelve on the sleeve. Jeff smiled and thanked her. Terry O'Reilly was standing next to Jeff, and he said, "Here, Jeff, let me help." Terry took the jersey and unfolded it and then gave it to Jeff. Jeff removed his cap, rolled up the sleeves, and put his arms through them and then put the jersey over his head and pulled it down. I started taking pictures. Several media outlets were there also taking pictures. We looked at Jeff standing in the hallway outside the rink doors when Gerry Cheevers approached him. I was thrilled to see Jeff speaking to the goalie, whom I had watched for years.

Jeff's high school coach, Derackk Curtis, and his friends were already on the ice skating while they waited for Jeff and Terry O'Reilly.

I stood behind the glass watching them skate and pass the puck. Jeff's hair was growing back, and he looked good on the ice.

While they skated, Kim and Steve, the PMC riders went outside the rink with us so they could be filmed preparing for the PMC. NESN filmed them circling the Sports Center on their bikes with us on the sidelines cheering them on. Again and again they rode around the front of the arena, and each time they passed, we cheered. The PMC was new for the Bruins and for us.

Kim was very friendly and genuine. She specifically made a point to find Jason to speak with him.

We went back inside the rink; it was hot and humid outside, and the rink was a good place to find relief. We entered and watched more of the street-hockey-style play from the players on the ice. I saw Jeff skate across the ice and sit up on the boards, resting. He was away from the play and on the other side of the ice. Until I saw him sitting on the boards, I was thinking everything was all right. He was skating and playing hockey with his closest friends, in the presence of the legend, Terry O'Reilly. I stared across the rink at him; I could see he was still sick.

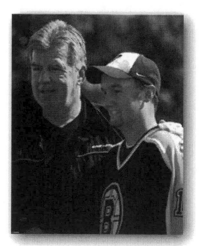

Terry O'Reilly and Jeff

CHAPTER 48

Third Clinical Trial Results

ON SUNDAY, JULY 17, 2006, my husband and John Jr., Jeff, Jason, and I drove up to Boston to stay at the Holiday Inn on Beacon Street in Brookline. It was a last-minute decision to stay the night before Jeff would have a chest x-ray taken to determine whether he had responded to this treatment. I phoned Nancy Helms, who had coordinated the Sunday dinners, and she phoned the Tomasinis, who were scheduled to bring us dinner that Sunday. I called Angelo, too.

"Hi Angelo. Nancy told us that you were making us dinner tonight. We just decided to go up to Boston this afternoon instead of making the long commute in the morning. Please don't worry about making dinner for us."

"You have to eat," he insisted. His voice was strong and persuasive. Angelo is kind hearted and a New Yorker, meaning, a Yankees and Rangers fan.

"Yes, but we can get something on the road."

"Oh, no! Jane has already started making the pasta. Brian will bring dinner by in an hour. Susan, you're not going to win this argument."

"Okay, Angelo." I smiled, knowing he was right, knowing I wasn't going to win. "Thank you so much, but are you sure?"

"Yes, I'm sure. Good luck tomorrow. We'll be thinking of you."

"Okay, thanks. Bye."

Brian arrived with bread, a pasta dinner, and salad. It was delicious.

After we finished eating our homemade pasta dinner, we headed to Boston. The ride was quick without traffic on a late Sunday afternoon. My husband dropped us off at the front door of the same Holiday Inn on Beacon Street, and we checked in. We had accumulated enough points to upgrade our room to a suite. When we entered the suite, we were excited to find a large living room, a kitchenette, and french doors to a large bedroom with a king-size bed, but most appealing to us was the air conditioning and two large flat-screen televisions hanging in the living room and the bedroom. Jeff and Jason pulled out the sofa bed, and Jeff viewed the movie choices.

"Let's watch *Sentinel*. It's a good movie," Jeff said. We gathered around the television, and Dad and John Jr. pulled up a chair to watch the movie.

"Jeff, can I stretch out next to you and watch?" I asked.

He moved over, and I lay next to him with our heads on the soft hotel pillows. Jason lay down next to him on the other side of the sofa bed. We watched the movie with little conversation, afraid to break the comfort and peace of the night. We didn't discuss the possibility of what we might face in the morning. The movie ended.

"Good night, dude," my husband said to Jeff. "See you in the morning."

"Good night, pumpkin," I said.

"Good night, John, good night Jay."

"Good night."

We lay in our own beds in complete silence until the roar of my husband's snoring began.

I prayed in the last moment before sleep fell upon me: Oh God, please, tomorrow, for the first time, let there be good news.

The next morning we ate breakfast at the hotel restaurant. When we had finished eating, I brought back a fork, a knife and a spoon to our room. I thought about taking it home to measure all the times I had stayed there, proof that I had been there throughout these horrible years. It was symbolic, an etching in stone or a carved message

271

in a secret place at the hotel to show that this really happened to us. We were here. Years from now we'd know that it wasn't just a bad dream.

I had become such a different person. I'd changed from the quiet and passive person I'd been before Jeff's diagnosis to someone more aggressive and outspoken. I needed to know why, and when I knew something didn't seem right, I questioned it. I tried not to miss a thing. I was convinced his life depended on my ability to care for him at every moment. I was determined that I wouldn't let him down.

We gathered back in the hotel room and packed our suitcases and went to the JFC. Jeff had the x-ray taken, and then we waited in the JFC for Sam.

I saw Sam walk quickly into the back of the clinic, just as he had done the last time we waited for the results after the second clinical trial. After another a long wait, one of the nurses came toward us and escorted us to one of the dreadful examining rooms.

Sam was different. I caught a glimpse of him walking quickly past our examining room. Hannah walked by with a smile on her face and quietly spoke the words, "It's good news." Sam returned and entered the room. I began to feel excited.

Sam was speechless, which was so out of character for him. He looked like he was about to explode, trying so hard to keep his emotions inside. He immediately walked over to Jeff, who was sitting on the examining table, and shook his hand and said, "The tumors in your lungs are all gone!"

Jeff's face lit up, and he smiled back at Sam. "All three tumors are gone?"

"Yes. You have responded to these drugs."

I jumped up out of my chair and hugged and kissed Jeff and then hugged Sam. Hannah came back into the room, and she hugged Jeff and all of us. I don't recall anything else Sam said to us at that moment as we finally had great hope of beating this disease. It was the happiest day of my life. I don't remember the next step in his treatment or even if we talked about it. I knew my husband, the eternal pessimist, would be cautious of the results and would want me to be the same. I could see it on his face. Not me, though. Jeff was cancer-free. We were on the other side of hope now. There was brightness that day. There was the possibility of Jeff beating this disease for the first time.

When we left the examining room, we were told to sit in the waiting room. I sat next to Jeff on the sofa. Sam came out of the back of the clinic, walked toward us and kneeled down in front of Jeff.

I asked Sam, "Are you excited?"

He looked up at Jeff and said, "They teach us to control our emotions throughout our years of medical school, but right now my insides are jumping up and down." Still looking at Jeff and not moving, he paused and said, "Jeff, you just hit a home run!"

Jeff smiled back at Sam, and Sam said, "I know you, Jeff, and I know that smile; it's awesome."

How quickly I forgot what it took to get us here; it was a new day, and everything was positive again. I had a million phone calls to make, and I felt like I was about to burst. I wanted to call everyone at the same time to let them know as soon as possible that Jeff was in remission.

The day we learned Jeff was cancer-free was July 17th, my son John Jr.'s birthday.

After one week of pure happiness and believing that Jeff was cancer-free, I received a phone call from Sam while I was at work.

"Do you have a moment to talk?" he asked.

He was serious. Jesus! What now? I thought. I walked outside our office and into the parking lot, pacing up and down in front of the parked cars with my cell phone glued to my ear.

"This is the most important decision you will make in your entire life," he began.

Oh my God! What now? I started to sweat with anxiety and fear.

"You will need to discuss this with Jeff for him to decide what the next course of treatment will be. It is his and your call. We can continue with these chemo drugs, or we can radiate Jeff's lungs to ensure that all the cancer cells are destroyed."

"How much more chemo can Jeff take?" I asked.

"We don't know," Sam replied.

"You can only treat the lungs with radiation once in a series of consecutive treatments. They cannot be radiated again."

I didn't want to make this life or death decision. I didn't want to make the wrong choice. I wanted Sam to tell us what to do, but he just gave us two choices, and maybe neither of them would cure Jeff's disease.

"Take some time to discuss this with Jeff and John, but not too much time. There is no wrong decision," he said.

I went back inside the office, terrified again. This was a very critical and difficult decision, a decision that most people will never face. It was a decision to choose the best treatment that might or might not be effective in beating Jeff's cancer. It was a decision we had to make together as a family.

We talked it over with Jeff. Radiation does work, but the risk of a secondary cancer later on in life was a possibility we had to consider. We assumed there were no other tumors anywhere in Jeff's body, however, we never did a full-body scan. I don't know why. Maybe we were afraid to find another tumor and thus end this treatment? Did Sam think this way too? If we did a full body scan and found another tumor, would that end our hope of treating this disease? Did it make a difference, because after the radiation on the lungs, we would still continue to administer these same drugs that Jeff had positively responded to.

We made the decision to radiate the lungs, thinking that we could kill any remaining cells.

The PMC was in one week. Kerry Collins called and asked whether the Bruins could stop at our house on Sunday morning, the second day of the ride.

Sam was also riding for Jeff and all his other patients. Sam had approached me last January to help him raise money for his ride. His goal was $100,000. I had said yes, of course. I was eager to help at that time, but as Jeff experienced several relapses, my focus remained on my son. "Don't worry about my ride," Sam said. "You have a lot on your mind right now." Sam said he planned on visiting Jeff the second day of the PMC to see his Hall-of-Fame basement; he'd never been to our house.

There was so much to do that week to prepare for the Bruins PMC team and the media that was expected.

I went to the Marshland Restaurant on 6A in Sandwich to speak with the owners, Kim Babiarz, Marty Finch, and Skip Cooke. Kim asked, "What do you need?"

"Bagels, muffins, and breakfast sandwiches?" I replied.

"Of course!"

I had the menu planned: bananas for potassium, water and Gatorade for hydration, crunchy peanut butter and jelly sandwiches for fuel. All I needed was coffee. John and I didn't drink coffee, so we didn't have a coffee maker or the experience to make a good cup.

I decided to ask Dunkin' Donuts to donate two boxes of coffee. They weren't expensive but I thought, why not ask. There were no customers when I walked through the door of Dunkin' Donuts on 6A the Friday night before the PMC. I approached the manager behind the counter and introduced myself. I began to explain why I needed the coffee. I thought the two women behind the counter would have no idea what the PMC was, but maybe they'd know who the Boston Bruins were.

"The Pan-Mass Challenge is a 192-mile bike ride this weekend to raise money for cancer research. The Boston Bruins Alumni team will be riding in honor of my son Jeff, who is battling cancer."

All I could see was a blank look on their face, and I imagined them thinking, what is this lady talking about and what does she want?

I continued, "The Bruins PMC team will be stopping at my house this Sunday morning for breakfast. I would like to ask if Dunkin' Donuts would be willing to donate two boxes of Joe for that morning."

The woman standing at the register listening to me was Brazilian, I thought, and she pointed to another woman standing close by and said, "Speak to the manager; she is right there."

The manager told me, "You have to call the regional manager for approval of any donations. I have her number if you'd like to call her."

I dialed her number, and it immediately went to voicemail. My back was to the two women behind the counter when I ended the message. I turned to face the counter and saw that the Brazilian woman had emptied the tip cup and was counting the money.

"I want to buy a box of Joe for you," she said.

The manager then spoke, "I want to buy the other one."

"Oh, no," I replied. "I left a message for the manager for a donation."

"No." they said. "We want to do this ourselves."

I insisted that they shouldn't, but they wouldn't relent, so I graciously accepted their kind offer. I didn't notice the customer standing at the counter until she ordered a cup of coffee. When her coffee was given to her, she gave the Brazilian woman a twenty-dollar bill and calmly said, "I would like to replace your tips for the box of coffee." She turned to me and said, "I know of your son and his battle with cancer."

"Thank you," I replied. "Thank you so very much!"

Back home, emotionally exhausted, I looked at my husband and said, "You're not going to believe what just happened."

CHAPTER 49

Pan-Mass Challenge
Weekend, August 2006

"LET'S STOP AND get the car washed," I said to Jason when we pulled out of the Hearth and Kettle Restaurant in Orleans. We were on our way home from Grandma and Grandpa's in Eastham after a day at the beach. Jason was seven, and it was years before Jeff's diagnosis. Across the street from the Hearth and Kettle, in the parking lot of a bank, was a group of teenagers washing cars. I pulled into the parking lot. My car needed a wash. The sign read, "All proceeds go to the Pan-Mass Challenge."

"Jason, what's the Pan-Mass Challenge?" I asked.

"I don't know."

"Well, let's wash the car anyway. It must be a fundraiser."

"Four thirty already," I turned over in my bed. It was Sunday morning, the first weekend in August of 2006, the second day of the PMC. The riders had spent the night at the Massachusetts Maritime Academy in Bourne and had set out at four thirty Sunday morning to finish the ride into Provincetown.

Jeff's friends, Brian Tomasini and Mike Bridges arrived with ice to fill the coolers of bottled water and Gatorade.

Patty and my sisters, Kathy and Joanne arrived and started making peanut butter and jelly sandwiches and setting up our breakfast buffet.

John left to pick up the food from the Marshland Restaurant and the coffee from Dunkin' Donuts.

My cell phone rang.

"Hi Susan, it's Kerry. The team is running late. I'll call you back to let you know when they will be arriving."

"Okay, I'll talk to you later."

I heard a car pulling into our driveway. I looked out the window and saw it was the NESN van. The cameraman and newscaster stood outside the van waiting for the Bruins. My cell phone rang again.

"Susan, Kerry. Jay and I are on our way to your house; we'll be there soon."

"Okay. NESN is here," I said.

Then another van drove up our driveway; it was NECN.

"NECN is here too."

"Oh, good, I'll be there soon," she replied.

I hung up from Kerry and went downstairs to see how Jeff was doing. He was sitting in his recliner, and Brian and Mike were sitting on the couch.

"How are you feeling, Jeff?"

"I'm okay."

His friends looked at me and smiled. He's not okay, I thought.

"Susan, Sam is here," my sister yelled down to me.

I ran up the basement stairs as Sam had rode to the end of our driveway and walked his bike up to our house.

"Hi, Sam!" I said.

He was wearing a helmet, bike pants, and his custom-made bike shirt that displayed his sponsors. Seeing him out of the clinic and away from chemotherapy treatment didn't change our admiration for him. He certainly looked different in bike gear, but he was still Sam to us. We looked up to him and hung tightly onto his sleeve, whether it was nylon or cotton.

John had returned from picking up the food and the coffee, and both were displayed on the kitchen table.

"Would you like some coffee, Sam?" I asked.

"Yes, I'd love some."

I made him a cup, and he grabbed a banana.

"Jeff is downstairs. You've got to see his room!"

John and I followed Sam downstairs. When Sam got to the bottom of the stairs, he looked at Jeff sitting

Dr. Sam Blackman and Jeff

in his recliner and said, "Wow, things have changed since I was a kid."

He walked around the room admiring Jeff's accomplishments as an athlete. Kathy took a picture of Sam and Jeff together in front of Jeff's wall of trophies, signed hockey sticks, plaques, baseball gloves, and bats.

Another voice from upstairs yelled down to us. "The Bruins' Hummer is here."

Kerry and Jay Southwood entered the kitchen.

"Hi, Kerry and Jay! Would you like something to eat?"

"No, thank you. The team is still running late."

"Would you like to see Jeff? He's downstairs."

We walked downstairs. Jeff stood up and said hello to them. As they walked around the room, they were amazed at the awards and trophies, but they couldn't believe all the autographed Bruins sticks and shirts.

"Where did he get the Derek Sanderson hockey stick? And the signed Bruins' team stick? And the signed Bobby Orr hockey stick?" they asked.

Jay picked up the Stephen Matheny Award that the MIAA Coaches had awarded Jeff last March. He knew a high school hockey player who had received this award a few years before Jeff. They didn't know that Jeff had also received the Bruins Sportsmanship Award at the TD Bank North Garden; the gold medal award was encased in a black velvet-covered box and displayed on a small table next to Jeff's couch along with other autographed Bruins pictures.

They didn't know much about Jeff and his love of the game until that day. I walked back upstairs. My husband was looking for me. The house was filled with people. It was six o'clock in the morning.

"Paul Stewart is here," John told me as I entered the kitchen from the basement door.

"Oh, God, do I know him?"

"He's the Head of the Boston Bruins Foundation. He had been a NHL referee for many years prior to his current position with the foundation. He's also a cancer survivor."

"This is my wife, Susan," John introduced me to Paul. He was admiring Jeff's hockey plaques we had upstairs.

"Susan, Sam is leaving," someone said.

Sam was walking down the driveway with his bike. I ran out the side door and caught up to him. I hugged him, thanking him for coming by to see Jeff.

"Good luck with your ride," I said.

Kerry approached me and said, "The team won't have time to stop at your house. We're going to meet them at the end of the street on Service Road."

"Okay, we'll bring the water and Gatorade to Service Road."

"We'll bring the sandwiches and oranges too," my sister said.

"Oh, I forgot about the oranges," I looked back at Kathy. Then I ran downstairs to tell Jeff that the team wasn't coming to our house and that we were going to greet them on Service Road.

I could see the relief on his face.

"Okay." He was so nervous and relieved. He put on his Bruins jersey and he and his friends, Brian and Mike left the house through the set of french doors that opened into our backyard.

We walked behind Jeff and arrived at the end of our street to meet up with other friends and neighbors. It was a clear and beautiful Sunday morning. The heat wave had ended the day before. Blue skies and no humidity, a great relief for the riders, I thought.

One by one the Bruins team stopped at the end of our road. The Hummer was parked on the side of the road as a marker for the team and the media. We cheered as other riders passed by. NESN and NECN were there with their cameras and began interviewing Don Sweeney. Then Terry O'Reilly and Judie Songin rode up on their recumbent bike. Terry sat up front and Judie in the rear seat. They needed Gatorade to replenish their empty bottles. Jeff  held Terry's bottle as he poured the Gatorade into the bottle. NESN and NECN filmed Jeff with the riders. Kim Jacobs put her arm around Jeff, and they talked. They smiled as they stood next to each other for a quick photo. She wore a Bruins bandana.

The Bruins saw Jeff looking healthy that day. It had been several weeks since we were told that Jeff was in remission. One rider asked, "How sick is Jeff? I ask because he looks so good."

"You don't know the type of cancer he's been battling; it's a tough cancer," our friend replied.

Kids in the neighborhood held up signs they had made and asked for autographs from some of the Bruins alumni.

The team had all arrived, and we gathered together in front of the Bruins Hummer for group photos. On the sleeve of their jersey were the initials JH encircled with a heart, in honor of Jeff.

After the photos, Jeff stood alone in front of the Hummer and was interviewed by NESN. I watched his interview later on television and listened as he said, "To have watched them play on television was something, but to see them here in person is great. The Boston Bruins have been my favorite team since I was five years old." He spoke well and without pause. I watched in pride. I knew it was hard for him, but he gave a great interview.

More PMC riders continued to pass us and we cheered.

The NESN sportswriter pulled me aside and asked, "How do you feel about Jeff being the Boston Bruins PMC pedal partner?"

"The Bruins have been Jeff's team since he was very young. He's a good hockey player and loves the game. To see them here this morning, riding for him, well, it's wonderful." I paused. "Being partnered with the Boston Bruins is the highest honor for Jeff. Hockey is his passion. Battling cancer and feeling alone is hard. To be associated with the Boston Bruins while battling cancer is the best possible pairing and it involves something he loves, hockey; it's a perfect match."

We thanked the team for stopping and for riding for Jeff. It was time for them to continue on down the Cape to the finish line in Provincetown. We stayed at the end of our street after the Bruins team had left, clapping and cheering as thousands of other riders rode past us and up Service Road. "What time is it?" I asked my sister.

"Seven thirty."

The PMC van slowly passed us, following the last few riders. Our neighbors, family, and friends returned to our house for breakfast. NESN and NECN drove off to follow the riders. When I got home, I went downstairs to see Jeff. I sat down across from him, still excited from meeting the Bruins PMC team, the media, and from cheering on the riders. I said, "Jeff, what a morning! You did great. These last two years have been amazing, haven't they? Now you, partnered with the Bruins team!" He was sitting in his recliner with his head back and legs up, resting. "Do you think you'll ride next year?" I asked.

"Yeah, I think I probably should," he replied.

"You know what?" I paused, first pondering the notion. "Jeff, I think I'm going to write a book." He looked at me from his recliner and said, "Who would want to read about me?"

"It's not about a race to the finish line; it's about a race to beat cancer," said Don Sweeney of the Bruins PMC team when the weekend came to a close and the riders were boarding the ship, *Providence Town II* to Boston. Out of thousands of riders, Don Sweeney was one of the top ten riders to finish at the Massachusetts Maritime Academy on the first day. He played fourteen seasons for the Boston Bruins in the 1990s. He is currently the General Manager of the Boston Bruins organization.

Jeff and Don Sweeney

CHAPTER 50

Senior Pictures, Second Annual Golf Tournament

JEFF STARTED HIS senior year in the fall and his radiation treatment on September 6, 2006. I told the photographer that we had only a small window of time to have Jeff's senior pictures taken. There wasn't a trace of any side effects from chemo. His facial hair had grown back, and he had a full head of hair without any changes in color, thickness, or texture. The pictures were taken in several different places and poses at the boardwalk and Town Neck beach.

Tom asked him to crouch down on his knee for a shot.

"I can't pose in that position," Jeff said politely.

Tom understood. He took several pictures of Jeff by the boardwalk, outside the sand dunes, and by the rocks with the waves gently touching the shore line as the background.

Saturday, September 24, 2006, was the second Annual Jeff Hayes Golf Tournament. That morning Jeff came to me and said, "Mom, I don't feel good."

"What's wrong?"

"I don't know. I just don't feel good."

I checked his temperature. It was normal.

"Try to take it easy today, pumpkin. It's a long day."

I knew he wouldn't leave the tournament early. Last year he told me he wasn't leaving until the last person had left.

When it was time to go, he dressed and drove to the course, a five-minute ride from our house. It was a cool and windy day.

Like the year before, there were two foursomes at each hole. That evening, the function hall was filled. Guests overflowed downstairs into the lounge. Everyone was excited that Jeff was beating the disease. John spoke again, and then I introduced Sam to the golfers and guests who sat at the tables that filled the large banquet room. The room was silent. The people in Sandwich followed

Jeff and Jack Lessard

Jeff's treatment and knew who Sam was. Sam approached the podium and began to speak.

"It has been an extreme pleasure to have been taking care of Jeff for the past year and a half," he began. "He's an extraordinary young man. I've also had the pleasure of getting to know the Hayes family as well. They've been thrown into this disease and the treatment and have had to learn a whole new language." He continued to talk about Jeff and Ewing's sarcoma. Then he thanked everyone in the room for all the support they'd provided Jeff and our family. At the end of his speech, we raised our glasses, and following Sam's lead, everyone repeated his words, "L'chaim! L'chaim!" We cheered and drank from our glasses. I thought it was amazing how he managed to get everyone in the room to speak Hebrew.

Sam left the podium, and our friends approached him, gathering around Sam and waiting in line to meet him. When I could finally get close to Sam, I told him that Jeff said he wasn't feeling well that morning.

"Really, what's wrong?"

"I don't know. He didn't have a fever."

"I'll go see him." He walked away from me, looking for Jeff.

Sam later told me he thought it was a feeling of excitement. "It's a Christmas morning, anxious feeling," he said after he spoke with Jeff.

It wasn't long after the tournament, in October, when things began to change.

CHAPTER 51

Jeff's Condition Begins to Change, October 2006

JEFF HAD FINISHED the radiation to his lungs, and he was taking the chemotherapy drugs that he had previously responded to. Sam and Hannah felt that he needed to be more hydrated. Just drinking more water or Gatorade wasn't working. They decided that Jeff would benefit from receiving fluids through his port, and they thought this was something I could do at home. Katherine instructed me to begin giving Jeff fluids in the morning before I left for work. She came to our house and showed me how to hook up the saline bag and access Jeff's port. I put on gloves and opened the syringe. I pointed the syringe up to the ceiling and clicked its side to release the air bubble. I watched it surface. I then pushed up on the syringe, and it stuck. I pushed again, harder this time, and out came the clear fluid in a blast that squirted the ceiling in Jeff's bedroom. He laughed. I laughed. Katherine laughed.

"That's okay," Katherine said. "We'll try another one."

Once I got the feel of the syringe and how to remove air pockets, I accessed Jeff's port by connecting the syringe to the attachment on his port. I rinsed the line with saline by pushing gently on the end of the syringe. I then removed the syringe and attached the tube that hung down from the bag of fluid. I released the clamp on the IV tube, and the fluid moved down the line into Jeff's port.

The next day I got ready for work and woke Jeff to start giving him the fluids. It all went well until I attached the syringe to the connector outside Jeff's port and blood starting coming out of the port. It was a light-red color. I began to panic.

"Just push on the syringe," Jeff said.

"Okay."

But blood still oozed out of the port.

"I think I'll call Katherine."

I dialed her cell phone and she immediately picked up.

"Hi, Katherine. I'm having trouble giving Jeff his fluids. There's blood coming out of Jeff's port. What should I do? Can you come over?"

"I'll be right there. Don't do anything," she replied.

Thankfully she lived only ten minutes away. "Jeff, she'll be here in a few minutes."

"Mom, it's okay. Sometimes blood escapes, and they usually just push it back into the port."

"Okay, but just in case, Katherine can look at it. I don't want anything to happen to you on my account."

Katherine arrived and did the procedure over with a new syringe and attached the IV line.

When I got to work that morning I called Sam and told him I couldn't do this. "This is too hard for me right now."

"Okay, don't worry. I'll call Hannah and let her know we need to come up with something else."

The next day Jeff went up to Boston with his friends to attend a college fair. He came home tired and with a bag full of college brochures. He was interested in Emerson College, New Hampshire's Plymouth State, University of Denver, Northeastern University, and Michigan State. Michigan State had been his favorite college sport's school. Jeff said he wanted to study sports medicine or criminal justice.

Homecoming weekend, Jeff's friends gathered at our house and sat in Jeff's living room. They were dressed in shirts and ties, dress pants, and shoes, not sneakers. It was the big dance before the first high school football game. They joked and laughed, waiting to leave for the dance. Jeff's date had purchased their tickets and was waiting for him at the door at the high school gym.

On Halloween, I left work early. When I got home, I turned the outside lights on and filled the candy bowl.

Jeff went out with his friend, Brian and was back home by nine o'clock. Trick-or-treaters had just stopped ringing the doorbell. Jeff entered the house through back door slider. He went downstairs, and I followed him.

"What's the matter?" I asked.

"I don't feel good."

I took his temperature. It was 100. Jeff's normal temperature was 97.6.

"Honey, we have to go to the emergency room." I ran upstairs to tell John.

John was sitting in his recliner, and his eyes were closed when I told him.

"Why, what's wrong?" he asked.

"His temperature is 100. I'm going to call Sam."

When I got Sam on the phone, he told me he would contact the emergency room and speak with the doctor on call.

When we arrived at the Cape Cod Hospital Emergency Room, Jeff sat with an intake nurse for his history and was brought to one of the curtained stalls inside the emergency room where his temperature was taken. Sue Whynot walked into the room. She was the mother of one John Jr.'s metro hockey teammates. I didn't know she was working, and I hadn't seen her for several years.

"I'm here to take Jeff for a chest x-ray."

It was good to see someone we knew. She wheeled Jeff's bed down the hall and through a door that closed behind them. I waited in the emergency room.

We were there until midnight. Nothing was seen on the x-ray, but they feared an infection in his port or in his lungs. Jeff was given Tylenol and antibiotics. He started to complain of back pain.

The fever remained constant. I gave him two Tylenol every four hours. The next day I drove Jeff to the JFC. It was a relief to sit in a familiar examining room and know that Sam and Hannah were there to care for him. For me, the enormous sense of responsibility and fear I felt lessened when we were at the JFC. We trusted Sam and Hannah. We were lucky to live close enough to Boston to get the care Jeff received at the JFC and at Children's Hospital, one of the best clinical settings and one the top Children's Hospitals in the world.

Sam sent us to the Brigham and Women's Hospital so that Jeff could receive a full-body scan in their Nuclear Medicine Department. The scan took over an hour. The technician was friendly, born and raised in Boston, and talked to us the entire time. She positioned Jeff, getting him to lie flat on the table, continually asking if he was comfortable. He watched *The Mighty Ducks* on a small television above the scanner. Most of the movies were for young children.

The large, circular scanner passed slowly over Jeff's body, starting from his toes and moving up to his head. I sat across from Jeff and behind the back of his head so that he couldn't see me watching over him. I was close to the monitor that viewed the skeletal images during the scan. I wanted to look, but at one point she turned the monitor completely out of my view.

During the last twenty minutes or so, a male technician came out from the back of the room. "You're doing great, Jeff," he said. "We're almost done."

When the scan was done, we were instructed to wait for Dr. Blackman in the small examining room next door.

We hadn't been waiting long when I looked up and saw Sam walking quickly toward us.

"Hi, Sam," Jeff and I said.

He sat down next to the examining table that Jeff and I leaned up against.

"There is a mass in Jeff's hipbone," Sam said, sitting across from us.

We didn't speak. We just sat there, shocked and nonresponsive. After several seconds, he said, "It will hit you later. I'm on my way to Sandwich for a speech. Head home now, and I'll call you tomorrow." He was puzzled, uncertain how to react to us staring blankly back at him and unresponsive.

Jeff and I left Children's for home; we were tired. It was getting dark, and the cars on the expressway were moving at a fast pace. I was blocked in the fast lane and noticed Sam's car behind ours in the right lane. He slowed down to let us in his lane. I couldn't react that quickly and let him pass. I knew his car. He had just purchased a new one and had told us the story a few months ago. He lived on the Jamaica Way. One night when he returned home, he pulled into his driveway, which was on a hill, and got out of his car. Immediately the car started to move in reverse, down the driveway and onto the Jamaica Way. It crossed over the two-lane highway and crashed on the other side. No other cars were passing by at the time. He told us that his first reaction was to get behind the car and try to stop it from rolling backward. "That was crazy," he said. "I don't know where my mind was when I got out of my car that night. Frantically, I tried to stop it by jumping inside the driver's seat, but I couldn't. I wasn't fast enough."

I moved our car over a lane and was behind Sam, driving to Cape Cod. Jeff and I didn't speak until I hit Route 3 in Braintree, and he turned to me and said, "I want to go to a Bruins game."

CHAPTER 52

Bruins Luxury Box, Hip Surgery

THE MOON WAS the only light. Looking out the window, I saw the strong wind sweep the loose leaves off the ground, forming a small, spiraling circle on the cement walk. The air was damp and cool. I felt tense and scared as I moved toward the front door. I put on my wool coat that fell just above the bottom of my floral dress—early 1940s style. I buttoned the top two large buttons on the coat and tied the laces of my worn ankle boots. My hat covered the top of my short, wavy brown hair. We had to get out of there quickly to run and hide. My sister was with me. I saw a soldier approaching the house. We were on a farm in a small province of France during WWII. I'd had this dream before. We quickly left through the back door and ran toward the barn. A light was shining from inside. As we approached, I saw hay inside through the large barn doors that were left open. We crouched down together, hiding just outside the doors in a dark space. There was a vehicle parked across from us. I heard gunshots in the distance. I was terrified, scared of being found and killed. I wrapped my arms around my sister, trying to keep as quiet as possible. From the corner of my eye, I could see the soldier's tall black boots. I looked higher and saw his dark face and his pistol. He walked several feet from us.

I woke suddenly. My body lay still and stiff, frozen in fear. The room was dark, without moonlight to illuminate the shapes in my bedroom. I turned over on my side, my eyes open, not wanting to return to that place. As I lay there, my fear began to fade, and I fell back asleep. When I woke the next morning, I remembered the dream and the fear that overwhelmed me, the sweat that formed in my grasp and between my fingers.

My phone rang. It was Sam.

"Susan, Dr. Ready can operate next Monday to remove the tumor in Jeff's hip," Sam said. "Can you come up on Friday for preop work and to meet with Dr. Ready?"

"Yes, of course," I replied.

Jeff complained of back pain on and off and looked tired. I leaned over his bed and felt his forehead while he lay propped up with pillows.

"Ouch! Jeez, Mom, what are you doing?" He raised his hand swiftly to push mine away.

"I'm sorry, honey. I didn't know." Oh, God, I thought. His forehead was sensitive to touch, painful for him. I had barely touched him with the back of my hand to see if he was warm. I felt awful, shocked by his reaction. I stepped away. His angry look disappeared.

"Can I get you some Tylenol? When was the last time I gave you some?" I asked. "Let me look in the binder." I left his room and opened the binder to the top sheet that read today's date and listed his medicines and the times he'd taken them.

"It's been a little more than three hours, honey. I think you can take two more now."

"Okay," he replied.

"Jeff, do you remember Dr. Ready? I asked. "He's going to remove the tumor in your hipbone on Monday."

"Yes, I remember him."

"Are you okay with this?"

"Yes, Mom. What time do we need to go?"

"Sam said nine o'clock Friday morning. We'll find out more about the surgery when we meet with Dr. Ready."

My phone rang again. It was the landline, and I ran upstairs to answer it.

"Hi, Susan; it's Kerry.

"Hi! How are you?"

"I'm well. How's Jeff?"

"Well, his fever hasn't let up, and we just found out he's scheduled for surgery this Monday."

"Will he be all right to go to a game?" She asked. "I've reserved a luxury box for Jeff and ten of his friends for Saturday night's game."

"I think so. He really wants to go to a Bruins game. In fact, I think that's all he wants to do. He takes Tylenol, and that temporarily takes care of the fever. I think he'll want to go; I'm sure of it!"

"Okay, then please ask Jeff and his friends to arrive early for the preskate. The tickets will be at the will-call window."

"Okay, that's great, Kerry. Thank you very much. He'll be thrilled."

"I've got tickets for you and your family too. They will also be at the will-call window."

"Really, thanks!"

"Okay, tell Jeff hello, and I'll see you Saturday night."

"Thanks again. See you Saturday." I hung up and ran down the basement stairs and into Jeff's bedroom. After I told him, I left his room, and he opened his laptop and began typing. He had to choose ten friends to go with him.

We arrived Friday morning at Dr. Ready's office. We followed the same insurance intake procedure that we had twenty-two months ago when we met Dr. Ready for the initial consultation. That was before we had heard of Ewing's sarcoma and how strong the treatment would be to fight it. I thought back over those months and all the unknowns. We were smarter now having been through it, but once again we were facing the unknown.

Sam called me again before the surgery.

"I wasn't thinking of the possibility of the mass being infection," he said.

"An infection and not tumor?" I asked.

"Yes, it could be an infection."

Sam was excited at the notion that it might not be another tumor. An infection would explain the high fevers. I began to think differently. The fevers hadn't made sense. A fever is a sign of infection. The disease might not have spread. My heart was sprinting. Before surgery, I asked Jeff's surgeon.

"Dr. Ready, do you think it may be an infection?"

"I don't know," he replied. That's why we are going in to take a look. It's the only way to find out. If it's not an infection, we'll take the tumor out."

Then he told me about tumor fevers. This was new, and I didn't understand. Jeff never had a tumor fever, even when we first learned of the tumor in his thigh and the tumors in his lungs.

"Tumor fevers? What do you mean?"

"Ewing's sarcoma can cause tumor fevers."

"Why is he experiencing them now?" I asked.

"I don't know. Let's go in and see what's going on," he replied.

We were frightened; things had turned so quickly.

Jeff invited ten of his closest friends to the Bruins game. Every one of those friends would have jumped in front of a bus for him. I was amazed at how they had kept in contact with him throughout his entire treatment; his cell phone had over a hundred contacts.

Jeff and his friends arrived at the TD Bank North Garden and picked up their tickets at the will-call window. They were wearing Bruins jerseys and hats. During the preskate, they got to sit on the bench and meet the players. Jeff took pictures on his cell phone.

Jeff had his own private luxury box with a full buffet of food. Between the first and second periods, two of Jeff's friends got to ride on each Zamboni. The mascot came in the box; everything was planned in advance by the Bruins.

Also between the first and second periods, members of the Bruins alumni entered the box, along with Charlie and Kim Jacobs. Charlie is the Chief Excucitve Officer of Delaware North's Boston holdings, and son of Boston Bruins owner, Jeremy Jacobs.

Jeff shook Charlie's hand and said hello to Kim, and he thanked them for inviting him and his friends that night. They spoke for a few minutes, and then Jeff returned to his seat. He looked pale and thin, but he never showed the pain he was in.

I was told near the end of the third period that Zack Fitzgerald, a Boston Bruins Foundation Coordinator, would be escorting Jeff onto the ice to have pictures taken with Marco Sturm and Mark Stuart after the game. When I saw Zach enter the luxury box, I walked down the short set of stairs to the front row of the box. Jeff was sitting on the end, closest to the stairs. I knelt down next to him. The game was tied.

"Jeff, you have to go with Zach down onto the ice for pictures."

He turned to me and said, "Mom, there's only two minutes left in the game, and the score is tied!"

"I know, I'm sorry, but you have to go now."

He stood up, met Zach and left the box. On his way down to ice level, the Bruins scored. I knew Jeff could hear the crowd cheering the win. I could only imagine how mad he was to have missed the goal.

Kerry escorted us all down to meet with Jeff then took us to the locker room to meet Patrice Bergeron. When we arrived outside the locker room, we waited for Patrice. The ice girls walked past the boys twice. I smiled watching the boys watch the ice girls.

Patrice came out of the locker room, his hair still wet from his shower. He approached Jeff and shook his hand. We took pictures of them together and with Jeff's friends. Jeff and Patrice talked, and then we were escorted back to the general public exits.

It was a great night, our last night out for a long time.

Kerry e-mailed me the next day to tell me that Patrice had asked for a copy of the picture taken of him and Jeff that night.

Matt Rumel, Kevin Ducie, Patrice Bergeron, Jeff, Greg Iadonisi Below: John Robertson, Will Buckley, Back: Ryan Conway, John Lessard & Zach Columbo

On Monday morning, John, Jeff, and I drove up to Brigham and Women's Hospital. We were praying that Dr. Ready would find an infection in Jeff's hipbone. Everyone was praying that day. Sam still thought it might be infection. Everyone knew of Jeff's surgery from the Internet and Facebook. John couldn't stay for the surgery so he left Boston and went to work.

The surgery was delayed. We waited all morning. At one o'clock they began to prep Jeff for surgery. A male nurse entered our curtained cubicle. He was tall and thin with black hair. He tied a tourniquet tightly around Jeff's upper arm. Despite many attempts, he couldn't access Jeff's vein, and I could see Jeff becoming impatient. What is he doing? I thought. He walked around the bed to attempt access in a vein on Jeff's other arm. He didn't speak to us. We had never seen a nurse have difficulty finding a vein in Jeff's arm; he had good, visible veins. Jeff stared at me and then looked up at the male nurse. This went on for a while. He's in, oh, thank God, finally, I thought. I was starting to think he might have to look for another vein in Jeff's foot.

He took the tourniquet off Jeff's arm and secured the needle in place and then left.

"What the hell was he doing?" Jeff said, gritting his teeth. "Don't let him near me again."

"I won't; don't worry."

Dr. Ready opened the curtain and walked up to Jeff. He was wearing Jeff's hockey lace on his shirt, tied in a loop. Mrs. Flynn had given him the lace. She was a post-op nurse who lived in Sandwich; her son had played hockey with John Jr. Dr. Ready marked Jeff's hip and initialed the spot. He told us again the reason for the surgery; to find out whether Jeff's pain and fever were from an infection or whether more tumors were present in his hip.

"See you after surgery, Jeff," he said and left us.

The anesthesiologist then came in to explain his procedure.

It was time.

"Good luck, Jeff," I said, standing next to him before they wheeled him into the operating room. "I'll see you after surgery. I love you, pumpkin."

My sister Janet and her friend, Steve sat with me. We were in a large waiting room that housed a library of books on one side and cubicles with televisions on the other. Sofas and chairs were placed throughout the room. There was a large desk in the middle of the room where the receptionist received phone calls from the operating room staff.

We sat for hours, watching the news and waiting. I thought over and over, how can I make the pain be an infection so that we can get back to the chemotherapy drugs that were working. Should I run down Longwood Avenue until I'm out of breath, until my legs become weary and I can't go any further; the physical pain unbearable so that right now, up in the operating room, they'd find infection? It's time, I thought, time to pray for forgiveness for anything that I may have done or didn't do that caused this to happen to Jeff.

At six o'clock Janet and Steve left, and I sat alone. An hour passed until I heard my name called. I approached the desk, and the receptionist asked me to wait in one of the small rooms at the entrance of the large waiting room. I hadn't noticed the rooms when I first arrived.

"Dr. Ready will be down shortly to speak with you."

"Is Jeff okay?"

"Yes. Dr. Ready will be down soon to see you."

I sat down on the love seat in the small room and left the door ajar so I could see Dr. Ready when he arrived. I waited for what seemed like forever until he entered, still dressed in his scrubs and surgical cap. He sat down in the chair next to the end of the love seat.

"It was tumor."

"Oh, no!" I stared back at Dr. Ready, then leaned forward, my head in the palm of my hands as I tried holding back the tears. Oh, God, I thought, why? Why can't we have good news? I felt sick and looked away from Dr. Ready.

I didn't know how I was going to tell Jeff. It's too hard. After all this time, it's just too hard to hit him with this news, I thought.

"I removed the tumor," Dr. Ready continued. "There were some signs of destruction of the tumor from the chemo drugs."

He put his hand on my shoulder. "I'm sorry. With Ewing's and in Jeff's case, it's like brush fires; when another appears, we have to put it out. We'll keep putting out the fires."

"Thank you," I looked back at Dr. Ready. "May I see Jeff now?" It was seven thirty.

"Yes, let's go back upstairs to recovery." When we arrived, Dr. Ready excused himself, and I walked toward the recovery room and decided to call Sam. I was angry and upset. Sam answered his phone.

"Sam, it's tumor."

"I know," he replied.

"How can God do this to him?"

"Susan, I know. Jeff hasn't had one break the entire time."

He was upset. I paced up and down the hospital corridor with my cell phone, trying to make sense of this with Sam.

"I just can't understand it." I said. "Poor Jeff. I have to go in there and tell him it's tumor. I know he's hoping for infection. I don't know how to pick him up after this. It's devastating, Sam."

"I know it's hard, Susan."

"How much more can he take?" I asked, not wanting a response. Sam listened with empathy.

"I'll see you and Jeff tomorrow. Good night, Susan." We ended the call.

I entered the recovery room and saw Jeff lying in the hospital bed, his eyes open as he watched me approach. He was the only patient in the large recovery room. All the curtains were open with empty beds. It was quiet.

I stood next to him.

"Hi. How are you doing, honey?"

"Okay. Was it an infection?" he asked immediately.

"No, it was tumor."

He looked up toward the ceiling. His eyes watered.

He must have been waiting awhile for me because he wasn't groggy and seemed to have recovered from the anesthesia.

"Well, Jeff, what will they ask you to do next? Jump out of a plane?"

He turned to me and said, "With or without a parachute?"

Mrs. Flynn, Dr. Ready's surgical nurse, walked toward us. It was good to see her. She was from Sandwich, the nurse who'd given Dr. Ready the hockey lace. She had stayed late to be with Jeff.

Jeff still had a fever. They gave him one Tylenol.

We left recovery and headed up to Jeff's room.

When we arrived, the floor nurse came in with her laptop on wheels and asked, "You're Jeff? Hi. I need to ask you some questions to make sure I've got the right patient. What is your date of birth?"

"September 23, 1988," Jeff replied.

I don't recall what medication Jeff was on other than one Tylenol for his fever. He was hooked up with an IV of fluids, but his fever remained. It was close to midnight. The nurse took his vitals. I had made my window bed with sheets and a blanket from the linen closet. I hadn't packed an overnight bag and didn't have pajamas or a change of clothes, so I took some scrubs from the linen closet on the floor and changed.

The nurse took Jeff's temperature and turned toward me with an alarmed look on her face. She took it again.

"What is it?" I asked.

She didn't reply; instead she turned the handheld device that recorded his temperature toward me: 104.7.

"What is it?" Jeff asked.

"It's high," I replied.

"What is it?" he asked again, angry.

"It's 104.7."

He calmly turned to the nurse and said, "Do you have any ice packs?"

The nurse responded quickly as she snapped out of her dazed fear. "Yes, I do! I'll be right back."

I began to fill the sink in Jeff's room with cold water and ran to find the ice machine and several facecloths. By the time I returned, the nurse had put the ice packs under Jeff's arms, and I put three facecloths in the cold water. I put a cloth on his forehead and one behind his neck, and with the other I wiped down his chest, his arms, and his legs and every bend in his body.

"Jeff, can you move your legs and bend your knees so that I can cool behind them? This one first." I wiped the back of each leg.

"Stomach now, ready? Is that cold?"

"No, it's okay."

"I'm going to change the cloth behind your neck now."

He wore only his boxers.

I did this on and off until the floor doctor arrived with another nurse. He looked frightened, as Jeff's temperature remained high.

"I'm going to order an x-ray."

I thought, how and where? His temperature is too high.

"Why don't we give him more Tylenol?" I asked. "It has worked for the last two weeks."

"Dr. Ready only ordered one Tylenol," he replied.

"Yes, but it works!" I cried.

"I will try to reach Dr. Ready." His look frightened me.

He left the room, and I never saw him again; nor did Jeff have an x-ray taken. Throughout the night I continued changing the facecloths and wiping Jeff down every ten minutes. The clock was hung over the sink, and I glanced at it throughout the night. Jeff remained calm, and we worked together keeping him cool. By three o'clock his temperature had come down to 101 degrees. I kept adding ice to the water and changing his facecloths; neither of us slept the rest of the night.

The sun began to rise, and the nurse was in and out watching Jeff. I lay down and fell asleep.

Two hours later I woke when my sisters Kathy and Janet walked into our room with a suitcase of clothes. I began to tell them of the night we had.

"I didn't have time to think, just to react," I explained. "His temperature was so high."

The nurse changed Jeff's bed, and I continued to cool him with a change of clothes; his temperature was still 101 degrees. We were now able to give him two Tylenol.

My sisters left to get us something to eat, and I lay on my bed. I looked up at the ceiling, relieved he'd made it through the night. Unable to move and lying straight out on the bed, I asked, "So, what do you want for Christmas?"

"It's too expensive." He replied.

"I don't care how much it costs. What is it you want?"

"PlayStation 3."

"Okay, how much is it?" I was curious now.

"It's six hundred dollars. It's hard to get. They're only making a certain number of them."

It's hard to get, I thought. Hearing that, just made me want to try even harder.

My cell phone rang; it was John, and I told him about the night we'd had.

"Dr. Ready said that his temperature would probably go up after the surgery."

"Yes, I know, but this was dangerously high."

Dr. Ready walked into the room, and I ended my call with John.

He approached Jeff's bedside and said, "Boy, I've never in all my surgeries received more phone calls on one patient than I have with you." His smile put us at ease.

"You'll probably have a high fever for a couple of days, Jeff. It's expected after this type of surgery." He examined Jeff, and after several minutes he walked toward the door, leaving to see his next patient. On his way out the door, he stopped midstride and looked back, asking, "Jeff, who coached..." I didn't hear the name the of the NHL hockey team. "And what year?"

Jeff replied immediately. Dr. Ready turned to Jeff and smiled, "You're right." And then he left the room.

"Well, I feel better that your fever is, I guess, normal, and we shouldn't worry. You were really amazing and calm last night."

"It was a long night; I'm tired," Jeff replied.

"Yeah, me too. Do you want something to drink, pumpkin?"

"Maybe some gingerale?"

"Okay, I'll get you some; be right back."

I walked out of Jeff's room and saw the nurse who had been with us all night. She was outside the door. I stood next to her as she entered data into her portable laptop. She looked up at me, smiled and asked, "Are you a nurse?"

"No." I said. "I had to wear these scrubs because I had nothing to change into."

"You were amazing last night," she said, now standing up straight and looking back at me.

The smile on my face changed and a tear rolled down my cheek.

"You were too. Thank you so much."

CHAPTER 53

Recovery from Surgery

W E STAYED AT Brigham and Women's Hospital for a few days. "You need to be able to walk around the nurse's station to go home," the physical therapist explained. He showed Jeff how to place the crutches on a step and support himself going up and down the stairs. Jeff's fever lessened; it never returned to his normal 97.6 degrees, but it never rose to 104.7 again.

One day at a time, I remember Hannah telling us. Jeff spent the week after surgery at home resting, anxious and worried. "I still have a lot of pain in my back, Mom." He'd moved from his recliner to the couch for relief.

"We have a follow-up appointment with Dr. Ready on Friday. Let's see what he says."

John and I both had missed so much work and needed to ask our friends to help us with appointments for Jeff. Michael, who had taken Jeff to his radiation treatment, took Jeff to this appointment with Dr. Ready.

"Who are you?" Dr. Ready asked Michael.

"Michael Cloherty, Jeff's uncle." He was John's best friend from college, and Jeff had often stayed overnight with Michael and his wife, Jackie, at their home in Waltham.

Dr. Ready examined the site of the incision and found nothing. "What did Dr. Ready say?" I asked Jeff over the phone.

"He said the pain was normal from the operation."

He was relieved and feeling good—I could hear it in his voice. It made me realize how much fear he kept to himself.

Dr. Ready had prescribed radiation treatment as a precaution to kill any cells that might have been missed during surgery, but we had to wait for the bone and surrounding tissue to heal.

I don't know what day it was in November when Jeff could no longer stand the pain in his mouth.

"Mom, can you call the dentist? My tooth is really bothering me."

It wasn't his tooth, I thought. I just couldn't bear the thought of what might be happening in his jawbone. The tissue around the socket where his wisdom tooth had been extracted was inflamed.

"I will call Sam, honey, and we'll see what he says."

Jeff's temperature remained around 99 degrees. He was now on OxyContin.

I sent out an e-mail to everyone I knew to help find Jeff a PlayStation 3 for Christmas. Kim Jacobs, Terry O'Reilly, and Judie Songin replied several times telling me that they were contacting everyone they knew, including owners of stores, to try to find one—even the manufacturer. Terry wore his Bruins jacket and visited several stores to try to persuade the owner that he needed a PlayStation 3 and why.

"He's never, ever done that for anyone," Judie wrote me in an e-mail.

When I returned home from work, I ran downstairs to see Jeff. He was sitting in his recliner watching television.

"Mom, I just heard on the news that someone shot someone else waiting in line for a PlayStation 3. Was that you?" Jeff asked.

"Very funny. It could have been me, Jeff. I'd kill for you. You know that, don't you?"

"Just make sure you get a PlayStation 3!"

Later that day I stood on the stairs leading down to Jeff's room. He was sitting on the couch with his legs stretched out and a pillow beneath his lower back. He looked pale and ill. I was on the phone with Sam.

Sam said, "Ask him if the pain is bone pain."

I yelled down, "Is it bone pain, Jeff? Sam is asking."

"No, I don't think so."

"He says no, Sam."

"Okay," he replied over the phone.

Sam prescribed him the slow-release Oxycodone. "He can take the long-acting pain-relief medicine and take the OxyContin for intermittent pain," he told me.

The day before Thanksgiving—the worst travel day of the year—I drove Jeff up to Brigham and Women's for a radiation treatment. The last couple of treatments had been quick; he was in and out within twenty minutes. On this day, however, the traffic was horrific. I decided to drop Jeff off at the front door and wait for him there. He left the car and entered the hospital, heading to nuclear medicine; I stayed parked along the sidewalk until one of the valet attendants asked me to move.

"You can't park here. This is a drop-off lane."

"Okay," I said.

I noticed a Jaguar parked two cars in front of me. "How come he gets to park there?" I questioned out loud, after shutting my car window. I started the car and drove outside the entranceway and onto Francis Street and then around the corner. I stopped at the red light. When the light turned green, I took a left turn back into the front entrance of Brigham and Women's and back into the drop-off lane. It took about five minutes with the traffic light. I looked around to see whether they had noticed my car down at the end of the lane. There were a few guys working valet. Again I was approached. The valet guy walked up to my car and stood next to the driver's side door. I opened the window. "You can't park here. Drive around please!" My car was idling. I put it in gear and drove my car around again. I did this again and again until I said to the valet guy, "When the owner of the Jaguar moves his car, I will move. That car has not moved once." I was getting pissed. It was the day before Thanksgiving; everyone who needed to be there before the holiday was circling the hospital or waiting to pick someone up. The traffic was bumper-to-bumper at the drop off and circling back to the entrance. Traffic getting from Boston to the Cape would be awful. It was now dark.

I had to move again. That was it for me. I was ready to knock out the next valet guy who approached my car. I circled around again and then parked across from the drop-off lane when a car pulled out and left. I pulled in and parked. I saw Jeff limping toward the car. He looked so tired and weary. I got out of the car so he could find me.

"That was fast," I said. I didn't want him to know that I had just battled the front line. I noticed the Jaguar pulling out of the drop-off lane a few cars ahead of me. He had been parked there the entire time and had returned to his car when it was convenient for him. I wouldn't have done anything, but thinking about rear-ending him felt good.

It took forever to get home. Jeff fell asleep almost immediately. He always waited until we reached the expressway, probably to be sure I was going in the right direction.

We had planned another trip to Waterville Valley for Thanksgiving but had to cancel.

On Thanksgiving, Jeff's temperature went up to 102.1.

I prepared a turkey dinner. Patty and Marty and Jeff's cousin Julie joined us. I made a plate with cut-up dark turkey meat, mashed potatoes, and corn and brought it down to Jeff. He and I ate together in his living room. He had little appetite; the pain in his upper right gum was getting worse, and his energy level was low.

We were anxious to get back to Boston, but with the holiday we had to wait until Monday. That entire Thanksgiving weekend he suffered quietly, waiting for relief. I continued giving him Tylenol along with Bactrim, OxyContin, and Oxycodone.

On Saturday I asked, "Jeff, how about if we stay up in Boston Sunday night and avoid the traffic Monday morning? There's a really nice hotel in Boston on the harbor, the Hyatt Harborside at Logan. Dad and I stayed there after our second trip on the *Spirit of Boston* cruise last September."

"Okay."

"We'll leave Sunday afternoon."

I called the hotel and made reservations. It was a relief to leave the house, knowing we'd miss the Monday morning traffic and could relax at the Hyatt Harborside Sunday evening.

Sunday dinner was homemade calzones from another hockey family. They were delicious and perfect for eating on the run. I wanted to know how to make them but knew it was probably one of those Italian family recipes, or no recipe that I'd never be able to reproduce with the same authentic taste.

I packed for Jeff and me. The medication log, which I left at home, was blank the day we left and for the week that followed.

When we arrived at the Hyatt, I told the hotel manager about Jeff and how John and I had stayed at the hotel after the Jimmy Fund Boston Harbor cruise. I told him about the last twenty-two months. He told me of a family member also battling cancer. He gave us a complimentary night.

We entered our room on the seventh floor, which overlooked the harbor, and Jeff made himself comfortable in the double bed closest to the bathroom. I sat in the chair next to the window, looking out into the harbor.

"Is this a five-star hotel?" Jeff asked.

"I'd say so, Jeff. Look at this view! And the room, it's first class."

There was a knock on the door. "Room service."

"Room service?" I looked at Jeff, surprised.

I opened the door, and the bellhop pushed in a linen-covered butler's table with a banquet-style bucket of ice filled with soda, water, and juice. There were two stemmed bar glasses placed upside down, cheese and crackers, whole fruit, two chocolates.

"From the manager, on the house," the bellhop said.

I looked around the room for my purse, handed him a tip, and thanked him as he left our room.

On the end of the butler's table was a sealed white envelope. I opened it. The front of the card was a photo of the Hyatt Harborside. Inside, the card read,

Jeff,

     Welcome to the Hyatt Harborside. I hope you have a pleasant stay. It is my pleasure to have such an outstanding young man staying with us. Please feel free to contact myself or Kelly if there is anything we can do to make your stay more comfortable.
With warm regards,
Phil Stamm, General Manager

I was losing count of Jeff's angels. Jeff was feeling pretty special, a VIP. He pulled out his phone to take a picture of the view from our window to send to his friends.

"What's your pain level, Jeff?" I asked.

"What time is it?"

"Enough time has passed; do you need some more pain medication?"

"Yes."

I snored that night. Jeff threw an empty water bottle at me during the night. I didn't feel it, nor did I hear him call my name.

As we checked out the next morning for our trip to the JFC, I said, "I think we should stay here every time we need to visit the clinic."

"That'd be nice," Jeff replied.

It was the usual routine, Jeff's vitals were checked shortly after we arrived. For the first time in almost two years his weight had dropped. Sam decided to admit Jeff. His blood levels were low, and he needed platelets, and Sam wanted to x-ray Jeff's hip. Once Jeff was admitted, we would discuss his treatment going forward. Sam asked Jeff to write down any questions he had for him.

That afternoon in Jeff's hospital room at Children's, we met with Sam and Hannah, a pain therapist, and a social worker.

"We have three choices of new chemo drugs we can try," Sam began.

I knelt down beside the end of Jeff's bed. He sat up in his bed with a pad of yellow lined paper.

Sam explained each set of drugs and their side effects. He gave Jeff and me a copy to read. The chemotherapy drugs that worked over the summer were not an option anymore, as another tumor had showed up in Jeff's hip. Any one of the three combinations was a shot in the dark. Jeff turned to me, as he always did, looking for the best choice. We made the decision we felt was best given the choices we had.

"Jeff, do you have any questions for us?" Sam asked. "Have you written anything down that you want to ask us?"

"Yes," he replied. "With this treatment, will I be able to return to school?"

Sam and I looked at each other. "Let's see how it goes."

We stood outside Jeff's hospital room, Sam, Hannah, Patty, and I.

"If he has to go, I'm going with him," I said, looking at Hannah. She didn't reply; her eyes began to tear. She looked away and then back at me, "Susan, you have two other kids."

"The weight loss isn't a good sign. We'll try this set of drugs and see what happens. Tomorrow I'm going to move Jeff into a larger, private room, and he'll have an x-ray taken some time this afternoon," Sam said.

"Can he still do the radiation treatment?" I asked.

Sam paused and said, "Yes, I'll set it up for tomorrow."

Sam and Hannah left, and Patty and I went back into Jeff's room.

"How are you doing, pumpkin? How's your pain level?"

"I'm okay, Mom."

"Would you like something to eat?

"No, I'm tired; I think I'll sleep."

I stepped out into the hall to make some phone calls, and Patty went outside for a walk. I called Doreen Lessard. When she answered her phone, I began to tell her that things didn't look good and that Jeff might not make it.

We cried together over the phone. Several days later I found out that when she told her husband, Jack, a captain with American Airlines, he grounded himself. He was too upset to fly.

Jeff was scheduled at ten o'clock that evening for new images of his hip-bone. He ate little at dinner. I helped him into his wheelchair, and we headed for nuclear medicine. Our floor nurse came with us.

We were taken to a large, well-lit room with a large reclining chair in the center of the room. A machine hovered over the chair with a wide metal bar suspended above; it was part of the x-ray machine. Next to the machine was a portable stand, waist high with a small keyboard, monitor, and pump where the doctor stood on and off throughout the x-ray. On one side of the room was a large protective window, and behind the glass I could see another room. Just inside and below the glass was the main control station and where the other technicians sat. There were four, sometimes five, people working together during this x-ray process, walking in and out of this room.

Jeff got himself into the chair. It was now after ten o'clock. One of the several technicians greeted us and told us that this was a new machine and they weren't sure how to get the images ordered. Another technician stood on one side of the chair in front of his small monitor; his back to me, as I stood on the other side of Jeff. Our nurse had accessed a vein in Jeff's arm and the technician proceeded to push the fluid into Jeff's vein in his right arm. Once he began, however, blood started flowing from Jeff's vein and down his arm. He then asked Jeff to hold his arm upright during the procedure. Our floor nurse went over and began to work on Jeff's injection site. She tried to stop the flow from the injection site and stop the bleeding from Jeff's arm. There was a sense of urgency as she struggled to get the needle back into his vein.

I quickly became frightened not only by the overall lack of knowledge in operating this new machine, but by all that had just happened at my son's expense. Did they know how critical his condition was? I wanted to ask.

"Why don't we try this in the morning when you may have a better understanding of how it works?" I asked.

"No, we need to get this done tonight!" one of the technicians replied.

Things got worse. Jeff's cheeks began turning red. It was like clockwork when his fever returned. I knew it was time for two Tylenol. I'd been treating his fever for weeks. I wish I had my pocketbook, I thought. I carried a bottle of Tylenol with me. I turned away from Jeff and looked back inside the window where the technicians sat. I saw them smiling and chuckling at something. I turned to the technician.

"Jeff needs Tylenol," I said. His back was turned toward Jeff and me. He didn't reply. He ignored me. He looked as though he was trying to figure out what was going wrong. I said to our floor nurse, "Jeff's fever is coming back, and he needs Tylenol."

"We don't have any Tylenol down here," she said, not looking at me.

"Please get some, because Jeff needs it now," I replied.

"We don't have Tylenol down here," she said again, her voice becoming stern.

"Then can you get me some cold cloths? His face is bright red."

I knew the routine of his fevers. I knew the remedy. Our floor nurse left the room and went behind the glass into the technicians' control room after she'd corrected the line in Jeff's vein. I was left there looking at the backside of the technician. Our floor nurse then opened the door of the control room and stood in the doorway. I looked her way and mouthed the words to her again, "I need Tylenol!"

"I told you: we don't have any Tylenol down here!" she yelled back at me, screaming the words in anger.

I was stunned. I'd never been yelled at by a nurse. I felt my face blush. Then I got really pissed. She was our floor nurse; she knew Jeff's condition. I tried to think of another way I could help Jeff. Again, I thought about the Tylenol I had in my pocketbook. Should I leave Jeff and go up to our floor and get it?

"I'll be right back," I said to Jeff.

"Where are you going?"

"I'm going to make a phone call."

"Okay, but don't be long."

I left the x-ray room. I called my husband and told him what they were doing to Jeff and that his fever was coming back.

"Call Sam," he said.

Sam's cell phone went right to voice mail. I left him a detailed message while I stood outside the room where Jeff sat at the mercy of these people who seemed uncaring and totally oblivious to my requests or the seriousness of Jeff's condition.

When I returned to the room, I pulled out my phone again and stood at the doorway prepared to get a wide-angle photo of the room; Jeff in the chair with his arm suspended in the air, with the technicians in the background. I didn't take it.

Our floor nurse came up to me and said, "Jeff has a high fever, and I have called upstairs for Tylenol."

You're kidding me! How many times did I tell her he needed Tylenol, I thought.

Within minutes a nurse from our floor arrived with Tylenol, which she gave to Jeff. Again and again they tried to take the x-rays, and finally it was over. By the time we left the room, Jeff's fever had gone down.

I stood next to Jeff in his wheelchair as we waited outside the elevator doors.

"I'm going to jail, Jeff."

He was so sick and just continued looking forward, not up at me. "Mom, just don't talk to her."

Our floor nurse approached us, hitting the lit elevator button again.

We stood in silence waiting for the elevator. The doors opened and we entered. I followed his advice and stood silent as our floor nurse sighed and said, "Thank God that's over."

I looked down at Jeff in his wheelchair, and he looked back up at me. I thought to myself, gee, I hope she's okay. It must have been such an ordeal for her! We rode the elevator up to Jeff's floor; I couldn't even look at her. When the elevator stopped on our floor, I pushed Jeff's wheelchair out of the elevator and to our room. Jeff got into the bed.

"Just let it go, Mom!" Jeff said.

The next morning when Sam walked into Jeff's hospital room, he immediately told us that he'd written a very long letter last night to that particular group of technicians and had also questioned our floor nurse.

Sam left orders to move Jeff into a larger room. John and Jason arrived later that morning. We stayed with Jeff. At noon John and I went to the food court, and Patty and Jason went to the hotel. When John and I returned, Dr. Grier, Sam's boss, walked into the room. I was standing at the end of Jeff's bed.

"Hey, Jeff, how are you doing?" Dr. Grier asked.

"Okay," Jeff replied, but he didn't look it. His face was drawn, and his color was pale. He looked weak as he lay in the hospital bed. The top half of the bed was elevated with two pillows comfortably supporting his head.

I began to tell Dr. Grier about the last several weeks and Jeff's pain. He stood next to Jeff at the head of the bed.

"We had to wait for the fourth hour to give him the pain meds. We couldn't keep up with the pain," I told him.

"You don't have to wait to give him Oxycontin. It's okay to give it to him when he needs it. He won't have a heart attack or stroke as most people think. The brain allows it because the body is in pain. You could have given it to him when he needed it."

"I didn't know that. I wish I had."

Sam entered the room.

Dr. Grier was commenting on Jeff's shirt, which he'd bought in Disney World. "Rules, what rules?" was written on the front of the shirt, and Grumpy, one of the seven dwarfs from *Snow White*, was sitting in the penalty box.

Later that afternoon, after Dr. Grier and Sam had left Jeff's room, my brothers and sisters started arriving. The room began to fill up. Jeff never had so many visitors all at the same time. Patty and Jason had returned. I wondered why he had a room full of visitors.

CHAPTER 54

Two Legends

IT WAS LATE in the afternoon. Since Jeff's treatment began, I'd lost my sense of time; our lives had change dramatically with the treatment. I can't compare the change in my life to what my son's life had become. I gave every thought and moment of time to my son. Nothing else mattered. He lived battling the disease, eager only to return home to his friends and to play hockey and baseball. Now the cancer was spreading, and we were losing time; we were losing Jeff.

The door opened to Jeff's hospital room, which was filled with family, and in walked Terry O'Reilly and Judie Songin. Terry was carrying a large gift bag with the face of a snowman on the front and the handles tied with ribbon made into a bow.

My brother was standing next to me and whispered, "I got a call from Judie; they wanted to see Jeff today."

Terry walked quickly up to Jeff's bedside and placed the bag next to Jeff. Terry started to open the gift while Jeff lay watching.

Jeff's smile was wide and lit up his thin, pale face. Terry smiled back, excited to present him with the gift. The room became full of surprise and pure joy to see both Jeff and Terry open a PlayStation 3.

"Judie said they had finally found one," my brother whispered to me.

"Thank you, Terry!" Jeff said in a sickly voice. "Can we play?" he asked.

"Of course we can," Terry replied, and took the game over to the television and hooked it up. Jeff got out of bed, and John placed a chair near the television for Jeff. Terry and Jeff played while everyone stood and watched.

"I'm not very good at this," Terry said.

"That's okay; it's a new game," Jeff replied.

An hour passed, and the room began to empty. Jeff thanked Terry and Judie, and John and I thanked them as well. It was unforgettable. When everyone had left, I unhooked the PlayStation 3.

"Mom, put it in the corner of the room with a blanket over it," Jeff said. "I don't want it stolen."

He watched closely as I put the PlayStation 3 in the corner of the room and covered it with a blanket.

"Do you think we can get bolts put on the front and side doors at home?" he asked.

I smiled and said, "I'll ask Marty if he will do that before we get home. I'm sure he can."

Jeff walked slowly back to his bed, leaning on the mattress to balance himself. He climbed into the hospital bed, and I straightened his blanket, leaving his feet uncovered.

"I need my rest now, Mom."

"Okay, pumpkin. At least now I don't have to go around shooting people for a PlayStation 3."

"Mom, how did the Bruins know I wanted a PlayStation 3?"

I e-mailed everyone I knew who could possibly help us find a PlayStation 3. It was very difficult, even for the Bruins, but they tried so hard.

I wondered if Sam knew about the PlayStation 3. I wasn't sure why he'd moved Jeff into a larger and private room. I left Jeff's room to go lay down in the teen room across from his room. I fell sound asleep on the small couch.

"Susan, Jeff wants to see you." Patty woke me. "Bob Sweeney from the Bruins just came by to see Jeff and gave him a Bruins sweatshirt. He's mad because you weren't there."

"Oh, jeez." I got up quickly, left the teen room, and walked into Jeff's room.

"Where were you?" He said, "You're never here when somebody comes."

"I'm sorry; I was sleeping across the hall. Wow! That's nice Bob came by to see you."

John had gone to the hotel and returned with something for Jeff to eat. The Bruins were playing tonight, and we planned on watching the game with Jeff, Jason, and Patty.

"Can we get the Bruins game on this television?" I asked.

"Yes, it's on NESN," John replied.

We finished eating, and I pulled up a chair next to Jeff to watch the game. Jason and Patty sat on the couch, and John sat in the cushioned window seat. It was quiet. We were accustomed to the change from the routine of the day to the stillness of the night. After the first period, Patty and Jason took the shuttle back to the Holiday Inn.

Between the second and third periods we watched an interview with Ray Bourque, a former Bruins defenseman. The third period started, and we watched, staring at the television. I heard the door open. I thought it was a nurse or a doctor. In walked Ray Bourque. It seemed as though he walked out of the interview booth and into our room. He stepped up to Jeff's bed and said, "You must be important. I received ten calls today to come see you tonight!"

"The Bruins have been very good to me," Jeff said, looking up at Ray from his hospital bed.

Ray pulled up a chair and sat down next to Jeff. "So tell me; what's going on?"

John and I listened and watched the game as Jeff and Ray talked. Jeff pulled out his cell phone and showed Ray the pictures he had taken during the pre-skate at the Bruins game he had gone to before his surgery. He talked to Ray Bourque as if he'd known him all his life.

"Here's Chara." Jeff gave his phone to Ray.

318

"Chara trains hard; he's a good leader," Ray said as he took the phone from Jeff. "He has a strict regimen of working out and working hard on his game."

I've never seen Jeff so comfortable talking as he was with Ray that night. I pulled out the sweatshirt Bob Sweeney had just dropped off and asked Ray to sign it. I looked for other items to have signed for John Jr. and Jason. Ray signed everything. John asked him about his son, Chris. John Jr. had played against him in Charlestown a few years earlier. We asked about his Italian restaurant, Tresca, in the North End and he invited us to come for dinner.

The third period ended in a tie, and Ray stayed for the shootout, which went longer than usual; neither team could score more goals in the shootout. Finally the Bruins won.

Ray said good night. I hugged him and thanked him. John shook his hand, and Ray wished Jeff good luck.

"Thanks for coming to see me," Jeff said.

"Bye," Ray said and left the room.

Moments later Sam walked into the room.

"Was that someone important?" he asked with a big grin.

Jeff raised his voice and said, "He's only one of the best NHL defensemen ever to have played the game!"

We were back home.

Sam prescribed methadone, three tablets every six hours, trilisate every six hours along with OxyContin every two hours, Tylenol every six hours, colace and senacol once a day, and the usual Bactrim twice a day.

My medication schedule was filled. Each line listed a different drug, and across the top were the times of day and night. I set an alarm clock each hour I needed to give Jeff medication. I put an asterisk in the box prior to the time I needed to give Jeff that medication. When I gave it to him, I recorded the dosage. The time between the pain meds began to get shorter as the days passed. With Sam's instructions, I changed the methadone to four tablets and gave him OxyContin as needed. His temperature remained around 100 degrees.

I slept every night on the couch outside his bedroom with the alarm clock on the end table and a tube of toothpaste on the floor beside the couch. I sat up in the middle of the night at the sound of the alarm, brushed my teeth, and with the flashlight lying on the bar top, I opened each bottle of medicine I had put out earlier, lined up in order, and put the pills in a small plastic cup, the cups used in the hospital to administer meds. I used Purell all the time. I opened a Sunny Delight, put a straw in it, and opened Jeff's door.

"What time is it?" he'd ask every time I entered his room.

I propped his head up with pillows. We had this down to a science: I placed the pill on his tongue and then let him sip through the straw.

"Why didn't we do this sooner?" I said to him softly.

The VNA visited regularly to draw blood and check his vitals. On Friday, after one week at home, John and I drove Jeff up to the JFC for a blood transfusion. Jeff's pain was becoming uncontrollable. Hannah entered the room and drew blood. "I'm going to give you a shot of morphine, Jeff, to help with the pain," Hannah said.

"Okay."

"Would you like to watch a movie?"

"Yes. What do you have?"

"*Iron Eagle.*"

"Okay." He looked very ill and thin.

She left the room and returned rolling in a small television. She inserted the tape and started the movie.

"Dad, close the door. There are swears in this movie, and there are little kids in the next room who may hear them," Jeff remarked.

Hannah and I looked at each other and then at John.

"Okay, Jeff," John replied and closed the door.

Jeff's blood levels were dangerously low, and they heard something in his lungs that made them order an x-ray of his chest.

After the x-ray at Children's, we returned to the same room and continued watching the movie. Jeff was still in pain, so Hannah gave him another shot of morphine. He then fell asleep, and John and I left for something to eat. When we returned, we waited for Sam.

When Sam arrived, he told us he had seen a small mass in Jeff's lung, an infection. He gave us a prescription for antibiotics.

"Sam, can you look at my tooth?" Jeff asked.

"Sure." After he did, he stepped back and said, "I'm going to call over to the dental clinic at Children's and see if they can see you this afternoon."

Sam escorted us outside Jeff's room. Once in the hall, he told us that he didn't think Jeff would make the week. I didn't believe it. It was as if I didn't even hear him. I focused on the dentist and taking care of Jeff. It was December 11, 2006, my husband's birthday.

We left the JFC with Jeff in a wheelchair and went to the dental clinic. It was dark outside when we took an elevator to the old, original section of Children's Hospital. Jeff was weak, dazed from the morphine, but he sat up straight in the wheelchair, his strength hard to believe.

I completed the history form, and Jeff was called into an examining room. The dental chair and overhead x-ray machine were the same I'd used when I worked for an oral surgeon twenty-five years before. I helped Jeff out of his wheelchair and into the dental chair. The dentist examined inside Jeff's mouth. He called in an intern to also take a look.

"I don't know what this is. I've never seen it before. I'd like to get a panoramic x-ray," he said.

We were brought into a small room where Jeff stood while the x-ray machine circled his jaw.

"I'll call Dr. Blackman tomorrow," the dentist said, and we left the clinic for home.

"It's disgusting," was what the dentist told Sam. That upset me, the insensitivity of the words he used to describe what he saw. It was Ewing's finding the fresh new flow of blood from where Jeff had his wisdom tooth extracted.

I added a new antibiotic to Jeff's medication schedule and gave it to him every four hours. I had become friends with the pharmacist at CVS and the women who worked with him behind the counter. Each time I returned for medication or chemotherapy drugs they'd ask, "How is Jeff?"

They were always prepared for what was needed or ordered. I don't know how. I just followed Sam's instructions to pick up the prescriptions. If they didn't have what was ordered, they got it from another pharmacy or had it delivered from Boston. I trusted them, and they made everything easier for me and gave me the support I needed to administer the drugs. They were professional and reliable; Jeff never went without what was prescribed. Thank God for the staff at the CVS on Quaker Meeting House Road in Sandwich.

CHAPTER 55

❦

The Deli

I ENTERED STOP & Shop and headed toward the deli. I didn't need much. I knew I couldn't be away from Jeff for too long. I could place my order in my sleep: roasted turkey breast, ham, and cheese, a half pound of each, and I'd be on my way home. As I approached the deli, I could see a crowd waiting to order. "Oh, shit!" I whispered under my breath, and then I looked around to see if anyone had heard me; no one seemed to have. The number forty-six appeared on the digital screen above the counter. I pulled the pink strip of paper out from the one-legged stand in front of the glass of cold cuts and prepared food: fifty-two.

"Number forty-seven," the man behind the deli counter shouted, and a woman standing alongside the glass raised her hand, "Right here! Half a pound of turkey breast."

It's the holiday season—hasn't she had enough turkey!

Wait, I need turkey breast too.

"What kind of turkey breast, ma'am?" The man asked. "We have Thumann's oven-roasted turkey," he paused and took a breath. "We have smoked turkey breast, honey turkey breast, cracked-peppercorn turkey breast, or Stop & Shop roasted turkey breast."

Oh, my God, I thought. What is this? Deli for beginners!

"Oh," she replied, "I didn't know there were so many different kinds. I'll have Thumann's turkey breast, sliced thin, please."

"Half pound?" the man asked.

"Yes."

Another employee sliced meat and then placed it on the scale and put it in a plastic bag. The price tag printed out, and she sealed the bag, placing the tag over the folded bag, and handed it to the customer. It all happened in slow motion while I watched.

"Anything else?" she asked the customer.

"That's it, thanks."

"Forty-eight!"

"Yes, that's me!" A man looked up from a small piece of paper he held in his hand—a list of cold cuts his wife had probably sent him to buy, I thought. Oh, God, here we go. Why do people do this on the busiest day? Don't they have better things to do than crowd the deli counter! I don't think I can do this. I don't think I can wait without killing someone.

"What can I get you, sir?" the woman asked.

The man looked down at his list again. "Prosciutto, please."

Oh no! It takes forever to slice prosciutto! One razor thin slice at a time, and then it's placed neatly and slowly on a strip of plastic paper, and the weight checked after every few slices.

How come they have only two people taking orders? I thought. There was a third, but he was working on preorders. There was a word used when the order was ready to be picked up. I tried to think of it. I'd heard it so many times over the loudspeaker throughout the store. "Your deli order is ready?" No, there's a word. What is it?

I knew I wouldn't be in the store long enough to pre-order and I would certainly forget the order and miss the announcement that my order was ready today or any day for that matter. That was a given. They'd have the Stop & Shop police out looking for me. "Hey lady, you didn't pick up your order." I'd lose sleep over it and turn myself in if they didn't find me first.

"Marguerite prosciutto?" the deli woman asked.

"Yes, I guess, thank you."

"One pound?"

"Oh no, half a pound, thanks."

The woman ordering the turkey breast was now on cheese. I couldn't listen. I knew what I wanted. It was the same thing every week: roasted turkey breast for John Jr., Saline ham for Jeff and Jason, American and Swiss cheese, sometimes provolone; that was it. I'd occasionally order roast beef or hot capicola for my husband, the Italian. I looked up at the specials board: Liverwurst or German bologna. Liverwurst, yuck. I remember eating bologna with American cheese and mustard on a bulky roll with a pickle and chips for my lunch at least once a week growing up. I had to share it with my friend, Lisa Bonazoli; she loved my bologna sandwich. Her mother didn't make her lunch, which I thought was odd since they owned a restaurant in Newton Center. What was that called…Bonazoli's Beacon, how could I forget!

"A half pound?" the woman behind the counted repeated.

"Yes."

My sons turned up their noses at bologna—snobs. "I'm not eating that," they'd say. "How about some Spam?" I'd say. "What's that?" they'd ask. I didn't know what Spam was, and come to think of it, I didn't want to know.

"Can I get you anything else, ma'am?"

"Yes, a pound of ham."

"We have imported ham, Virginia ham, honey-baked ham, cooked ham, brown-sugar-cured ham, black forest ham."

I wanted to scream, "Get the Saline ham! It's the best!" Odd, he didn't mention it. It's from Virginia; a farm that exclusively makes this ham. I'd eaten it one time for lunch during the summer in Eastham. It was delicious. I asked Dad what kind of ham it was. He said, "It's the best-tasting ham." I've been buying it ever since.

"How 'bout the honey ham, please," the woman replied. I was glad I didn't divulge my ham secret; she'd probably get the last slice, and I'd be pissed.

"How much?" the deli man asked.

"Half pound, sliced thin," she replied.

The man with the honey-do list was still ordering when another deli employee showed up. Must have been on break I thought. Okay, here we go; let's get this thing rolling!

He looked up at the current number and said, "Forty-nine!"

I looked at my pink slip: fifty-two. Yup, it hadn't changed.

"Anything else?" the deli man asked the woman waiting on her honey ham.

"No, that's it, thank you."

"Here you go. Have a nice day!" He looked up at the current number and called out "Fifty!"

I started to get a little excited that I might be ordering within the next hour when I heard the customer say, "I'll have two pounds of Thumann's roast beef." He was wearing a Patriots game shirt.

Oh, God.

"Deli kiosk order number one hundred and twenty-five is ready for pick up at your convenience," I heard over the loud speaker. That's it, deli kiosk! I couldn't think of the word. I hope Jeff is okay, I thought. What time is it? Time was never an issue until I was without Jeff.

"That's it," I heard from the honey-do man.

"Number fifty-one!"

A woman raised her hand and said, "Hi. I'll have a half pound of salami."

Oh, please don't ask!

"What kind?" he asked.

Oh, my God! I looked up at the ceiling.

"Genoa, please."

"How would you like that sliced?"

"Thin, please."

"Fifty-two!"

I thrust both arms up in the air as if I'd just scored. "That's me!"

He smiled. "How are you, ma'am?"

"I'm fine, thank you."

"What would you like?"

"Half a pound of Land O'Lakes American cheese, white, please."

He looked for the cheese, tossing different brands around in the bin across from the counter and then said, "Oh, sorry, we're out. I have to go out back and get a new one."

Oh no you don't, I thought. I'm not waiting until you come back from eternity and then start trying to open the wrapper on the cheese and then find out that you'll have to wait for the cutter because someone else is using it. "Oh no, that's okay," I said. "I'll have the Stop & Shop brand, then."

I finished my order, standing up against the glass as he handed me my Saline ham.

"That's it, thank you."

When I got home, I went right to Jeff and sat down on the couch next to his recliner.

"Hi, honey. How's the pain?" I asked.

"Okay. Where were you? You've been gone a long time."

CHAPTER 56

Twelve Days of Christmas

THE NEXT MORNING, I went out to our mailbox and found an envelope inside with a note and a lottery scratch ticket. The note read, "Dear Jeff, this is the first day of Christmas." It wasn't signed. The next day, there was another envelope in the mailbox. I gave it to Jeff, and he looked at me oddly.

"What's this?" Jeff asked.

"The second day of Christmas, I guess."

"Who is it from?"

"I don't know. Someone put it in our mailbox, but we haven't seen who." John and I tried to think who it might be; we never saw anyone putting mail in our mailbox. Jeff opened the envelope to find two theater tickets and a scratch ticket.

"Two theater tickets, a scratch ticket, and a partridge in a pear tree!" I sang. Jeff gave me a peculiar look.

The next day, I was downstairs with Jeff while he watched television. He was out of bed and sitting in his chair.

"Was there anything in the mailbox?" I smiled when he asked. I'd completely forgotten about the mysterious next day of Christmas gift.

"I haven't checked yet, honey. I'll go see."

Sure enough, a gift bag was hanging on the mailbox. I brought it down to Jeff.

"The Third Day of Christmas" was written on the tag of the gift bag. I handed Jeff the bag.

He smiled and opened it to find three T-shirts, two theater tickets, and a scratch ticket.

He scratched the ticket and won.

"Mom, can you cash this, and put the money in my bank account?"

"Sure, honey. Do you want me to get you some more scratch tickets?" I asked.

"No, just put the money in my account, okay?"

He sat in his recliner during the day with two pillows on each side of him and one supporting his head. I covered him with his blanket, and he watched television. He ate scrambled eggs, macaroni and cheese, and soft noodles and drank strawberry milk when he could. I started to give him Ensure. He complained of the pain in his mouth, and I felt bad that I couldn't do anything to relieve his discomfort.

"Do you remember the coffee cake you bought for us a long time ago?" he asked.

"Yes, Entenmann's. Would you like me to get one for you?"

"Yes, that's my favorite."

I went back to the Stop & Shop only for Entenmann's coffee cake and hurried home again, keeping my distance from the deli. When I got home, I cut him a square, heated it in the microwave, and lightly spread butter on each side, just like my mom had done for me.

I couldn't remember the last time I had my haircut. I was looking like a homeless person.

"Jeff, I need a haircut. My bangs are falling over my eyes!"

"Your hair looks fine," he replied.

"I think I'll run out to the hairdresser."

"Mom, it looks okay to me."

"Okay, honey, if you say so."

I was home for good. I'd phoned my bosses to tell them I was taking a leave of absence.

"Mom, your favorite movie is on, *A League of Their Own*. Want to watch it with me?"

"There's no crying in baseball," I replied. "Remember when the right fielder didn't throw the ball to the cutoff man, and Jimmy Dugan yelled at her, and she began to cry? There's no crying in baseball." I smiled and sat down to watch the movie.

"Oh, Jeff, this is my favorite part." Jimmy walked up to Dottie Henson, who was leaving the team with her husband. He'd just returned home from the war. He'd been injured. She was standing next to their car, facing Jimmy. She said, "It's too hard."

"Of course it's hard," Jimmy replied. "If it wasn't hard, then everyone would do it. That's what makes it so great."

"That's right, Jeff. It isn't easy. Look at all your baseball trophies!"

"It's not that hard, Mom."

Near the end of the movie, Jeff's nose began to bleed. That happened more often now; his platelet count was low. I gave him some Kleenex to help stop the bleeding. As he held pressure on the side of his nose, he asked, "Mom, am I going to die?"

Oh God, I thought, he's eighteen! I didn't know what to say. I had to speak; the silence was frightening.

"Jeff, look around your room," I said. I got up and sat on the edge of the couch. "Look at all that you have achieved in your life thus far. All your championships, those close games, winning because you would never give up. You've been very successful in all that you set out to do. It's extraordinary, Jeff, unlike most kids your age who've never experienced anything close to what you have, and look at all the friends you have. We are so proud of you and love you so much." I paused. I felt awful, physically ill.

From the very beginning, I never thought the treatment wouldn't work. I wasn't prepared to answer this emotionally difficult question let alone concede to his fear. I wanted to protect him from the thought; the fear of dying. I wanted him to believe there was still hope. I didn't know how to escape from this frightening possibility, so I tried to help him realize the extraordinary life he's led.

"We have to take one day at a time and try to beat this disease. You are amazing, and you have been this whole time." He stared at the television and didn't reply.

"We're not going to stop fighting, Jeff."

Judie and Terry O'Reilly wanted to get Jeff the latest PlayStation 3 games, his favorite games. They drove down from their home north of Boston so Terry could play the new games with Jeff. Terry also brought highlight tapes of his games and the fights throughout his career playing with the Bruins.

When they arrived they had their beautiful terriers in the car with them. Judie walked toward our house and asked, "Can I let my babies loose?"

"Of course," I replied. "There's plenty of open space for them to run." Her two terriers jumped out of their vehicle and ran around the front yard. Terry got out of the car and said, "How long have you lived here?"

"About fifteen years," I said from the front door.

They came in, and we went downstairs to see Jeff. Our neighbor, Mary Jo, had just brought us some homemade lobster chowder, a favorite of Terry's. Patty had come over and heated it up for him. Our close friends Jack and Doreen were downstairs with Jeff and had brought a small oak table to house the PlayStation 3 and its games. Judie and Terry were amazed at Jeff's display of trophies, awards, and autographed hockey and baseball memorabilia. Jeff sat straight up in his recliner with the control in his hands as he played a game with Terry.

The phone rang as everyone was downstairs visiting.

It was Sam. There had always been a sense of urgency when Sam called. Now we were beginning to speak more often over the phone. He was checking on Jeff.

Jeff's friends came by to watch the tapes, and the room was full. Terry and Judie had to leave to attend a family party. Terry left his fighting videos for Jeff. I remembered watching some of those games years ago. The games and Terry's fights were classics. Jeff guarded the videos. He was proud that Terry left them for him. Watching the fights and knowing Terry now, I thought fighting seemed out of character for him. He's a kind and gentle man. I've got to call my Dad, I thought. Terry O'Reilly had come to our home to visit and play Jeff's favorite games on PlayStation 3!

I figured out the secret Santa on the sixth day of Christmas. I kept it a secret from Jeff. The sixth gift was frozen stuffed shells. Sue Bolton had made Jeff stuffed shells one Sunday, his favorite. She had bought them in Boston. I kept it a secret from Jeff. Six stuffed shells, five matchbox cars, four baseball cards, three T-shirts, two theater tickets, a scratch ticket, and a partridge in a pear tree. Our freezer began to fill with stuffed shells.

I was unable to do any Christmas shopping. Baseball and hockey families shopped for Jeff, John Jr., and Jason. My sister Joanne provided much of what Jeff needed on a weekly basis: new sheets, comforter, clothes, and at one point, a portable commode. She also bought and wrapped Christmas presents for my sons.

The Lessard boys bought a four-foot-tall artificial Christmas tree for Jeff's room, and each of his friends decorated the tree with a special ornament: a mobile of a hockey helmet with Merry Christmas written on the back and hockey skates and gloves hanging down from the helmet, a Bruins ornament, a Red Sox bulb, a Patriots bulb, and a soccer player from Mike. Soccer was Mike's sport.

It was the seventh day of Christmas: seven white socks, six stuffed shells, five matchbox cars, four baseball cards, three T-shirts, two theater tickets, a scratch ticket, and a partridge in a pear tree.

"Jeff, a big box was just delivered; it's from the Bruins," John shouted coming down the basement stairs.

Jeff was sitting up in his recliner. John handed him the box, and he opened it. The box was filled with many different gifts from the Bruins. A signed Chara jersey, a mini Bruins helmet signed by the team, several Bruins signed caps, Bruins pucks with their logo, and other autographed memorabilia. On the top of all the gifts was a CD.

"Mom, can you bring me the portable DVD player? Jeff asked.

I left the basement, found the DVD player, ran back down the stairs, and handed it to Jeff. I plugged in the power cord, and Jeff inserted the disc. It was a Christmas message from Patrice Bergeron. He stood in the stands of an empty TD Bank Garden. "Hi, Jeff. How are you? I hope you will be up and about again soon so that you can come in for another game. I hope you like your gifts. Good luck. Merry Christmas, Jeff." Along with Patrice's messages were highlights of Patrice and some of the Bruins games.

Jeff watched it again and again. I thought about that night he'd met Patrice, when the Bruins gave Jeff his own luxury box to watch a game with ten of his friends. It seemed so long ago, but it was only last October, less than two months ago.

"Mom, can you call Sam and ask him if he could give me something to stay awake to watch the Bruins?"

I called Sam, and he prescribed Ritalin. I went to CVS and picked up the prescription, and I added it to my medicine log. One night after a game, Jeff walked around the basement for what seemed like hours. He was unsteady, thin, and feeble, and John and I walked with him, hoping the effects of the Ritalin would wear off soon; I feared he'd fall. He kept walked and talking. It was out of character for him. It scared me. He was able to stay awake for the game, and that's all he wanted to do. When he finally settled down, we got him into bed, and he fell asleep. The next day he was sore and very tired. I decided to ask Jeff to tape the games and watch them the following morning.

The eighth day of Christmas arrived, and another Christmas gift bag hung from our mailbox.

"Jeff! It's the eighth day of Christmas! Here you go! I stood over him, watching to see what Sue Bolton had given him along with all the other days of Christmas.

"Did you find out who's leaving me these gifts?" Jeff asked.

"Nope, still don't know, pumpkin. What is it?"

"Reese's Cups," he said. "And don't sing."

"Reese's Cups, your favorite! I'll just hum, honey."

Katherine came the next day, on the ninth day of Christmas, which also brought nine one-dollar bills. She drew his blood and then drove directly to Cape Cod Hospital for a quicker analysis. This was the start of continuous blood transfusions.

On Saturday, the tenth day of Christmas, ten packs of gum. I called the Hyatt Harborside at Logan for reservations so we could stay there Sunday night for a blood transfusion on Monday.

The hotel manager gave us the room for ninety-nine dollars whenever we needed to stay on a Sunday night. I checked in. Jeff sat on the other side of the large foyer across from the check-in counter. I asked the hotel employee at the counter if I could order a food and beverage tray like the one brought to us during our last stay. I wanted Jeff to get the same VIP treatment we experienced during our first stay. I didn't want him to know I had ordered it for him. We took the elevator up to our room, staring out at the view of Boston.

Jeff placed his cell phone on the table next to his hotel bed and pulled out his laptop.

"Room service." There was a knock on the door.

He looked up at me and smiled.

As if the food and beverage tray was brought in, he sat in his bed, writing his friends.

"I'll have a Sprite, Mom," he said not looking up.

It had become difficult for him to eat solid food like the cheese and crackers on the tray. I thought he might be hungry, so I asked, "Would you like some mashed potatoes?"

"Yes!" He replied with a smile.

I called room service and said I would be down to get them.

I took the elevator down to the restaurant. I walked past the door that led to the pool and a Jacuzzi next to the fitness room. I'd brought my bathing suit. I thought I might take a swim after I returned with Jeff's mashed potatoes, and that's what I did.

The view from the pool and fitness room was beautiful through the full-length glass windows overlooking the harbor and the lights of the city. I skipped the pool and sat alone in the warmth and powerful bubbles of the Jacuzzi. I looked out at the Boston skyline. The thoughts racing through my mind began to lessen as I relaxed and found peace. I sat for a while, which I had been confined to doing in all the different hospital rooms. I looked over at the empty pool, thinking, how can I not swim? I left the Jacuzzi and walked slowly to the pool and into the water, feeling the chill after leaving the warmth of the Jacuzzi. I swam a few laps and went back to the Jacuzzi before going back to the room.

I gave Jeff his medicine, and we watched a movie together.

The next morning we headed to the JFC.

Jeff's vitals were taken, and his blood was drawn. We were then taken to one of the small examining rooms again. Sam checked Jeff's lungs. The infection had cleared. Jeff had made it past the predicted one week of surviving this horrific disease, but it was apparent by his blood levels that the cancer had penetrated his bone marrow.

"He can have my bone marrow," I said desperately to Sam as he stood next to Jeff. Jeff looked at Sam. Sam looked down at the floor and said, "That would surely kill him."

Jeff's mouth was bleeding from the empty socket as he sat up in the bed. I placed a paper towel over his chest and periodically changed the gauze, which was soaked in blood at every change. The nurses hadn't covered his chest when I left the room, and his shirt was stained with blood when I returned. I'd always placed a paper towel over Jeff's chest and then wrapped the blood-soaked gauze in the paper towel after removing it from Jeff's mouth, protecting his shirt and disposing of the gauze in the paper towel. I'd practiced this procedure from my years as a dental assistant. The bleeding subsided after a while.

"We need to change his pain medication. Do you have your schedule of Jeff's medication with you?" Sam asked.

I had brought it with me this time; I don't know why, but I had left it in my car. When I got to my car, I opened the binder and removed the pages from the past few weeks and brought them to Sam.

"You're a chart person, I can see," he said. "I'm going to sit down right now with the pain management team to evaluate his meds, and then I'll be back."

Sam returned later with one of the pain medication specialists.

"This is a grueling regimen for you to administer these medications. We've changed it so that you can sleep and Jeff can get the relief he needs," they told me. Sam started Jeff on morphine and methadone for pain, hydrocortisone and Tylenol for his fevers, and Ativan and the usual Senna and Colace for bowel movements. The chemotherapy drugs we had chosen were no longer an option. It was dark outside, and Sam and I were standing next to Jeff when I said, "I'm just too tired to drive home right now in rush-hour traffic. Can I lie down for a little bit before we leave?"

"Mom, it's okay. Go lie down, I'll wait," Jeff replied immediately.

"There's an empty room next door," Sam said.

"Okay, honey, but just for a little bit so that I can drive us home after."

I went into the room next to Jeff's and fell asleep. It seemed as though I had been sleeping for hours when Sam entered my dark room.

"Susan, it's Sam."

I opened my eyes to see him sitting next to me.

"Hannah and I have discussed an alternative way to get you and Jeff home. We don't want anything to happen, knowing you're tired and Jeff is sick. We decided it would be best if you and Jeff went home in an ambulance."

I lay there while Sam spoke. Turning my head toward him, I said, "Three years ago my Mom had a stroke while receiving chemotherapy for pancreatic cancer. An ambulance took her to Cape Cod Hospital. She stayed in the hospital for a few days, and then they discharged her; there was nothing more they could do. I rode with her in the ambulance to their home in Eastham. One morning at home, at the end of the six weeks, she woke angry and said, 'I'm still here!'"

Sam smiled, sitting across from me in the dark.

"That's something I would say."

"She died the next morning."

"I'm sorry."

There was silence for a few moments. I sat up.

"We have called for an ambulance, and they'll be here shortly."

"Does Jeff know?" I asked.

"Yes."

"I'll go to my car to be sure I take everything I might need."

I called John to tell him we were coming home in an ambulance. Sam called Katherine and asked her to be there when we arrived. They prescribed a morphine pump for Jeff so that he could press for a bolus of relief when he needed it.

It was a long ride home. I watched Jeff as he lay in the stretcher while we rode in the back of the ambulance. He was wearing his red L.L.Bean jacket and his white Notre Dame cap. His eyes were closed. He didn't speak. I thought about the ride I'd taken with my Mom. I'd sat next to her, as I now sat next to Jeff. She never spoke. I didn't know what to say to Mom three years ago, and I didn't know what to say to Jeff now. I sat in silence watching over him. No words, I thought, could make a difference for Jeff or Mom. Were they thinking the same thoughts, knowing their battle with the disease might be ending? I hoped they weren't feeling anything.

When we got to Sandwich, John helped Jeff into the house and down his stairs. He sat in his recliner. I walked into our kitchen and saw Katherine and three pans of lasagna on my kitchen counter. I felt nauseous at the sight of them.

"Lasagna! Oh, my God. Katherine, lasagna!" The stress of Jeff's condition and my tiredness had come down to anger against pans of lasagna. Otherwise, I would have eaten all three pans.

Katherine listened and then said, "Let's go downstairs and get Jeff's pump set up."

Kathy Grant, the high school nurse, told me, "In September and especially at the end of October, he told me he was getting weary, which was not like Jeff. He was starting to get tired of it spreading, and that's when I saw a little bit of a change. Not a change in his will to fight it, but a change in that I may have to accept this. And this was hard for him. 'I'm chasing it now,' he said."

CHAPTER 57

Blood Transfusions and Christmas Day

"Mom." Jeff walked out of his bedroom; it was an early morning in December. I was lying on his couch. I jumped up at the sight of blood coming from his mouth. I quickly grabbed the roll of paper towels on the bar and cleaned away some of the blood. He then pushed a large blood clot to the front of his mouth, and I wiped it from his lips. He couldn't speak until I had packed the upper gum with gauze and the bleeding was under control.

"I think it may be time to go to the hospital," he said, looking at me, wanting to know how bad it was.

"Oh, no, honey," I said while I cleaned his face. "This is a good sign; your blood is clotting. I continued to clean his mouth as he stood outside his bedroom door.

I didn't know when the right time would come when he would need to go to Children's Hospital. I thought I could still take care of him. I knew he wanted to be home. I continued to give him all his medicine and the one chemotherapy drug Sam gave him for hope. I couldn't bear the thought and the reality of this disease taking over his body.

He went to the bathroom and then sat in his recliner. I covered him with a blanket and put pillows around him.

"I'm going to call Sam, Jeff, to let him know about the bleeding."

I told Sam that I thought the clotting was a good sign, that his blood platelets were high enough. There was a long pause over the phone.

"Susan, I'm going to have Katherine come by to draw blood."

"Okay."

"How is his pain?" Sam asked.

"It seems to be okay right now, but he's becoming thin and more tired. It's difficult for him to eat anything solid, and he's having trouble moving his bowels."

"Have him try some Boost or Ensure, and I will have Hannah call you about moving his bowels. We can give him something else to help with that."

"Okay."

"I'll call you when I get the results of his blood counts."

"Thanks, Sam."

A few hours later Sam called to say Jeff needed platelets.

"I'm going to call Jordan Hospital and order a transfusion for Jeff this afternoon. I will call you right back."

The phone rang. It was Hannah.

"Susan, we have called in a prescription for something else for Jeff to take to move his bowels. It's very important for him to go the bathroom. Please let me know if it works; it's pretty strong."

My phone rang again.

"Susan, it's Sam. Jeff will need to go to Jordan Hospital for blood typing so that they can order his platelets, and we'll give him more red and white cells while he's there. They know you're coming."

"Jeff, we have to go to Jordan Hospital for a blood transfusion."

"Now?"

"Yes, honey. Are you okay to go?"

"Yes." He pulled the white featherbed comforter off himself. He was wearing his nylon gym shorts. I stared at his legs, seeing them for the first time. He had no muscle tone. It frightened me. His skin fell around his thighbone. His legs were atrophied and skeletal. I just wanted to cry. I'm losing my son, I thought.

I stood up to help him out of the chair, unable to speak. I helped him dress into some warm clothes. He had the morphine pump that he carried with him.

The blood bank was in Canton, about one hour north from Jordan Hospital in Plymouth. My husband came home from work and took Jeff. They waited all day for the blood to arrive from Canton to Jordan Hospital.

That was our first meeting with Kitsy. She ran the IV unit at Jordan. The room was hers. It was like a sitcom but not a fun place to be. Patients smiled when they entered the large room, knowing she would be there to greet them. Reclining chairs and two beds were placed in a semicircle around the perimeter of the room. Fifteen patients filled the room for most of our visits.

Her voice was lively and loud. Most of her patients were older than me, and she called them by name as if they were family. Jeff was the youngest, and she took to him immediately. He needed platelets every three days after that first visit. The blood screening was done in another part of the hospital. A screening was necessary for each transfusion. Jeff took the bed next to Kitsy's station, where she could keep an eye on him. He slept during the transfusion.

Christmas was approaching.

Jeff started to complain of pain in his neck and shoulders. We drove up to the JFC. He wore a zippered sweatshirt with the hood covering his head and falling just above his eyeglasses. He wore his Boston College sweat pants and a blanket over his legs, his sneakers untied. He was in a wheelchair. I was surprised that he would wear a zippered sweatshirt until I realized it was too painful for him to put on any of his hooded sweatshirts that didn't zip up the front. My sister Joanne had bought him two hooded, zippered sweatshirts months ago, which lay on his dresser, never worn until now.

When we arrived at the JFC, I left Jeff in his wheelchair across from the reception desk and went out back to get a nurse. I looked up for a moment and saw the mother of the boy who had lost his leg to osteosarcoma. She was sitting on the couch where we had waited so many times in the last two years. She waved to me, and I waved back. It was a sad gesture between two mothers caring for teenage sons with cancer.

I imagined she saw the change in Jeff. We hadn't seen each other in a long time. I wheeled Jeff into an examining room and waited. Ann, the nurse who had asked Jeff and me two years ago to be the first adolescent cancer patient to receive chemotherapy at home, entered the room. She asked Jeff where his pain was and examined him. Sam and Hannah were not there that day. She ordered blood drawn, and we waited in another room where Jeff could lie down.

While Jeff rested, I waited outside his room. I looked up when I saw Ann walking toward me from the end of the hall. It felt as if she'd never reach me. The hall was quiet. No one was around. When she approached, she stood in front of me and said, "We need a miracle."

I leaned up against the wall across from Jeff's room. His door was closed. I looked up at the ceiling and said quietly, "God, this is a good time for a miracle; we really need one now, please." How does one earn a miracle? Are we worthy? Exhausted and scared, I thought this can't be the end of all hope. I wanted to keep going, to keep trying to save Jeff's life.

"I will talk to Sam when he returns," Ann said.

Jeff and I left for home.

Each morning he got out of bed and walked slowly to his recliner. I covered the chair beneath him with a white featherbed comforter before he sat down. That afternoon his friends Jess Robertson and Greg Iadonisi arrived with a small money tree that his friends had all contributed to; it was decorated with folded ones, fives, and ten-dollar bills. They stayed for a short while, and after they left, Jeff and I removed the money and counted it for a deposit into his savings account.

Jeff started to become distant from his friends, not wanting to see them. Their visits became less frequent. He was very ill; his physique was changing and his strength waning. It was hard for him to sit and play PS3 without becoming tired or for fear of another nosebleed. Jeff was very proud. His friends wanted to see him, asking to come by and take him out for rides or to hockey games or out for something to eat.

342

They didn't realize that the disease was spreading, that each day it was getting worse. It was consuming him at a fast rate.

The following day at eleven o'clock in the morning, I walked down his stairs and sat on the couch next to him. He sat stiff in his recliner, just staring at the television but not watching.

"Are you in a lot of pain?" I asked. "Hit the button again."

"I just did, Mom."

He was quiet. I sat down on the couch next to him. He got out of his chair and walked slowly and cautiously into his bedroom to lie down. I knew his pain was mounting; he was trying to overcome it.

"I'm going to call Katherine; you need a higher dosage. Jeff, keep pushing for another bolus. Try to keep in front of the pain, honey."

I started to get anxious waiting for Katherine, knowing Jeff's pain was getting worse. When she finally arrived, the pain had escalated, and Jeff began to scream, rolling over on his side as he lay in the middle of his bed. She reprogrammed the pump and gave him more. I called Sam.

"Sam, the pain is unbearable for Jeff. He is screaming, rolling over in his bed."

"Let me talk to Katherine."

Sam instructed her to give Jeff a bolus of morphine every thirty seconds until the pain subsided. She got off the phone and knelt down next to his bed with the pump in her hand. I stood in the doorway watching the second hand on my alarm clock next to the couch in Jeff's living room.

"Now!" I said to Katherine.

Another thirty seconds passed so slowly. Jeff remained on his side in a fetal position, crying from the pain.

"Again!"

I kept my eyes on the clock.

"Again!" I said, remaining calm, waiting for thirty seconds to pass. "Now!"

I waited for that second hand, trying not to answer before the thirty seconds passed.

"Now!" I waited.

"Again!"

I could feel the clicking of the second hand slowly moving from one small black line to the next.

"Again!"

We did this for what seemed like fifteen minutes until Jeff quieted and turned over on his back.

"Is that better, honey?" I asked softly. His face was red, and his eyes cleared of tears that had fallen.

"Jeff, keep pushing that button when you start to feel anything," Katherine instructed.

I called Sam. He must have been pacing with his phone in his hand, waiting for my call. He picked up right away.

"Sam, he's better now," I exclaimed.

He immediately replied in a stern voice. "Susan, you've got to tell Jeff never to let his pain get this bad again. We may not be able to bring him back next time. He's not on a lot of morphine, so he has plenty of room to increase his dosage."

"Okay, Sam, I will."

I didn't know where on the scale of safe dosage he was or how much more he could take.

"I'm going to try to get down to see Jeff as soon as I can," Sam said.

"Okay, I think he'd like that. Thanks, Sam."

Katherine got up from the floor and walked out of Jeff's room. She walked around the mud room. "I've never done that before," she finally said.

"There's been a lot of firsts for all us." I paused, relieved Jeff's pain was under control. "Everything's been a first for me. You did great, Katherine. Thanks."

I walked back in to see Jeff.

"Are you okay, honey?"

"Yes."

The stress on his face and redness in his eyes had faded. I helped him get more comfortable, propping him up with several pillows and some at his side. He rested quietly, watching television on the TV suspended on the wall across from his bed.

"Can I have something to drink, Mom?"

"Of course. What would you like?"

"Can I have strawberry milk like Grandma's?"

"Yes, I'll be right back, honey." I now had Mom's strawberry milk down pat.

Katherine drew more blood and left for Cape Cod Hospital. Later that day Hannah called and told us Jeff needed more platelets. He was scheduled for a transfusion in the morning at Jordan Hospital.

Jeff moved to his recliner later that day. I tried some scrambled eggs for dinner. I continued to give him his medicine as scheduled and as needed.

He needed help getting out of his chair. I picked up his pump and bent over so that he could support himself with his arm over my shoulder. We walked slowly from his chair to his bedroom. As he sat on the edge of his bed, I removed his slippers and helped him into bed. I placed the pump next to him and covered him. He liked a fan blowing on him at night, so I adjusted it to his liking.

That night, all night, I stayed on the couch outside his bedroom, worrying about how he might not be able to get up in the morning and travel. Would he be able to make the drive to Jordan Hospital to receive the platelets he needed to survive? I couldn't sleep. I scripted in my mind many versions of what I would say to him when morning came. I thought I would tell him that it was okay if he couldn't make the trip to Jordon Hospital. I didn't, however, know how to tell him it was time to go to Boston. It was late into the night when I finally fell asleep.

"Mom! Mom, wake up!"

I jumped off the couch, waking at the sound of Jeff's voice. I ran to his bedroom. He was sitting on the edge of his bed, dressed and ready to go.

"Mom, why are you still sleeping? Get dressed! We have to go."

"I'm sorry, honey. I must have overslept. I ran up the basement stairs thinking, how did he get dressed and go the bathroom? I ran up the second set of stairs and to John Jr.'s bedroom.

"John, get up! I need your help getting Jeff in his wheelchair and out the back door. Wake up!"

John Jr. pushed Jeff out onto our lower deck, up the small hill on the side of our house and to the driveway.

I couldn't believe it; I stayed awake all night thinking we'd never make the trip in his condition.

When we arrived at Jordan Hospital, I pulled up alongside the entrance and parked there while I ran inside the lobby to get a wheelchair. I waited as the doors opened, and I pushed the wheelchair outside next to our Explorer and opened Jeff's door. I helped him out and pushed him into the hospital lobby.

"I'll be right back, Jeff."

I parked the Explorer and ran back to Jeff.

"Mom, we need to go to the lab first for blood typing."

"Oh, right. I forgot."

I followed the signs leading to the lab. I parked Jeff next to a row of chairs, and I walked to the receptionist, who stood behind the glass partition.

"Jeff Hayes is here," I said and gave her my insurance card.

After a few minutes, Jeff was called in behind the door and to a cubicle where his blood was drawn from a vein in his arm, not his port. We then left for the IV unit and Kitsy.

"Hi," I said as I wheeled Jeff into the IV unit.

"Hi! Jeff, how are you? I've got your bed all ready for you. Come on in."

Jeff got out of his wheelchair and climbed into the bed. I held his morphine pump until he was lying down and then placed it by his side. Jeff and I were getting used to the pump and carefully maneuvered it when he moved. It was connected to his port. I checked frequently to be sure the power never read low, and I carried batteries with me. I had watched Katherine closely when she reprogrammed Jeff's dosage.

I needed to know how the pump was programmed in case Katherine couldn't get to our house when Jeff's dosage needed to be increased.

There was a long wait for Jeff's platelets, and I have never been one to sit still for long periods of time.

I walked down to the lobby and down a long corridor where some vendors had set up handcrafted items for patients and visitors. One of the tables displayed round wooden clocks, and I spotted one with the Bruins logo in the center of the clock. I bought it immediately and walked quickly back to the IV unit to give it to Jeff.

He smiled and said, "Thanks, Mom."

"Do you like it?" I asked.

"Yup."

He was lying with his arm out straight and an IV line accessed in his vein while blood ran down the line from a package of platelets hanging above his bed. I was relieved the platelets had arrived earlier than I'd expected.

"Are you tired, honey?" I asked.

He nodded and closed his eyes to sleep.

We were there all morning. I watched the platelets empty through the IV line until the last drop was gone and the bag deflated. Jeff was wheelchair bound; he could no longer walk on his own. I placed the wheelchair next to his bed, and he carefully stood up and sat in the chair. We said good-bye to our new friend, Kitsy.

"Bye, Jeff. I'll see you again soon."

I pushed Jeff back to the lobby and covered his lap with a soft flannel blanket I had brought from home, and then left to get the Explorer.

I still had trouble finding my way driving to and from new places. I guess I wasn't paying attention, or maybe it was because I was thinking about how Jeff was feeling all the time.

"Which way do I go, Jeff?"

"Take a left here and go straight," he replied.

The next day at home, we received a visit from Simone Rinaldi, a pain specialist. Sam and Katherine had arranged our meeting with her to discuss Jeff's pain level, type of pain and their plan to guide us in maintaining the correct dosage of medication to keep Jeff comfortable. She also worked with the company who designed our morphine pump.

The cancer was spreading quickly. We started to research experimental methods and unproven drugs we heard about from friends of friends who had tried these treatments with positive results. My sister researched an experimental tea and had a bottle delivered to our house. Dr. Grier from the Dana-Farber warned me that some people would prey on parents who were desperate to find a cure; he said their motives were ethically questionable. Sam told us that if there were a drug out there that he thought would help Jeff, he would know about it.

I asked Jeff if he wanted to try the tea.

"What does Sam think?" he asked.

"Sam doesn't think there is anything out there for us to take, but I think it's worth a try. I will drink it with you, Jeff."

He and I tried it. It made Jeff's stomach sick, and he wouldn't drink it again. I felt no effect.

I spent the next morning with Jeff. Patty was upstairs in the kitchen when our friend Tom Fair walked through the side door and into our kitchen. He was standing at the door when I walked up from the basement. I didn't hear him come in. He placed an envelope on our kitchen table and said, "We wanted to help somehow." He didn't stay long and said good-bye. The envelope had $2,000 in it.

The weekend before Christmas, my sister Kathy came by with a money tree from my Mom's side of the family. My Mom was one of twelve. Jeff read each note attached to a five-, ten-, or twenty-dollar bill before removing the money. As he opened each note carefully, he asked, "Who is this?"

I explained to him that it was a great aunt or a cousin from Grandma's side of our family. "Do you remember the big Christmas parties we went to when you were little, and Santa Claus came and brought you a present? One year you danced with all your other little cousins until your face was bright red."

"I don't remember that, Mom."

"Yes, and you also sat quietly waiting for Santa to arrive. Santa was my cousin."

Slowly he removed each note and read it. The tree was well organized, decorated with money and carefully placed messages. Special Christmas clips held the notes and money attached to separate branches on the tree. Jeff really enjoyed how big his family was. He was so methodical, opening each note, reading it, and carefully handing it to me. The money he kept on his lap.

Our neighbors Elaine Berry and Karen Rutherford came by with a collage of gifts from our neighbors. The large rectangular board was covered with gift cards and money. We purchased a portable DVD player from Best Buy with one of the cards.

My brother John and his wife, Patty, and their teenagers, Johnny and Niki, came that evening to see Jeff. They brought money raised by their friend John Smith, who ran a marathon in Florida in support of Jeff. John wears all the T-shirts, the golf tournament jackets, the baseball cap, and the hockey lace wristband that were designed over the last two years on Jeff's behalf. Recently we found in our mailbox a supply of blue rubber wristbands that read "Pray for Jeff," and we mailed one to John.

On Monday, Jeff and I went back to Jordan Hospital for more platelets and red and white blood cells. We had been going every three days for platelets, and Sam ordered the red and white cells so that Jeff would feel better for Christmas. Sam had told us that Jeff might not make it to Christmas.

I decided that during this transfusion, after I got Jeff settled in with Kitsy, I would go to Kohl's Department Store, which was five minutes from the hospital. This was my only chance to go Christmas shopping. Katherine was unavailable, so she had given me the pain specialist's phone number in case I had a problem with the pump.

I pushed Jeff in his wheelchair into the IV unit at Jordan Hospital, and Kitsy immediately greeted us. Jeff got into the bed, and Kitsy examined the veins in his arms, hands, and legs. It was getting more difficult to use the same veins, so she decided to access his port for the transfusion. She was unsure how to remove the connection to the pump and hook up the platelet IV without interrupting Jeff's pain medication and losing the morphine flow.

She assured me that she would be able to make this work and sent me on my way. I made it to Kohl's and bought all the sportswear clothing of the Bruins, Boston College, and the Red Sox that I could find. I was on my way back to the hospital when my cell phone rang. I hadn't been gone long. It was Kitsy. She sounded distressed and nervous telling me that the pump alarm was sounding and not working.

"I'm five minutes away; I'll be right there," I replied. "Is Jeff okay?"

"Yes. I'll see you when you get here," she replied.

Five minutes seemed like an eternity as I sped down the street toward the hospital. I found a parking space immediately and ran to the IV unit.

When I arrived, I pulled up a chair next to Jeff's bed and held the pump in my hands.

I looked up at Jeff and asked, "Are you feeling any pain, honey?"

"I'm okay, Mom. Can you fix the pump?"

"Yes, pumpkin, but I'll need to call the pain specialist who came to visit us. She knows how to reset the pump."

I pulled out the cell phone number Katherine gave me and dialed her number. There was no answer.

"She's not answering, Jeff, but I'll keep trying."

I looked at the pump and called up the main menu, looking for instructions to reset the pump. Unsuccessful at my attempt to reset the pump, I tried calling the pain specialist again. There was still no answer. I called Katherine. She told me to keep calling. I dialed again, and she answered. I immediately asked, "Where were you? The pump is not working, and I need to reset it immediately. I'm at Jordan Hospital, and Jeff is having a transfusion. I tried calling you several times."

"I'm sorry. I was in the shower."

"Oh. Well, we need to reset the pump as soon as possible. How do I reset it?"

She gave me instructions to reset the pump, and nothing worked. She then suggested that I check the IV line from the pump. I placed my cell on the bed and opened the piece of the pump that secured the line. I placed the line back into the spot where it lay flat on top of the pump and then secured it in place with the safety piece. Once I secured the safety piece, the pump immediately went back into its normal working mode.

"Jeff, press the button."

The pump released his dosage.

"It's working," I said over the phone.

The pain specialist explained the need for the line to be secured and then apologized for not being available when I called.

"I need you to be there to answer my call in an emergency like this. Jeff cannot miss a dosage." I said good-bye and ended the call. After I hung up, I felt bad that I'd said that. I looked up at Jeff.

"Are you in any pain, Jeff?" I asked.

"No, I'm okay."

I could see the relief on his face as he laid his head back down on his pillow. I checked the power meter on the pump and then placed it next to Jeff.

When we got home, Jeff stepped cautiously out of the Explorer and put his arm around my shoulders, and we walked together into the house and down the stairs to his basement. He sat in his recliner, and we went over his medicine and when he needed to take it.

OUTSIDE THE LINES WITH
Allie Flynn
Dan Crowley, the columnist, asks, "Who has been your inspiration?"

My inspiration started with my father, who has been building a rink in our backyard for years, making me want to become a better skater than he was, and always trying to improve. Spending my free time out there taking shots and skating also helped my game without me even real-izing it. Also to all the girls who wanted me to play and finally got me to, I am glad that I finally listened to you. Also, having the privilege to know Jeff Hayes inspires me to live life to the fullest and to try my hardest all the time on and off the ice.

CHAPTER 58

Newspaper Articles

"Courageous Teen Proves Inspiring" by Rob Duca, *Cape Cod Times*, December 24, 2006

One of the first things people usually ask when they discover that I cover professional sports is, "Do you get to meet the athletes?" Invariably, the following words from their lips are, "You are so lucky."

The next time someone says that to me, I think I'll tell them, "I'd be a whole lot luckier if I met more people like Jeff Hayes."

Too often, I write about obscenely rich, pampered athletes who still manage to find something wrong with their lives. I write about a Manny Ramirez, disgruntled and demanding to be traded, or a Terrell Owens, the poster boy for the Me Generation. Or an Isiah Thomas, a thug behind a choirboy smile; or a host of cheaters, liars and law-breakers, from Mark McGwire to Barry Bonds.

But not always. In February I wrote a profile of Hayes, then a junior hockey player at Sandwich High who only hoped to step onto the ice, however briefly, when the Blue Knights faced Bourne in the annual Canal Cup. The backdrop to the story was that Hayes was battling cancer, and that's not the kind of story anyone wants to write, unless the subject has beaten the disease. Unfortunately, Jeff still remains in the throes of the struggle.

I wondered what I would encounter when I went to his home for an interview. This was someone who had every reason to be angry, bitter and disillusioned. But isn't it remarkable how those with genuine courage surprise you? I found a polite, soft-spoken kid with an infectious smile and a refusal to curse his situation. His hair was gone due to

353

chemotherapy and many days found him too weak to go to school, but his voice was absent outrage.

"Stuff happens to everyone," he said, making it sound as if he had been sidelined with a sprained ankle. "You do what you've got to do. Don't complain. Just do what your doctors tell you. I'm in good hands. I'll be fine."

A few nights later he stepped onto the ice for 27 seconds, displaying more grace, dignity and strength in that short stretch than most pros do over an entire season.

You can have the Manny's and T.O.s; I'll take meeting Jeff Hayes every time.

CHAPTER 59

Christmas Eve

T HE TWELVE DAYS of Christmas gifts ended on the tenth day; it was Christmas Eve day. Around noontime, I had just gotten out of the shower and happened to look out my bedroom window. I saw some of Jeff's friends and their parents walking up our driveway carrying wrapped Christmas presents. I immediately dressed and called Patty to come over.

"Patty, please come over quickly. There's a group of parents and kids at our door."

Jeff was sitting in his recliner as I guided everyone down to his basement living room. They presented Jeff with gifts and sat and talked, telling him that when he got better he could get back out on the ice to use the new Bruins autographed stick they had bought him. Matt Melia and his dad, Jim, sat next to Jeff handing him the gifts. Jim is a Barnstable policeman, and he gave Jeff a black, long-sleeved Barnstable County Sheriff's T-shirt with the law enforcement emblem on the front. Don Bolton, the husband of the secret Santa who dropped off the twelve days of Christmas presents, also presented Jeff with gifts. Patty prepared food upstairs in the kitchen. John and I served shrimp platters, cheese and crackers, and drinks to our guests all afternoon.

Privately, in Jeff's bedroom, I talked to Mary Jane Melia about Jeff's condition. She handed me a silver medal of a saint.

After everyone left, our doorbell rang. It was one of the employees from the CVS Pharmacy delivering a turkey dinner. She stayed just long enough to place all the trimmings of the turkey dinner on our kitchen counter; it was enough to feed us for the next two days. The doorbell rang again. Nancy Helms and her sons, Chris and Josh, entered the kitchen with trays of hors d'oeuvres. Our counter was filled with food. The doorbell rang again. A group of girls, Jeff's friends, held candles and sang Christmas carols. I hugged each one of them and invited them in to see Jeff. Nancy, Holly, and Jeff's best friend, Mike, then arrived. The Lessard family arrived shortly after them. Nancy Helms continued cooking hors d'oeuvres, and we passed the food around. More Christmas ornaments were brought and placed on Jeff's tree. Many gifts had been brought earlier in the week from families in Sandwich. They were for Jeff, John Jr., and Jason. They filled the bottom of our tree and overflowed into our living room. It was nine o'clock in the evening when everyone started to leave. The house became quiet. I gave Jeff his medicine and tucked him in.

"Now, don't get up too early tomorrow morning," I said as I left his room to change. I unplugged his Christmas tree and feel asleep on the couch, still praying for a miracle.

CHAPTER 60

Christmas

"MERRY CHRISTMAS, MOM." I woke at the sound of Jeff's voice. "Merry Christmas, pumpkin. You're up early." He was sitting up on the edge of his bed.

It was eight o'clock. I helped him up off his bed and up the stairs into our living room filled with wrapped presents and envelopes on the tree. Jeff sat in the oversized chair and rested his legs on the ottoman. I covered him with a blanket. I looked for the spot where I had dropped the plug to the Christmas tree lights. I found it lying on a pile of presents and plugged it into the outlet. Jason appeared from the kitchen. I hadn't heard him come down the stairs.

"Merry Christmas," Jeff said to Jason as he walked into the room. Jason's eyes were still filled with sleep.

"Merry Christmas, Jeff," he replied with a sad and surprised look on his face—surprised, I imagined, at seeing Jeff up so early.

John and John Jr. soon appeared, and we began our family tradition of handing out the presents. Jeff opened his gifts, and then started opening the envelopes containing gift cards from friends and families in Sandwich.

Sam thought Jeff would never make Christmas, I thought to myself, but he did everything he could so that Jeff could be with us this day.

When Jeff finished opening the envelopes, I saw a look of melancholy on his face as he watched John Jr. and Jason still opening gifts. I wished I'd had more presents for him. I wished the gifts were endless for him.

I sat near the tree passing out the remaining gifts to my husband, John Jr., and Jason. When the gifts had all been opened, I began to

357

pick up the discarded Christmas paper and put it into a large garbage bag.

"Mom." I looked up and across the room at Jeff. "You're not going to Mass, are you?" Jeff said with a terrified look on his face.

I stopped packing bows and paper and looked back at him and said, "Oh, no, honey, I'm staying here with you."

"Okay," he said and pulled out a gift from its box, a pair of Bruins flannel pants.

My husband began his Christmas morning entertainment by examining everyone's presents, and I started breakfast. Jeff got up and sat at the computer, checking out the new flat screen John Jr. had just connected to the computer.

I stood in the kitchen, terrified and incredibly sad at the thought that Jeff wouldn't be with us next Christmas. I hated the thought of him not here with us this day next year and all the days for the rest of our lives. I walked back into the living room and sat with him. He was so sweet, looking at his gifts. He was thin and pale, lost in his blanket. Again, I tried to bury the thought of the years to come without him on this morning.

The phone rang. We let the answering machine take the call and listened to Sam wishing us a Merry Christmas. It was the only call we received that day.

Jeff stayed upstairs all day and sat with us during dinner. Patty, Marty, and Julie joined us with more gifts. The day turned into night, and it became quiet as I sat next to Jeff on the couch, and my husband sat on the love seat across from us. I covered Jeff with a blanket and put a pillow behind his head. We watched television together.

"Mom, I think I'll go downstairs now," he said. His voice was tired and weak.

"Okay, honey. I'll help you downstairs. John Jr. and Jason came in the room to say good night to Jeff.

I came back upstairs after a while and sat on the couch; my eyes were burning and sore. It was two years from the time when Jeff entered the kitchen on Christmas Eve and told me he thought there was a tumor in his leg. Not possible, I thought.

I remember a time when Jeff was strong and full of life. It was in the spring before his diagnosis and during his freshman year in high school, when he was healthy. I heard a car pull into our driveway as Jeff stood in the doorway.

"Where are you going, Jeff?"

"Out."

"Oh, that place. I spent a lot of time there at your age. Grandma always said to me when I told her I was going out, 'Susan, out is a pretty big place. Can you narrow it down a bit?'"

"I'm going to the Helms' house to the graduation party," he said and then walked out the front door. John Robertson waited in his car parked in our driveway, the engine running.

"Okay, we'll see you there." I wondered why John Robertson was picking him up. He was John Jr.'s friend and had played hockey with John Jr.

Shortly after Jeff left, John Jr. left as another car pulled into our driveway.

"I'll see you at the Helms'" he said.

The Helms' house was where all the kids gathered after games and on the weekends. It was Saturday, and Nancy and Ralph Helms were throwing a party for their eldest son, Chris, who had just graduated from Bridgeton Academy.

John and I left for the party a couple of hours later, around one o'clock in the afternoon. As we approached the house, a group of teenagers stared at us. We got out of our Explorer and walked toward the house. I felt a little uneasy as the kids seemed to be studying us. The deck and inside the house were filled with parents. I went inside, and John stayed out on the deck. Ralph was cooking on the grill.

After a while, I walked out onto the deck, and my husband looked up at me. He was talking to Brian Kolb, John Jr.'s friend.

"Jeff's been in a fight," my husband told me.

"What?" I walked over to him and Brian.

"There were about one hundred kids behind the Stop & Shop on Cotuit Road," Brian began.

"I guess a kid from Yarmouth kept telling Jeff and the hockey team that they sucked. These kids had been at the bowling alley in Yarmouth. This had been going on for weeks. Apparently, a fight between this kid and Jeff was planned for today. Jeff was to fight him at noontime. As everyone watched, Jeff and the kid stood looking at each other, standing in the middle of the crowd of kids. Jeff pulled on his shirt, like a hockey hold, and then beat the shit out of the kid."

"Oh my God! Where is he now?"

"Well," Brian continued, "after Jeff beat this kid up, his brother, who was twenty-one years old, wanted at Jeff. He was big and older than us. So John Jr. stepped in and said, 'Don't touch my brother.' The guy then punched John in the eye, and he went down."

I began to shake, pissed and worried about John Jr. Then I worried about the other kid.

"Just as John went down, the cops came, and everyone scattered," Brian continued.

"Where are they?" I cried, angry that they would do something so stupid.

"John went home, I think. I don't know where Jeff is," Brian explained.

I left the deck and went inside to Nancy Helms's bedroom to call Jeff.

"Where are you?" I asked when he answered the phone.

"I'm at the Lessards' house," he replied.

"Get home now."

John and I drove home. I found John Jr. lying on the couch in our basement with a bag of ice on his eye.

"What happened, John?" I sat down next to him on the couch.

"Jeff came to me one day last week and asked if I would come to a fight between him and another kid from Yarmouth. He wanted me to come in case he needed me." He lifted the bag of ice off his eye. "So I got some of my friends to come with me. Mom, Jeff beat the shit out of the kid."

"Oh my God, John!"

"Mom, don't you know how strong he is? Jeff can beat the shit out of me. He's really strong."

"No, I guess I don't. But there's no violence in this house, and that's not what we try to teach you guys. Fighting in a parking lot, John! Something worse could have happened. What if that kid is really hurt? Then what? For what reason, what good reason, if any, would you guys fight?

"Let me see your eye." He had a shiner.

"You need some Tylenol," I said.

"I'm okay. I already took some."

I heard the slider door shut and my husband speaking to Jeff. I left John Jr. and went upstairs.

"Jeff, how did you know that kid didn't have a knife or some other weapon on him? You can't take that chance," my husband said raising his voice.

"Dad, you always told me to protect myself, and that's what I did."

Jeff ran quickly up to his bedroom, two steps at a time to the top of the stairs. I looked at my husband's face and then followed Jeff up the stairs. I walked into his room. He was already sprawled out on his bed. I sat down beside him. He didn't have a spot of blood on him and appeared to be all right. I sat quietly next to him for a minute before I spoke.

"You can't feel good about this, Jeff," I said softly.

He shook his head, and his eyes began to tear. I stayed sitting beside him as he stared up at the ceiling, not looking back at me. I stood up and left the room.

The cancer continued to spread.

It was quiet on New Year's Eve until nine o'clock when our doorbell rang. Jeff's friends Jess Robertson and Greg Iadonisi were at our front door.

"Happy New Year," I said. "Please come on in."

"We couldn't keep away, Mrs. Hayes," Greg said. "We wanted to see Jeff."

"It's okay, you guys. You're always welcome here." John and I invited them down to Jeff's bedroom as he lay there alone watching television. We left them alone with Jeff and returned upstairs.

Their stay was short, and when they left, I sat drinking a glass of wine with John and then returned to sit with Jeff while we watched Dick Clark's celebration and then the ball drop; it was 2007.

I stayed in the moment in the days that followed. A new year—what good would that possibly bring? I lived every moment with Jeff, not knowing how much into this new year he'd be with us.

"Here," I said, opening the palm of my hand. He picked up the one chemo drug Sam still prescribed—the small dosage of hope. I gave him the rest of the meds, and he lay back in his bed, surrounded by pillows and his featherbed comforter. My sister Joanne had rearranged the room by moving Jeff's dresser across from his bed and bringing in one of the matching recliners, which she placed next to his bed.

"Would it be okay if I slept tonight on the recliner next to your bed?" I asked.

"Yes, Mom. I like to keep the television on all night, though."

"That's okay, but you know I might be snoring."

"I know."

The next day Jeff complained again about the pain and discomfort he was feeling in his mouth. I didn't know what to tell him.

"Jeff, let me ask Katherine or Jean if they have a portable suction machine we can use to take out some of the mucus in your mouth, and then I'll call Sam again about your tooth."

The VNA and the medical supply company immediately supplied us with everything Jeff needed. It seemed as though the people who supplied us the medicine from CVS and medical supplies from the VNA and Cape Medical Supply where on call just for us. We never waited long for anything. Jeff wanted to use the suction machine as soon as it was delivered. I was surprised they had one at their disposal. I suctioned the mucus from his mouth. It looked similar to the machine from a dentist's office, only it was a small, portable machine with a tube and plastic tip. It didn't relieve the pain, but it did help to keep his mouth clear.

We traveled back up to the JFC to see Sam and Hannah. It was afternoon before Jeff was lying in an examining room. Hannah comforted Jeff and drew his blood.

"Jeff, you are going to need some platelets," she told him when she returned after receiving his blood analysis. She directed her next question to me. "Because it's later in the day, do you think on the way home you and Jeff could stop at Jordan Hospital and have them draw some blood and then go back the following day for a transfusion?"

"Yes, we can," I answered.

Sam entered the room. He hadn't seen Jeff in weeks. His voice was soft and low. Sam's weary and fatigued physical appearance at the end of this day and the sorrow on his face, made me realize the despair he was feeling. He knew that he'd done everything he could for Jeff to fight the disease that had now taken over his body.

"Hi, Jeff. How are you doing?"

"Okay. My tooth is still bothering me, though."

"Let me take a look." Sam examined Jeff's mouth and said, "I'll give radiation a call and arrange a time when we can treat that part of your mouth with radiation. Maybe that will help with the discomfort you are feeling. Would that be okay with you, Jeff?"

"Yes," he replied.

"I'll call Jordan Hospital and let them know you guys are coming this afternoon for blood typing," Hannah added.

Jeff sat up, got off the examining table and into his wheelchair. I pushed him out of the room and down the hall toward the exit. I could feel Sam and Hannah watching us. I turned for a moment, looking back at the room we'd just left to see them standing in the doorway; the look on their faces was of complete anguish and sadness as they stared back at us. I felt defeated for the first time; there was nothing more they could do. They were keeping him alive and comfortable for as long as they could. We exited the JFC into the parking garage.

When Jeff and I arrived at Jordan Hospital, I followed the same routine of parking at the entrance and getting Jeff a wheelchair from the lobby and then wheeling him back to the lobby to wait while I parked the car.

I pushed him down the hall toward the small clinic where Jeff had his blood drawn. The door was open, but the clinic was closing. I knocked on the reception glass to attract a nurse.

When she appeared, I told her why we were there.

"There's no one here who knows how to access a port," she replied.

"What?" I said.

"Just a minute, Mrs. Hayes, I'll see if I can find someone."

It was four thirty in the afternoon and starting to get dark. Jeff and I were both exhausted and sat there for a while, waiting for the nurse to find another nurse or doctor capable of accessing Jeff's port. I got up and looked through the glass past the receptionist. What is taking her so long? I thought.

When she finally appeared, we listened, hoping she'd found someone so that Jeff could receive platelets tomorrow.

"There is a nurse in the emergency room who knows how to access a port," she said.

"How do we get to the emergency room from here?" I asked.

She gave us directions, and we headed in that direction. Inside the emergency room we waited for someone to give us instructions on what to do next. There was another long wait.

"Are you Mrs. Hayes?" A nurse appeared from another room.

"Yes, and this is my son, Jeff. We are waiting for a nurse to access Jeff's port for blood typing. He is scheduled for a transfusion tomorrow."

"I can do that for Jeff." She directed us down the hall to a bed that was vacant in the hallway.

"Jeff, can you get onto the bed for me?"

Jeff got out of his wheelchair, moving carefully, and climbed onto the bed. As he lay there, she placed a tray on the counter top across from us and put on gloves to access Jeff's port. She was pleasant and nice. The blood was drawn quickly, and we set out for home.

It was dark when we left Jordan Hospital. Jeff was sitting with the passenger seat reclined. As I drove over the Sagamore Bridge, I heard an ad on the radio promoting Jordan Hospital's new cancer unit.

The next day Sam called and asked whether Jeff and I could come up to Boston for radiation treatment on his jaw.

"Sam, we are going to Jordan Hospital for platelets. Should we come after that?" I asked.

"What time are you going to Jordan Hospital?" he asked.

"We're leaving now."

"Can you go to Brigham and Women's after Jeff's transfusion?"

I turned to Jeff and asked whether he was okay to go to Boston, because Sam had scheduled radiation treatment on his jaw to ease the pain in his mouth.

"Yes," Jeff replied from his recliner.

We left for Jordan Hospital. Each day that passed weakened Jeff, his weight dropped, and his strength decreased, but not his will to live. After hours with Kitsy in the infusion room, Jeff was out of immediate danger with platelets and the ability for his blood to clot. I drove to Brigham and Women's Hospital.

Jeff lay in bed in the large waiting room for patients receiving radiation. None of the beds were occupied, and with the curtains open around each bed, the room appeared to be larger than it was.

I realized that Sam was ordering this treatment to make Jeff comfortable for his remaining days of life. Maybe it would stop the tumor from growing so quickly in his mouth.

A technician approached us and sat down to talk to Jeff. She was wonderful and compassionate. Angelic, I thought. She knew by looking at Jeff that the disease was in the latter stages, but she made him feel that hope was not lost as she carefully explained the procedure to him.

At that moment I felt a relief and calmness come over me. She had softened my heart, and I retreated from my heightened stress and constant worry. I listened to her speak. She didn't rush through her explanation, and she smiled as she spoke.

The radiation didn't take very long, and I sat waiting next to Jeff's bed. I thought about the traffic and getting Jeff home again. When he returned, he remained in the wheelchair, and I pushed him out of the hospital and to the parking garage. He slept all the way home.

When I drove up to our house, several cars were parked in the driveway. Jeff woke up, and we looked at each other, wishing we had no visitors.

The next day I called Sam.

"What do I do, Sam? I don't know what to do. He is so sick and weak."

"Susan, just sit with him and spend as much time as you can with him."

That night at bedtime, I entered Jeff's bedroom.

"Mom, can you sleep here again tonight, in the recliner?"

"Yes, of course I can, honey."

CHAPTER 61

~

Mom, I Think It's Time to Go to the Hospital

JOHN JR. HELPED Jeff into his wheelchair and pushed him out through the french doors and onto the deck in our backyard. He pulled the wheelchair up the small hill on the side of our house as I pushed from behind. John Jr. helped Jeff into his truck and I drove to Jordan Hospital.

Kitsy had Jeff's platelets when we arrived. There was no wait this time for the blood bank in Canton, and she accessed Jeff's port for the transfusion. I sat with Jeff for two hours; the time it took to replenish his platelets. They were keeping him alive.

"Good-bye, Jeff. See you in a few days." Kitsy looked at Jeff and smiled.

When we returned home, I offered him an Ensure and gave him his meds.

Jeff wore his glasses all the time now, removing them only to sleep. I thought back to when he was in the fifth grade and came home from school to tell me he couldn't see the blackboard during class. We took him for an eye exam and realized he needed glasses. I had wondered too, how he could hit a baseball so well in Little League while struggling with his vision. I remember when he was five years old and his doctor performed surgery on Jeff's ears and water gushed out. He said that it was as if Jeff had been living under water with all the fluid in his ears. Jeff never complained either time until the pain from his ears or the strain on his eyes became too much for him.

The weekly get-well card from Jan Simpson, Jeff's homeroom teacher, and her students arrived in the mail.

Jan told me that a student had approached her and asked, "Have you heard anything about Jeff?"

"I've heard that he is not doing well," she replied.

"Oh, Mrs. Simpson, Jeff is going to be all right. I know it!"

She looked back at him with a look of sadness and worry that was clearly defined on her face; he cried out loudly as the rest the class looked on, "Oh, my God, he's not going to make it!" The kids, up to this point, had no idea how bad Jeff was and how fast the cancer was spreading.

Jeff slept on and off during the day.

I closed my eyes and began to bargain with God. "Dear Lord, you can have my life for his," I pleaded. "Please don't take him from us. I will do anything." Every night I prayed until I fell asleep repeating the Our Father and Hail Mary.

Our visiting nurses, Katherine and Jean, visited Jeff daily and drew blood. It was Friday, January 5, 2007. Jeff wanted to shower. I followed him as he slowly walked into his bathroom. He removed his tee T-shirt, and I wrapped his chest under his arm and around his back with Saran wrap to cover his port. I left the bathroom just before he stepped into the shower and stood outside the door listening until he was done. When the bathroom door opened, the Saran wrap was on the floor with his clothes, and he was dressed in clean boxers. I reconnected his pump and helped him dress. From his bedroom he walked slowly to his recliner.

"Mom can you get me some nail clippers, my electric shaver, and a comb?"

"Sure, honey. I'll be right back."

I returned with the items, and then he asked for a mirror. I couldn't find a small mirror, so I took down the one that hung over his bathroom sink. I stood in front of him with the mirror as he shaved and combed his hair. I watched him groom himself; not a hair was out of place. He was a perfectionist; you could see it by looking around his room. Every award, trophy, plaque, and picture was hung perfectly straight and spaced evenly. The mirror was getting heavy as I waited patiently for him to finish. He carefully placed his eyeglasses on the table next to his recliner and said, "Okay, I'm done, Mom."

Oh, thank God, I thought.

I hung the mirror back up in his bathroom, and he went back to his bedroom to lie down. The doorbell rang. My husband was upstairs and greeted Doreen and Jack Lessard. They visited with Jeff downstairs and then sat with us. Nancy Bridges arrived shortly after the Lessards. Despite Jeff's weight loss, his weakness, and atrophy, his color was good, and his mind was clear. He looked good after showering, I thought. Maybe he'll be with us longer than everyone thinks.

Saturday he was quiet, and we sat watching television most of the day until the Bruins played that night.

"What's up with Thomas?" I asked. It was between periods, and the Bruins were losing.

"Mom, they have a really good goalie coming up, and they have Chara; he's a great defensemen." He paused before he spoke again. "The Bruins are going to be great in a couple of years."

I followed Jeff's medicine schedule as usual. He walked slowly into his bedroom to change into his nylon Adidas shorts, and I left to put my pajamas on. He had six pillows and a featherbed comforter under and around him. He repositioned himself frequently, searching for a position where he could rest without pain. I turned out the lights, leaving the television on, and climbed into the recliner next to Jeff's bed. The pain intensified as the hours passed. After watching him restlessly trying to find comfort, I whispered to him, "Jeff, why don't you try sleeping on the recliner, and I'll lie in your bed?"

"Okay," he answered softly. Carefully he moved from the bed to the chair, and I placed pillows around him and behind his head. Able to close his eyes for only a minute at a time, he lasted for maybe fifteen minutes in the chair.

"Should I call Katherine?" I asked.

"No, not now."

He moved back to the center of the bed and sat up straight. I got up into his bed and sat with my back pressed against his with my legs crossed Indian style and my fists pressing firmly against the mattress so I could support him. I put a pillow between our heads. He continually pressed for a bolus of morphine that was set for every ten minutes. The TV played nothing but infomercials. Jeff didn't sleep the entire night. He again tried to position himself as he had originally, with his pillows around him. The light from the early morning sunrise shone in through the french doors. At six o'clock I called Katherine, and she came over.

"I'll call Sam," she said, "and ask him to up Jeff's dosage."

Sam gave Katherine orders to increase Jeff's morphine dosage, and Sunday he slept most of the day and night, waking only to drink, take his medicine, and go to the bathroom.

Jean arrived early Monday morning. I stood in Jeff's bedroom doorway as Jean talked to Jeff. I called Sam.

"Sam, he slept all day yesterday and seems better today," I said over the phone.

"What does he want to do? Does he want to stay home?"

I moved my cell phone away from my ear and asked Jeff Sam's questions. Jeff looked back at me from his bed and said, "Mom, I think it's time to go to the hospital." I was standing in the doorway, looking back at Jeff.

"He wants to come up to the hospital, Sam." I began to feel frightened. I walked into the other room.

"It's eight o'clock, Sam. We'll be there around eleven."

"Okay. I'll be here waiting for you."

I said good-bye to Sam and walked into Jeff's bedroom.

"Jeff, do you need to go the bathroom?" I asked.

"No, I don't need to," he answered.

He hadn't gone since the previous night. I was worried.

"Do you need some help getting up, honey?

"Yes."

"Wait there, I'll go get your brother."

As we entered Jeff's room, I explained to John Jr. how he would have to lift Jeff out of the bed. Jean went to get the wheelchair. John Jr. looked down at Jeff.

"Hey, kid, how are you doing?" he asked softly.

"Okay, I guess," Jeff replied.

Jeff was still lying in the middle of his bed, propped up with his pillows. It appeared he couldn't move. Jean was sitting in the recliner.

"John," I said, "sit across from your brother, and get as close as you can. I want you to wrap your arms around him from under his arms and very gently, when he's ready, lift him up. Jeff, I want you to wrap your arms around John's shoulders, and as he lifts you up, hold on to him. Okay, ready? John, get closer to Jeff, and on three, slowly and carefully pull him up."

"One, two, three," I said slowly. Jean looked on.

I watched as Jeff put his arms around John Jr. and rested his head on his shoulders. He had no strength. John Jr. slowly pulled him up. They stayed in that position for a few moments. Jeff's head lay resting on John Jr.'s shoulder, his eyes shut. My eyes filled with tears, and I swallowed. I couldn't speak; my heart was breaking. Moments passed, and I said, "John, carefully help Jeff move his legs over the edge of the bed."

I went over to Jeff's dresser to get him some clothes. I thought carefully for a moment about what he should wear. I grabbed a favorite T-shirt, sweat pants and a front-zipper maroon hooded sweatshirt. Jean

372

sat in the recliner, instructing John on how best to help Jeff into the wheelchair once he was dressed.

"Are you sure you don't need to go the bathroom, Jeff?" I asked again.

"No, Mom."

"John, go get dressed, please. I'll need your help getting Jeff to the truck."

"Okay, Mom, I'll be right back." He paused before he got up.

"Are you okay, Jeff?" John Jr. asked, kneeling next to him.

"Yup, I'm okay. Can you tape *24* for me tonight?" he asked his brother.

"I will. Don't worry."

I helped Jeff get dressed, and when John Jr. returned, he gently lifted Jeff out of the bed and into the wheelchair. I was already dressed, and I called my husband to tell him we were heading up to the JFC. I then called Patty to let her know. I threw some clothes in an overnight bag for Jeff and got a small throw to cover his legs.

I looked around Jeff's living room at all his trophies lined up by height on the shelf his Uncle Marty had built. I looked over at his awards and all the pictures of the Bruins and Terry O'Reilly and the Bruins jerseys hanging on his walls. I stood still for a moment. He might not return home again, I thought. The room felt empty and silent. A starched white hospital pillow case lay on the seat of his recliner. I lowered my head and spoke softly, "Oh God, please guide us and keep him safe." I turned and said good-bye to Jean, who was standing outside Jeff's bedroom.

John Jr. had wheeled Jeff out the french doors. I turned and walked out the door behind them. John Jr. pulled Jeff, and I pushed him from behind, up the hill and around the front of our house to the driveway. Carefully John Jr. helped Jeff into his truck and covered him with the blanket. It was mild outside and no snow on the ground. I was thankful for that.

"Jeff, hold on a second; I'll go get some pillows."

Jean was typing notes in her computer as I entered Jeff's bedroom to grab some pillows.

"Thanks, Jean, for your help." She hugged me, and I left, running back up the stairs and out the door. I placed a pillow behind Jeff's head and back. He was struggling to find a comfortable position sitting in his Mountaineer. I started the truck, and we drove up to Boston.

The song "Amie" by Pure Prairie League came on the radio as we drove through Plymouth.

"Mom, is this an old song?" Jeff asked. I could tell he liked the song.

"Yes," I replied.

"Oh."

"Do you like it?" I asked.

"Yes, but it's old."

"There are old songs, classics that are great songs; they're timeless. The age of a song doesn't make it a bad song; it's your taste in music. Like what you like."

He didn't reply; he was in pain.

"Keep pressing for a bolus of morphine, Jeff."

"I am, Mom."

When we reached Marshfield, he asked me to stop. He couldn't get comfortable. I took the Marshfield exit and pulled into a parking lot near the Christmas Tree Shop. I helped him out of the truck, and he stood there for a while working through the pain.

"Are you okay, honey?"

"Yes, we can go now."

With his hood over his head, I helped him back into the truck. I placed the blanket over him and put a pillow behind his head. I got back on Route 3 North toward Boston. We stopped again before the expressway, and Jeff got out of the truck. He was having trouble getting in and out. I was in awe of him and felt completely helpless. He didn't complain about the pain and I didn't ask because I knew he wanted to handle it on his own. I didn't know where the cancer had spread. I didn't know if it had hit other organs or just his bones.

When we arrived at the JFC, I parked across from the entrance and called Hannah.

"Hi, Hannah. Jeff and I are parked outside the front door of the Dana-Farber. Can you come and help us?"

"Susan, just stay there. Sam and I will be down soon."

Jeff and I waited for fifteen minutes. I called her again.

"Hannah, are you coming down?"

"Can you drive up to the parking lot and park outside the entrance to the clinic? I'll meet you there."

"Okay, we're on our way."

OUTSIDE THE LINES WITH
Emily Masi
Dan Crowley, the columnist, asks, "Who has been your inspiration?"

My love for sports comes from my father and my older brothers, Anthony and Alex. I always played sports with them outside and signed up for soccer and basketball as soon as I was old enough. I have found inspiration in my teammates through their commitment and enthusiasm. Also, Jeff Hayes has been a huge inspiration to all athletes at Sandwich High School, defining perseverance and true strength.

CHAPTER 62

Short Ride to Children's Hospital

I DROVE UP THE ramp to the parking garage and parked in front of the entrance to the Dana-Farber. The entrance leads to the JFC. Hannah walked out toward our truck and opened the passenger's side door.

"How are you doing, Jeff?" she asked.

"Okay." He sat in the front seat with his hood on. Sam then approached the truck, walked around the back and got in the back seat behind me. I saw Hannah look at Sam, her face solemn as their eyes met. They didn't speak.

"Jeff, we're going to drive around to the emergency room entrance at Children's. We're not going into the JFC. They are preparing a room for you at Children's," Sam explained.

"Okay," Jeff replied.

"I'll meet you at the emergency room entrance, okay, sweetie?" Hannah said to Jeff.

"Okay."

"We'll take care of you there, Jeff," Sam continued.

I started the truck and drove to the emergency room entrance at Children's.

It was a two-minute ride to Children's, and when we arrived, Sam immediately got out of the truck and ran to the other side. Hannah was waiting curbside. Jeff opened the door, and Sam helped him out of the truck.

"I can't feel my legs," Jeff said to Sam.

Hannah was standing in front of Jeff, and after hearing his words she ran into the emergency room for a stretcher.

"When Hannah comes back, we'll do this slowly, and she and I will help you onto the stretcher. Are you okay right now standing?" Sam asked, standing close by Jeff's side to support him.

"Yes," Jeff replied.

Hannah returned within minutes. She and Sam helped Jeff step up onto the curb and get onto the stretcher. I watched from the driver's seat, tears filling my eyes, trying not to lose control. Jeff lay in the stretcher with his hood covering his head. Sam stuck his head through the doorway of the passenger's side and said, "We're taking Jeff to Seven West. I'll see you there."

"Okay."

Sam and Hannah quickly pushed Jeff in the stretcher through the emergency room entrance. I watched until they disappeared through the doors, and then I drove back up to the garage to park, and then ran over to Children's. As I entered Seven West and walked to the nurse's station, I could see Jeff lying in a bed in a room directly in front of me. The blinds were open. I entered the room.

"Are you okay, honey?"

"Yes, Mom."

Sam was outside the door talking to a group of nurses. He had already examined Jeff before I arrived. I walked out of Jeff's room to talk to Sam.

"The cancer didn't hit his spine; it hit his spinal cord. Jeff's bladder was huge. I thought the cancer would have spread to his backbone, and I feared it would break. Instead it hit the nerves in his spine. He couldn't feel the need to urinate, so we are draining his bladder right now."

He and I walked into Jeff's room.

"Jeff, your bladder was so enlarged I thought it might explode," Sam said. "Do you still have no feeling to urinate?"

"No," Jeff replied.

I was as relieved as Jeff was to be at Children's. The cancer was hitting him hard and fast. I realized now why the wait had been so long:

Sam and Hannah had been moving patients to free up a bed for Jeff across from the nurse's station.

I sat with Jeff in his room. He was hooked up to an IV and given his meds.

"We had a suction machine at home for Jeff's mouth," I said to Jeff's nurse. "Can we get one here?"

"Yes, I will get one for you," she replied.

Sam was in and out of Jeff's room, and I asked him about Jeff's mouth.

"I will call over to the dental clinic and see if someone can come over to see Jeff."

"Can I still have the radiation on my jaw?" Jeff asked Sam.

Sam paused and said, "Yes, I can arrange that."

Jeff slept for a while. My husband, John arrived. My son John Jr. drove Patty and Jason up.

Sam asked John and me to meet with him in a small private room on the floor while Patty, John Jr., and Jason sat with Jeff. We entered the small room with Sam and sat down.

"I don't think he is going right now. He might be able to go home by the end of the week," Sam began.

I felt relieved that we'd have more time with Jeff. John sat on a chair, and I sat on the love seat. Sam sat next to me.

"You need to think about what you want to say to Jeff before he leaves us," Sam said as tears rolled down his face.

Oh God, I thought. The room became just the chair I sat in. I looked back at Sam, wanting to tell him what I thought I should try to explain to Jeff that might help him transition into the next life. Finally I answered, "I've been thinking about what to say, Sam," unable to hold back my tears.

"That's good," he replied. "We have a group of people who can help you talk to Jeff. Would you like me to have them meet with you?"

"I don't think so, Sam. Thank you." There are several groups of people who specialize in pain management. There are social workers like ours, Deb Berg, who was with us several times throughout Jeff's treatment, and then there are counselors for moments like this. But I wanted no part of it. I didn't want to speak with people I didn't know about something so personal. I didn't want to be influenced by them to say something they thought I should say. I will probably regret not asking for their help; they were experienced in helping patients and parents with end-of-life comfort and advice.

"You said you thought Jeff might go home by the end of the week," John asked Sam. "What do you think will happen?"

"I don't know. Let's take one day at a time for now," Sam replied.

We cried together.

John Jr., Jason, and Patty sat with Jeff all afternoon. That night my brothers and sisters came to see Jeff. Then John took Patty and Jason to the hotel. It was dark, and we talked quietly sitting in Jeff's room.

Around seven o'clock, Jeff's door opened, and five young dental students entered the room. They introduced themselves, all wearing long white doctors' coats. The room was filled with my brothers and sisters.

"Hi," I said. "This is my son, Jeff. He has been having discomfort in the upper left quadrant of his jaw. He had his wisdom tooth extracted last year, and for the past several months he's been complaining about pain in that area."

One by one they examined Jeff's mouth. Jeff lay patiently. When they finished, they stood together at the end of Jeff's bed. I sat in a chair next to Jeff.

"Mrs. Hayes, we are going to try to come up with something to help alleviate Jeff's discomfort. We will be back in about eight hours."

I looked up at the clock behind them. "You have twenty minutes to come back and tell me what needs to be done." My brother John looked at me and smiled.

"Yes, Mrs. Hayes. We'll be back in twenty minutes," the more experienced dentist replied.

My family began to leave one by one, and I sat with Jeff.

"Mom, can you get me my slippers?"

"Sure, honey." I put his slippers on his feet, and he bent his knees.

"My legs keep sliding down on the bed; my slippers help keep my legs up."

"Okay, honey."

The door opened again and the five dental students entered the room.

"We're going to put a topical anesthetic on Jeff's gums to numb them."

"Okay, great," I said.

One of the students applied the anesthetic.

"How does that feel, Jeff?"

"Good, Mom."

They left me with a small bottle and some applicators to apply the anesthetic when needed. I thanked them and they left. I should have done that a long time ago, I thought. It was the only thing Jeff complained about. It was awful for him, a tumor growing from his jaw into his mouth.

I put my pajamas on and made my bed on the bench built into the wall.

"Mom, can you come sit next to me?" Jeff asked.

"Of course I can, honey." I sat down beside his bed.

"I can't breathe, Mom." His eyes looked into mine. I hadn't seen him struggling to breathe like this before. I couldn't believe how quickly things were changing.

"Okay, honey. I'll go get Sam. I'll be right back!" I opened the door and stopped suddenly. Gismo was standing across from Jeff's room. I stood still. I'd never seen him on our floor. Where have you been? I thought. I'm frightened. It was odd to feel comfort, to feel anything, from a robot, but he reminded me of hope. I looked up from Gismo to the nurse standing behind the nurse's station. "Is Dr. Blackman here?" I asked.

"Yes, I'll get him for you," she replied and walked away. Within moments Sam appeared from a room behind the nurse's station.

"Jeff is having trouble breathing," I explained.

"I'll order oxygen for him," he replied.

We walked back to Jeff's room and stood alongside his bed.

"We'll get you some oxygen, Jeff. That will help you breathe," Sam told him. I told Sam about the topical anesthetic.

"Does it help?" he asked.

"It seems to," I replied.

A nurse entered the room and hooked up the oxygen and placed the mask over Jeff's nose.

"I'm going to be at the nurse's station across the hall all night if you need me," Sam said.

"Okay, thanks," I replied.

OUTSIDE THE LINES WITH
Mike Bridges
Dan Crowley, the columnist, asks, "Who has been your inspiration?"

Jeff Hayes has been my inspiration. He has taught me to play each game as if it were my last. Two years ago the doctors found a tumor in his leg and he hasn't played hockey or baseball since. One of the best moments in my life was last year at the Canal Cup when Jeff got to play the first shift. Although it was only a minute or so, to see how far he had come, it made me so happy.

CHAPTER 63

I Don't Understand Why

THE ROOM WAS quiet. My husband John, John Jr., and Jason were staying at the hotel with Patty. I sat in a chair with my head resting on the middle of the Jeff's bed. I watched him as he slept peacefully until I could no longer keep my eyes open. I picked my head up as the nurse entered the room. I had fallen asleep for a few hours. I looked up at Jeff. He was still sleeping, so I walked over to the window bed and lay down to sleep. It was still dark and I didn't want to disturb his sleep.

I woke again when I heard Sam enter our room. He was wearing scrubs. I sat up. Jeff was sleeping. Sam sat next to me. He kissed the side of my head and hugged me as I cried quietly next to him. It was seven o'clock in the morning. I thought, how horrible it must be to gasp for air, to feel like you are suffocating.

When Sam left, I changed out of my pajamas, and John, John Jr., Patty, and Jason arrived.

"Hi, kid. How are you?" John asked.

Jeff had placed the mask beneath his chin. "I'm having some trouble breathing, Dad."

I could see the sadness on my husband's face as he looked back at Jeff.

"It's okay. Try to breathe into the mask when you need to."

"Hi, Jeff."

"Hi, Auntie."

"Would you like something to eat?" Patty asked. "I brought you a bagel and strawberry milk."

"No thanks, Auntie."

"Hey, kid. How are you doing?" John Jr. asked.

"Okay."

"Where's Jay?" I asked Patty. She gestured for me to come near her and she spoke softly. "He's down the hall; he doesn't want Jeff to see him crying."

Hannah entered the room, and we talked. Then I left her alone with Jeff.

I walked down the hall on Seven West alone. When I saw Hannah leave Jeff's room, I greeted her. "Can I ask what you said to Jeff?"

"Yes, of course. I asked him if he was ready to go," Hannah began. "And he said, 'Go where?'"

I smiled sadly back at her. "He doesn't know, does he?" I asked.

"Well, I told him that his body just can't take anymore, and that's when we know it's time. He looked at me and said, 'I know it's coming.'"

"Oh why, Hannah, why? I just don't understand. I don't know why!" Tears began to fall, and I looked back at her. She said, "Susan, all I can think of is that he's needed somewhere else."

We hugged. She left for the JFC, and I went to Jeff.

His breathing was very shallow. He was still wearing the T-shirt I'd given him to wear before we left home. We sat with him all morning. I applied the topical anesthetic over his upper gums. I thought it might be refreshing to brush his teeth for him, so I left his room to get him some toothpaste and a clean toothbrush. There wasn't a nurse around, so I went to the storage room across from the nurse's station and found the door open, which was unusual; it was always locked. There were several shelves filled with toiletries, soap, shampoo, a comb. It was well stocked. I saw a clear plastic wrapping that packaged something white. Out of curiosity, I picked it up from the rear of the shelf and read the package: Body Bag. Oh my God. I quickly put it back, grabbed a toothbrush and toothpaste, and left the room. I walked around the hall, still startled and terrified. I sat down outside Jeff's room until I could regain my composure enough to help him brush his teeth.

Sam entered the room and told us that he was going to move Jeff to another room, but until the room was available, Jeff would be moved to a temporary room down the hall.

The temporary room looked like an operating room. There was a long counter top with a sink, and another entrance to the room from a door next to Jeff's bed.

John, Patty, Jason, and I gathered around Jeff's bed. John Jr. had to go back to the Cape but said he would return later. Someone knocked on the door. John opened it. Coach Derackk and one of Jeff's friends, the goalie, Matt Ryan from Sandwich High entered. Jeff took his mask off and smiled. They talked hockey. Jeff's mind was clear as they joked and shared recaps of recent games. They visited for most of the afternoon and then left just before Jeff was moved to a large single room with windows that reached from the ceiling to the floor. Couches and chairs were lined across the front of the windows, and Jeff's bed faced the windows from across the room. We had never been in this room before. John Jr. arrived and sat with Jeff. It was late in the afternoon, and more of Jeff's friends were on their way up.

"I'm going to lie down in the teen room for a while," I said to Patty.

"Julie is coming up; she's bringing Jeff a portable fan," she replied.

"Oh, great idea, he'll like that."

I left Jeff's room and entered the teen room down the hall. Thankfully the room was empty. I made myself comfortable on the small couch and fell asleep.

"Susan," Patty said, kneeling next to the couch. "Jeff is looking for you. Bob Sweeney from the Bruins just left."

"He was here!" I sat up.

"Jeff said you are never there when someone visits."

"He's right; I'm always somewhere else. He gets so upset. Is he mad?"

"No, but he wants you to come back to the room."

"Okay." I walked quickly toward his room.

"Mom, where were you?" He asked softly when I entered his room.

"I'm sorry, honey; I was napping."

"Bob Sweeney came to visit again."

"That's really nice; I'll stay close in case someone else comes."

Melanie and Bob Hill walked in. Bob stood next to Jeff, holding his oxygen mask and handing it to Jeff when he needed it to breathe. Melanie sat across from Jeff's bed. Jeff and Bob used to play catch for hours up until Jeff entered high school, before his diagnosis.

Nancy Bridges arrived with her son, Mike, and a carload of Jeff's friends. The room was full. I was thankful that my husband initiated the conversations with everyone; he was much better than me at carrying on long conversations with people. I just can't talk that much.

I wasn't in Jeff's room when the boys arrived. When I saw them sitting across from Jeff, I said hello. They seemed visibly shaken by the change in Jeff's condition from the last time they had seen him. They remained stoic, but I could see the sadness. I looked at one boy I didn't recognize and wondered who he was.

"It's me, Will, Mrs. Hayes. I got my hair cut," he said quietly and smiled.

These were the friends that Jeff had been so eager to come home to over the past two years.

They sat along the window looking up at Jeff. They watched him struggle to breathe, and after a few hours, each one stopped by Jeff's side to say their good-byes. Melanie and Bob said good-bye then left.

Sam came in after they had gone and spoke to John Jr. and Jason. "Now is the time you need to think about what you would like to say to Jeff. This is your chance to let him know how you feel and how much he means to you. If you don't, you'll regret it the rest of your life."

I don't think John Jr. and Jason knew yet what they wanted to say to their brother.

John Jr. approached Jeff.

"I love you, Jeff. I'll see you in the morning."

Jeff stared back at his brother. "Love you too."

An old memory came to me.

I'd told Jeff to be home at eleven o'clock. He was only a freshman and hanging out with seniors who drove. It had only been an hour, and I began to worry.

"John!" I called out to my son. "Go find Jeff and make sure he's all right."

"What?" he replied.

I walked into the room where John Jr. sat watching television. "Go find Jeff, and make sure he's okay."

"Mom, I'm not going out to look for him."

"Why not?"

"Mom, you know Jeff always does the right thing."

I stood in the middle of the room, looking back at John Jr., and then said, "John, go out and find Jeff."

"Okay, but I know he's all right."

Sam walked into Jeff's hospital room.

"Jeff," I asked. "Do you have anything to tell Sam?"

"Yes," Jeff replied.

Sam walked away from me and over to Jeff's side.

"I have two sharp points coming out of my head, right here. What's that, Sam?"

Sam looked back at Jeff, his voice low and soft, and I thought Sam might start to cry. He paused before he looked down at Jeff and answered, "That's the disease." Jeff turned away, not saying a word and looked up at the ceiling.

"Is there anything else you want to tell me, or anything I can get for you?" Sam asked.

"No, nothing," Jeff said quietly.

Julie arrived with a small portable fan and placed it just behind the top side of Jeff's bed. He had always loved cool air blowing on him.

"Great idea," Sam said, looking at Jeff.

I left the room to put my pajamas on. When I returned, I sat in a chair next to Jeff. He looked out the window into the night at the streetlights glowing from below. His breathing worsened and became more labored. I knew we were losing him.

We stood at Jeff's bedside, John, me, Sam, and the pastor, as his last rites were read, then all of us, including Jeff, recited the Our Father. When the pastor left, a nurse approached us and asked, "Would you like Jeff's handprints?"

I looked across to Patty.

"Yes, she replied.

The nurse left and soon returned with watercolor paint and several sheets of paper, some with clouds and a blue sky and a couple of sheets of five-by-seven linen-colored paper that were already matted.

I placed Jeff's hand in the paint and then pressed onto the paper. He gave me a look of, "What the heck, Mom!" He didn't speak.

After the nurse cleaned up, Jason approached Jeff, and Patty left the room. I stood next to Jeff, and John stood at the end of the bed as Jason spoke to Jeff and told him how proud he was of him. He continued to speak, and as we listened, our eyes filled with tears.

Jeff's body could no longer withstand the progression of the disease. It was just before midnight on January 10, 2007 when John and I had to say goodbye to our beautiful son. We remained by his side. He didn't look terribly ill and his will to live never ceased. Oh, Jeff, I can't imagine life without you.

We told him over and over again how much we loved him, how deeply we would miss him, and how lucky we were to have had him as our son. We told him how proud we were of all he had accomplished in his life and how amazing he was to have made such a difference in so many lives. And when it was time, we told him it was okay to let go, and not to worry about us because we knew that he'd always be there watching over us. Heaven is a beautiful place, and you have no need to fear anything.

Good night, we love you so. Jeff left this life just after midnight. I kissed him good-bye.

I looked up at the ceiling, thinking Jeff was now looking down upon us and at peace.

OUTSIDE THE LINES WITH
Brian Fleckles
Dan Crowley, the columnist, asks, "Who has been your inspiration?"

My hero and inspiration in my life has been Jeff Hayes. Jeff is one of the bravest, strongest kids I have ever met in my life. He has taught me to live every day to the fullest, and to always be grateful. Jeff showed us that life is fragile. So I use that when I go out and play sports. I go into golf matches like it's that last one I might ever play and I cherish that. I will never forget Jeff, and I thank him for making me the person I am today.

CHAPTER 64

❧

So Many Times We'd Left Together

IT WAS WELL after midnight and I knew we needed to make the difficult call to John Jr. since he was back on the Cape and planning to come up to see Jeff later in the day. I knew he'd be asleep and I didn't want to wake him only to have him be all alone with the news. I thought it would be best to call him first thing in the morning.

My sister Kathy arrived, and we stayed with Jeff until four in the morning. When she left, our friend Michael, who had circled Children's Hospital for hours before he could find it in his heart to come inside, joined us. Jack and John Lessard and Brian Kolb came in to see Jeff. Jason and I gave them their privacy and returned after they left. The floor was quiet, and it was time to go. Sam had already gone. Michael drove Patty and Jason back to the hotel, and Julie drove home. After leaving Jeff, we entered the hallway. Michael had returned and walked toward us, kissed me on the cheek, and told us he'd be downstairs waiting for us when we were ready to leave. John and I walked past Jeff's room. I looked back into the room one last time, and I saw the nurses tending to him. The elevator doors opened to the lobby floor. We walked past the brightly painted wall with the names of the donors. The lobby was empty. We left through the revolving doors and went out onto the sidewalk in front of Children's. We didn't speak. We stood there while Michael drove up to the curb, and then we got into his SUV. As he slowly drove away, I stared back at the doors that remained still. It was almost dawn. I thought about all the times Jeff and I had gone through those doors. In the beginning, he was in a wheelchair; then later in his treatment, he walked through those doors. This early morning, we left without him.

Michael dropped us off at the Holiday Inn on Beacon Street. John and I went to our room. Patty and Jason stayed down the hall. I changed and lay down on the bed draped with Jeff's clothing that the nurses had given me before we left. As I lay there, looking up at the ceiling, I could feel a heaviness, an invisible presence several feet from the foot of my bed and suspended in the air. "Jeff, are you there?" I asked softly. I stared back at the aura, knowing he was. I stared into the darkness until I fell asleep.

"What time is it?" I asked, hearing John walk out of the shower and into the room.

"Seven thirty," he answered. "Are you okay?" he asked.

"I feel like this isn't real," I replied, fighting back the tears.

His cell phone rang. I lay there watching as he held his cell phone to his ear.

"The kids have walked out of the school!" He said looking back at me.

"What!"

"There's a memorial down at the rink," he continued.

"At the rink!" I repeated.

"There was an announcement at school. The flag is at half-mast, and Father Rodney is there with the kids."

"Oh my God, John, the poor kids. We have to call John Jr.!" My phone rang. It was my brother John.

"How are you doing?" he asked.

"I don't know yet."

"The Bruins called; they want to help," he said. "What do you need? How can I help?"

"The Bruins called?" I repeated. "I don't know, Johnny. I just woke up, I can't think. John's on the phone with someone. The kids all walked out of school. Um…" I thought for moment, trying to make sense of all that had just happened in the few minutes I'd been awake.

"Do you think you could drive Jason and Patty to the Cape?" I asked.

"Sure, I'm on my way."

"Okay, thanks." I hung up and set my phone down. John was still on the phone. I thought about the kids walking out of school. My phone rang again.

"Susan, it's Sam."

"Hi, Sam. We just found out that the kids walked out of school."

"They did! How many?" he asked.

"I don't know."

"Are you okay?"

"I don't know. Everything seems to be happening so fast. Have you seen Hannah?"

"Yes, everyone at the clinic is pretty upset. Susan, do you and John need anything?"

"I don't think so, Sam. Thanks."

"Okay, I'll talk to you later. Bye."

"Bye, Sam."

"Who was that?" John asked.

"Sam, and my brother John. And the Bruins called."

"They did!"

"Yes." My cell phone rang.

"Hello."

"Hi Sue, Nance. I'm so sorry. What can we do?"

"Have you heard about the school?"

"Yes, Casey called me. I had to pick him up at school. Do you need anything?"

391

"I don't think so, Nance."

"I'll call you later, okay?"

"Yes, thanks. Bye."

"John, we need to call John."

"You're going to tell him over the phone?"

"I'm sure he's heard. I don't know what to do."

"Wait until we get home."

"Okay. I'm getting in the shower."

"Do you want me to get you something to eat? Michael is on his way."

"No thanks."

"I'll be right back."

"Check on Jason and Patty. No wait; I'll call them. My brother Johnny is coming to pick them up and take them to the Cape."

"What room are they in?"

"Gee, I don't know. I'll call the front desk. I've got to call Joe, too."

"Work?"

"Yes, then I'll jump in the shower."

"Be right back." He walked toward me, and we hugged, both fighting back the tears. Then he left. Tears started to fall instantly. I think I'll shower before I call my boss. Oh, wait I thought, I need to call Patty. I stood in the room alone. It was suddenly quiet. I felt frightened and deeply sad. I lay down on my bed, covering myself with Jeff's clothing.

I heard a knock on the door a few minutes later and heard Patty's voice softly call for me.

I got up and opened the door. "Hi. Where's Jason?" I asked.

"He's still sleeping. It took him a while to fall asleep. He's so upset and angry," she replied.

"Let him sleep. I'll check on him after I shower. Oh, I've got to call Joe." I picked up my cell and dialed.

"Hi, Joe," I sat down on the edge of my bed, trying not to cry as I told him we had lost Jeff. Joe had been a vision of strength for me over the last two years. I'd always felt strong in front of him; he gave me that strength.

"I'm so sorry," he replied. Can we do anything?"

"I don't think so."

"I'll call Bill and let him know, and I'll let our clients know too."

I hung up knowing that Joe would always be there for me; he and Bill had been so generous and understanding during the last two years, and I was grateful. Joe and Jeff talked sports when Jeff visited the office, and I remember one day when Joe and I watched Jeff as he walked away, looking through the tall glass door as he walked down the front walk toward the parking lot and to his car. He wore his white fighting Irish cap, beige cargo pants, his navy windbreaker, and white leather Adidas shoes. He had an athlete's physique. We stared until he got into his car and drove away. We said nothing; we both just watched him from inside the office then quietly went back to our desks.

The door opened and John entered. I got into the shower, and Patty went to check on Jason. I took a quick shower, not one of my long "safe from the world" showers.

"What happens now? Where's Jeff?" I asked John after I'd dressed.

"Peter called. He wants me to meet him and John Devito. Michael is going to take me. Can Kathy take you home?"

"I guess. I'll ask," I replied. "John, I don't want to leave without Jeff."

"Don't worry; it's okay. John Devito has made arrangements with a funeral home in Yarmouth to bring Jeff back home to the Cape, so he'll be close."

"Okay."

My phone rang, and Kathy was on the line. "Okay," I said. "Kathy, can you drive me home? Johnny is taking Patty and Jason home, and John is going with Michael, Peter, and John Devito. Okay, thanks," and I hung up the phone.

Johnny arrived, and Patty and Jason left with him. My sister Kathy picked me up, and we left the Holiday Inn for the last time. I walked out of the lobby and through the doors. The day seemed empty. There was

Susan Hayes

traffic, daylight, and nothing else. I sat in the passenger seat, looking out at the road.

When Kathy and I arrived at my house, I went upstairs to see John Jr. I sat next to him on his bed. "John, Jeff passed away last night."

"Mom, please leave me alone," he said, curled up and lying still. I left his room and walked downstairs through the kitchen and downstairs to Jeff's bedroom. I lay in Jeff's bed, clinging to his clothes. Marty, my brother-in-law, came down.

"Susan, you okay?"

"Yes. I'll be up in a minute."

Food began to arrive. Baskets, flowers, plants, they all kept coming. The Falmouth hockey team sent an enormous gift basket filled with several plants, small white cancer Care Bears, and several mini hockey sticks made from small wooden sticks with black hockey tape around the blade and the number twelve and Jeff's name on the shaft.

I lay on the couch surrounded by family. Joanne covered me with Jeff's comforter. I could hear their soft voices and their attempts to hold back their tears. I saw Peter peek his head into the room just as I closed my eyes.

On Facebook, friends remembered Jeff.

Noelle Kern at 8:01 a.m. wrote:

In the end my friend, we will all be together again. We'll all miss ya Jeff.

Ryan Carroll at 3:05 a.m. (University of Massachusetts Dartmouth) wrote:

"And the road that young man paved
The broken seams along the way,
The rusted signs, left just for me.

394

He was guiding me, love, his own way.
Now the man of the hour has taken his final bow,
As the curtain comes down,
I feel that this is just goodbye for now."

Jeff Hayes...I love you kid...lets go pig on some pizza and cheesy bread from Papa G's...and then kick back and play some twoods...one of these times I'll beat you...just like you'll out eat me at Papa G's...you are, and will always be an irreplaceable part of my, and many other's lives...you've taught us all so much, how to fight, how to stay strong, and most importantly how to live. Thank you for being a huge part of my life #12...look over us up there, I'll see ya.

Kyle Kruse at 4:49 p.m. (Franklin Pierce) wrote:

RIP Jeff, I'll never forget how we ruled canal youth hockey on defense our midget year! You will be missed by all—Kyle

Danielle Tropea at 1:41 p.m. wrote:

If you could see me now;
I'm walking streets of gold.
If you could see me now;
You'd know I'd seen His face.
If you could see me now,
You'd know the pain's erased.
You wouldn't want me to
Ever leave this place.
If you could only see me now
My light and temporary trials;
Have worked out for my good.
To know it brought Him glory;
When I misunderstood.
Though we've had our sorrows;
They can never compare;

What Jesus has in store for us;
No language can share.
God only takes the best…Rest in the sweetest of peace #12

The next morning Patty and I left for Dennis to see a florist to select the flowers for Jeff's service. Peter had asked me to pick out Jeff's clothing for the wake. John was with Peter and John Devito, and then we met at our church, Corpus Christi Parish in Sandwich, to speak with Father Rodney.

Our mailbox was filled and overflowing with sympathy cards in the days that followed. Aside from the hundreds of Facebook messages, cards were sent by the dozen. We received a letter from the Living Memorial Program that read, *I hereby certify that a tree has been planted in a national forest as a memorial to your loved one.*

There were many letters from Sandwich students, friends of Jeff. I read them all. John handed me a folded piece of paper he'd just read. I opened this letter, which had a watermark underneath the typed words that read, "I'm sorry" in various sizes all over the page. I began to read:

> *Dear Hayes Family;*
>
> *I'm very sorry for your loss. I really didn't know Jeff that well, I just knew of him. Although I always got updates on him with my frequent visits to the school nurse's office. Everyone always spoke so highly of Jeff; I never heard any bad words spoken. I regret not being able to get to know him like a lot of others did.*
>
> *Anyway, this is just a little gift for your family. I'm not even sure if it will be of much importance. This past Thursday the Teen Cancer Group that I'm part of, got to go to the game and meet Patrice*

Bergeron. And I thought, since Jeff was so into hockey that maybe after the game when we met Patrice I'd get something signed for you guys. When I asked him to sign it, his face seemed to drop and so did the girl's next to him. I don't remember how he said he knew Jeff, but he did. He seemed terribly upset after hearing this news. So along with everyone else Jeff touched, I think he touched Patrice too.

While Jeff was going through his treatment, I was going through treatment myself for T-Cell ALL Leukemia. So even though there's no way I feel what you're feeling now, I do understand what going through treatment is like. I know you probably have many people telling you this, but if you ever need anything or just need someone to talk to, my number is (508) XXX-XXX, I can also be reached at (508) XXX-XXX.

Along with Jeff, you and you're family will be in my prayers.
Sincerely,
Katherine Tompkins

I opened the package. Inside was a white Bruins T-shirt. On the front, above the Bruins logo, in black marker it read, "In Loving Memory of Jeff, Patrice Bergeron #37."

Sam called. He called every day, but this call was extraordinary. He said, "Jeff's two corneas were given to two different people, one in Massachusetts and one in Texas. Two people can now see now because of Jeff."

Friday, January 12, 2007, the Sandwich *Enterprise* front page pictured Jeff. It was Jeff's senior high school picture I'd given to Jack Lessard. The headline read: "Jeff Hayes Remembered as 'a Fighter.'"

On Saturday, January 13, 2007, the *Cape Cod Times* front page read: "He Battled Cancer Like He Played Hockey: Sandwich Friends, Teammates Mourn the Loss of Senior Jeffrey Hayes, a Champion on and off the Ice Rink." It pictured Matt Ryan, the Sandwich High senior who visited Jeff on the last day of his life. In the picture, Matt is painting the wall of the boy's locker room at Gallo with the words, "Today We Play Like Champions #12—'Just Win Boys' Jeff Hayes—We Love You Man."

The *Upper Cape Codder* read:

Everybody Loved Jeff Hayes. Heroes seem harder to come by these days. Yet for an enormous number of people in and around Sandwich, finding someone to admire was as easy as looking at Jeff Hayes. "Everybody loved Jeff Hayes," said Dave Aycock, Hayes' former baseball coach and tutor. "They didn't just love Jeff Hayes the hockey player or the baseball player. They loved Jeff Hayes the person."

Immediately, a tribute to Hayes was erected outside the Sandwich boys' locker room at Gallo. Flowers were laid at the foot of the door that Hayes had walked through so often, while pizza boxes and other memorabilia formed a mountain of memories to a friend and a teammate.

"As recently as Thanksgiving, Jeff had really believed that he would be at graduation in June, that he would be playing baseball for me," said Aycock, who spent countless hours tutoring Hayes last fall. "He said he didn't know if he would be ready to play the outfield but wanted to at least take some innings at first base."

Calling him "The best pitcher in his freshman class," Aycock said there's no doubt that Hayes was talented enough to have been a three year varsity starter. "Who knows what would have happened. He had so much ability."

Coping with the reality that their friend had died, Brian Tomasini said, "None of us are really sure what to do right now. We're trying to stick together. Nobody wants to be alone right now. But Jeff is probably looking down and laughing at us, saying there's other things we should be doing. That was Jeff."

Much has been written about and discussed regarding Jeff Hayes' ability to skate to the puck and throw a baseball. Still, people continue to talk about a young man whose career was cut short far too soon; but more telling than his athletic ability, say many people who knew Hayes, was his way of bringing people together. "He was a born leader. Kids are coming together, some of them football players, cross country runners, baseball players some of them who don't play sports at all— girls and guys, just coming together in his memory. It's amazing to see," said Angelo Tomasini. While Hayes touched the lives of innumerable people in Sandwich, his memory lives on beyond town borders as well.

"People in Bourne are devastated," said Robert Kruse, whose family has known the Hayes family since their boys began playing hockey and baseball with and against each other as youths. "We're lost for words." Kruse remembers Hayes as a "great athlete and a great kid. Jeff was the kind of kid who was quiet, but when you spoke to him, you always got a very cordial response. He was always very, very polite," Kruse said.

Hayes last had the opportunity to play on the same ice as his Sandwich hockey teammates last February, during the Canal Cup contest between Sandwich and Bourne. For 27 seconds of the first period, the amount of time Hayes spent on the ice, Gallo Ice Arena seemed as if it might collapse from the thunderous applause Hayes received from the fans on both sides of the stands.

"A lot of people hear Jeff Hayes and they think hockey, baseball or cancer," said his former coach. "There was so much more to him than those three things."

"I was in math class with Jeff, so I knew him a little bit." Taylor Pacheco began to speak about Jeff and the day he passed.

I noticed he was getting more and more sick, and then he wasn't in class. Some of us talked to the teacher. I'd received text messages that he wasn't doing well. I remember the day he died, before we heard it over the loudspeaker, and all of us were told to come down to the auditorium; we all knew at that point, because we were all in touch with his friends. I remember exactly what I was wearing and the guy I was dating at the time. I remember sobbing, my head lying against his red sweatshirt; it was so heartbreaking.

Later, my friend Katherine Bahrawy came over to me. I was sitting in the auditorium, crying, and she said, "We need to do something."

"Okay, what do we do?" I replied.

"Well, we could do some fundraising so all of us can come together; we need to help out," Katherine continued. "Or, we could do a T-shirt. We just made Blue Knights Pride T-shirts; let's do T-shirts! Let's do something that everyone can wear. Lets incorporate hockey, and that'll be easy."

"I know Mr. Tomasini at the sports shop downtown; let's use him," I said.

Katherine drew up what she thought was a good design, and together we added two hockey sticks crossed, Hayes, True Hero, One School, One Heart, and we brought it to Mr. Tomasini. We picked out the shirt color, and within a week we had boxes in Mrs. Booras's office; students were attacking us for these shirts. We initially ordered five hundred shirts and reordered three times. We sold them for twelve dollars. We sold them at hockey games, in the front lobby, and at the school store. It wasn't about how much we made. That wasn't the point. In the end, it was about how many we were selling, how quickly we ran out, and calling Mr. Tomasini for more.

I called him and asked, "Mr. Tomasini, can we order five hundred more, because I don't have any more smalls and people are waiting in line."

Everyone was very supportive; all the teachers, every student.

Even if you didn't know Jeff, you knew his story, you knew his friends, and you knew how it touched anyone with cancer. The whole school came together. We were such a good school at that point; everyone was behind him and all his struggles leading up to it. So for all of us to do something that included hockey was awesome. It brought us all together. My best friend had cancer before Jeff, and I looked at him when the news came over the loudspeaker. He was sitting across from me in class, and he was sobbing. This wasn't just about Jeff. This touched everyone who has ever had to deal with cancer.

"A Night to Honor a Fallen Knight," was the caption on the front of the *Cape Cod Times* sports page.

It was Saturday, January 13, two days after John Lessard had seen his best friend at Children's Hospital after he'd passed. John was the only other senior playing; he and Jeff, had Jeff played, would have been the team leaders their junior and senior years. John had a great season in honor of his friend and carried Jeff's number twelve jersey from the locker room and through the tunnels of teammates and Bourne Canalmen who'd come pay tribute. He skated around the rink raising Jeff's jersey to the roar of the crowd. The rest of the team followed a moment later, and after the warm-ups, the announcer asked for a moment of silence to honor Jeff. The game ended in a tie. Coach Derackk Curtis said after the game, "That was our best game since I've been here. We were focused and played with emotion."

My sisters arrived at my house with three new suits they'd just bought at Macy's for me to try on for Jeff's wake and funeral. John and Jason met Julie and my brother John at Men's Warehouse for new suits generously purchased by Michael and Jackie. I was putting together what Jeff would wear. That was all I needed to do. Peter had taken care of everything else.

So many people were expected for the wake, too many for a funeral home to accommodate, so it was decided the wake would have to be held at Corpus Christi Parish.

The day of the wake, Father Rodney Thibault met us at the entrance to the church. I took comfort from him; he was a young priest, and I stayed focused on him and followed his lead. We sat in the front row during the short private family service, and then we were escorted to the side of the church where Jeff lay wearing his Sandwich High hockey jersey. His friends stood behind us to provide privacy for our first viewing. Then we stood next to Jeff in the receiving line, which had now stretched through the center aisle, around the pews and out the front door of the church. Thousands of people came to pay their respects and show their love for Jeff. In a small room off to the side of the lobby, Jack had set up a video presentation he'd created. There we displayed a memorial of Jeff's trophies, his skates, his baseball glove and bat, the Stephen Matheny Award, his youth hockey jacket and pants, his high school picture, and many other personal items. Two tables were filled with what Jeff loved in life.

Many students passed through the line. I looked up at one point to see the Bourne hockey team in line. It was incredibly moving to see them all wearing their matching high school varsity jackets. Bob Sweeney, the Director of the Boston Bruins Foundation as well as other representatives from the Boston Bruins came. Peter approached me during the wake and said, "Johnny Muse has given me a Boston College hockey jersey that he would like to put in Jeff's casket. He's written a message on it for Jeff. He wanted to know if that was all right with you."

"Of course," I replied, looking around for Johnny. I didn't see him.

"I'll take care of it," Peter replied. My brother-in-law and Jeff's godfather, Peter was amazing. He had organized the wake, purchased the cemetery plot, and helped with the funeral arrangements with his long-time friend, John Devito. He stood next to, and watched over Jeff's casket for six hours.

As I stood in the receiving line next to John Jr., who had insisted on being first in line to receive our visitors and accept their condolences, a pretty girl with strawberry-blond hair, who had tears in her eyes said, "I was Jeff's first girlfriend in third grade. He gave me a Barbie doll." I hugged her and smiled. "Thank you for telling me that, and thank you for coming." Then I wondered, as the next young girl gave me hug and then the next, where did he get a Barbie doll? He is something else, my Jeff.

Sam and his wife, Julie, were next in line, and I gave him a hug and looked at Julie.

"You came."

"Yes, of course," she replied. We hugged.

"Thank you."

I saw players from both the Falmouth and Barnstable hockey teams make their way through the line. All John Jr. and Jason's friends came too. There were family, friends, and some people we didn't know; an entire community had come to wait in line to pay their respects. It was truly amazing. I don't remember the line ending. At one point, I left and went to the rectory for a break. Someone had filled a table with food. I sat there for a while before returning back to the receiving line, which was still streaming out the front door. My brothers and sisters stood in line for us when John Jr., Jason, John and I needed to rest.

When it did end, we said good night to Jeff and left for home. Tomorrow would be our last time to see Jeff.....one day at a time.

On Tuesday, January 16, 2007, a limo arrived at our house. The parking lot at Corpus Christi Parish was completely full when we pulled in. We entered the church. There were so many people. Dad was the first one I saw when we stepped into the lobby.

"You're doing great," he said and gave me a hug. My sister Marianne had flown in from Denver with her young son, Baden and was also there to greet us. She hugged me with tears in her eyes. I turned to my right and saw my boss, Joe, his wife, Cindy, and their son, Bill; he was a couple years younger than Jeff. We hugged, and I said, "Thank you, Bill, for coming."

"I wanted to," he replied. He was the first one to show his compassion and sincerity that morning among so many of Jeff's peers. I couldn't begin to know the maturity of these teenagers and the love and respect among them. Jeff had brought them all together in one place, a sacred place.

The church was filled when we walked down the aisle to the front row. The pallbearers, Jeff's closest friends, John Lessard, Brian Tomasini, Mike Bridges, Ted Vrontas, Will Buckley, Zach Columbo, and Greg Iadonisi slowly pushed Jeff's casket into the church. John Lessard wore his hockey jersey, and others wore their baseball shirts; others dressed in a suit coat and tie. They stopped in front of the altar then returned to their seats. John and I walked up to Jeff's casket and placed his gold cross from Uncle Chuck and his silver saint medal from Nancy Bridges on the casket and returned to our seats. Father Rodney approached John and me, I kissed him; he then shook John's hand and returned to the altar.

"I don't have an answer as to why Jeff was taken from us," said Father Rodney said as he began the mass. "Jeff is in heaven where he can once again don his hockey jersey, lace his skates, and score goals. I do not have a prescription to take away your grief," he continued. "I'm confused too. Why someone so young? Why? I don't have those answers."

As he spoke, I listened carefully. The church was filled to capacity, but I could only see Father Rodney. His presence was so powerful and so comforting. His voice was strong and clear. He'd gone to the high school the day that Jeff had passed, and he had told me how scared he was when he approached the school and saw all the students outside and then in the auditorium, hugging each other and sobbing. He didn't know how he'd be able to comfort them. It wasn't until he started listening to the kids that he realized this was where he needed to be and that he could offer them solace. Not all were Catholic, he'd said.

I looked over at my sister Marianne who was in the children's room to the right of the pew where we sat. She had tears in her eyes holding her young son, Baden. John, Jason, Patty, and Marty sat with us. My family sat in the pews behind us. A dozen classmates also participated in the mass as lectors and communion servers.

The service was beautiful. Gary Linehan, Jeff's history teacher and friend, spoke first followed by Holli Bridges, Jeff's friend from childhood who had accompanied him to the prom. Coach Derackk Curtis followed. My sister's poem was read last by my niece, Julie. It was titled, "Where are the Words..." The end of the poem read:

> *He never let on with words that make only sound,*
> *he made you look deeper for that which was more profound.*
> *For like the saying goes, still water runs deep,*
> *more meaning, more soul in the silence he may keep.*
> *For to those words and to these Jeff is beholden:*
> *Speech is silver and silence is golden...*
> *And when we ponder on his life, his essence and style*
> *We'll all be rewarded by his warm and gentle smile.*

At the end of the mass, the pallbearers stood on each side of the casket and pushed it forward down the center aisle following Father Rodney and Father Bouchard. John and I, John Jr., and Jason followed out the front doors of the church and to the limousine. I sat in the limousine, my head against the window, watching so many grieving as they exited the church. I saw Kim Jacobs look my way. "I love you." Her silent words reached me, and tears rolled down my cheeks. The limousine driver started the car, and we pulled away slowly. The procession was miles long. When we came to the first turn onto Quaker Meeting House Road, a Sandwich policeman, standing in the middle of the road blocking traffic, saluted as we passed. It was an incredibly proud moment. I stared back at him until he was out of my view. John, John Jr., and Jason watched intently until we came to the next turn. "Mom, look again!" I looked out the window as we turned onto Route 130. The policeman's face was solemn and his poise was steadfast and unyielding. He saluted as we made the turn. Another policeman stood saluting at the entrance to the cemetery.

The driver parked along the edge of the grass, and we remained in the limousine. The endless line of cars continued to enter slowly, looking for places to park.

Jeff's friends carried the casket to the plot. John Devito, the funeral director, opened my door, and Father Rodney took my hand as we walked across the cemetery. The sky was gray, and light snow began to fall. It was cold. John Jr. stood on my right, and I wrapped him into my long coat. He stood shivering, looking down. Jason stood on my left, and my husband stood next to Jason. Father Rodney and Father Bouchard stood next to the casket and in front of us. We waited. I turned to see hundreds of people walking toward us. I looked back at Father Rodney and then Father Bouchard, who was holding the Bible against his chest. I saw their eyes redden and fill with tears, as they struggled to stay composed watching the crowd form around us. I swallowed and held on tight to John Jr. The light snow stopped and the sky seemed to brighten as Father Rodney delivered the valediction.

As the crowd slowly departed, we said our final and painful goodbye to Jeff. I waited until everyone was gone to be alone with my son.

CHAPTER 65

❧

The Next Day

THE NEXT DAY the headline in the *Cape Cod Times* read, "PAVE PAWS Cancer Link Gets New Look from State." Next to the headline was a picture taken after Jeff's mass. It showed Jeff's hockey team in their jerseys, standing in a line and forming a passage as the lectors held up the cross above their heads and exited the church.

In a column next to the article, bold letters declared: "13—The number of local cases of Ewing's Sarcoma, found mostly in children. Most have been diagnosed in the past five years. One case is in Edgartown, the rest are on the Cape. 3—Is the incidence rate for Ewing's Sarcoma per 1 million children; according to the National Institute of Health."

The article, written by Robin Lord, said that

State officials planned to expand their study of childhood cancer rates on Cape Cod to include a look at whether PAVE PAWS radar facility in Sagamore could be playing a part in the unusual number of cases of a rare form of bone cancer in the region. Suzanne Condon, Assistant Commissioner at the State Department of Public Health, said yesterday that Cambridge based research group, Broadcast Signal Lab will be hired to measure the levels of radiation from the PAVE PAWS radar station in Sagamore that is hitting the homes of more than a dozen Cape residents who have been diagnosed with Ewing's Sarcoma in the past five years. This will be the second time Broadcast Signal has studied PAVE PAWS.

The study proved nothing. We were not given any findings that showed a possible connection to this rare cancer. I had my theories that I shared privately. I was disappointed reading the thick
report that has been mailed to us from the Massachusetts Department of Health. I'd met with Suzanne Condon several times to discuss the study. She was always willing to meet and discuss her findings with me. I appreciated her candor and the interest she'd shown in what I referred to as a cluster. Her report concluded it wasn't. It has never been determined why 13 cases were diagnosed during those years. To this day it still remains a mystery. The cause is still unknown.

A week passed. I went food shopping in Marston Mills, the next town over. I didn't buy much; we still had two refrigerators filled with trays of food dropped off not only on Sundays but also during the week. It was early afternoon. Both John and John Jr. were at work, and Jason went to school. Joe and Bill had told me to take as much time as I needed away from work.

It was another mild January day. It was unusual that we had no snow, but nothing would be the same again. I walked up the deck stairs to our house and stopped. I felt something heavy above and behind me. I could no longer hear the sounds around me. There was a soft rumbling, a masculine noise in my mind, a black cloud filling my head. I couldn't hear the outside world, just this rumbling. The noise was intermittent; it came and went as if there was a pause between words, but there were no words.

I turned to look above me. The handles of the plastic bags holding my groceries slipped from my grip, and the bags fell from my hands onto the deck. I slouched over and then stood up straight. The noise stopped. I no longer felt the presence or the heaviness. I could see only the bareness of the trees and the winter grass. I could now hear the sounds around me that had momentarily gone silent. I wasn't certain about what I'd just experienced, but could it be? Jeff had been gone for a week.

I picked up my groceries and went inside. I thought about Mom and the chickadee I'd seen hovering outside my window a week after she'd passed. I'd never believed in connecting with someone in spirit. I still wasn't sure I had. I didn't know if what happened to me was real or imagined; but I did know that something had just happened.

Days turned into weeks. I was lost. Driving at times with Patty, I'd take turns down a road to nowhere.

"Where are you going?"

"I don't know."

"That's okay," she replied. "Just checking."

I was glad for her company, but there were days when I preferred to be alone.

One day, I drove to the cemetery and parked my car across from Jeff's row. When I opened the car door and stood up, I heard the rumbling again just as I had on my deck; the same intermittent, muffled sound that I couldn't make clear or understand. I felt the heaviness. I looked up behind me, and it stopped, just as it had before. Now I knew for sure. I smiled, thinking, he's probably pissed I didn't get it the first time. "I hear you," I said softly. "Hi, honey!" I thought about what he might be saying: "Mom, it's me! Didn't you hear me the first time?" I felt warmth in my heart, and it made me smile. He was gone in an instant, though, just as I turned around to look up toward him. I wondered why he couldn't stay.

I visited Jeff every day, clearing the flowers that had wilted. I never felt him near me or heard him again after that day. I hoped he'd return, but that second time was the last. I walked across the grass to the end of the row. A marker that one of Jeff's friends had placed there pictured a boy on skates dressed in uniform with a hockey stick in hand. Jeff's name, and the years he'd lived, where written next to the number twelve. I put fresh flowers down next to the marker.

We arrived at Gallo Arena on February 3, 2007, for the Canal Cup; it was less than one month since we'd lost Jeff. We entered through the rear of the building where the Zamboni exited the rink. Up in the stands and along the boards at ice level, we saw a crowd of students wearing the blue True Hero shirts. Our family and friends, my boss Joe and his wife, Cindy stood with Jeff's closest friends at ice level with us. We waited at the entrance of the Zamboni doors. Terry O'Reilly and Judie Songin approached us from behind the crowd. They'd come to surprise us and pay tribute to Jeff. As I turned, looking at them in surprise, a tear ran down my cheek, and we hugged. John Jr. and Jason, stood close, shaking Terry's hand and hugging Judie. Kevin Flanagan began the ceremony.

It was one year after that same meeting between Sandwich and Bourne, when Jeff had skated for twenty-seven seconds at the start of the annual Canal Cup. Tonight, his brother John Jr. left our side and stepped onto the ice, skating laps around the rink in front of a packed crowd, holding the framed jersey his brother once wore. The roar of the crowd echoed through the rink and was deafening as we shed tears for our beloved son, in the arena he loved. Jeff's framed jersey was then mounted outside the boy's locker room and the number twelve was retired that night.

KNIGHTS OWN CANAL CUP—Sandwich routs Bourne following tribute to fallen teammate, by Dave Colantuono—*The Upper Cape Codder*

On a night when a community came out to support their team, that team gave their community something to cheer about. Taking to the ice just minutes after a touching tribute to fallen teammate Jeff Hayes, the Sandwich hockey team swarmed all over rival Bourne Saturday, controlling the action throughout the 25th annual Canal Cup.

Led by the electric play of the Lessard brothers, the Blue Knights skated to an easy 7–1 victory. Senior co-captain John Lessard netted four goals while younger brother Garrett notched four assists as the Blue Knights followed through on a Hayes premonition.

"Last year at the Canal Cup dinner, Jeff said I think we should beat them 7–1," said Sandwich coach Derackk Curtis following the game.

Skating in front of an overflow crowd, the Blue Knights carried the action from the drop of the puck, keeping the Canalmen on the defensive through much of the first period. "We were a little surprised they came out in a 1-2-2 forecheck," said Coach Curtis of the game's opening moments. That surprising style led to the first goal of the game, as Bourne's leading scorer, Joe McCabe, stole the puck in the neutral zone and beat Sandwich goalie Kevin Desmarais for the struggling Canalmen's lone highlight.

Then John Lessard's power play goal at 6:44 in the first period tied the game. Following the equalizer, the 6 foot 1 forward skated by and touched the newly painted number 12 under the Gallo ice in tribute to his fellow captain. Much of the high octane effort came from the younger Lessard, who was a force throughout much of the game. Just a sophomore, the 5 foot 6 center was often found working along the boards to dig out the puck in the offensive zone. In most cases the recipient of that hard work was older brother John who always seemed to be in the right spot to onetime the brotherly setup.

After reading the article of the game I'd watched from inside the board-room at the rink, I thought about the final score Jeff had predicted last year. I tried to imagine him sitting among his teammates the night be-fore the Canal Cup last year when they asked him to predict the score. Where did 7–1 come from? How did Bourne score that lone goal?

"We've gone through a lot of adversity lately," said Curtis as he stood by the newly framed memorial. "It was nice to get the win for the Hayes Family."

The Sunday dinners continued. The mass cards and letters from stu-dents continued. KerryKares continued giving, and Kerry Collins from the Boston Bruins Foundation contacted us in March.

"Hi, Susan, it's Kerry. How are you doing? We want to host a trib-ute at TD Garden, formerly TD Banknorth Garden, in honor of Jeff," she continued. "We've been thinking about how we could do some-thing to honor him, and we decided to host a special night and pay tribute to Jeff. At the same time we'll present a check to the Dana-Farber with the proceeds raised from the PMC. It'll be on March 15. We want to show video of Jeff between periods. Can you send us some video?" she asked.

"Yes, of course," I replied.

"You, John, and your sons will be our guests, along with a group of your family and friends, in a luxury box that night. We'd like you and John, along with Terry O'Reilly and Bob Sweeney, to present a check to the Dana-Farber between periods."

I was stunned, then excited and honored, but speechless as she con-tinued with more details.

"We'll offer Sandwich residents tickets for twelve dollars to watch the Bruins play the Washington Capitals next Thursday night."

"Thank you, Kerry! Wow, I don't know what to say." I was silent with thoughts of Jeff and his team, the Bruins at the TD Garden; it couldn't be more fitting. "I'll have our friend Jack Lessard, who has lots of video of Jeff, send what he's produced over the past two years. I'll call him."

"Okay, great," she replied. I couldn't wait to tell John as I listened to Kerry.

"We'll put out a press release to the town, and I'll call you with more details later."

"Okay," I replied. "Thank you so much for doing this for Jeff and all of us."

We ended the call, and I sat down. My eyes were sore but hardly dry as I thought of Jeff. I knew what he'd say; he might even smile. No, he would give me that half smile, holding it in for as long as possible before he could no longer, and then a full smile would fill his face with pure, unassuming joy. That's all he'd give me; that's what I'd learned to love.

On Friday, March 9, 2007, the front page on the *Cape Cod Times* read, "A Night for Jeff—Boston Bruins to Host Tribute to Late Student:"

The entire town is invited. "We want to see a sea of blue there," Jay Southwood, Boston Bruins Foundation Event Manager said. "The tribute is a first for the Bruins. Previously, these nights have been reserved for former coaches or players. Jeff became friends with several Bruins players and Kim Jacobs, wife of Bruins Principal Charlie Jacobs, when she rode in the PMC. Jeff was paired with us because he was a hockey player," Southwood said. "We went into it blind. We didn't know we were getting

such a great kid. The team took to Jeff because he inspired players with his hard-fought battle against Ewing's."

"The kid had a lot of guts," said Paul Stewart, Director of
Development for the Bruins Foundation. "In hockey terms, he
had a lot of jam."

The night of March 15, I arrived at the Boston Harborside Hotel. The
city skyline was amazing. "Is this a five-star hotel?" I remember Jeff asking the first night we'd stayed here. I turned and walked toward to the
hotel desk to check in. While I waited, I looked behind me and across
the lobby at the two empty chairs, one Jeff had sat in while he waited
for me to check in the last night we'd stayed here. I pictured him, sitting
alone. He looked very thin and very sick. Oh God, I thought, as I turned
to look toward the voice of the hotel employee. "You're all set," she said.

My words quivered in reply. "Thank you very much." I turned to
take one last glance at the empty chair. I had wanted to come back here,
knowing he loved this hotel, and on the night when the Bruins would
pay a special tribute to him. I knew it'd be hard. I took the glass elevator
up many floors, staring out at the view.

I entered the room alone and sat on the end of the bed, staring out
the window. My cell phone rang. It was George Brennan from the *Cape
Cod Times*. We had scheduled this interview days before.

After we spoke, I dressed and waited for John in the lobby.

Our tickets were at the will-call window at the TD Garden. I felt like
a VIP. Our family and friends filled the luxury box as we watched the
Bruins and the Capitals warm up on the ice. Dad was with my brothers
John and Paul. I approached him. He looked excited and nervous; he too
had been a Bruins fan most of his life. "Hi, Dad," I said.

"Hi," he replied. "How are you?"

"I'm okay."

He looked around and out onto the ice, seeming to watch the players warming up, and asked, "Where do I pay?"

"Dad, it's free," I said.

I motioned to him to have something to eat; a buffet was set up for us. "Dad, are you hungry? Please have something to eat."

Some of the Bruins PMC team entered the box, and Bob Sweeney approached us. "Hi, Susan."

"Hi, Bob. How are you?"

"Good, thanks. I wanted you to know that we'd like to ride again this year for Jeff," he said.

"Oh, that would be great!"

Looking out from the luxury box, we could see hundreds of seats filled with Sandwich students wearing the navy True Hero T-shirts.

"What an amazing turnout; it's unbelievable," Bob commented.

At the end of the first period, John and I joined Terry O'Reilly, Bob Sweeney, and a representative from the Dana-Farber and walked out onto the long stretch of carpet and into the bright lights of the arena. I'd seen singer Rene Rancourt walk out on that carpet at the start of the Bruins games many times. I turned and waved to the students cheering in the stands.

"The Boston Bruins Pan-Mass Challenge team presents a check in the amount of $100,000 to the Dana-Farber Institute" was announced over

the loud speaker. Two cameramen were taking pictures. When the short ceremony ended, we turned, and I followed John off the ice, looking up at the blue section and waving to all the people from Sandwich. John and I were escorted to the elevator and made our way back to the luxury box.

At the end of the second period, John, John Jr., Jason and I left the luxury box and went to section 323. Cameramen followed us. I walked up to the balcony and waved to all the students to come and sit together to watch the video of Jeff on the Jumbotron. Students came up to me to give me a hug before finding a seat. We looked up high on the large screen suspended above center ice and watched the video of Jeff from his youth to the last year of his life. I'd seen Jeff skate many times when he could during treatment, wearing the Bruins number twelve jersey. The pictures of him shown on the Jumbotron were hard to watch, and it was difficult not to feel the emotion while sitting among the hundreds of blue T-shirts.

The Bruins and Capitals waited to step out onto the ice, and John and I were escorted back to the luxury box. As we passed the concession stands, all we could see was the name Hayes and the number twelve on the back of navy-blue T-shirts on the kids waiting in line. Walking down the corridor to our luxury box, and within our view, were groups of students; it was truly a "Blue Knight in the Garden" in honor of Jeff.

The third period ended in a tie. There was a shoot-out after the five-minute overtime. It was the only part of the game I watched. The Bruins won. The Washington Capitals had signed a hockey stick for us, and Kerry presented it to us before we left the TD Garden.

The next morning, back at the Hyatt, when our baggage cart arrived, we placed our luggage on the cart and left for the elevator. In the lobby, while I waited for John to get the car, a man approached me. I'd hung Jeff's number twelve Bruins jersey on the cart above our luggage, and he'd noticed.

"Jeff Hayes," he said. "I heard about him while listening to Lyndon Byers on his radio station, WAAF." LB played for the Bruins and rode on the PMC team.

"Yes," I said. "Jeff's my son."

"I'm so sorry. LB talked a lot about him. Sorry for your loss."

"Thank you." He walked away as John pulled up in front of the hotel.

"I'm gonna ride in the PMC, on the Bruins team!" I said to John. "I can do it!"

"You need a bike, kid," John replied.

"Yeah, a bike would be good, but that's not what worries me. I need time to train."

"Well, get a bike and ride."

"I will."

Our delivery of Sunday dinners came to a natural end. Nancy Helms invited us and all the parents who had prepared dinners for us to her house for a cookout.

In April, John, Jason, and I went to Siesta Key in Florida for five days. John Jr. stayed home. We rented a condo. We needed to get away. We need peace. This was Dad's doing. A few weeks before, Dad and I were finishing up our once-a-month lunch, and he stopped me as I approached his car. "Susan, take this." He handed me a check. "Go on vacation; go somewhere and get away." After Florida, John flew home to Boston, and Jason and I met Patty in Baltimore. From the BWI Airport we took the Light Rail to Camden Yards. I thought about the trip Dad, John, Paul and me took a few years earlier. I remembered Pedro warming up with Varitek before the game that day; we stood behind the bullpen watching. Pedro would windup and look in our direction every time. I smiled thinking about the picture of Pedro I'd received after the trip. Neither Dad, nor my brothers would come clean as to who had sent it to me.

We took in a Red Sox–Orioles game at Camden Yards that evening. The next day we took the train to Washington, DC, and visited museums, the war memorials for WWII, Korea, and the Vietnam Memorial. I spent a lot of time there. I found it remarkable and wanted to show my respect for the soldiers who had died for my freedom. It was moving for me, heroic, a grand memorial worth embracing with grateful thought.

Back in Baltimore the next day, we left our hotel and walked toward the harbor. We saw a white stretch limousine parked alongside the road before the harbor. "I bet that limo is for Red Sox players," I remarked.

We were hungry and entered the Cheesecake Factory restaurant. The hostess gave us a beeper to alert us when our table was ready.

"Mom," Jason whispered.

"What?"

"There's David Ortiz!"

I looked up. Standing next to the hostess desk was Big Papi.

"Don't!" Jason whispered.

"What?"

"Don't go talk to him," Jason said.

Jason watched as I looked back at Papi. "I'm leaving," he said and got up and walked outside.

Um, I don't know why my kids are embarrassed. I walked up to Papi. "Hi," I said. "I'm from Boston."

"Hi! Then you must know this guy," Ortiz replied. I turned, and Jason Varitek turned, looking back at me as he walked quickly past us. "Hi!" he said and then disappeared from view.

A small man approached me. He was short and dressed in oversized pants and untied sneakers; his head was shaved with the outline of Fenway Park on the side of his head.

"You can't talk to him, ma'am," he said.

"Oh, I'm sorry. I didn't know." I walked away and sat back down on the bench, still holding the beeper in my hand. Big Papi then came and sat down on the same bench with me. It was just he and I sitting, waiting for a table. He was listening to music and wore all white with diamond earnings and gold jewelry. I tried not to stare. His buzzer went off, and I watched him walk past me. Jason returned with Patty, and my buzzer lit up. The hostess led us to a table outside on the edge of the patio right next to Big Papi's table. On the other side of Big Papi's table was Jason Varitek sitting with a man I didn't recognize.

We sat down. The waiter approached our table to greet us, but Patty and I had our cell phones extended to get some pictures.

Last September, Jeff had been chosen as one of the patients from Children's Hospital to sit in Varitek's seats at Fenway Park. Jeff and several young children and their parents met Varitek outside the locker room at Fenway Park before a game. I took pictures that day of Jeff and Varitek standing next to each other. I glanced over at Varitek, and he looked back at me. I thought he might recognize me, remembering the woman who took several shots of him and Jeff that day. "I want to go over and talk to him," I whispered to Patty and Jason.

"No, Mom, leave him alone," Jason replied. "Don't go over there."

We saw Manny Ramirez sit down at Big Papi's table and dig into the food spread out on the table.

Our lunch was served. "We don't need go to the game now," I whispered to Jason, biting into my sandwich.

He smiled. "Mom, we're going to the game."

Before we'd finished our lunch, Manny left, and Big Papi paid their bill. Varitek and his guest left shortly after.

I wanted to call Dad and tell him about lunch. He'd remember our trip to Camden Yards. Last time it was Pedro, today David Ortiz, Manny Ramirez, and Jason Varitek. Patty, Jason, and I stopped at the curb before crossing the street outside the harbor. I dialed Dad's number. There was no answer. I knew my sister was staying with him. He hadn't been feeling well. I hit redial. No answer. I called my sister's cell. No answer. "Grandpa is not answering, Jay," I said, looking out onto the traffic, waiting to cross the street.

"He's not home, Mom."

"He has to be home; Janet's staying with him."

I called my brother John. No answer. I then called my brother Paul, and he answered.

"Hi, Paul. Where's Dad?" I asked.

There was a long pause. "What do you know?" he replied.

"I don't know anything," I said. "Where's Dad?"

"Maybe you should talk to John."

"Paul, tell me. Where's Dad?"

"He's in the hospital."

CHAPTER 66

Dad

IN FEBRUARY, DAD had a stent put into an artery in his heart. It took him a week to fully recover. His diabetes complicated things. Right after we'd left for Florida, Dad had gone into the hospital with an infection. He needed to be on a ventilator, so the doctors placed him into an induced coma. He'd been in the hospital for a week now. My siblings had been with him before I'd returned home from Baltimore. When I arrived, I too sat with him. A few days passed, and after work I visited him again as I had each day since I'd returned. I walked toward his hospital bed. Standing next to him, I said, "Hi, Dad."

Suddenly, his eyes opened. They were bright blue. He turned his head slightly toward me. "Hi," I said again, excited and surprised to see him awake and amazed at the color of his eyes. They had always been hazel.

The doctor had apparently brought Dad out of the coma long enough for us to see him awake. He was still on the ventilator. I stayed and talked to him until he fell asleep. I wished I hadn't been alone when he woke. I called my brother John. "He's awake, Johnny!" I said excitedly over the phone.

Dad was moved to a private room, and on Saturday, May 5, 2007 we gathered in his room. It was the night of the Kentucky Derby. In years past, we'd stayed with Dad in Eastham to watch the race; playing a pool with all the horse's numbers; each of us had a different horse to win.

When I arrived at Cape Cod Hospital, I saw Paul sitting by the elevator. "It's too sad," he said when he saw me. I entered the elevator and went to Dad's room. My brothers and sisters were there. I walked up to Dad's hospital bed wearing Mom's pink, striped shirt I'd saved and a pink sweatshirt tied around my shoulders. I whispered in his ear, "Hi Dad. You will see Mom soon, and Jeff will be there too." He opened his eyes wide, and I stayed close, whispering into his ear. He seemed to understand; he seemed to be listening. I pulled up a chair and sat close to his bed, clearing the tube of his catheter. We stayed with Dad until late in the day.

"This might be too hard for you," my sister Kathy said to me. I stood next to the door in Dad's room, looking back at him. I wanted to stay but couldn't. I kissed him on the cheek and left.

It's the biggest regret of my life.

At one thirty in the morning, my brother Johnny called after the hospital had phoned him: Dad had passed.

The house in Eastham was empty. I decided to spend a couple of nights down there after work. At night, the house was lit only by a timer on the living room lamp. I felt better guarding it, or at least giving the appearance that someone still lived there. Jason was in high school and came down with me after work. We'd get up early the next morning and drive back to Sandwich.

It was quiet at night, especially during the winter. Jason stretched out on the living room couch and read. I sat in the den, writing on Dad's computer. I'd been writing at home after work, most nights until midnight, committed to telling Jeff's story.

There were nights when I'd go to Eastham alone to write. I wasn't frightened. I left the television on in the family room. The time passed quickly as I wrote. I didn't hear a thing. I looked at the time on the computer screen—ten o'clock already. I was tired. I saved what I'd written and turned off the computer. I'd always slept on the couch in the family room after Dad passed. I walked through the living room, past the kitchen, and through the opening that led to the family room. I walked past the closet and stopped, startled as music began to play. "Somewhere My Love"—the musical notes came from nowhere. I looked around and then up in the direction of the sound and realized it was coming from a ceramic white dove high above me on the top of the closet. There were cathedral ceilings and a shelf on each side of the closet. The music kept playing. I ran and got a kitchen chair and placed it next to the closet door. Standing on the chair, I reached for the white dove. It sat atop a mahogany platform. I'd never noticed it before. There was a crank on the side of the platform. A thin cobweb laced the wings of the dove. I picked the dove up, and it continued to play as I stepped down off the chair and stood in the family room. When I put the white dove and its platform down on the table, the music stopped. I called my sister Kathy and then my brother Johnny.

"You have to turn the small piece on the side of the platform to wind it up to play music. It's a music box." I paused. "It hasn't been touched in years," I said over my cell phone. I turned the crank and played the music into the phone. "It happened. It played by itself," I insisted.

No one was going to believe me, I thought.

"I love you," my sister-in-law Patty said after I'd spoken to my brother John and she got on the phone.

"I love you too. Good night." I hung up and put the white dove on its platform and back above the closet. It was quiet again. I stood in the middle of the room. I could see my reflection in the french door; the backyard was in complete darkness. I left the room and put my pajamas on, pulled a set of sheets out of the linen closet, covered the couch, and went to bed. I lay there with the television on. I thought about the tiny chickadee hovering in front of my bedroom window on a cold November morning, one week after Mom passed. Then Jeff, the odd noise I'd heard, and the presence I'd felt just those two times. It was clear to me now, if not before, the message, 'I'm ok and you will be too.' I felt an overwhelming sense of contentment. I smiled and embraced it with an open heart.

"Good night, Dad," I whispered. "I won't run the water too long, and I'll pick up after myself before I leave."

On May 17, 2007 Jeff was named an honorary member of the National Honor Society. We joined the thirty-one inductees for a special ceremony in the library at Sandwich High School. The next day we met with Principal Ellin Booras and Class President Dave Shorten to talk about graduation day. We sat in Mrs. Booras's office for an hour discussing the program planned for the Class of 2007 and how Jeff would be included in the ceremony.

"It should be an extraordinary day," Mrs. Booras concluded.

"Jeff taught us a lot and was an inspiration to all of us. I knew him from baseball," Dave added. "When I played Babe Ruth," he continued, "I didn't talk to the jocks, the guys who were good players, Jeff's friends. They were on the all-star team, and I didn't have their skill. They stayed together, on and off the field, and kept to themselves. I was on the same Babe Ruth team as Jeff. The better players where spread evenly on each team. Jeff showed me how to throw a curveball. He talked to me and spent time with me, showing me how to throw a baseball, unlike the other guys he played with. We played catch during practice. When we weren't on the field, I'd walk by him in the hall at school and he'd say hi and we'd talk. We didn't hang out together, but he was always friendly to me at school."

CHAPTER 67

High School Graduation, June 2007

W E ARRIVED EARLY and sat in the front row, hoping for a breeze through the hazy, hot sun, just a whisper from a light wind blowing across the open field. I was sticking to my seat. There were six hundred chairs set up theater-style on the high school lawn next to the baseball diamond. We wanted to be seated with the class. Jeff had graduated; that's all he wanted to do.

The seniors walked out the side door of the school from inside the gymnasium. They lined up in rows on the bleachers directly in front of us. The commencement began with Salutatorian Sarah Jensen:

> By being in these bleachers today, we have accomplished arguably our biggest goal yet in our lives. As we take that large step into the unknown, we look around and see so many friendly and warm faces next to us. I truly believe the reason we reached this goal is because of each other's comfort, love, and friendship. Together, we felt the pains of death, as we said good-bye to a classmate, a teammate, a crush, but, most importantly, a best friend. We relied on one another when everything we took for granted in life seemed to slip away. We learned how to mourn. We miss you, Jeff; we know you're here with us today.

Jeff's name was mentioned by several who spoke. Principal Ellin Booras praised the Class of 2007 as one of "extraordinary integrity and recognizable maturity." She spoke in front of us, and I focused my attention on her. "Very few classes grow up as you did on our watch. Most young people progress to the next developmental milestone after they leave us.

You emerged from the chrysalis of adolescence right before our eyes. Perhaps it was Jeff's interrupted young life and the magnitude of courage that prodded you to grow up somewhat prodigiously. Your support of him throughout his journey is the trademark of your goodness."

Class President Dave Shorten also spoke of his friend Jeff. "Jeff's passing has, better than anything else, brought us together, reinforced the fragility of life, and therefore made us aware that we should take this opportunity we have been afforded for the next step. The people around me are inspiring. They have taught me to live, to think, and to love."

During commencement, two beach balls passed along the bleachers and into the air above the graduates. The number twelve and Jeff's name were written on each beach ball. Occasionally, students would turn or look down, and I could see the number twelve or Jeff's name atop their caps.

The speeches ended, and Mrs. Booras approached the podium to announce each graduating senior. We stood up when she said "Jeffrey Thomas Hayes" before the rest of the class was announced. We walked to the podium amid a thunderous applause. I approached her first. We hugged, and she handed me Jeff's diploma. Then John and my sons hugged her as I waited. The four of us stood together in front of the bleachers. Suddenly and in the moment, I raised Jeff's blue-encased diploma skyward. I smiled, looking up into the sky and then out at the crowd of people now standing. I held it up for several moments, in front of the parents with whom we'd shared the last twelve years, and some of whom were closer to Jeff's story and shared more of our personal battle with the disease. I thought about what Jeff had accomplished and how difficult it was during his illness. "You did it, honey! Here it is!" The crowd and the students continued their standing ovation as we walked back to our seats.

I smiled and looked up beyond the bleachers to the top of the tall pole where the baseball field lights are mounted. I saw a lone bird sitting there in the heat and humidity. I thought that little robin would have been standing on the side of a birdbath dunking his tiny head in the water or resting on a tree branch to keep cool; it was such a hot day. I knew it was you, Jeff, letting us know you where there.

At the end of the ceremony, after all the seniors had received their diplomas and had thrown their caps up into the air, Jeff's friends formed a semicircle on the baseball field between first and second bases and wrote the number twelve in the dirt in front of them, posing for a picture in memory of their friend.

OUTSIDE THE LINES WITH
John Lessard
Dan Crowley, the columnist, asks more from Jeff's best friend

Yes. Jeff was my best friend, still is. I love that kid. I had known Jeff ever since kindergarten, where we immediately became good friends. We would hang out together almost every day. We'd do all sorts of things from hockey, going out, and beating our arch rivals Rum, Duce, and Conway in whiffle ball any chance we could get. We still hang out. I go down to his resting place and hand out with him when I get an opportunity to. Jeff was the greatest kid I have even known. Always smiling, a great friend and never complained.

The kid was an athlete as well. Jeff was a competitor. He played hockey tough and he pitched tough. But when the contest was over, he would go back to the nice and caring kid that he was. Having Jeff as a friend was a privilege. Sometimes you take that for granted because they are always in your lives and you think that they will always be around. I learned you can't think that way because bad stuff can even happen to the nicest of kids. Jeff touched us all. I have never been to a wake that had a constant line of people paying their respects, one that wound up and down the church aisles. That is how much of an effect he has had on the school, the town, and families all over. I will always remember him as my best friend and it hurts not to have him lacing the skates up right next to me every time I go out onto the ice. But in a way, I know he still is.

Who has been your inspiration?

There have been many inspirational people in my lifetime but not one of them compares to Jeff Hayes. That kid taught me how to fight and be a strong person even through the toughest times. For someone to go through that amount of trouble and pain and not complain about it one bit is amazing—truly amazing. So every time I am on that ice and I think I am tired or hurt, I think of number 12 and realize that what I am going through does not even belong in the same category of what he had to endure. He is definitely my hero, definitely everyone's hero.

**Ted Vrontas, Zach Columbo, Will Buckley,
Mike Bridges, Brian Tomasini, John Lessard**

CHAPTER 68

Riding in the PMC

IN AUGUST I'D be riding on the Bruins PMC team with Judie and Terry O'Reilly, Bob Sweeney, Kim Jacobs, Shawn McEachern, and others from the Bruins organization. I bought a Cannondale bike from The Bike Zone in Hyannis. It was June and I needed to train. I'd started spinning at the Sandwich Racquet and Sports Club. The owners, Jack and Laurie Kelleher, were the parents of Brendan, a baseball team-mate of Jeff's. They hosted a "Spinning to Beat Cancer" fundraiser. My brother Paul, who taught spinning at a Boston sports club, ran the event, and Jeff's friends and my family filled the twenty stationary bikes we'd moved into the large parking lot outside the club.

NECN reporter Scot Yount contacted me for an interview to produce a segment on Jeff for the opening ceremonies of the Pan-Mass Challenge. I sat in Jeff's basement apartment with Scot and his camera-man. He looked at Jeff's recliner where I'd kept Jeff's pillow covered by the white hospital pillowcase, Jeff's number twelve sweatshirt that I'd placed over the arm of the recliner, and the pair of his Adidas shoes I'd left on the floor in front of his chair. I hadn't put Jeff's things there for the interview; they'd been there since the day he passed.

"That's an incredible memorial right there," Scot remarked, looking at the chair as I climbed up onto one of Jeff's bar stools set in the middle of the living room. He looked around at all Jeff's trophies, certificates, medals, and all the Bruins shirts and signed items. "Can you scan the room and get all this?" he asked his cameraman.

"Yes, it's quite a room," the cameraman replied. When the interview ended, they followed me in their NECN vehicle up and down my street as I rode my bike. Oh God, I thought as I looked down at my rear tire, it was flat. They smiled. "I've got enough film," Scot's cameraman said.

"I hope this isn't a sign of what's to come," I said.

The Pan-Mass Challenge starts in Sturbridge. It's a two-and-a-half-hour drive by car from Cape Cod, and a whole day ride on a bike back to Bourne. When you think about it, and I didn't, that's a long way to pedal.

The Sturbridge Host Hotel & Conference Center was a small village with several buildings, a conference center, and restaurants. We arrived late Friday afternoon to register and pick up my PMC bike shirt. The first day of the ride, everyone wears the PMC shirt. On the second day, riders wear their team shirt if they're part of a team. We saw the Bruins Hummer parked close by and met up with Kerry. She gave me my Bruins shirt, and then we had dinner with some of the other Bruins riders at a restaurant on site.

Quickly, John, Jason, and I walked from the restaurant to the conference center and arrived just before the start of opening ceremonies. We walked through the doors into an enormous dark theater. The only light I could see was along the front of the stage and above the small stage set up in the middle of the auditorium. My eyes adjusted to the darkness, and I saw Sam in a crowd by the door. We made our way to the front of the auditorium, and Sam sat in the row behind us, next to the stage. NECN was ready to go live to air the opening ceremonies of the PMC. There were thousands of riders watching and no air conditioning. My long hair covered the back of my neck, and I began to feel the sweat as a man with headphones directed us to our seats. The NECN host stood on the stage in front of us and began the live telecast. I turned from my seat and looked behind me at my cousin Rita and her husband Paul sitting two rows behind me with the rest of Bruins team. We watched two video stories, and then Jeff's story was aired. Jeff's voice was heard while the video showed me riding my bike down our street. Jeff was shown with the Bruins the year before when they had stopped at the end of our street and he was interviewed, standing in front of the Bruins Hummer. He looked amazing, and I thought how fast the disease had spread within months of that interview. It was heartbreaking.

I couldn't remember what I'd said during the interview that day. It was odd to watch myself on the large screen. I was surprised how articulate I was and how clearly I spoke, pleading to an audience I couldn't see. "We need to do something to stop this disease in children; we need to do more."

I'd worried constantly over the past several months about whether I'd be able to bike the 192 miles and whether the emotion of the weekend would overcome me. When the video ended of Jeff's story, the NECN host walked toward me and asked me to stand. The lights that now shone down on me intensified the heat and I looked over at my cousin. "You can do this," she whispered to me. I looked back at the host and began to speak into the microphone. At the end of the live interview, the NECN host held out the microphone to me one last time and said, "Well, you have all these riders to help you along the way."

"That's good," I replied with a nervous smile, "because I'm gonna need every single one of them!"

After the ceremony ended, the social director and Christine, a nurse from the JFC, approached me. I was surprised and happy to see them. I felt comforted knowing they were there; we never felt alone when it came to the Jimmy Fund staff. They were there for Jeff and us all the time, in every way.

John, Jason, and I walked toward the exit. They kept walking, and I was stopped along the way by riders who had just watched Jeff's video. They shook my hand and said my name. They were amazing, and I began to feel more relaxed and less alone.

We walked into a pub on site and sat at a round table in the corner with some of the riders on the Bruins team. I walked up to the bar to get a couple of beers for John and another friend from the team.

The bartender put two Budweisers in front of me, and I handed him twenty dollars. He put his hand up and said, "No, you're all set; the man at the end of the bar bought these beers." I looked across the bar and saw a young man look back at me. "Thank you," I said softly. He nodded.

My alarm went off at four thirty on Saturday morning. I was awake anyway. I shut off the alarm and heard Jason and my husband stir for just a moment while I got up. I dressed and looked out the hotel window. I could see my brother Paul getting out of his truck. I didn't know how long he'd been there. He was riding with me. He wanted to help me get through the hills and the long ride to Bourne. He'd helped me train. I walked outside toward Paul's truck.

Paul had my bike in the back of his truck with his, and we drove to the conference center together.

Everyone pedaled toward the starting line. The darkness was fading, and I couldn't see the sunrise. I sat on my bike seat with one foot on the ground, staring up at the thousands of riders making their way up the gradual hill in the thick haze. The muggy morning air couldn't restrain them or keep them from moving forward; they were riding to beat cancer. I watched the sea of colored shirts filling the two-lane highway at a harmonious pace. No one spoke; they just pedaled up the hill. Oh God, I thought. Here we go! I pushed down on my pedal and lifted my other leg over the bike seat and pushed down on the other pedal. I followed Paul toward the hill, blending in with all the riders.

Hours passed, and I felt like I was climbing the same hill. Paul had stayed with me for a while and then disappeared in front of me. I wanted him to go at his own pace. I rode at mine. It was hot, but not as bad as I'd imagined. Maybe it was the breeze felt by riding. I kept drinking from my Camel, a small backpack with ice water. The water didn't last long, and the empty pack was hot lying on my back. I called John and told him where I was. Soon he was driving alongside me with Jason in the passenger seat.

"You okay?" he yelled from the driver's seat.

"Hills are tough," I replied.

"I'll meet you up further where you can stop for a minute."

"Okay," I said and changed the gear on my bike. "What is this, Mount Everest?" I gasped.

"Keep going! See you in a couple of miles!"

We met at the next water stop, and I filled my water bottle and ate a banana. I remembered last year when Sam stopped at our house and ate a banana and drank coffee. I couldn't imagine drinking coffee today. I rested in the heat and then started on my way. The road became flat and easier to ride. There was shade as I rode through neighborhoods in the early morning.

I'd lost contact with Paul. The pack of riders thinned out after the first five miles. I hit another hill. The hills seemed to get longer and higher as the morning went on. I stopped on the side of the road to rest.

"Hi, Susan!" A rider shouted, pedaling steadily up the hill. I looked up to see him smiling and waving back at me, and I thought, last night, after Jeff's video, there I was in front of thousands of riders.

"Hi," I yelled back as a woman who looked eighty years old passed me. "Oh, great," I said out loud, but there was no one to hear—it was just me on the side of the road. I watched the woman ride up the hill without changing gears. I lifted my leg over the seat and stepped down on the pedal and rode up the hill. "I'm having what she's having for lunch!"

"Hey, Susan, nice bike!" I heard and looked up to see a man riding past me on the other side of the road. I watched him until I realized he was riding a Cannondale. "Thanks!" I yelled back. His pace was fast as he rode up the hill; I'm not sure he heard me. How do people recognize me? I wondered. I'm wearing a helmet. It's probably because I'm the only one stopped on the side of the road.

It was eleven thirty when the signs for the Dighton lunch stop appeared. I rode through a rural neighborhood. Tall pine and oak trees lined each side of the street, shading a path in the midday heat that led to the entrance of the elementary school. I followed other riders past the medical tent and the enormous tent where we'd eat lunch. I found an empty spot in a row of many bike racks that filled one side of the open field. The doors to the Porta-Potties that lined the front of the racks opened and shut continually.

Rows of banquet tables were filled with a variety of sandwiches, fruit, energy bars, cookies, brownies, multigrain chips, hard-boiled eggs, and buckets filled with water and juice drinks. I filled my plate with a peanut butter sandwich, a banana, a cookie, and a brownie and approached a table with an empty seat.

"Hi, may I sit here?" I asked.

"Sure, have a seat!" a man said with an accent. "I'm Jack."

"Susan." I looked down at my plate and then at his. "With all this food," I said, "I'm not sure what I should eat."

"Well, you shouldn't eat the brownie and the cookie," he said, looking at my plate and smiling back at me. "Eat the sandwich and the banana. That's all you need, and drink lots of water."

"Okay, thanks!" I said, not realizing that I was staring back at him. I turned away and took a bite of my sandwich while he drank from his water bottle.

I should call Kerry, I thought, and let her know I hadn't pedaled out of control and into a ditch somewhere. I hadn't seen anyone on the Bruins team since we left Sturbridge. Kerry was driving along the route, following the team in case someone was injured or had a flat.

I reached into the back of my bike shirt and pulled out the small laminated list of the team and their cell phone numbers. I looked closely at the list, trying to read it. I didn't have my glasses.

"Excuse me. I'm sorry to interrupt your lunch again; you've been so kind, but I wanted to call the rest of my team, and I can't read the names or numbers on this sheet without my glasses. Can you look for Kerry Collins on the list and read me her number, please?"

"Oh, of course, let me see." I handed him the list. "Here she is," he said and read me her number.

"Thanks!" I dialed, and Kerry's phone went right to voice mail. I left a message.

"Well, I'm off," Jack said. "Have a good ride."

"Thank you. You too," I replied. "And thanks for your help."

It was hot back out in the sun and in the open field. I found my bike and rode back onto the PMC route. I pedaled in the mix of riders. I didn't know anyone.

People stood along the route, sitting outside their homes, holding signs. I passed a man who held a hose out to shower us in the heat. The hills were difficult, and changing the gears didn't help much. I came to another hill and stopped for a moment.

"Hey, Susan, come ride behind me. I'll pull you up the hill!" a man called out.

"Oh, thank you! I'm okay."

"All right," he replied and sped up the hill.

Wow, I thought, and I got back on the route.

"Keep going, Susan—you can do it!"

I looked over, surprised to see Jack riding up behind me.

"Hi!" I replied.

"You didn't think we'd just have lunch together, did ya?"

"Yes, I mean no! I knew we'd meet again, but I wondered how I'd find you with so many riders. What are the odds?" I looked forward, passing a rider to keep up with Jack.

"Yes, it's a long shot. This is my good friend, John." I looked at the rider to the right of Jack and pedaling alongside him.

"Hi, John!" I said.

"Hi, Susan."

"Where are you from?" I asked.

"Connecticut. This is my third PMC."

"How do you know each other? Jack's from Australia."

"We met my first year. Jack's been riding for eight years."

"I'm riding with the Boston Bruins team—well, I'm on the team; they're ahead of me."

"We saw you last night," John replied. "I have a little girl."

"How old?" I asked.

"She's three. She's amazing."

"That's great. I always wanted a girl." The road flattened out, and we rode together for the next five miles until we reached the next water stop, and I saw my brother John holding up a sign at the entrance. "Thanks for riding with me, you guys. I hope I see you again."

"We'll see you in Bourne! Bye, Susan." They sped past the water stop and stayed on course for Bourne.

I pulled into the stop where some of my family and friends were waiting. Patty and Marty approached me after I set my bike down. "Hey, how's it going?" they asked.

"The hills are tough," I replied.

"You won't believe how many people have come up to us looking for you. They asked to have their picture taken with our signs and the picture of Jeff."

"Really!" As she spoke, I saw Julie Blackman walking toward me. "Hi, Julie! How are you? Where's Sam?" I asked and gave her a hug. She had met Sam in his spinning class; I should have realized she would be riding on Sam's team. Then Deb McNamara, Abby Lincoln, and Judie and Terry O'Reilly pulled into the stop. We didn't stay long. I got my bike and rode the rest of the route with Deb, Abby, Judie, and Terry to Mass Maritime Academy. We rode through the receiving line of volunteers who cheered continually as many riders passed through. The campus was full of spectators and riders. Another enormous tent was set up with food stations, beer, live music, and massages inside the tent. I found the Bruins Hummer parked past the tent and close to the ship docked nearby. A man approached me. I was standing with some of the Bruins team who had arrived much earlier in the day. He introduced himself and began to tell me his story and why he rode. I described Jeff's struggle and referred to cancer as "the beast."

"That's what we called it." He smiled. "The beast."

It felt good to listen to his story. We understood each other. That bond is so strong. I began to shed the outermost layers of the protective shield I'd built up like a coat of armor to protect me from the pain. Letting go of the heaviness felt good; my neck and my legs didn't. I headed toward the parking lot to meet up with John. I heard a voice call out my name. I turned to see my niece, Julie and her friend, Sarah. They were riding in from another route and were wearing their PMC bike shirts. It was great to have had the chance to see them with all the other riders; it was hard to find anyone.

I left Julie and Sarah and then was approached by friends I hadn't seen in twenty years. I wondered if I kept walking I'd see more friends; and I did. These were family members. Again, I heard my name. It was Michelle and Melissa, my cousin Rita's two daughters; they were volunteers. Michelle was carrying a large, beautiful bouquet of flowers for me.

I took the shuttle bus to a parking lot off campus, and John picked me up. Traffic along the canal was bumper to bumper; it was Saturday, when the summer weekly rentals changed over. It took us two hours to get home to Sandwich from Bourne. The first day was done.

I started the second day of the ride from the intersection of Chase and Service Road in Sandwich where the Bruins would stop. It became a memorial stop for Jeff. Those who stayed at Mass Maritime Academy started at four thirty in the morning. We cheered all the riders, waiting for the Bruins team. One by one, each rider pulled to the side of the road, and when all had arrived, a picture was taken with the team and all Jeff's friends. The initials, JH are written on the inside of a red heart on the sleeve of the Bruins bike shirt.

The team left our water stop. I couldn't believe I was riding the tail wind of Kim Jacobs and Don Sweeney...and I still had a pulse! They're amazing athletes. We rode through Barnstable to the Brewster water stop. The roads were flat as we weaved our way through several Cape towns. The weather had cleared. The humidity was gone, and the air was dry. It was a beautiful sunny day. From Brewster, I rode with Steve Caldwell and LB, Lyndon Byers. I waved to Lura, my niece, and my brother John when we passed behind Arnold's Seafood in Eastham. I was sandwiched tightly between LB and Steve. It was the best cycling of the weekend until the hill at Lacount Hollow Beach. Steve, who didn't have any gears on his bike, stayed with me until the water stop in Truro. We rode into the stop and met up with some of the team.

"She's doing really well!" Kim said as Steve and I approached.

"No, she's all done," Steve replied.

I didn't have anything left. I looked back at Kim, and my eyes watered. I felt tired and spent, but mostly disappointed in myself.

The team left, and John picked me up, and we drove to the start of the dunes in Truro. I rode the small hills through the dunes to a spot where the team was waiting for everyone to join them. We were all going to cross the finish line together. I rested my bike on the rail of an old wooden fence; I could see the ocean beyond the sand dunes. The team was tired and quiet, ready to ride the last few miles to the finish line.

"Hey, Susan! Is Susan there?" I saw John, the rider I'd met with Jack the day before on our way to Bourne. He'd crossed the finish line and was riding back out of Provincetown. I was standing with the team wearing my Bruins bike shirt. I saw him pass when he called out my name.

"Hi, John! Bye, John," I yelled from the side of the road. He was riding fast, and I hoped he heard me. He faded down the road and out of sight, and I felt sad. I'd miss him and our ride together.

We waited until Judie and Terry O'Reilly pulled up to the side of road; they had a flat tire hours ago.

This was it. We were all together as a team. I picked up my bike and rode along with them toward Provincetown. The ride in was surreal. I had done it. I sat up straight on my bike, riding alongside the Bruins team. We rode for Jeff and all those stricken with cancer. I smiled as we crossed the finish line, proud to be part of the Bruins PMC team. Brian

Hayes was alongside me, and I felt a bond with him. He'd been at Jeff's golf tournament. He, along with all the riders, was kind and compassionate; they knew Jeff's story. Deb McNamara is a very special lady and always kept us smiling. She rode the first year on the Bruins team while battling cancer herself. The following year she visited the JFC and remembered a fourteen-year-old girl she'd seen there. "I walked out of her room," Deb told me, "and said, 'F—— that, I'm riding again next year!'" I was so proud of Deb's strength and human spirit. She is truly a remarkable woman.

I saw my cousin Rita and Paul waiting for me as we crossed the finish line. It was wonderful to see them. I imagine it was very difficult to have made the trip and follow my ride for both days. I'm grateful to them for their support during a very difficult and emotional two days.

I stood in the middle of the Bruins team for a group picture, and then the team disbursed. They left for massages and a shower before the ride back on the *Provincetown II* to Boston. I stood alone, wondering how everyone had disappeared so quickly.

A NESN man approached me and asked me about the ride and my son Jeff. After the interview, and without me seeing him, a little boy wrapped his arms around my legs. I looked down. He didn't say anything. He held on tightly. I bent over and wrapped my arms around his shoulders.

"Hi, honey. Thank you for the hug," I said as he let go and looked up at me. I could see he was bald underneath the cap he wore. He must be undergoing treatment, I thought.

"I'm Drew," he said, stepping up on the sidewalk and turning around as he spoke. "Look at the back of my shirt; it says, 'Kick Cancer in the Butt!'"

I laughed and said, "That's right, Drew. We're gonna kick cancer in the butt!" He was smiling and laughing, proud to be wearing a shirt that he felt was badass. I guessed he was around seven years old. He took off his badge that was pinned to his T-shirt.

"Look, that's me!" He showed me his badge with a picture of him in a red superhero outfit. It read, "Drew's Crew, Powered to Pedal for a Cure!"

"Here, this is for you," he said and handed me his badge.

"Are you sure, Drew?" I asked.

"Yes, I want you to have it."

"Thank you very much. I'll keep it forever." I hugged him as his mom walked toward us.

"He's remarkable," I told her. "I love him."

"Me too," she replied.

I said good-bye and walked away. "Thanks, Jeff," I whispered.

On Monday, I stayed home from work. My neck was sore, and my arm was numb and tingled down to my fingertips. My doorbell rang. I opened the front door, and I couldn't see the deliveryman behind an enormous floral arrangement. The card read, "Thanks for riding with the team. Our thoughts and prayers are with you always. Love, Kim Jacobs."

CHAPTER 69

~

Sandwich Clinches State Title

WHEN THE BLUE Knights boarded the bus at the Gallo Ice Arena at eleven o'clock Sunday morning, the day of the state finals, they thought they were heading for the TD Garden and their MIAA Division II game against Wilmington. When the bus turned onto Route 6 heading east, several of the players shouted out that they were going the wrong way. When the bus turned off at Exit 2, some asked, "Where are we going?" When the bus passed the Cotuit Road turnoff, there wasn't a sound; they knew just where they were headed.

At eleven fifteen Sunday morning, the Blue Knights team bus pulled into the Sandwich Town Cemetery off Route 130. They had a date with destiny in Boston, but not before a visit with fallen teammate Jeff Hayes, who died during the season last year.

"Jeff's battle with cancer taught this team how to be strong and face life head-on," said Coach Curtis. Over the years they had taken strength from Jeff's fight, and today they stopped by Jeff's grave to remind themselves of how hard he had fought and how much he would want them to bring home a championship.

The coaches brought along two twelve packs of Jeff's favorite soda, Mountain Dew, and the team formed a semicircle around Jeff's stone and raised their drinks in a toast to their fallen comrade. "We toasted to him and poured a little on Jeff's grave," Coach Curtis said. "Jeff would have given anything to be with us."

It got quiet. Then Coach Curtis called out, "For Jeff, today we play like champions!"

When the final buzzer went off to end the game, John and I stood in the stands in the midst of hundreds of students wearing True Hero blue T-shirts as they jumped out of their seats, cheering for their team and their school. The roar of the crowd filled TD Garden, and we watched Coach Curtis walk out onto the ice to celebrate with his team. They had beaten Wilmington 1–0. It was their championship.

"I know now that he was there with us," Garrett Lessard said after the game. "Especially on a couple of those saves that Pat made. I thought those were going in. He was definitely there helping us out. Jeff would have loved this; he loved winning. It would have been his dream come true."

"Yes, he was there," Bolton noted. "I believe it, I really do."

"Without a doubt he was there on the ice with us," Assistant Coach Mohre added. "He was with us all the way, smiling, laughing, and crying."

Each of the members of the state championship Blue Knights team was awarded a gold medal. They made sure Jeff Hayes received one too, and Coach Curtis placed it atop Jeff's gravestone the following day.

The *Cape Cod Times* front page pictured the Blue Knights in celebration, huddled together on the ice in triumph. In the background of the picture, a Wilmington player is seen skating away from the Blue Knights and the number twelve is clearly visible on the back of his jersey.

Beating Cancer

Winning or losing the battle against cancer isn't determined solely on a life saved or a life lost. It's the life lived. Skating for 27 seconds, showing strength and unselfishness among your teammates and peers; walking tall when no one knows how sick you really are; being humble and worried about others around you, beats cancer. Living a short life but inspiring so many, beats cancer. An enduring smile beats cancer.

A life lost but not forgotten is the profound basis of this story. Live. Make a difference. Treat others with kindness and respect. Be polite. Be courageous and honest. To have lost his life living with honor is the greatest achievement and legacy one could impart as a guide for us to live by.

I'd written so much, over 138,000 words to help me heal. I decided to take a few Chapters across the street to my neighbor, Elaine Berry, she's a teacher at the Oak Ridge School. Several days passed and then one day while I stood in my kitchen cleaning, I heard a knock on the door. It was Elaine. I invited her in and we sat at the kitchen table.

"I've made notes," she began. I could see the post-its placed on the pages as she turned them; there were comments in pencil too. "This is good," she said, looking back at me. "I'd like to try and get you into the Sandwich Writers' Group. Do you think you'd like to sit in with them and read some of what you've written? I know the wife of one of the writers in the group. His name is Mark Wiklund. Should I reach out to him?" Elaine asked.

"Sure, that would be great," I replied.

Elaine came with me. We waited at the bottom of the stairs in the library, across from two closed doors. I heard footsteps and turned to see who it was.

"Oh, hi Mark," Elaine said when he approached us. "This is Susan Hayes. Susan, Mark Wiklund."

We waited for the rest of the writers to arrive and then entered the room. I listened as they took turns reading a short piece they had written. Some of these pieces were parts of larger works. Some were short, written to fuel their desire to continually write. One person in the group was a poet.

They saved me for last. My legs were shaking under the table when the last writer finished reading. Mark said, "Okay, Susan, why don't you read a little of what you've brought." All eyes were on me.

"Yes, thank you but I must tell you, I'm not a writer, I just have a story to tell."

"Then tell it!"

Epilogue

A Letter to Jeff

Dear Jeff

I never use an alarm clock. I turn the news on when I awake every morning and before I get out of bed. When the traffic report comes on, I change the channel before I see the expressway, especially at the gas tanks, remembering all our trips to Boston.

At night, I sit on the couch looking out the window, staring at a star I'd noticed after you had to leave us. Even as winter ended and the bare trees became full again, I could still see its radiance from the window next to the couch. It was brighter than any other, and I found it remarkable that I could see it perfectly from where I sat at the end of each day.

Jeff, I've loved you, John Jr., and Jason from the very first moment; I will love all of you until there are no more years left for me.

I hope you're okay with the story, Jeff. You didn't say a lot. You didn't let on how bad you felt and how hard it was not playing hockey or baseball, but we knew. We are so proud of you. I'm saying now what I couldn't say to you then, and how I wish I'd told you more and how I hated to see you in pain. You battled the disease like a brave soldier, hunkered down and worried about those around you. You did it without resentment or self-pity. You battled with strength, courage, and grace. You were amazing. Thank you, honey, for all that you've left each one of us; we will never forget you and all that you taught us. I'm so sorry.

445

I knew when my star no longer appeared in that same spot outside my window that I needed to find that brightness here in my life. I've finished the story, remembering how you told me I never finish anything. I thought about those words many times when I couldn't write another word. But I did. There were times when I couldn't stop, and then there were times I sat with the laptop in front of me, not writing a word, just staring at the screen.

The Boston Bruins won the Stanley Cup in 2011. You were probably there, but we couldn't get tickets. I imagined how excited you would have been. A couple of years after their Stanley Cup championship and at the end of a shortened season; a lockout, the Bruins played the Toronto Maple Leafs, Dr. Ready's favorite team, in the first round of the playoffs. They took the series to game seven and scored three goals in the last ten minutes of the third period to win the game. Patrice scored the game-winning goal. Then they beat the New York Rangers in the next series. But then, wow, you should have seen what they did to Pittsburgh! They took the best player in the world, so they say, Sidney Crosby, and their other star player, Malkin right out of the series. Crosby and Malkin didn't score a point, let alone a goal! The Bruins played great defensive hockey. It was the best series I'd ever seen them play. They swept the Penguins. By the time the Stanley Cup finals began between the Bruins and the Blackhawks, both teams were pretty beat up, but evenly matched, I thought. The Chicago Blackhawks—they're a good team, Jeff; they won the Stanley Cup. You couldn't hate them, like the Canadiens or the Maple Leafs. Patrice was amazing throughout every series and played the fifth game of the finals with a cracked rib, torn cartilage, and a punctured lung.

Throughout his four years at Boston College, your good friend, John Muse played in goal. We went to one of his games. He had a small blue-and-white jersey with the number twelve painted on the side of his helmet. The team won the Eastern Conference and Frozen Four Championships three out of the four years John played.

Jason graduated early from the Biochemistry Molecular Biology program at the University of Massachusetts Amherst, making the Dean's List all but one semester, missing it by one-half of a point. He wants to help find a cure for the cancer that took your life. He called me the night before his last final.

"Mom, I can't sleep. I can't concentrate," he said to me over the phone. "I can't stop thinking about Jeff." It was right before Christmas.

I told him to talk to you. He asked me when, and I said, "When you're alone, talk to him and tell him how you feel. Tell him to send you an angel. I ask him all the time; in the morning when I wake and find it hard to start the day, I ask him. Some mornings, I ask for several, and I say, 'Jeff, I'm gonna need more than one angel today. Can you send me several?' And you know what, he does. And throughout the day, I recognize who he's sent. They're all around me."

John Jr. named his boxer, Tuukka, after the Bruins goalie and before Rask even played. Tuukka is the goalie you told me about years ago. You said, "Mom, don't worry the Bruins have a great goalie coming up; he's young." You were right. He's really good.

John Jr. doesn't let on how hurt he is. I've read all the messages he's left for you in the blue book in the mailbox next to your resting place. He misses you too.

The year you died, a memorial bench was approved by the town to be permanently placed at the Sandwich Boardwalk parking lot. It's placed at the edge of the marsh. Brian led the group of students in the DECA Program at Sandwich High, and they raised money to purchase the bench. Many people have told me that they sit there and look out over the marsh and out into the ocean. You'd be so proud. And every Christmas, two ten-foot steel angels are placed around Sandwich. They are lit up at night and were created by Michael Magyar, a local artist and glassblower. One is you, and the other is Maggie Smilie, the other teenager who died the same year. Over the years, Michael has created many figures and angels. They light up 6A during the holidays; it's festive and symbolic of many landmarks in Sandwich.

The Sandwich Enterprise reminds us each year at Christmas who the angels represent.

Mike and Brian rode in the PMC on the Bruins team the year after me. They looked like they'd just walked out of a magazine posing for the 192-mile bike ride, not even sweating when they rode up to me at the lunch tent in Dighton. Mike played in a soccer championship game that Sunday night after the two-day bike ride.

Brian now teaches and coaches at Sandwich High. He told me a story after we attended your anniversary mass. He said, "Jeff's math teacher, Mr. Germaldi, returned to his classroom after a long absence battling an illness. He searched his desk drawer trying to find the math exam Jeff had taken; the one he'd saved for six years. Jeff had passed in the test at the end of class and showed Mr. Germaldi the last page where he'd signed his name; his signature. Jeff had told him, 'I signed the exam so that when I'm famous, you'll have my autograph.' Mr. Germaldi was so relieved that he'd found the exam."

Mike Bridges has a large cross tattooed on the middle of his back with the number twelve centered within the cross. John Lessard has a small hockey lace with the number twelve tattooed on his arm. Several of your friends got tattoos; each one different. I have your full name and two red hearts above my ankle, and Auntie has an angel above your name in the same spot as me. We had a few drinks after the tattoos that day; it was the first anniversary after you left us.

All your cousins wear the number twelve when soccer, baseball, and hockey seasons start and uniforms are handed out. They make sure they get your number. Uncle Peter has sponsored Jerome's and Josh's Little League teams named after you. Even your cousin from Denver, Baden Johansen, wore number twelve for his first Little League game. He chose it himself.

Marty Cosgrove hosts the Jeff Hayes Memorial Hockey Tournament for Sandwich High, the first Sandwich hockey tournament ever. All your aunts, uncles and cousins were part of the opening ceremony, and we showed a video of you while your family stood on the red carpet at center ice. All the tournament teams, including the Blue Knights, stood on the ice, and at the end of the ceremony they raised their sticks and shouted, "Jeff Hayes!"

The second year of tournament, we got the Stanley Cup! Phil Pritchard from the Toronto Hall of Fame took the Stanley Cup to Newtown, Connecticut, the town where twenty-six people were gunned down. Most were elementary school kids, killed in cold blood; it was heartbreaking. Months after the deadly shootings, Phil took the Stanley Cup to the people of Newtown, then in the same day, brought it to your tournament at Gallo. We raised money to support the three scholarships we've given out for nine years now: the Jeff Hayes Memorial Scholarship and two #12 Scholarships. We always award a female student athlete one of the scholarships because the first year we awarded scholarships, you had chosen two seniors as your finalists; one was a girl.

I also want to tell you, the Bruins PMC team riders still stop at the end of our street. They have for the past ten years now. They wear a red heart on their sleeve with your initials in the center. Our pastor, Father Harrington from Corpus Christi

2015 Bruins PMC Team with Susan

Parish, walks down Service Road at six o'clock in the morning, and when all the riders on the Bruins team arrive; he blesses the team and speaks of you.

Julie ran in your honor at the Boston Marathon in 2011 on the Dana-Farber team. We met Heather Reardon from Cohasset who ran in your honor in 2012 and 2013, also on the Dana-Farber team. Like Julie, we were paired with her by the Dana-Farber as a memorial partner. The year 2013 was the horrible year of the bombings. Heather's parents and her husband Pat were at the finish line, but luckily they weren't hurt. Heather's parents left the city right away, and Pat searched for Heather; she walked six miles after they stopped the marathon, and it took her hours to meet up with her husband. I watched the race from the fire station in Newton. I ran with Heather a few hundred yards before Heartbreak Hill then Julie took over and ran with Heather for a while. I left for home right after that.

On my way home, Jason called me, then John, then Dad, and then Joe and Cindy called to see if I was okay. I didn't know two bombs had gone off at the finish line. It was horrific.

The following year, Sarah Jensen ran in your honor on the Dana-Farber team. Dad and I had decided that after Heather told us she was pregnant, we weren't going to have someone run in the "In Memory Program" for you. Then we thought, let's ask Sarah, one last time. I called Sarah. When she answered, she said, "I can't believe you're calling me right now." She began to cry.

"I'm sorry," I replied.

"Oh, no," she said. "It's because I'm at Logan Airport, waiting to board a plane to LA for an interview for medical school. I have six interviews, and this is my first. You see, my personal statement for admittance was all about Jeff." She said yes, she'd love to run the Boston Marathon on the Dana-Farber team. At Northeastern University she raised the most money for the National Cancer Society out of all the colleges and universities across the country. She's amazing, Jeff. She chose UCLA's medical school.

I've been walking in the Jimmy Fund Boston Marathon Walk for nine years. My friend David Schneider supports me each year and donates $1500, and many friends from work send donations so that I can earn

Pacesetter status. After the bombings, Auntie Patti Fay formed another Team Jeff, bigger than ever, just like the first year when you were here.

Every month since you've been gone, we receive a letter from the Dana-Farber stating that Bob and Melanie Hill have made a donation in your name. Uncle Chuck's daughter, Charlene also sends a donation to the Dana Farber in your name. Mary, Chuck's third daughter lives her life to the fullest in memory of you and how much you've meant to her.

Dad battled colon cancer a few years after your battle. His treatment was surgery and seven months of chemotherapy—nothing as long or as arduous as yours but scary for him. Uncle Marty fought throat cancer, and that was terrible. I gave him your tallest baseball trophy when he was going through the worst of it. He's been in remission for two years now.

I want to make a difference, Jeff. I want to help other families facing this horrible disease. If by telling this story, I can help, then something good has come of this tragedy. I feel a deep sense of caring and commitment to other children and adolescents who may have the same fears we faced. Random acts of kindness, supporting the community, and, of course, the Boston Bruins Foundation would be my mission, in your name. Currently, Schuyler O'Brien, a young man from the Cape who was diagnosed with Ewing's one year prior to you is studying for his PhD at the University of Utah. He is a four-time survivor. We want to raise awareness of this disease and hopefully increase participation in his study, Project Genesis.

There's so much to tell you and so much of this life you've missed. I try to understand our life here and where you might be. What is the meaning of the universe, and what happens to our spirit when we leave? Sometimes I think we've been here before, lived another life, reincarnation. I'd like to put in an order for the person I'd like to be next time. Then I think, I can be whomever I want, now.

So this is it, Jeff. I'm ending the story, although it never truly ends. We continue to fight for a cure for cancer. I have an evil vengeance against the disease because of all the people it has affected and taken from us, especially you and Grandma. I'll do everything to avenge it. I'm sorry I couldn't keep my promise that I wouldn't let anything happen to you. I tried with all my heart. My thoughts are of you, honey, every day. You've made such a difference in so many lives. Your cousin Lura named her son Owen Jeffrey after you. One of your high school classmates, also used Jeffrey as her first son's middle name. I find that remarkable.

I'm counting on us meeting again; then you can tell me what you thought of the story. Thank you for placing a dime in places where it's so unexpected. I'm not sure why it's always a dime, never a nickel or a quarter, or even a penny, but I know they're from you. There are only a few who understand and find a dime, but once they do, and it keeps happening to them, they believe.

Thank you for the messages. I wonder where you might be in a place that's timeless from what I believe to be eternal happiness--where I know you've laced up your skates and can feel a cool breeze touch your face, stride after stride.

I love you,

Mom

About the Author

AFTER THE DEATH of her son Jeff, Susan began writing as a way to keep her son close and help herself heal. Never did she expect that one day she would be publishing a memoir. She met with the Sandwich Writers' Group to read a short piece from her story, and it was the reaction of the writer's, her need to keep the memory of Jeff alive, and her capacity to write that gave Susan the strength to relive her devastating loss and compose a beautiful and inspiring story.

Susan is from a large Boston family of twelve. This is where she believes her compassion, courage, and strength was born and raised; in the number five spot of ten children. She holds close the values that were instilled during her childhood and understands the importance of life's struggles along the way. She treasures the joy she experienced growing up in a large family and later raising her three sons. Her heart is filled with thoughts of Jeff.

Susan is currently working on a series of short stories. She is, and will always be, a loyal Boston Bruins fan.

Please visit: www.jeffhayesstory.com
For Information on:
Supporting Families with Cancer
The Boston Bruins Foundation
Project Genesis
Jimmy Fund Walk
Pan-Mass Challenge

Susan's Blog

The Website features, Articles, Videos and a Photo Gallery

50693758R00260

Made in the USA
Charleston, SC
29 December 2015